Ethics and Statecraft

The Moral Dimension of International Affairs

THIRD EDITION

Cathal J. Nolan, Editor

Foreword by Joel H. Rosenthal

PRAEGER™

An Imprint of ABC-CLIO, LLC

Santa Barbara, California • Denver, Colorado

Library of Congress Cataloging-in-Publication Data

Ethics and statecraft : the moral dimension of international affairs / Cathal J. Nolan, editor ; foreword by Joel H. Rosenthal. — Third edition.
  pages cm
Includes bibliographical references and index.
  ISBN 978–1–4408–3340–3 (hardback) — ISBN 978–1–4408–3354–0 (paperback) — ISBN 978–1–4408–3341–0 (ebook) 1. International relations—Moral and ethical aspects. I. Nolan, Cathal J.
JZ1306.E877   2015
172′.4—dc23   2015021213

ISBN: 978–1–4408–3340–3 (hardcover)
ISBN: 978–1–4408–3354–0 (paperback)
EISBN: 978–1–4408–3341–0

19 18 17 16 15   1 2 3 4 5

This book is also available on the World Wide Web as an eBook.
Visit www.abc-clio.com for details.

Praeger
An Imprint of ABC-CLIO, LLC

ABC-CLIO, LLC
130 Cremona Drive, P.O. Box 1911
Santa Barbara, California 93116-1911

This book is printed on acid-free paper ∞

Manufactured in the United States of America

Contents

PART II: PEACEMAKING

PART III: TRANSFORMATION

PART IV: EMERGING ISSUES

Foreword: Biography, Ethics, and Statecraft

Joel H. Rosenthal

Fifteen years into the twenty-first century, "globalization" is the distinguishing characteristic of our age. According to Klaus Schwab, founder of the World Economic Forum, "The new reality of our networked society is that global, regional and industry developments are completely intertwined. Technological revolutions are changing the context for decision-making and disrupting our conventional decision-making processes."[1]

What does globalization mean for statecraft? Does the empirical fact of wider, deeper, and faster connectivity change anything? Even if one is skeptical of the Davos view of the world—and there is much to question in this elitist, top-down perspective—it is clear that national interests and global responsibilities are becoming harder to separate.

National interests have an extra dimension these days. Threats come less from rival powers than they do from failed states, dysfunctional institutions, and weak coordination in addressing basic human needs in places near and far. Collective action is urgent yet elusive. Defense of human dignity is both a particular and universal challenge. As a result, the most revered statesmen are no longer judged solely by what they do for their countrymen. They are also judged by what they do for the world.

The virtue of this volume is that it enables the reader to see what is constant and what may be changing in the practice of diplomacy. Today there are modern-day Wilsonians such as former British Prime Minister Gordon Brown, who argue that "global problems require global solutions." These solutions will require "global institutions based on a global ethic."[2] Others such as Michael Ignatieff prefer a realist strategy rooted in local circumstance. The goal is simply minimal agreement on basic values—from there, perhaps clever and effective statesmen can scale up to address global-level issues such as climate change and genocide prevention. According to Ignatieff,

"The more evident our common needs as a species become, the more brutal become the human insistence on the claims of difference."[3] We ignore this fact of human nature and experience at our peril.

Whatever one's preference—Wilsonian or realist—there is an emerging consensus that enlightened self-interest is a standard worth striving for. In a global world, there is no escape from the interests of others.

One of the first things one notices in assessing ethics in statecraft is the "level of analysis" problem. Shall we look at the *international system* as our target of analysis, the *nation-state*, or the *individual statesman*? Naturally, all must be considered together, although it is reasonable to single out any one for alternate analysis. One way to deal with this problem is by using the conventions of history and biography. This approach allows for giving due weight to all three levels, while placing an emphasis on the individual and the role of conscience. There are few more compelling sources for the study of ethics and international affairs than the true stories and historical experiences of statesmen who made hard choices in reconciling principle and power. In the tradition of Aristotle and Plutarch, we can learn from example and from biography: one cannot deny the moral impact of good stories.

The challenge for us is to make some sense of these stories, perhaps to extract some generalizations that may allow us to get beyond individual examples as a string of anecdotes. There is of course a legitimate question as to how theoretically rigorous one can be in this area: the theme of moral statesmanship is by its very nature not conducive to "scientific" study that would please natural scientists and social science quantifiers. Yet as this volume demonstrates, this theme is nevertheless thematically cogent and worthy of systematic study.

One of the objectives of this volume is to bridge the gap between the literature of moral judgment on specific events (e.g., the Holocaust, the Vietnam War), and the literature that assesses individual leaders. The literature of events enjoys the benefit of credible normative criteria such as human rights standards or the application of just war theory. But, as Brian Job of the University of British Columbia has noted, "the quality of debate often breaks down when individual leaders are examined. Decisions are either explained away as a result of someone's idiosyncratic or pathological nature, or are portrayed as if the individual in office had no individual input in determining the course of events (i.e., he or she was 'the product of his/her time and culture')." Fortunately we are not in completely uncharted territory in dealing with this problem.

One look at the great literature of Western civilization reveals the central place of the perennial themes of free will versus chance, character versus fate, and the individual versus destiny; they are the animus of Tolstoy's *War and Peace*, Melville's *Moby Dick*, and Machiavelli's *The Prince*, among many others. Many pages have been devoted to the theme of how the great individual such as Napoleon, Ahab, or the prince moves within history. The individual sometimes seems to be at the mercy of overwhelming historical forces, while at other times it appears as though one great man can move history by a singular force of will. Tolstoy outlines the problem of biography and history in his infamous and ponderous "Second Epilogue" on the subject, "What forces move history?"

> In 1789 a ferment arises in Paris, it grows, spreads, and is expressed by a movement of peoples from west to east. Several times it moves eastward and collides with a counter-movement from the east westward. In 1812 it reaches its extreme limit, Moscow, and then, with remarkable symmetry, a counter-movement occurs from east to west, attracting to it, as the first movement had done, the nations of middle Europe. The counter-movement reaches the starting point of the first movement in the west—Paris—and subsides.
>
> During that twenty-year period an immense number of fields were left untilled, houses were burned, trade changed its direction, millions of men migrated, were impoverished, or were enriched, and millions of Christian men professing the law of love and their fellows slew one another.
>
> What does this all mean? Why did it happen? What made those people burn houses and slay their fellow men? What were the causes of those events? What force made these men act so?[4]

In the course of his 1,000-plus-page narrative and discursive conclusion, Tolstoy makes it plain that modern history must consider a variety of irreducible factors.

Given this perspective, how then can we possibly theorize about these matters of free will, contingency, historical force, and moral choice? At least five points emerge in a review of the literature in this field that may serve to organize discussion and study: (1) the construction of narratives; (2) the distinction between perfectionist and nonperfectionist ethics; (3) the theme of necessity and choice; (4) the issue of individual versus collective morality; and (5) the role and resonance of international moral norms.

In his 1992 article entitled "The Cold War's End Dramatizes the Failure of Political Theory," John L. Gaddis observes that modern theoretical approaches to the study of international relations have failed on their own ambitious terms: they have failed to increase the reliability of prediction, and they have failed to remove uncertainty from political action. Because of the nature of international relations, variables cannot be reduced or isolated for close study—the conditions required of a controlled experiment cannot be achieved. In something of a prescriptive conclusion, Gaddis writes, "in practice we tend to fall back upon the only simulative technique that successfully illustrates the general and the specific, the regular and the irregular, the predictable and the unpredictable. We construct narratives."[5]

The narratives examined here—consisting primarily of the biographies and specific experiences of statesmen—are an integral part of how we might improve our understanding of ethics and international affairs. These narratives reveal the timeless philosophical quandaries all humans face, yet they account for history and context: they consider ethics in terms of both principle and practice. As William Kilpatrick, a professor of education at Boston University, writes: "the connection between narrative and morality is an essential one, not merely a useful one. The Ph.D. needs the story 'part' just as much as [anyone]. In other words, story and moral may be less separable than we have come to think. The question is not whether the moral principle needs to be sweetened with the sugar of the story; but whether moral principles make any sense outside the human context of stories."[6] There is a natural instinct for those of us interested in ethics and international affairs to get down to cases, to merge theory and practice through example.

This focus on narratives, as well as ethics and decision making, enables us to get to the root of ethics, which is human agency—or real people acting in history. Despite their focus on the international system, the conditions of anarchy and the primacy of power and interests, realists such as Hans J. Morgenthau and Kenneth W. Thompson conclude: "Ethical rules have their seat in the conscience of individual men. Government by clearly identifiable men who can be held personally responsible for their actions is therefore the precondition for the existence of an effective system of international ethics."[7]

This assertion leads to a second theme in discussing statecraft, and that is the issue of perfectionism versus nonperfectionism. Max Weber calls this the distinction between the "ethics of ultimate ends" and the "ethics of responsibility."[8] Without delving too deeply into this distinction here, most people are willing to cede some ground to Weber and the realists on this point, and most understand statecraft to be concerned with moral choice that frequently if not regularly requires the balancing of competing moral claims and the choosing of the lesser of two evils. Decision making always involves reconciling the desirable with the possible: the political arena is not the realm for the blind pursuit of moral imperatives without regard for consequences. For this reason, saints, by their very nature, do not make good politicians, and politicians are generally not suited for sainthood. One will find very few pure Kantians among statesmen anywhere—that is, statesmen who strictly adhere to principles over consequences, and the virtues of reason over the lessons of experience.

This gets to the heart of the matter concerning statecraft, and a third theme—the problem of necessity and choice. The frequent justification given by statesmen for their action is, "I had no choice but to do x." As Arnold Wolfers puts it in his essay on "Statesmanship and Moral Choice":

> Machiavelli and Machiavellianism have stood for a doctrine that places princes and sovereign states under the rule not of ordinary morality, but of the "reason of state," considered an amoral principle peculiar to the realm of politics. German writers have been particularly insistent that ethical standards that apply to private individuals cannot measure the behavior of states which are said to be guided by necessity.

Wolfers goes on to note that in general, "the English speaking world . . . has been unwilling to admit any peculiar ethics of state behavior."[9]

This generalization aside, Wolfers is correct in conveying the basic tension between an almost nihilistic Machiavellian realism that posits all action in terms of national interests and maximizing power, and a more nuanced view that seeks to reconcile morality and power, and does not see power accumulation and balance of power as exclusive moral ends in themselves. "In every case," writes Wolfers, "the interpretation of what constitutes a vital national interest and how much value should be attached to it is a moral question. It cannot be answered by reference to alleged amoral necessities inherent in international politics; it rests on value judgments." This is where the character of the individual statesman comes into play.

If nothing else, it is imperative for us to expand the inquiry into the "choice" part of the dialectic between necessity and choice. While the enmity of the international system may not give the statesman the complete freedom that he would ideally like, he is rarely boxed in to such an extent that all of his choices are gone. Is it possible that in many instances where statesmen justify their actions in terms of being boxed in to the point of "no choice," the box is of their own making?

A fourth theme is the one suggested by the title of Reinhold Niebuhr's well-known book of 1932, *Moral Man and Immoral Society* (a book, one should note, that was about socialism and domestic politics, not international affairs). Niebuhr makes much of the distinction between the moral behavior of individuals and the moral behavior of social groups. The question, easily extrapolated from this argument, is: how can one live a moral life (and make moral choices) in the context of an immoral or amoral world; and for our purposes, how can a statesman pursue a moral foreign policy in the context of nationalism, self-interest, and international anarchy? It is a theme that has had considerable resonance over the years, often referred to in debates over individual and collective morality.

The essential point of this debate concerns social dynamics. How much weight, if any, do we want to give to Niebuhr's observation that "group relations can never be as ethical as those which characterize individual relations"? Niebuhr observes that "one of the tragedies of the human spirit [is] its inability to conform its collective life to individual ideals. As individuals, men believe that they ought to serve each other and establish justice between each other. As racial, economic and national groups they take for themselves whatever their power can command."[10] The statesman, of course, stands at the apex (or vortex, depending on how you look at it) of this dilemma—he or she is an individual, with a conscience of his or her own, acting on behalf of a social group.

In discussions of this sort, the Italian Cavour's aphorism: "What rogues we would be if we did for ourselves what we do for our country" immediately springs to mind. But as Greg Russell points out in his study of Hans Morgenthau and political realism, upon further reflection, the choice is not so stark: "What changes for the nature and role of moral judgment on either [the individual or collective] level is not the action itself, but the social environment within which . . . norms must function" (in our case, this environmental imperative refers to the security-power dilemma—the consistent drive for power as a measure of ensuring national security).[11] As for Niebuhr, David Little's analysis is apt: "The interesting question is not whether there is an irreconcilable conflict between individual and collective morality as Niebuhr says there is . . . The interesting question concerns the shades of difference between what is morally expected of individuals in comparison with nations and other groups, and that requires more careful analysis than Niebuhr gave the matter."[12]

A fifth and final point relates to the standards or yardsticks by which statesmen themselves make judgments, and by which we ourselves might make judgments. Obviously, much is left to conscience and how an individual perceives his or her options, circumstances, and duties. Yet part of how statesmen (and we as individuals) perceive "right" and "wrong" depends on how we understand the "rules of the game" in international affairs. What role do international moral norms play in shaping the words and deeds of policy makers? One of the objectives of this volume is to describe this interaction, and in this way, describe the connection between normative and empirical concerns.

By international moral norms, we mean the prescriptive principles of desirable behavior to which most nations can and do agree. These norms embody the ideals and principles by which a community—even a world community—defines itself. The evolution of international moral norms (and their effect on statecraft) tells us much about world history and our current situation. Much of this story is told in Dorothy V. Jones's book *Code of Peace: Ethics and Security in the world of Warlord States*, where she outlines the origins and evolution of principles such as the sovereign equality of states, the presumption of nonintervention, the recognition of human rights, and the principle of self-determination, and explains that these principles have not been created in a vacuum.[13] As Jones illustrates, these principles have arisen from the hard-won lessons of war and peace throughout world history, and especially in the twentieth century. They have shaped the beliefs and actions of statesmen, and in turn, they have been shaped and reshaped by them.

This volume gives due consideration to the aforementioned three levels of analysis, as well as the five points outlined above. At the very least, it provides a modicum of discipline and organization that enables us to extract some generalized wisdom from case studies such as the ones that are explored. Current tools of diplomacy and statecraft such as finance (sanctions), technology (drones), and law are best understood as presented here, fully embedded in historical context with actors making decisions in real time. In this way, this volume opens an important pathway to the study of ethics and international affairs and is a genuine contribution to our understanding of the connection between moral principles and national leadership.

Three takeaways for every reader are guaranteed. First, readers will gain a greater appreciation of the intrinsic connection between values and interests. By viewing statesmanship through the lens of biography and ethics, one can see that interests are a matter of judgment, subject to human reason and experience. Second, readers will see why discussions of ethics that focus solely on the individual or the institution are insufficient. It is the interaction between the two—the individual acting within a system and set of circumstances—that is worth considering. Third and finally, the stories themselves remind the reader of the human element of statecraft. Models of international relations theory cannot substitute for the passions, aspirations, and anguishes of those in the breach. The high stakes and real-life drama should never be forgotten or diminished.

NOTES

1. Klaus Schwab, "From Our Founder," World Economic Forum, http://www.weforum.org.

2. Gordon Brown, "Wiring a Web for Global Good," *TED* Talk, http://www.ted.com.

3. Michael Ignatieff, *The Needs of Strangers* (London: Vintage, 1994).

4. Leo Tolstoy, *War and Peace* (Chicago: Encyclopedia Britannica/Great Books Edition, 1952), pp. 675–76.

5. John Lewis Gaddis, "The Cold War's End Dramatizes the Failure of Political Theory," *The Chronicle of Higher Education*, Vol. 38 (July 26, 1992), p. A44

6. William Kilpatrick, "The Moral Power of Good Stories," *American Educator*, Vol. 17 (Summer 1993), pp. 24–30.

7. Kenneth W. Thompson, *Political Realism and the Crisis of World Politics* (Washington, DC: University Press of America, 1982), p. 157.

8. See Max Weber, "Politics as a Vocation," in Hans Gerth and C. Wright Mills, eds., *From Max Weber: Essays in Sociology* (New York: Oxford University Press, 1946).

9. Arnold Wolfers, *Discord and Collaboration: Essays on International Politics* (Baltimore: Johns Hopkins University Press, 1962), pp. 47–65.

10. Reinhold Niebuhr, *Moral Man and Immoral Society* (New York: Charles Scribner's Sons, 1932).

11. Greg Russell, *Hans J. Morgenthau and the Ethics of American Statecraft* (Baton Rouge: Louisiana State University Press, 1990), p. 156.

12. David Little, "The Recovery of Liberalism: *Moral Man and Immoral Society* Sixty Years Later," *Ethics & International Affairs*, Vol. 7 (1993), p. 198.

13. Dorothy V. Jones, *Code of Peace: Ethics and Security in the World of Warlord States* (Chicago: University of Chicago Press, 1991).

Preface to the Third Edition

Cathal J. Nolan

The editor and contributors to the first and second editions of *Ethics and Statecraft* were pleased with the positive reception it received, and the wide readership it garnered. Academic reviewers praised the book for its clarity of presentation, the soundness of its scholarship, and an appropriate focus on individual human agency as the fulcrum of ethical concern in foreign policy strategies and decision making. Students responded with eager attentiveness to important issues.

This is a scholarly era wherein far too much political science is marred by scientistic pretension and obscurantist writing, and perhaps too much history is devoted to domestic social and cultural change without much reference to international affairs and the global influence of issues of war, peace, intervention, and disparate economic development. This volume stresses clarity of prose, presentation, and thinking, bringing together the abiding concerns of the past with developing issues of real moral and political import in the early twenty-first century.

It is not an accident that the earlier editions saw wide university adoptions not just at the graduate level, but in introductory politics and social science and philosophy courses. This fact confirms the editor's and original contributors' judgment that the study of important debates of lasting and trenchant moral significance, clearly presented, both deserves and will retain the attention of modern college students.

Most pride is taken from the fact that professors at several institutions of higher learning who used the book in class said that it helped awaken students to their own place in the ongoing drama of human history, world politics, and some of the key moral debates of these and even all times. Similarly, the strong response of the educated reading public confirms that good political history about important ideas and decisions, which is also written well, consistently attracts the attention of intelligent men and women who are concerned with the moral significance of great events of the past, and the abiding issues of their own times and place.

Changes made in the third edition improve the logic of presentation and enhance the general usefulness of the book. The new edition incorporates important new chapters on emergent issues of international ethics, or issues that have recently taken on real salience: the responsibility to protect minorities by preventing atrocity and genocide, human security, new rules and duties in war zones, humanitarian intervention, drone ethics, and targeted sanctions.

To better fit these new essays into the book, the original framework has been changed to situate chapters that play to one another over four grand themes: the ethics and statecraft of war, the moral obligations and pitfalls of peacemaking, the ethics and statecraft of major international reform ("transformation"), and the laws, norms, and statecraft of key emergent issues and trends in international relations. In addition, original chapters by Carl Hodge, William Tilchin, and David Armstrong were revised and updated.

Cathal J. Nolan

March 1, 2015

Natick, Massachusetts

Acknowledgments

I am grateful to Hannah Metheny and Amy Noel Ellison, doctoral candidates in history at Boston University, for their devoted and careful editorial assistance in helping to prepare the manuscript of the third edition of this book. I am pleased to include a number of essays from earlier editions that readers appreciated and applauded, and I thank the newest authors to join the book for their wise contributions. I am grateful for encouragement to undertake a new and expanded edition provided early on by Steve Catalano, senior editor for security issues, politics, and military history at Praeger Publishers and ABC-CLIO. I also thank him for his patient support and sound advice throughout the editing process. I am most grateful to my wife, Valerie, for her years of close support and constant companionship. My debt to her is ineffable.

Cathal J. Nolan
Boston University

Introduction

Cathal J. Nolan

> Those who would treat politics and morality apart will never
> understand the one or the other.
> —John, Viscount Morley of Blackburn, *Rousseau* (1876)

An animating concern, and part of the underlying logic, of the scholarly
enterprise leading to this book is to rekindle academic inquiry at the intersec-
tion of political analysis, diplomatic history, and philosophical investigation.
That is why mostly senior diplomatic historians and philosophically minded
political scientists were asked to contribute to this collective study. Their
essays are of high quality, confirming that there is a bright future for interdisciplinary and normative inquiry in this field: among students and scholars
there exists an untapped reserve of interest in reviving a philosophically and
historically informed understanding of world politics.

Another concern of this text is to call attention to the ethically ambiguous
role of decision makers acting under the constraints and imperatives of real-
world situations that impose real consequences, rather than to dwell on
abstract moral propositions or the construction of theoretical models.
The explicit purpose of this volume is to show that the individual leader is a
major conduit by which ethical considerations enter into the decision-
making process of states, and thereby affect the course and nature of
international politics. This text thus offers an unusual concentration on his-
torical/political biography, suggesting that it is a necessary part of any consideration of the ethics of statecraft. This approach cuts to the heart of the
question of the place of ethics in international affairs—the contention that
the foundation of ethics is human agency, which is always acted out in a context of ambiguity, competing moral claims, and unforeseen consequences.

The subjects of this text were selected based on their involvement with a
range of hard moral issues that are central to the conduct of statecraft, with

representative examples of leaders in peacetime, wartime, and times of sweeping political change. There are no clear clear-cut cases here, and solutions to ethical dilemmas are not obvious. Contributors do not engage in airy academic scribblings about "contending moral paradigms" and other such fashionable clichés. Instead, they express empathy with the difficulties, as well as opportunities, that changing circumstances and public responsibility present to the ethical practice of statecraft. This volume sets out questions of international ethics as they are encountered by decision makers in real life: as dirty, gray, uncertain choices, which once made are likely to be forever unsatisfactory to the moral purist or political ideologue. As a result, the chapters present moral issues in foreign policy for what they really are: great and difficult dilemmas—not hurdles on the path to political sainthood—faced by flesh flesh-and and-blood human beings who must act with limited knowledge and under enormous pressures of time and political constraint, who yet remain responsible for consequences of huge import. Cases from the highly important Anglo-American legacy in international affairs are included, along with cases from other national traditions. Some chapters present a striking counterpoint to the liberal-internationalist concerns and assumptions that dominate recent English-language writing on ethics and world affairs. Readers will therefore encounter a different (and often misunderstood) moral tradition, one attached to political realism. Encapsulated in the ideas of prudence and virtue, this tradition upholds a set of qualities that inform independent moral judgment and are rooted in caution, consideration of opposing interests, deliberation, forethought, foresight, preparedness, wariness, and—if and whenever possible—candor with adversaries as well as allies.

Contributors were asked to look—straight in the eye—at real real-life moral dilemmas faced by prominent national leaders, about whom we know a fair deal but who operated under conditions of restricted knowledge and limited power to effect change. The global stature and wide influence of these leaders rendered their actions (or inactions) of considerable moral and political gravity. Their central participation in decision making, and the pivotal nature of the events with which each was involved, make them stand out as appropriate choices for sober reflection. These are not the small-fry of history and politics. To the contrary, we all live within the consequences—moral, political, and otherwise—of their actions and decisions. Otto von Bismarck dominated not only his nation but his era, elevating Germany through war to the pinnacle of the European state system, from where he also presided over the "Eastern Question" and oversaw the final partition of Africa. Theodore Roosevelt and Woodrow Wilson continue to cast shadows over the twentieth century, in particular its grand experiments with international organization, collective security, and decentralized international governance. Flawed as their visions surely were, as the twentieth century closed, at least both

Wilson and TR surpassed in lasting significance their contemporary and fellow visionaries of a new world order, Vladimir I. Lenin and Leon Trotsky. Franklin Roosevelt and Winston Churchill led two great democracies in the biggest war either nation ever faced. In doing so, each had to address ethical problems of extraordinary complexity and consequence. Their moral accomplishments are dealt with here without mawkishness, just as their uneasy compromises, deliberate deceits, and personal and moral flaws are discussed without the majestic condemnation born of hindsight that the living too frequently dispense in judgment upon the dead. And so with the other leaders: Konrad Adenauer and Eduard Shevardnadze were also statesmen of major significance, whose complex choices and actions are subjected to sustained moral reflection by specialist scholars. The volume also contains an expanded set of important thematic essays: on warmaking, peacemaking, and humane relations and interests among nations.

The Carnegie Council on Ethics and International Affairs made a generous offer to sponsor a conference on biography, ethics, and statecraft, using the existing structure and essays in the book, already under commission, as the framework. Council sponsorship enabled most contributors to meet under the auspices of the Institute of International Relations, University of British Columbia, in Vancouver in October 1993. Papers were delivered before an invited, international gathering of interested scholars, government officials, and Council officers. Debate was lively, as presentations were subjected to close scrutiny by assembled historians, moral philosophers, political scientists, and political theorists, with each bringing to bear the varied methodologies and insights of their disciplines. Although unanimity on specific or final moral judgments sometimes eluded the gathering—as perhaps it should on such profound issues as war, peace, and political transformation—an important consensus developed on the set of questions necessary to think systematically about issues of ethics and statecraft. The conference thus highlighted a number of core themes that appear in nearly all the essays, as diverse as their subjects are. It was generally agreed that these themes emerged out of the essential practice of statecraft, as reflected in the case studies. It also was made clear that the ethical dimension of world affairs cannot be properly or fully understood without explicitly stating and directly addressing the questions that are raised at the level of individual decision makers. Since then, other scholars have joined the debate ongoing in these pages and in the world. Together, contributors old and new advance and update the issues of the twentieth century for reconsideration in the twenty-first. And they take on new issues emerging from rapid legal, technological, and geopolitical change.

Of what did this scholarly consensus consist? First, it was accepted that analysts must assess the extent to which ethical concerns can be considered separate from diplomatic practice. They must ask: to what degree do these concerns arise from the nature of foreign policy and specific situations encountered in the real world by national leaders, rather than descend out of an Olympian cloud of abstract reasoning or absolute principle? This was seen as the critical issue by most participants. Moreover, it spoke directly to the second but related question: what criteria should be used to judge the ethical content of actual decisions? Many argued forcefully for historical and situational empathy and discrimination. Others asked if this was enough, suggesting that formal moral theory still has a role to play in assisting leaders to make difficult choices, and analysts to assess the choices actually made. Moral theory might provide an "Archimedean point" for articulating first principles for deducing ethical action and making judgments. Or it might at least help to articulate a moral sense, and enable consideration of the inevitable trade-offs and contradictions of difficult problems. In this context, all participants praised the case study approach for allowing close examination of a leader's motives and means, as well as the consequences of his or her actions and decisions. Examining actual decisions made by men and women on the great moral questions in world affairs highlights the extant role of volition in foreign policy, no matter how otherwise constrained a policy context might be. These studies thus help account for the three components critical to any application of moral reasoning to problems of statecraft: What were the motives of the decision makers involved? Did they have reasonable, alternative means at their disposal that might have allowed them to effect different choices than the ones they actually made? And what were the real, as well as perceived and potential, consequences of the choices they faced?

A final element of the consensus was that analysts of ethics and international affairs must address the issue of what qualities are truly desirable in men and women involved in public affairs, without assuming that private virtue guarantees moral success on the international plane. It was generally accepted that the realm of statecraft often raises different moral questions and may call for qualities other than those celebrated in the private domain. Put another way, the common assumption that good public policy will necessarily flow from having people of private virtue in positions of authority seems erroneous. The record suggests that the road to foreign policy (and even moral) disaster may well be paved with the good intentions of decent people. Thus, while it is a necessary beginning, it is not a sufficient basis for judgment to ask whether leaders remained true to their internal or declared principles once great power was theirs. We should ask as well if they adhered to, and sought to advance, the normative conventions of international society and international law, or of some developed moral theory that reached beyond their personal outlook. And we must be prepared to accept that peculiar circumstances may permit leaders to depart, with absolution, from some moral conventions if their decisions serve competing ethical purposes and needs.

Similarly, leaders who achieve admirable moral ends while also conducting an instrumental foreign policy may do so in spite of a gravely flawed private character. They may even be successful (morally speaking, not just politically) because of behavior that would be widely excoriated if it aimed solely at private ends. Gentlefolk are quite properly found ethically wanting if they read each others' mail; they ought not in general to lie, either, or use force to impose their will on others. Yet, under certain circumstances, governments and national leaders are likely to have a moral obligation to use such means in the service of higher public goods. Bluntly stated, private sinners may well make excellent national leaders—and remarkably often, as matters turn out. Equally, under specific conditions private vices may actually take form as public virtues. This is one of several paradoxes concerning the ethics of statecraft to emerge from comparison of the case studies in this volume.

A lake of ink has been spilled concerning the differences between "realists," in the academic sense, and "idealists." In the 1920s and 1930s, a raft of self-declared realist scholars and commentators vehemently rejected what they saw as the excessive legalism and moralism underlying the Versailles settlement. Wilson's foreign policy came in for special condemnation, for its putative ignorance of the realities of the balance of power and the role of force in world affairs, and for what was seen as a foolhardy effort to displace these hard realities with mere moral constructs. Conventional academic wisdom soon had it that world politics was inescapably a stage where players engaged in a raw contest for power. In this nearly unmitigated realm of Darwinian struggle, nations could expect to cling to existence only by embracing *Realpolitik*, or even *Machtpolitik*, assumptions and prescriptions. Several generations of political science students were taught that the fundamental, underlying reality of world affairs is a Hobbesian anarchy wherein the "condition of Man ... is a war of everyone against everyone."[1] Evidence of interstate concern for a political order cognizant of questions of justice was dismissed, as a facade concealing harder antagonisms. This veneer had to be stripped away, coarser realists said, to reveal the unchanging reality of coercion through the naked exercise of power, unrestrained except by countervailing power and an equilibrium of brutality and fear. This vulgar worldview was served up both as a depiction of reality and as a quasi-philosophical justification for a smug amoralism about foreign policy. Those fond of the pedigree (though not necessarily the content) of the classics then quoted, to justify their amoralism, Thucydides's famous statement of moral and political pessimism: "know that in human reckoning the question of justice only enters where there is equal power to enforce it, and that the powerful exact what they can and the weak grant what they must."[2] Yet the most profound realist writers were always aware of the moral realm, and qualified hard portrayals of world politics at its worst by pointing as well to large-scale social and normative features of the states system, such as international law and organization.[3] They were joined by others, working overtly within a normative framework, who suggested that in the modern era there was at least as much caricature as fact in coarse, amoral images of international affairs.[4]

In short, differences between realists and idealists are not the truly unbridgeable academic divide. It is instead the gulf between humanistic and scientistic (not scientific) approaches to social science that cannot be spanned. The rise within the social sciences of a crude, yet pervasive, positivism has been profoundly damaging to normative understanding of the meaning of world affairs. This scientistic prejudice of much contemporary political science threatens to suffocate the essential humanism that suffused classical political and social science inquiry, including classical realism.[5] Politics is a plain, blunt subject demanding plain, blunt words. Yet too much modern political science writing is tedious and pretentious, and suffused with arcane methodologies that obscure the truly important intellectual, practical, and moral purposes of political study. This results from an extreme narrowness of philosophical vision—or even consciousness—of many of its practitioners, who explicitly and proudly reject any concern for the normative dimension of world affairs. Among positivists, the classical notion that philosophical inquiry is a key pathway to understanding social and political matters is seen as quaint at best, and at worst as threatening the ongoing project of compiling a "science of politics." Such disregard of the normative realm is further aggravated by an attendant affliction of a historicism, in which the very nature of history and the craft of historians are miscast. The former is viewed as a rudimentary compilation of data, while the latter are seen as data collectors, without much to offer by way of analysis or theory. Only gestation of historical data under the more rigorous, quantitative methods used by doctors of politics, it is suggested, can lead to the birth of a "theoretical" and "scientific" understanding of public events. Above all, any effort to use moral reasoning to uncover the meaning of political actions is dismissed as methodologically archaic, as it is supposedly irretrievably subjective and nonscientific. In addition to their inherent humor, these are profoundly flawed and damaging (to the truth) conceits; for in neglecting the normative realm positivists necessarily fail to understand the essential nature of power politics as well.

The contributors to this book include some who might be described as realists, and others who may be read as idealists. But it is much more important that for all—as for most people on a near-instinctual basis—it is entirely natural to explore the ethical dimensions of statecraft, and to consider matters of political power and interest as imbued with normative content. A shared premise—one that positivists utterly fail to grasp—is that no adequate understanding of international relations is possible in the absence of normative inquiry. There is also recognition that moral norms as governing ideas already significantly shape international relations and the context of statecraft in the real world.[6] Thus, a key purpose this volume serves is to begin to close the artificial chasm that has opened between realist and idealist scholarly communities, that hitherto have used different analytical languages and arrived at dissimilar conclusions about the essential nature of world politics, but are not as far apart in their normative concerns as is often thought. In this regard, it bears repeating that the most profound realist thinkers have always clearly understood and noted the importance of normative concerns in international relations, just as shrewder idealists have not been unaware of the role of power and the interplay of interest in the affairs of states.[7]

In addition, there is a shared cognizance among the contributors of the special problems of morality and foreign policy decision making. In particular, there is a common appreciation of three considerations: (1) the centrality to normative analysis of historical and situational context; (2) the need to focus not just on the motivations of key decision makers, but also on the means available to them; and (3) the requirement to assess potential as well as actual consequences of moral choices. Because of this understanding of the complexity of the ethics of statecraft, the contributors to this volume are not unduly shocked by political expedience any more than they are overly impressed by mere moralizing rhetoric. National leaders are neither utterly condemned for their less savory actions nor raised up in hagiography for their fine words and unsupported declarations of good intentions or noble aims. Instead, they are treated with temperate judgment, derived from the historical, psychological, and situational empathy each author brings to bear. The innate human tendency to harshness of judgment of past actions is thereby mitigated by consideration of the extraordinary circumstances and pressures with which these individuals contended, and the sharp limits on their knowledge of others' intentions, and of real outcomes. The result is a set of portraits of key leaders struggling with great moral issues in critical political settings. Many are sympathetic, yet—in the spirit of Oliver Cromwell's famous command to his court painter—they still depict their subjects truly, with "roughnesses, pimples, warts and everything."

NOTES

1. Thomas Hobbes, *Leviathan*, Part I, Chapter 4 (1651). That is not to deny that realists had valid targets in that era, and since. It is certainly true that much writing by "world federalists," some normatively inclined international lawyers, and others, has deserved the characterization of naïveté and excessive abstraction cast upon it by realists.

2. Thucydides, "Melian Dialogue," *History of the Peloponnesian War* (New York: Washington Square Press, 1963), p. 181.

3. For example, see Hedley Bull's influential and important treatise, *The Anarchical Society* (London: Macmillan, 1977); and Hans J. Morgenthau, *Politics Among Nations: The Struggle for Power and Peace*, 6th ed. (New York: Alfred A. Knopf, 1985).

4. See the important corrective to neorealism's overstatement of the idea and the reality of international anarchy represented by Terry Nardin and David R. Mapel, eds., *Traditions of International Ethics*, Cambridge Studies in International Relations #17 (Cambridge: Cambridge University Press, 1992).

5. This contrast emerges clearly in any comparison of the flexible insights of humanistic, "realist" writers such as Hedley Bull or Martin Wight, with the arid models of the state system offered up by a positivist "neorealist" like Kenneth Waltz.

6. Among key works on these themes, the most ambitious in its normative conclusions is Dorothy V. Jones, *Code of Peace: Ethics and Security in the World of the Warlord States* (Chicago: University of Chicago Press, 1991). Also see Louis Henkin et al., *Right v. Might: International Law and the Use of Force* (New York: Council on Foreign Relations, 1991); and Henkin, *How Nations Behave: Law and Foreign Policy* (New York: Council on Foreign Relations, 1968; 1979). A more skeptical, though still sympathetic, view of the evolution of international norms is Cathal J. Nolan, "The United States, Moral Norms and Governing Ideas in World Politics," *Ethics and International Affairs*, Vol. 7 (1993), pp. 223–39; and Nolan, *Principled Diplomacy: Security and Rights in U.S. Foreign Policy* (Westport, CT: Greenwood, 1993), passim.

7. For instance, see Morgenthau's discussion of the moral basis of the balance of power in *Politics Among Nations*, pp. 233–40. An important study of moral content in modern realist thought is Joel H. Rosenthal, *Righteous Realists: Political Realism, Responsible Power, and American Culture in the Nuclear Age* (Baton Rouge: Louisiana State University Press, 1991).

Part I

War

1

"Bodyguard of Lies": Franklin D. Roosevelt and Defensible Deceit in World War II*

Cathal J. Nolan

Truly, to tell lies is not honorable. But when the truth entails
tremendous ruin, to speak dishonorably is pardonable.
> —Sophocles, *Cruesa* (fragment)

Truth . . . never comes into the world but like a bastard.
> —John Milton (1643)

In war, the truth must be protected by a bodyguard of lies.
> —Winston Churchill (attributed)

This chapter sets out to accomplish a difficult task: to defend lying, on occasion, by a democratic government. This proposition is unpleasant, which is why I have stated it so baldly; to do less would be to dissemble, and thereby defeat the purpose of the exercise. Most of us feel, I assume, a certain political—if not natural—squeamishness at any suggestion that lying in public affairs is defensible, especially in a democracy. Beyond that shared disquiet I suspect that this proposal is more difficult for Americans to accept than it is for some other, perhaps more cynical (or is it just more tory?) peoples. That is so not only because of a rooted, democratic political culture, but also due to the experiences of the Vietnam War and Watergate. Those events left an often painfully naïve generation seared with cynicism, by the supposed "revelation" that presidents lie. A growing sense of the dangers of presidential deceit was reinforced for many in the 1980s, by what were widely seen among foreign policy analysts as exaggerated reasons for intervention in the Caribbean and in Central America, and by the Iran-Contra affair.

---

*I am grateful to Professor Emeritus Edward M. Bennett, of Washington State University, for his insightful comments on an earlier draft of this chapter.

Other generations under other circumstances have been more tolerant of deceit, most notably during wartime. Prior to Vietnam the argument was more acceptable among policy elites that lying to the public by high officials was excusable, if vital national interests were at stake that plain folks—either through prejudice or lack of knowledge—did not apprehend. Since the end of the Vietnam War, something of a consensus has developed that lying by public officials was a proximate if not a primary reason for the escalation of immersion in that disastrous conflict, and hence that lying is itself a threat to the national interest. That thesis has considerable merit, certainly regarding Vietnam and probably generally as well. And yet, does it hold true for all cases? If moralistic overreaction would deny legitimacy to any other instance of deliberate deceit, might this not result even in dangers to the public good? Aware of the opposition this notion is likely to engender, I nonetheless suggest that moral absolutism condemning all lying in public affairs is an emotionally gratifying position, but hardly an intellectually satisfying one.

The practices of deceit dealt with here are not the usual stuff of warmaking, about the moral legitimacy of which there should be little disagreement. Assuming that a cause is genuinely just, the propriety of lying to the enemy is a moral given because of the obvious need to conceal one's capabilities for reasons of defense. Passive deception of an enemy in wartime is an integral component of virtually every military plan. Terms such as "camouflage," "feint," or "stratagem" are particular references to the overall need to confuse and deceive an enemy, so that one can better kill its troops, incapacitate its armies, and destroy its ability to resist. Disinformation and propaganda go further: they are forward measures to deceive the enemy. But they may also cross a line into active deceit of one's own population, in order to sustain national morale. Surely in these areas at least, we ought to abstain from a position of moral absolutism that holds it improper to ever lie to one's own people, even when the nation is at war. In warfare there are usually much higher moral goods at stake, such as the preservation of life (primarily on one's own side, of course), and more important, of national values and perhaps national identity.

But let me push the argument further, to suggest that the special conditions of wartime statecraft mean that leaders may actually be morally obligated to lie. Most clearly, they must deceive their own people about troop movements, ship sailings, productivity figures, and strategic plans. This type of lying to one's own simply reinforces the deceptions one is attempting to foist upon the enemy. Moreover, releasing misleading or false information, maintaining extreme secrecy, and other such wartime deceits are generally accepted by the vast majority of citizens. "Loose lips sink ships" was the way a famous World War II slogan had it, a caution that was as often as not roughly enforced on the factory floor or along the waterfront by workers themselves.

It is not these mundane wartime lies—if I may be permitted that phrase—with which I am concerned (they do not, in fact, unduly concern me on any level). Rather, I am interested in the grand, strategic lies in which statesmen take recourse in the face of public resistance to their policies. Specifically, I wish to consider the calculated deceits that Franklin Roosevelt purveyed and culti- vated to get America into World War II, to sustain its war effort, and then to commit it to postwar activism. What were the uncomfortable facts of his moral dilemma? Were his deceptions defensible? If so, what were the benefits and losses the nation incurred? In what ways did he deceive the American public? To what extent were his lies pardonable by circumstance? And what price, if any, was paid for them later?

My argument is simple: even between democratic leaders and the peoples they lead, deceit may be defensible when the nation is *in extremis*. Indeed, in times of great crisis and danger, such as that faced by the United States and civilization itself before and during World War II, lying to the public in order to get it to move to a position from which it would otherwise have fled may well have been the most morally defensible course of action. In short, what some others have rejected as Roosevelt's moral duplicity, I will argue, amounted to moral leadership in a wider sense. After all, his prewar manipula- tion of public opinion was essential to a statecraft that pursued immediate defense against a manifest danger, as well as longer-term, enlightened self- interest. But I am not in the business of hagiography, and I will consider as well the eventual foreign policy costs of this lying. For expedient deception, even of political allies, was a practice that with Roosevelt became habitual. His reliance on personal charm to advance political goals, and his reputation for Tammany Hall scheming, are both well known. With a political twist, he appears to have believed with Terence that "obsequiousness begets friends; truth hatred." Roosevelt was a man to whom dissembling came easily, and who did not like to tell disagreeable truths boldly. He thus continued to lie about his broad foreign policy goals to enemies and allies alike well after Pearl Harbor. Furthermore, to support his wartime and postwar plans, he deliberately deceived the American public about the internal character of the Soviet Union, a maneuver that proved quite harmful in the end.

LIES AND THE NAZI THREAT

Professor Sissela Bok has written a wide-ranging and widely read treatise on lying.[1] She refers to Roosevelt's statecraft only once, mainly for purposes of comparison to Lyndon Johnson's conduct of the war in Vietnam. Yet what she has to say should, by contrast, help illustrate some of the points I wish to make. She agrees that the case of a public unwilling to face up to the immi- nent danger from Nazi Germany before World War II is:

a difficult one, and one on which reasonable persons might not be able to agree. The threat was unprecedented; the need for preparations and for support for allies great; yet the difficulties of alerting the American public seemed insuperable.

She asks "would this crisis, then, justify proceeding through deceit?" Her answer is a curiously theoretical and emotive one, given what we actually know about World War II:

> To consent to such a deception would, I believe, be to take a frightening step. Do we want to live in a society where public officials can resort to deceit and manipulation whenever they decide that an exceptional crisis has arisen? Would we not, on balance, prefer to run the risk of failing to rise to a crisis honestly explained to us, from which the government might have saved us through manipulation? ... Only those deceptive practices which can be openly debated and consented to in advance are *justifiable* in a democracy.

She concludes that the deceit practiced by Roosevelt was probably inexcusable, and certainly unjustifiable; that the price paid in terms of broken domestic trust was too high; and—rather predictably—that the secrecy and deceit of the Vietnam War and the Nixon administration "grew at least in part because of existing precedents," by which she means Roosevelt.[2]

There is more than a little sophistry in that argument. Leave aside that advance consent by a democratic public to its own deception is a *non sequitur*. It is more telling that Professor Bok has removed the debate from the realm of facts and real-world consequences to that of merely emotionally gratifying preferences. Of course the adult citizen in a democracy prefers being consulted to being duped. But that merely side-steps the larger moral issue of whether it is pardonable for leaders to dupe citizens anyway, if the security, core values, and independent life of a free nation are at stake, as they arguably were after 1938. More important, it is ethically glib to rank the threat from Nazi Germany in World War II with later misperceptions of the degree of threat to the national interest from the local communisms of Indochina. The hazard to the United States from Nazi Germany was of the first order, surpassed as a national danger in American history only by the disaster of the Civil War. Roosevelt did not merely "perceive" or "decide" that Nazi Germany was a fundamental threat to America's interest in an open and expansive world order, and ultimately to the survival of its liberal values at home as well. Aggressive, expansionist Germany under the control of Adolf Hitler and the Nazis *in fact* posed a potentially mortal danger to the United States. One may justly criticize several subsequent presidents for screening their decisions and actions from public scrutiny by facile comparison to the dilemma faced by Roosevelt, and for using rationalizations about mortal threats to the national interest when they knew that the existence of such threats was patently untrue. It is no doubt correct to hold that misinformation and misdirection of the public is neither politically necessary nor morally justifiable to support a mere brushfire war against some regional threat from a nation one-tenth one's own size and power, and when one's own citizens are in no way directly threatened. But that is a far cry from trying to prepare a nation, beguiled by isolationism and in full, wounded retreat from an earlier holocaust in Europe, to face an almost certain and ferocious onslaught against its physical security and national belief system by a Great Power like Nazi Germany. Yet that was the vital task Roosevelt faced, and it is against that real-world background that he must be judged.

It is therefore startling and more than a little disturbing that Professor Bok asks us to forego any consideration of the consequences of losing World War II—to put it most plainly—apparently solely to preserve our collective innocence from public lies. I submit that such arguments about abstract, public well-being are utterly inadequate as a guide to moral judgment of public officials or public affairs when the nation is truly *in extremis*. How can we accurately or fairly address the moral significance of Roosevelt's deceitful actions without some corresponding effort to assess the likely consequences of inaction? In this case, of all cases, the consequences of failure to use nearly any and all efforts to resist the Nazi evil would have been truly horrific. There is every reason to believe that had U.S. industrial might not been matched to Soviet manpower and Britain's strategic location (as a giant airfield and invasion platform off the coast of Europe), the Axis powers could well have triumphed. Had events gone just marginally differently than they actually did, the result would have been Germany's hegemony and a corresponding nazification of Europe, the Middle East, much of Africa, and possibly India, too. It is not trite to remind ourselves of the implications for the United States had American inaction permitted Germany to win World War II on such terms, for such considerations played themselves out in the minds of policy makers of the day. Indeed, it is not only worthwhile to spell out the broad consequences of that nightmarish outcome, it is essential to any fair assessment of the moral probity of Roosevelt's choices and actions.

At the least, a German victory would have meant: the utter destruction of European Jewry as well as mass executions of Gypsies, homosexuals, "mental defectives," and others not to the taste of the Nazi elite; the re-enslavement of Slavic peoples, and the enslavement of Africans as well; extinction of the liberal idea in Europe; subjugation of dozens of nations, which must have led to endemic, violent resistance in following years; global dominance by the fascist powers, not just militarily but in terms of trade, international organization, and the setting of international legal and moral norms; and an ineluctable pressure upon the United States to form a "Fortress Western Hemisphere" security zone, replete with construction of a severe "national security state" and deteriorating respect for national independence and domestic liberties in the Americas. Furthermore, Germany, left to harvest the fruits of its victories in Europe, Russia, the Middle East, and Africa, would soon have acquired nuclear weapons, a prospect truly horrifying when it is coupled with the fact that German scientists and engineers already enjoyed a 5- to 10-year head start on missile and jet technology. In short, had Roosevelt failed to prepare the United States to enter decisively into World War II, Nazi Germany was likely to have won that war on terms that amounted to global dominance. The world must then have descended into a Cold War of a wholly different order. In this alternate Cold War, the United States would have been desperately—and possibly fatally—disadvantaged by not controlling western Europe or Japan. It would have faced, alone, an adversary far more adventurist, expansionist, and belligerent than the Soviet Union ever proved to be; and one in control of a greater industrial, resource, and technological base than even that of the United States. Those are the most "frightening," to use Professor Bok's word, and pertinent moral facts about this case; not whether Americans should have to live with the realization that victory came about in part because their leaders lied in order to prepare the nation to fight and to supply its allies.

I do not think the scenario I have given for American inaction and German victory is far-fetched. Of vastly greater importance, neither did Franklin Roosevelt. He understood the consequences of Nazi victory, even without an American defeat, in comparable terms to those just listed (with the exception that he lacked full knowledge of the coming Holocaust against the Jews). He did not believe with the isolationists that America could remain secure, or ultimately survive as a liberal power in a fascist, lawless world.[3] Earlier and perhaps more deeply than some other Western leaders, he found Nazism utterly repugnant. He saw it as entirely antithetical to his personal, Christian values and liberal-capitalist ideology. Once he also became convinced that Nazi Germany presented a fundamental threat to the nation, his diplomacy aimed consistently at encouraging an encircling alliance of antifascist powers. He wanted to bring together the Western democracies, the Little Entente,[4] and the Soviet Union in an anti-German and antifascist front. However, he was constrained by domestic opposition to seek to keep the United States from formal membership in any alliance, or overt commitment to collective defense. The compromise he settled on was to make actual, through rearmament, some of the latent military power of the United States, for purposes of deterrence. While some might see that primary reliance on other states opposing Hitler as weak at best and cynical at worst, it is more accurate to say that Roosevelt's determination to see Nazism off the world stage was genuine, but that he remained hamstrung by the strength of isolationist opinion.[5]

On the other hand, it took him a number of years to develop an assertive diplomacy toward Germany. During his first term, as the crises in Europe and Asia built, he was more concerned about reforms at home than threats from abroad. In 1934, he used the lure of trade to correct an atrophied U.S. policy toward the Soviet Union by granting recognition. In part he hoped to engage the Soviets in his desired defensive front against Germany, just as Stalin hoped to engage the United States against Japan, but Roosevelt did not follow the opening with any sustained effort. Through most of the 1930s, the United States offered Moscow, as it also offered London and Paris, little more than diplomatic encouragement.[6] FDR spoke of a "moral embargo" on arms sales and of a "quarantine" of aggressors and the contagion of war. He also hinted to the Western democracies and the Soviet Union of his support for collective security, although the United States remained outside the League of Nations, and Congress refused to permit adherence even to the World Court. When tested by the outbreak of the Spanish Civil War, Roosevelt so feared a backlash from American Catholics in the 1936 election that he refused to lend any support to the Republican government in Madrid (which was strongly opposed by Catholics). Although strict neutrality permitted him to aid the Republican government as the legitimate government of Spain, he chose not to do so. That was a policy he came to regret even as he continued to speak publicly in defense of the arms embargo Congress imposed on both sides. Instead of attempting to educate public opinion to the national interest in supporting Madrid, he decided to avoid a domestic fight he felt certain he would lose. He then worked to counteract the embargo covertly by sending limited aid to the Republicans, shipped through France during 1938 and 1939.[7]

Following the Munich Conference of September 29–30, 1938, Roosevelt broke with British and French appeasement—a policy he had never fully endorsed in any case. But he still had to concern himself with the appearances of neutrality, even as he became more assertive about defense preparedness and formulating a forward policy to deter and, ultimately, to defeat Hitler. He used executive authority whenever possible to bypass Congress and begin rearmament, not just for reasons of defense, but in the hope of bolstering Britain and France and thereby deterring Germany. He hoped to have the democratic nations of Europe do the job themselves, but thought it might stiffen their spines to believe they would have U.S. backing in the event of war. He therefore sent instructions to William Bullitt, then ambassador to France, to tell the French government that "if a war should break out we will certainly not take part in the beginning, but we will end it."[8] This message was sent with the clear knowledge that U.S. opinion at that point would not support even significant aid to Britain or France, let alone entry into combat. In addition to generating false hopes in Europe of American engagement, the man who had firmly stated that the only thing Americans had "to fear is fear itself," turned at home to generating false fears of an imminent German invasion of the hemisphere. Prior to the outbreak of war in Europe he repeatedly warned of German plans to invade Latin America, although he knew that the short-term threat was virtually nonexistent.[9] Nor did he hesitate to cast wide aspersions of treasonable disloyalty on the part of the German, Italian, and Japanese populations of Latin countries and the United States itself, hinting suggestively to favored journalists that he had information these people were organizing as Fifth Columnists for the fascist states (which a small minority of them were). He undertook this rather scurrilous deceit, too, in order to shatter the complacency of a nation still deluding itself that its prosperity and internal affairs were independent of European or Asian security, and the global balance of power.[10]

Roosevelt's scare tactics brought American public opinion slowly to the realization that at least hemispheric defense was prudent. This enabled him to gain approval from Congress for a huge increase in military spending, portrayed as entirely defensive in nature and as directed toward hemispheric defense. On the surface, it still looked like Roosevelt was prepared to lead only where public opinion was already inclined to follow. In fact, he had begun to manipulate public opinion on a grand scale, and always in the direction of increasing preparation for a direct clash with Germany. While he said in public that American rearmament was solely defensive, the very scale of that rearmament gave the lie to his statements. He admitted in private, and German intelligence concurred, that America was rearming not just to secure the Americas, but toward the day it could provide the Western democracies and their allies with an overwhelming military superiority over the fascist states. Beginning in 1938, U.S. war production was put on a path toward the point where it would be able to both supply Britain and France and build up a huge American army and a dominant navy. Professor Robert Herzstein puts the case succinctly: "The fact is Roosevelt wished to create a long term threat *to* Germany, and that required a major military buildup. In order to obtain the rearmament appropriations he needed, [he] conjured up a short term threat *from* Germany."[11]

Roosevelt wanted to form an antifascist coalition to deter German aggression, or at least confine the conflict should deterrence fail. However, intense domestic opposition to membership in any alliance or collective security system meant that he had to preserve the appearance and formal strictures of isolationism, while simultaneously encouraging other states to band together to oppose Germany. It was not a winning hand, but it was the only one the public and Congress would deal him. To strengthen it he called upon his fabled charm, his considerable guile, and a talent for easy deceit. Was he wrong to do so? Could he have achieved the same ends, of rearmament and strengthened deterrence, by appealing to the higher reason and better natures of average Americans? The record strongly suggests that any direct statement of the threat and appeal to the national interest in stopping Germany would have been disbelieved, and would have failed. The evidence further suggests that such an approach actually would have deepened the public's impulse to plunge its head into the isolationist sands, so as not to face the prospect of involvement in the carnage that lay ahead.[12] Thus, when Roosevelt first asked for revision of the Neutrality Laws and repeal of the arms embargo those laws imposed, he was rebuffed by Congress and public opinion alike. Despite these setbacks, even before the Polish crisis of 1939, he was determined to use U.S. force against Germany if deterrence failed—not right away, and not if Britain and France could do the job alone, but ultimately. He believed that the last resort would not arrive for several more years, due to the twinned strength of the Royal Navy and the French Army (then the largest and still considered the finest in the world). He hoped Allied resistance would give him time enough to turn the tide of domestic opinion firmly his way, and more important, build U.S. military strength for the coming "rendezvous with destiny."[13]

Roosevelt thus continued to lend merely verbal support to Britain and France in their pale efforts to limit the European conflict short of war, and distantly to court the Soviets as well. As late as midsummer 1939, he still hoped that promises of American support might do some good, and that deterrence might yet suffice to deal with Hitler. Of course, it did not. With the outbreak of war, the debate in the United States shifted to competing interpretations of neutral rights, and the degree to which support should be given to the Western Allies. Thus, in November 1939, an arms embargo provision in the 1935 Neutrality Act was repealed. While still far short of adopting a full rearmament posture, this at least represented movement in the direction of national preparedness for war. Roosevelt used the crisis to further accelerate rearmament (which was gaining popularity anyway for the return to prosperity it caused), and to call for conscription and the unprecedented creation of a million-man, peacetime army. Throughout 1940, he walked a tightrope between launching additional preparedness measures and rising suspicions that he was planning to enter the war on Britain's side. He repeatedly denied the charge, although by then he was determined to do just that. In the 1940 campaign he was forced by the good showing of a surprisingly adept opponent, Wendell Willkie, to pledge that "your boys are not going to be sent into any foreign wars."[14] That especially mollified traditionally Democratic voters in German, Irish, and Italian American communities, which contained the highest percentage of isolationist if not actually pro-Axis members. His promise was altogether expedient and political, though not entirely disingenuous: Roosevelt did intend to keep the country at peace if he could; he just had severe doubts that this was possible any longer, or that peace was still in the best interest of the nation. Besides, in his own mind and in confidential talks with foreign leaders, he made the distinction that he did not consider the war in Europe as truly "foreign," because it touched upon so many vital U.S. interests. However, Roosevelt believed that if he told the American people the whole truth all at once, instead of leading them gradually to the understanding that they were seriously threatened, he would be defeated in the next election, and those who followed would be less inclined to prepare the nation to face the threat—or worse, might not even believe it existed and might prepare for it not at all.

Prior to 1940, Roosevelt refused to formally guarantee U.S. support for any anti-German policy that might entail the immediate risk of war, while privately giving repeated assurances to the Allies that the United States would join them in the longer term. It was not until after the German *Blitzkrieg* had overrun Poland, Norway, Denmark, the Low Countries, and France, and chased the British Expeditionary Force back across the Channel, that the grip of isolationism on U.S. policy was loosened. Even then, isolationists in Congress still insisted on a "cash-and-carry" policy: belligerents were required to pay in advance and themselves carry away munitions and other goods, in the forlorn hope that a repeat of the U-boat crisis of 1915–1917 could be avoided and neutrality upheld. But facts, as John Adams once remarked, are decidedly "uncomfortable things." By midsummer 1940, Hitler's legions occupied nearly all Europe, a fact that was enough to discomfit all but the most irreconcilable isolationists. With Germany threatening to seize the French Mediterranean fleet and French bases in West Africa, and the British stretched beyond their naval means in the Atlantic, Mediterranean, and Pacific, the threat to the Western Hemisphere was a clear and present danger.[15] America's historic isolation and security, enjoyed by grace of the Royal Navy since the end of the Napoleonic Wars, was gone. Moreover, its principal allies in the last war with Germany—Britain, France, and Russia—were, respectively, barely in the fight, defeated, or still in cahoots with Hitler. Yet at any point between Munich and the 1940 election, had Roosevelt told the American public that he intended to fight Germany if Nazism could not be defeated in any other way, he probably would not have survived politically. This was, therefore, no time to be overly concerned about honesty in government, or even about constitutional niceties.

Although reelection gave him greater security, from the election to Pearl Harbor, speaking entirely forthrightly about foreign policy still would have undermined Roosevelt's political base to the point of defeating that policy— he was, after all, preparing to take the country into a war while proclaiming the very opposite.[16] Nonetheless, following the fall of France in June 1940, and despite the defeatist cables he received from Ambassador to London Joseph Kennedy, FDR became driven by an overwhelming sense of the need for urgent action to support Britain. His crafty solution to the public relations problem was to depict every step he took toward greater engagement in the conflict with the Axis as motivated by peaceful intentions, constituting a move *away* from war. For example, in August 1940, he responded to desperate pleas from Britain by approving the "destroyers-for-bases" deal in which 50 old destroyers were swapped for 99-year leases on seven British island possessions in the Western Hemisphere. Three days later, he flatly denied that the grant of destroyers to bolster Britain's convoy defenses was his central aim, which it was. Instead, he emphasized that he had strengthened America's own coastal and hemispheric defenses by acquiring outlying naval bases. He did not add that this would further project American naval power into the Atlantic, where it might be—and later was—deployed to supplement Royal Navy and Royal Canadian Navy action against the German U-boat threat.[17] That was a highly effective lie and major deceit by omission, which placed his critics in the position of seeming to oppose even direct defense of the United States. Omitted from discussion was his long-term, strategic—some would also say imperial—intention to have the United States displace Britain as the dominant naval power. Nor did he suggest that the new bases were to be used by the U.S. Navy to enforce a "Hemispheric Security Zone," intended to relieve the British of part of their convoy duties and which thereby promised soon to bring U.S. warships into direct conflict with German U-boats.[18]

If Roosevelt expressed his fears in private to only a select few, he spoke in real confidence of his long-range plans to only three highly trusted men: Henry Stimson, Harry Hopkins, and Sumner Welles.[19] Given this discipline, the administration proved adept at damage limitation when called out about one of its many deceits. For example, the Germans published certain captured Polish documents that showed Roosevelt had, in 1939, vehemently encouraged the Poles to resist further appeasement, and had helped persuade the British and French to honor their guarantees to Poland. This made Roosevelt look as though he favored war, not peace. He responded with a favored, and once again effective, deceptive technique: a disclaimer, designed for domestic consumption but made by a foreign head of state or government, of what both Roosevelt and the foreign statesman knew to be the truth. In this case, he sent Sumner Welles to Paris to visit Eduard Daladier. The French Premier agreed to release a letter stating that during the 1939 crisis, Roosevelt and Bullitt had always made it clear to him that the United States would not enter the war.[20] The documents (which were real enough) were made to appear tainted by their passage through Nazi hands, and with

Daladier's partial truth about the Bullitt mission in circulation, this worked to avert a crisis of confidence in the integrity of Roosevelt's assurances. As a result, the majority of Americans continued to believe that their president was working to keep them out of the war at all costs, when he was actually doing everything he could to ensure that they eventually entered it.

By mid-1940, Roosevelt's fears about German hegemony had proved prescient, but so too had U.S. rearmament been underway for several years. Because of his foresight, ostensibly neutral America was already building a head of economic steam toward a full war economy; one that would stand the Allied cause in good stead once full U.S. engagement in the war came about. Moreover, his disingenuous public relations campaign was working, and began to provide him at last with broadened foreign policy options. Public opinion toward Germany was increasingly hostile, and hardening fast. It still favored any policy portrayed as reducing the chance of U.S. entry into the war, but Roosevelt had reason to believe the time had come to take additional, forward steps against Germany.[21] U.S. policy began to display an openly anti-German character. By the spring of 1941, Roosevelt felt free to offer Britain virtually all aid short of war. He authorized huge arms sales and approached the military about a plan to share equally with Britain all U.S. war production. All that remained was to devise a means by which Britain could defer payment for all the munitions and equipment American factories and shipyards were turning out, for London had liquidated its overseas holdings and drained its treasury. The solution was Lend-Lease.

Lend-Lease was a brilliant expedient, one that Churchill ranked (with accuracy) among history's "most unsordid acts."[22] It also was a means for effecting an Anglo-American alliance in all but name, and thus dramatically increased the likelihood that the United States would be drawn into the European war: Why should Hitler any longer seek to appease Roosevelt (as he had been doing since 1939, for instance, by restraining his U-boat captains in the North Atlantic) when American goods and loans were already flowing to the United Kingdom, and American escort ships were engaging U-boats from the Gulf of Mexico to Iceland? Yet Roosevelt successfully sold Lend-Lease to the American public as a policy that would keep the United States *out* of the Anglo-German war. Any contrary suggestion by his critics and political enemies, that he was considering "sending armies to Europe," Roosevelt said, was "deliberate untruth."[23] Once again, he got away with it. The American public was eager for the relative prosperity of an economy placed on a wartime footing although it was still peacetime, and it was warming to the idea that as long as the British were going to do the actual fighting that stopped Hitler, the United States should supply the tools—as Churchill later put it, speaking disingenuously himself. That logic applied with even greater force to the vast manpower reserves of Soviet Russia, which Hitler's armies attacked in June 1941. Roosevelt's decision was therefore immediate and clear: with the enthusiastic support of Churchill, he offered Lend-Lease to Stalin. However, to gain congressional approval he would have to maneuver against opposition from American conservatives and Catholics. In August he took the remarkable step, for the leader of a supposedly neutral nation, of meeting with Winston Churchill to draft and sign the Atlantic Charter. That document amounted to joint Anglo-American war aims, premised as it was on "the final destruction of the Nazi tyranny."[24]

LIES AND THE SOVIET ALLIANCE

Already by March 1939, when Nazi Germany swallowed the remainder of Czechoslovakia, there could be no question that the main threat to U.S. interests and values was headquartered in Berlin and not Moscow. Hence, announcement of the Nazi-Soviet Pact on August 23, 1939, shocked and angered Roosevelt but did not shake his conviction that Germany posed a singular danger. However, the related Soviet invasion of eastern Poland, in late September, deepened anti-Soviet opinion among many ordinary Americans. Millions of Polish Americans, in particular, reflected bitterly on another partition of their ancestral homeland. They were supported by other Catholics concerned for the welfare of Polish coreligionists, still bitter over the Spanish Civil War, or just following the severe line toward Moscow laid down by the popes since 1929.[25] Catholics were joined in anti-Sovietism by millions of other Americans, stunned at what they regarded as the naked cynicism of Stalin's deal with Hitler.[26] More than the assault on Poland, the Soviet Union's unprovoked aggression against Finland ("Winter War") in late 1939 had embittered relations with the United States and deeply angered Roosevelt personally. FDR was in a quandary. He had not invoked the Neutrality Act to cover Moscow's participation in the partition of Poland in September 1939, fearing that would only drive Stalin deeper into Hitler's embrace. He similarly was reluctant to do anything over the invasion of Finland that might push the Soviet Union closer to Nazi Germany. On the other hand, he was moved by the plight of the Finns and personally angered by Stalin's naked and brutal opportunism. He decided to ban sales to the Soviet Union of certain strategic metals, appealed directly to Stalin not to bomb Finnish cities, revived his earlier call for a "moral embargo" on sales of aircraft to aggressor countries, and opened fresh lines of credit to enable Finland to purchase munitions.[27] Roosevelt decided against breaking diplomatic relations with Moscow, although the House of Representatives nearly took the matter out of his hands de facto when it came within three votes of denying appropriations for the Moscow Embassy. Lastly, FDR endorsed the expulsion of the Soviet Union by the League of Nations, a feeble moral gesture made at the final meeting of that tragically hapless organization.[28]

Roosevelt's desire to assist the Finns, however minimally, was at odds with America's still prevailing mood of isolationism. Congress thus resisted the effort to aid Finland, supported in its obstruction by a general public, which disapproved of Soviet actions and admired Finland but remained nervous about any measure that involved America in the war in Europe. In December 1939, one poll recorded that 88 percent of Americans had extensive sympathy for Finland. Yet a poll taken two months later revealed that 77 percent opposed entry into the wider European war even if it seemed likely that Nazi Germany would defeat Britain and France. And isolationists in the Senate vehemently opposed aid to Finland out of fear that the United States might be dragged by a Nordic side door into the larger war in Europe.[29] Roosevelt's anger at the Soviet Union and frustration over Senate myopia came together in February 1940, when he declared in a moment of rare public frankness: "The Soviet Union, as everybody who has the courage to face the facts knows, is run by a dictatorship as absolute as any other dictatorship in the world."[30]

A profound ambivalence ran through Roosevelt's thinking: deep anger toward and moral alienation from the Soviet Union, coupled with recognition that nonetheless he would have to work with Stalin if the Nazi threat was to be countered. That conclusion was not altered even by events of midsummer 1940. France fell under the German jackboot in a mere six weeks in May and June, following the even more rapid conquest of Norway, Denmark, and the Low Countries. Stalin took advantage of war in the west to occupy the Baltic States, in accordance with a secret protocol to the Nazi-Soviet Pact and a follow-up treaty in which he had traded rights to the Polish provinces of Lublin and Warsaw to Hitler in exchange for Lithuania. He also forced Rumania to give up its provinces of Bessarabia and Bukovina.[31] Despite anger in Washington over these moves, strategic considerations outweighed the temptation to indulge in futile moral gestures, such as breaking diplomatic relations. As ruthlessly opportunist as Stalin appeared to be, Roosevelt and even the public realized Hitler's appetite for conquest was more immediate, and probably insatiable.[32] The conviction was deepened that Germany was a fundamental threat far outweighing the distant distaste most Americans felt for the Soviet Union.[33]

When Hitler unleashed Operation Barbarossa against the Soviet Union on June 22, 1941, Churchill and Roosevelt immediately decided to give all possible assistance to Stalin, including Lend-Lease.[34] Roosevelt's public education efforts over the previous years and months—in which he had played to anti-Soviet sentiments when necessary, but overall had sought to convince Americans that the main threat came from the Axis—were beginning to pay off, greatly aided by the force of events.[35] However, there was one large block of anti-Soviet opinion that neither Roosevelt nor Hitler could so easily dissolve. American Catholics continued to cling to such fierce anticommunist convictions that they posed a significant obstacle to getting approval of supplemental Lend-Lease appropriations for the Soviet Union through Congress. Roosevelt was hoist on his own petard: he had repeatedly stated that religious belief was a major source of "democracy and international good faith."[36] He had also counted freedom of religion among the "Four Freedoms" on which he said he wanted to base postwar order and reconstruction, in an expedient oversimplification that was comforting to millions and thus politically effective.[37] He could hardly now admit that antagonism to organized religion informed Soviet domestic law and practice. In September 1941, he thus began a sustained campaign to convince Americans that religious liberty was unfolding in the Soviet Union.

In September 1941, Roosevelt expressed convenient optimism about the future of religious liberty in the Soviet Union in a letter sent to Pope Pius XII to solicit papal aid in obtaining Catholic acquiescence in Lend-Lease to Stalin:

> I believe there is a real possibility that Russia may as a result of the present conflict recognize freedom of religion. . . . I believe that the survival of Russia is less dangerous to religion, to the church as such, and to humanity in general than would be the survival of the German form of dictatorship. Furthermore, it is my belief that the leaders of all churches in the United States should recognize these facts clearly and should not close their eyes to these basic questions and by their present attitude on this question directly [sic] assist Germany in her present objectives.[38]

In this correspondence Roosevelt made use of his personal representative to the Vatican, Myron C. Taylor, appointed in December 1939, in anticipation of just such difficulties with American Catholics. The Pontiff, despite his deep failings with regard to the nature of Nazism and fascism in Europe,[39] knew better than Roosevelt the real conditions under which believers lived and labored in the Soviet Union. He replied with polite generalities, avoiding mention of conditions in Russia. FDR was satisfied because the Pontiff drew a fine distinction between wartime assistance to the Soviets and forbidden support for communism, which left the moral opening FDR wanted for American Catholics to back Lend-Lease.[40]

Roosevelt's natural skill at deceit now began to ill-serve him and the nation. Instead of pushing Lend-Lease through the narrow opening permitted by Pius's reply, Roosevelt adopted a broad tactic of lying about the real conditions for religious believers in the Soviet Union, in order to manipulate American Catholics (and some others) into supporting Lend-Lease. A baleful pattern now developed wherein Roosevelt dissembled and deceived even when the possibilities of straight talk had not been exhausted. For example, in late September 1941, he suggested during a press conference that reporters acquaint themselves with the freedom of religion clause of the Soviet constitution (Article 124), which also declared the right of the state "equally to use propaganda against religion." He next described this limitation as "essentially what is the rule in this country, only we don't put it quite the same way." He concluded, "Since the Soviet constitution declares that freedom of religion is granted, it is hoped ... an entering wedge for the practice of complete freedom of religion is definitely on its way."[41] Of course, he knew better. Just six months earlier, his administration had privately protested NKVD[42] desecration of the Catholic Church in Moscow, which serviced American Embassy officials as sanctioned by mutual recognition agreements signed in 1933. Roosevelt had personally negotiated, and proudly trumpeted at the time, clauses in those agreements purporting to guarantee a right to religious worship for U.S. Embassy officers.[43] When an outcry arose over the inaccuracy of Roosevelt's characterization of Soviet domestic practice, the State Department sought to stifle it with a statement attesting that freedom of worship was denied equally by Communists and Nazis.[44] That was true, but entirely beside the point.

There can be no doubt that the clear intention behind Roosevelt's glib depiction of the state of religious affairs in the Soviet Union was an effort to forestall Catholic and other religious opposition to his extension of Lend-Lease to Stalin. He was quite explicit about this in private, as when he told Soviet Ambassador Constantine Oumansky, "If Moscow could get some publicity back to this country regarding the freedom of religion [in Russia] it might have a very fine educational effect before the next lend-lease bill comes up in Congress."[45] Embassy staff were then ordered to request formal Soviet assurances that freedom of religion would be respected in future. These were readily provided, since Stalin's need for Lend-Lease supplies was great and his intention to honor paper promises was nil. In transmitting the Soviet reply, the Embassy warned, with considerable restraint and understatement, that "the Soviet Government will give lip service and make a few gestures to meet the President's wishes but is not yet prepared to give freedom of religion in the sense that we understand it." Pressure was also coming from outside the administration. House Majority Leader John McCormack advised Roosevelt that a great advantage could be had "from a psychological angle" if the United States intervened on behalf of a number of Polish priests being held in Soviet concentration camps. Assistant Secretary of State Adolf Berle agreed to press for their release, because he said it "would mean definite assistance in allaying some of the Catholic opposition to aid to Russia."[46] The Soviets were told that freedom for the Polish clerics was sought "not with the intention to interfere in Soviet internal affairs [*sic*]," but in the hope that Moscow would in turn facilitate Roosevelt's effort to extend it the maximum of assistance.[47] This remarkable exchange utterly ignored the fact that the Polish priests were arrested during the 1939 Soviet aggressive invasion of eastern Poland, made in accordance with the Nazi-Soviet Pact, and that the United States had never recognized the Soviet annexation as legal.

The most practiced student of Catholics and American foreign policy, George Q. Flynn, argues that Roosevelt's efforts were only superficially cynical, that "the president seriously hoped to promote religious freedom in Russia."[48] While that may have been true on one level—Roosevelt had a deep sentimental and romantic streak—on another plane he was undoubtedly deliberately false. After all, in 1942 he candidly admitted to Treasury Secretary Henry Morgenthau, "I am perfectly willing to mislead and tell untruths ... if it will help win the war."[49] But there was more to it than that. As Robert Dallek noted:

> Roosevelt knew full well that there was no freedom of religion in the Soviet Union. Nor was he blind to the fact that he could extend Lend-Lease help to Russia without demonstrating her devotion to religious freedom. But ... convinced that only a stark contrast between freedom and totalitarianism would provide the emotional wherewithal for Americans to fight, Roosevelt wished to identify the Russians, regardless of Soviet realities, with Anglo-American ideals as fully as he could.[50]

The appropriate criticism thus is not that Roosevelt lied. The real problem was that he may have lied *unnecessarily*, before he really tried an all-out campaign of using the presidential bully-pulpit to convince anti-Soviet Americans that massive material aid to Russia was in the direct and vital interest of the United States—which, of course, it was. Instead, as the war progressed additional deceits built upon the first, until real damage was done to the long-term interest of having a willing, because informed, public behind the great efforts of war and peacemaking that lay ahead.

After the Axis invasion of the Soviet Union, and Imperial Japan's attack on Pearl Harbor and various British and Dutch outposts five months later, the American public naturally revised its opinion of the Soviet Union.[51] As also happened in 1917, many Americans evidenced a need to regard their new Russian ally as moved by democratic ideals similar to their own, whatever the truth about "Why Russia Fights." Too many downplayed or dismissed entirely the bloody purges of the 1930s, the persecution of religious and other minorities that had begun under Lenin right at the outset of the Bolshevik Revolution, and more recent Soviet aggression against Poland, Finland, the

Baltic States, and Rumania. By 1943, the shift in public opinion occasioned by the German assault, but also assiduously shepherded by FDR, was complete: majorities of Americans, of nearly all class or religious backgrounds, reported favorable views of the Soviet Union. They even upheld belief in a bright future of peaceful postwar cooperation with Stalin.[52] What brought about this remarkable change? Naïveté and ignorance about the true character of Stalin and the nature of his terror regime played a real part. So, too, did a natural sense of shared wartime burden and common moral purpose with the peoples of the Soviet Union, who were indeed engaged in a heroic defense against an utterly barbaric and genocidal enemy in Nazi Germany. Whatever the real character of Soviet government, many Americans—including Catholics who, like their pontiff, otherwise remained deeply suspicious of Moscow—looked mainly to the undoubted heroism, suffering, and sacrifice of millions of ordinary Soviets. They just could not believe that such appalling suffering and enormous effort to defeat one great tyranny would be cynically abused and magnified by another.[53] Yet, sharing enemies and wartime suffering does not fully explain how the Soviet Union came to be seen by a large majority of Americans not just as an ally in a mutual war against fascism, but as a viable partner in reconstruction of the postwar order along free and democratic lines.

The leading cause of this crucial change in public opinion was that Roosevelt set out to cultivate a false impression that Stalin endorsed Anglo-American ideals and war aims, as set out in the Atlantic Charter. Americans were repeatedly told that the Soviets accepted that the peace would be reconstructed according to Roosevelt's vaunted "Four Freedoms," of speech and religion, and from want and fear (of aggression). Just as he had earlier sought to mollify Catholics by claiming that freedom of religion was coming in Russia, Roosevelt next played to the tendency of the general public to oversimplify by Americanizing the objectives and interests of wartime allies, regardless of reality. In this he was joined by other administration officials. In *Mission to Moscow*, a bestseller published in 1941 and later turned into a smash Hollywood film, former ambassador to Moscow (and apologist for Soviet purge trials and other "excesses") Joseph C. Davies wrote:

> The Russia of Lenin and Trotsky—the Russia of the Bolshevik Revolution—no longer exists. ... [The] Russian people, the Soviet government, and the Soviet leaders are moved, basically, by altruistic concepts. It is their purpose to promote the brotherhood of man and to improve the lot of the common people. They wish to create a society in which men may live as equals, governed by ethical ideals. They are devoted to peace. They have made great sacrifices attempting to achieve those spiritual aspirations.[54]

Davies elsewhere proclaimed that communism in the Soviet Union was established "after all, on the same principle of the 'brotherhood of man' which Jesus preached." Far from disagreeing about the internal nature of Soviet society and the putative altruistic and spiritual motivations of Generalissimo Stalin, Roosevelt endorsed Davies's views in private as well as in public.[55] At the same time, he ignored dissenting voices among the experienced officers of the State Department, such as George F. Kennan. Sometimes, this refusal to listen to opposing opinion extended to rejecting unpleasant facts, such as those attending Soviet responsibility for the Katyn massacre of thousands of Polish Army officers.[56] Powerful private citizens who embraced the president's policies, such as Henry Luce, editor of *Time* magazine, reinforced the administration's distortions and willingly participated in his manipulation of public perceptions.

Nor was the administration alone in its belief in the expediency of misinformation about the Soviet Union. Encouraged by Roosevelt, some important Republican figures cooperated in the effort. Thus, after just two days in Moscow in 1942, Wendell Willkie told his Soviet hosts that the visit made him realize how unfairly their system had been represented to the American people. Ambassador William H. Standley reported back to Washington that Willkie said to the Soviets:

> Enemies of the Soviet Union caused many Americans to believe that the Soviet Government did not permit freedom of religion ... and was persecuting those who practiced religion. He now knew that the stories of religious persecution ... were false. ... It was now his understanding that the Soviet Government was opposed to priest craft [*sic*] as distinct from religion. He personally also had little respect for priest craft and ... hoped that the American people could be brought to understand what the real situation was in the U.S.S.R.[57]

Willkie boasted that millions of Americans had confidence in him because "they knew that he was a man who frankly told the truth and the whole truth and that he could be trusted." Without blushing, he next promised to lie by omission, saying that "if he saw something which he did not like or which [if] made known in the United States might create an unfavorable impression, he would remain silent to it."[58] Willkie published *One World*, an account of his whirlwind global tour, the following year; it sold several million copies and had a huge impact on public opinion during World War II. In the chapter dealing with his brief sojourn in Moscow, he delivered a paean of praise for Stalin, whom he described as "a simple man, with no affectations or poses." He added: "Russia is an effective society. It works."[59] The top political leadership of the United

States, led by the president, together presented to the American public a vision of easy cooperation with a rapidly, and genuinely, liberalizing Soviet ally. This great nation, Americans were told, was under the stern but deeply wise leadership of "Uncle Joe" Stalin, who shared their hopes for a postwar order of international peace and cooperation through the new United Nations Organization. After that, there would be hell to pay later when the truth finally came out about what "Uncle" had been up to at home and in the Baltic States, Poland, Silesia, and eastern Prussia. All these territories were liberated from the Nazi yoke by the Red Army's tanks and troops, but they were also immediately occupied by the ruthless secret police, informer network, and torturers and firing squads of the NKVD.

CONCLUSIONS

Roosevelt faced an unprecedented challenge to U.S. security at a time when American isolationism was deeper than it had ever been—and when there was a direct correlation between the degree of strategic threat and the deepening of the public's desire to avoid war. That situation went a long way to excuse his choice of manipulation and trickery to convert Americans to accept, first, the necessity of prudent self-defense measures, and eventually, to adopt an interventionist stance. In this case, the ends of rearmament and otherwise preparing the nation to face and defeat Hitlerism surely justified a few expedient means. That said, not all his lies were defensible, even given the stakes involved. There was no good reason, for instance, to smear whole ethnic populations with presidential innuendo about disloyalty. Nonetheless, if Roosevelt deceived Americans about the long-term implications of his principled opposition to Nazism—and he did deceive them, often and deeply—he yet served the nation well. Those were extraordinary days, and the danger faced called for special dispensation from normal moral burdens.

Roosevelt should be commended for shouldering that most onerous of public duties: personal responsibility for morally ambiguous solutions to the problems of statecraft. He did not fear moral ambiguity as some might have (as Neville Chamberlain did, for instance), to the point of impaling the national interest on their personal principles and narrow conceptions of honor. Nor did he indulge in questionable practices for their own sake, or because he enjoyed power more—as some do—when it was exercised deviously. Instead, he accepted the paradox that in times of great and genuine emergency it may be the higher calling of a statesman to deceive in order to lead, and otherwise secure the nation. Like Abraham Lincoln before him—the only president to face a comparable or greater threat to the nation—he appreciated that *in extremis* it is sometimes necessary to violate the letter of the law in order to save the rule of law. Both men trod roughly on the Constitution at times, and Roosevelt trod also on the truth, in the name of higher good. Yet both thereby helped to preserve the idea and the rule of law for better days. If Roosevelt had one great flaw that Lincoln did not, it was that even with the United States definitely in the war and the enemy's defeat assured, he could never quite bring himself to stop dissembling and re-engage the truth. Lying is a requisite of diplomacy. But the best diplomats and national leaders nonetheless lie only rarely and in extreme cases, because they know that when deceit is overdone it destroys the essential ingredient of trust which is itself requisite to the effective implementation of policy. Roosevelt thus can be applauded for his early, essential lies, but also deplored for his later, petty ones. That said, he still may be properly judged to have been not only a great states-man on narrow, *Realpolitik* grounds, but, on the whole, also a moral practi-tioner of the ethically exacting art of statecraft.

NOTES

1. Sissela Bok, *Lying: Moral Choice in Public and Private Life* (New York: Pantheon Books, 1978).

2. Ibid., pp. 179–81. Original emphasis.

3. He did, on the other hand, believe that coexistence with the Soviet Union was unpleasant but entirely possible, as it had proved to be since 1920 and would again after 1945. On Roosevelt's view of the threat from Nazi Germany see Robert E. Herzstein, *Roosevelt and Hitler* (New York: Paragon House, 1989), pp. 215–403 pas-sim; and Waldo Heinrichs, *Threshold of War* (New York: Oxford University Press, 1968). On FDR's view of the Soviet Union see Edward M. Bennett, *Recognition of Russia* (New York: Blaisdell, 1970) and *Franklin D. Roosevelt and the Search for Security* (Wilmington, DE: Scholarly Resources, 1985); Robert Browder, *Origins of Soviet-American Diplomacy* (Princeton, NJ: Princeton University Press, 1953); and the author's *Principled Diplomacy: Security and Rights in U.S. Foreign Policy* (Westport, CT: Greenwood, 1993), pp. 45–89.

4. The "Little Entente" was an East European alliance that lasted from 1920 to 1939. To the original alliance between Czechoslovakia and Yugoslavia signed in 1920, there were added two additional bilateral pacts with Rumania in 1921. These separate agreements were incorporated into a single alliance treaty in 1929. The main purpose of the Little Entente (an informal, popular name echoing the prewar *entente cordiale* of France, Great Britain, and Russia) was to prevent Austria or Hungary from attempting to reclaim the old Habsburg lands taken away in the treaties of St. Germain (with Austria, 1919) and Trianon (with Hungary, 1919). With the rising threat from Hitler's Germany, efforts were made by the Little Entente powers to nego-tiate mutual defense arrangements with France. A turn to the hard right in Yugoslavia after the assassination of Alexander I, especially its willingness to collaborate with plans for aggrandizement by Nazi Germany, shook the Little Entente. The Munich Conference and then the occupation of the rump of the Czech lands by German forces gutted the Little Entente of any use it might have had to buffer Germany, by removing

Czechoslovakia from the chessboard of Europe and drawing its other members closer to the Axis.

5. See Manfred Jonas, *Isolationism in America, 1935–1941* (Ithaca, NY: Cornell University Press, 1966; Imprint, 1990). On the evolution of FDR's thinking about Nazi Germany, see the essay by William E. Kinsella, "The Prescience of a Statesman: FDR's Assessment of Adolf Hitler before the World War, 1933–1941," in Herbert Rosenbaum and Elizabeth Bartelme, eds., *Franklin D. Roosevelt* (Westport, CT: Greenwood, 1987).

6. Bennett, *Search for Security*, various passages.

7. George Q. Flynn, *Roosevelt and Romanism* (Westport, CT: Greenwood, 1976), pp. 29–62; Frank Freidel, *Franklin D. Roosevelt: A Rendezvous with Destiny* (Boston: Little, Brown, 1990), pp. 268–72.

8. Waclaw Jedrzejewicz, ed., *Diplomat in Paris, 1936–1939* (New York: Columbia University Press, 1970), pp. 168–70; Herzstein, *Roosevelt and Hitler*, pp. 244–45.

9. That is not to say there was no long-term threat, for there was. In 1940 Hitler instructed the German Navy to develop contingency plans for the seizure of Atlantic islands, preparatory to establishing bases within the Western Hemisphere. See Stetson Conn and Byron Fairchild, *The U.S. Army in World War II: The Framework of Hemisphere Defense* (Washington, DC: U.S. Government, 1960); and Alton Frye, *Nazi Germany and the Western Hemisphere, 1933–1941* (New Haven, CT: Yale University Press, 1967).

10. Herzstein, *Roosevelt and Hitler*, p. 240ff; Robert Dallek, *Franklin D. Roosevelt and American Foreign Policy, 1932–1945* (New York: Oxford University Press, 1979), pp. 173–75; Freidel, *Rendezvous with Destiny*, pp. 209–20. Roosevelt continued to use this tactic after 1940, but by then, with Hitler's acquisition of the French coastal ports and Italian and German access to colonies and bases in North Africa, the threat was real.

11. Herzstein, *Roosevelt and Hitler*, p. 245.

12. See "Gallup and Fortune Polls," *Public Opinion Quarterly* (March–June 1940). More generally, see Robert A. Divine, *The Illusion of Neutrality* (Chicago: University of Chicago Press, 1962); and Jonas, *Isolationism in America*, pp. 244–72.

13. The strongest case made in this respect is in Herzstein, *Roosevelt and Hitler*, pp. 284–317. Roosevelt was not the only statesman to overestimate the resistance that would be presented to Germany by France. Stalin too would make that mistake, with near fatal consequences for himself and his empire.

14. Quoted in Dallek, *Roosevelt and American Foreign Policy*, p. 250. Also see Herzstein, *Roosevelt and Hitler*, p. 352.

15. See Note 9, *supra*. For an idiosyncratic, revisionist viewpoint see Bruce Russett, *No Clear and Present Danger* (New York: Harper & Row, 1972).

16. On Roosevelt's titanic struggle with Congress see Jonas, *Isolationism in America*, pp. 206–72; Divine, *Illusion of Neutrality*, pp. 243–83 passim, pp. 297–303, 315–19; and John C. Donovan, "Congressional Isolationists and the Roosevelt Foreign Policy," *World Politics* (April 1951), pp. 299–316.

17. Dallek, *Roosevelt and American Foreign Policy*, pp. 243–47. On Roosevelt's stormy relations with the press see Graham T. White, *Roosevelt and the Press* (Chicago: University of Chicago Press, 1979).

18. Herzstein, *Roosevelt and Hitler*, pp. 347–48.

19. Heinrichs, *Threshold of War*, p. 20.

20. This episode is recounted in Herzstein, *Roosevelt and Hitler*, pp. 318–20.

21. "Gallup and Fortune Polls," *Public Opinion Quarterly* (March and June 1940).

22. The most comprehensive study of Lend-Lease is Warren F. Kimball, *The Most Unsordid Act: Lend-Lease, 1939–1941* (Baltimore: Johns Hopkins University Press, 1969).

23. Quoted in Herzstein, *Roosevelt and Hitler*, p. 357. Also see Henry L. Stimson (with McGeorge Bundy), *On Active Service in Peace and War* (New York: Harper & Row, 1947), p. 366.

24. Draft and final versions, along with a firsthand account of the Charter's composition, are in Winston Churchill, *The Grand Alliance*, Vol. 3 of his *The Second World War* (New York: Bantam, 1962), pp. 366–80.

25. Flynn, *Roosevelt and Romanism*, pp. 141–42.

26. See "American Institute of Public Opinion—Surveys, 1938–1939," *Public Opinion Quarterly* (October 1939), p. 596.

27. *Public Papers and Addresses of Franklin D. Roosevelt*, ed. Samuel I. Rosenman (New York: Macmillan, 1941), Vol. 8, pp. 586–94 (hereafter *Roosevelt: Public Papers*); and Robert Sobel, *Origins of Interventionism* (New York: Bookman Associates, 1960), pp. 91–94.

28. Alexander DeConde, *History of American Foreign Policy*, 3rd ed. (New York: Scribner's, 1978), Vol. 2, p. 584.

29. "Gallup and Fortune Polls," *Public Opinion Quarterly* (March–June, 1940), p. 102. For a summary of press and other reactions to the attack on Finland, see Thomas R. Maddux, *Years of Estrangement: American Relations with the Soviet Union, 1933–1941* (Tallahassee: University Presses of Florida, 1980), pp. 114–27; also see Donovan, "Congressional Isolationists," pp. 299–316.

30. "Address to the American Youth Congress," February 10, 1940, *Roosevelt: Public Papers*, Vol. 9, p. 93; and see Dallek, *American Foreign Policy*, pp. 208–13, where this anecdote is placed in the broad context of Roosevelt's struggle with Congress and public opinion.

31. "Soviet/German Friendship and Frontier Treaty," September 28, 1939, in Jane Degras, ed., *Soviet Documents on Foreign Policy* (New York: Oxford University Press, 1951), Vol. 3, pp. 377–79. The Baltic States were annexed in August 1940. For recently released documents from the Soviet archives see "The Baltic Countries Join the Soviet Union," *International Affairs* (March 1990), pp. 134–42; and (April 1990), pp. 97–124.

32. See Ralph B. Levering, *American Opinion and the Russian Alliance, 1939–1945* (Chapel Hill: University of North Carolina Press, 1976), pp. 15–38; Thomas R. Maddux, *Years of Estrangement*, pp. 128–46.

33. *Inter alia*, see George Herring, *Aid to Russia, 1941–1946* (New York: Columbia University Press, 1974); Raymond Dawson, *Decision to Aid Russia, 1941* (Chapel Hill: University of North Carolina Press, 1959); and Robert Jones, *Roads to Russia* (Norman: University of Oklahoma Press, 1969).

34. Maddux, *Years of Estrangement*, p. 147; Heinrichs, *Threshold of War*, pp. 92–117. Text of the Lend-Lease agreement in Stanley Jados, ed., *Documents on Russian/ American Relations* (Washington, DC: Catholic University Press, 1965), pp. 86–88.

35. See "Gallup and Fortune Polls," *Public Opinion Quarterly* (Spring 1942), pp. 152ff. Following the Nazi-Soviet Pact, Stalin's invasions of Poland and Finland, and the additional annexations of neighboring territories in 1940, 35 percent of Americans polled (in October 1941) still believed the Soviet Union and Nazi Germany were equally detestable tyrannies. Another 32 percent thought there was little to choose between them internally but considered Soviet Russia slightly better than Nazi Germany. The key result came in answer to the question about which side Americans wanted to win the war; with Nazi panzers then surging toward Kiev, Moscow, and Leningrad, most Americans preferred a Soviet victory.

36. For example, see his "Annual Message to Congress," January 3, 1940, *Roosevelt: Public Papers*, Vol. 8, p. 1.

37. Freidel, *Rendezvous with Destiny*, pp. 360–62.

38. "Letter from President Roosevelt to His Holiness," September 3, 1941, in Myron C. Taylor, ed., *Wartime Correspondence between President Roosevelt and Pope Pius XII* (New York: Macmillan, 1947), pp. 61–62.

39. Pius XII, né Eugenio Pacelli (1876–1958), was a career Vatican diplomat who rose to cardinal and then to secretary of state to the Holy See. He had lived in Germany, where he negotiated the Vatican's concordat with Hitler. His failure to speak publicly against the Holocaust has been bitterly criticized. Although Pius was informed about the genocide underway against Jews, Roma, and others under Nazi occupation, he did not speak openly against Nazism. Nor did he publish a major condemnation of anti-Semitism prepared by his predecessor, Pius XI. More pointedly, while tolerating the hiding of some Jews in Catholic monasteries and convents, he never commanded his clergy to speak against fascism, despite its antireligious and pagan philosophy. Nor did he command the faithful to oppose, to the best of their moral abilities and the limits of their personal courage, the murderous policy of the Nazi regime, not even when SS death brigades came into Rome itself in 1943 to cart off Italian Jews to the death camps. Pius's reticence was motivated by a complex of factors. He was, of course, concerned with political calculations relating to the vulnerable position of the Catholic Church in Nazi-occupied Europe. Second, he and the Curia were powerfully influenced by a deep detestation of communism and of the Soviet Union, probably more so than by any personal antipathy for Jews, though that possibility may not be discounted entirely. Finally, Pius feared the destruction of his life's work, which had been to consolidate papal power over national Catholic churches in Italy and Germany and worldwide. Even if all that is true, his silence still deafens. And there lingers the possibility that his passivity had darker, more sinful motivations of personal anti-Semitism. See John Cornell, *Hitler's Pope: The Secret History of Pius XII* (New York: Viking, 1999).

40. "Reply of His Holiness to President Roosevelt," September 20, 1941, in Taylor, *Wartime Correspondence*; and Freidel, *Rendezvous with Destiny*, p. 376. Also see George Q. Flynn, "Franklin Roosevelt and the Vatican," *Catholic Historical Review* (July 1972), pp. 171–94; and Flynn, *Roosevelt and Romanism*, pp. 165–69.

41. Press conference, September 30, 1941, *Roosevelt: Public Papers*, Vol. 10, pp. 401–2. See Article 134 of the 1936 Soviet Constitution, in Ian Brownlie, ed., *Basic Documents of Human Rights* (Oxford: Clarendon Press, 1971), p. 27.

42. Narodnii Kommissariat Vnutrennikh Del (NKVD), or People's Commissariat of Internal Affairs. This was the name of the Soviet secret and political police from 1934 to 1954. In 1934 the OGPU (formerly the GPU, formerly the Cheka) was expanded into the NKVD. The NKVD carried out the great purges of the 1930s and during the war maintained Rifle Divisions numbering tens of thousands of political troops, whose principal task was to shoot Soviet soldiers who retreated or deserted, along with nationalist partisans or anyone else in momentary disfavor with their master in the Kremlin.

43. Department of State, *Papers Relating to the Foreign Relations of the United States*, 1941, Vol. 1, pp. 998–1000. Hereafter cited as *FRUS*.

44. "Aid to Russia," October 13, 1941, *Roosevelt: Public Papers*, Vol. 10, p. 418. On the protest against desecration of churches, see *FRUS*, 1941, Vol. 1, pp. 998–1000; and Flynn, *Roosevelt and Romanism*, pp. 159–60, for an account of American Catholic and editorial reaction.

45. *FRUS*, 1941, Vol. 1, p. 832.

46. Ibid., pp. 997–1005.

47. Ibid., p. 1004.

48. Flynn, *Roosevelt and Romanism*, p. 158.

49. Quoted in Dallek, *American Foreign Policy*, p. 336.

50. Ibid., p. 298.

51. Levering, *American Opinion and the Russian Alliance*, pp. 39–62.

52. Ibid., pp. 97–145; and see Warren B. Walsh's compilation of wartime polls, "What the American People Think of Russia," *Public Opinion Quarterly* (Winter 1944–1945), pp. 513–22.

53. On the brief wartime lull in Catholic antipathy for the Soviet Union, see Wilson D. Miscamble, "Catholics and American Foreign Policy from McKinley to McCarthy: A Historiographical Survey," *Diplomatic History*, Vol. 4, No. 3 (1980), pp. 223–40.

54. Davies, *Mission to Moscow* (New York: Simon & Schuster, 1941), p. 511. A rare, and mostly misguided, positive view of Davies is Elizabeth Maclean, "Joseph E. Davies and Soviet-American Relations, 1941–43," *Diplomatic History* (Winter 1980), pp. 73–93.

55. See John L. Gaddis, *The United States and the Origins of the Cold War, 1941–1947* (New York: Columbia University Press, 1972), pp. 35–36; quoted at p. 36.

56. For example, see the account of how Roosevelt treated dissent over his handling of the Katyn massacre, in Crister S. Garrett and Stephen A. Garrett, "Death and Politics: The Katyn Forest Massacre and American Foreign Policy," *East European Studies Quarterly*, Vol. 20, No. 4 (January 1987), pp. 429–46.

57. *FRUS*, 1942, Vol. 3, pp. 645–46.

58. Ibid.

59. Wendell Willkie, *One World* (New York: Simon & Schuster, 1943), pp. 83, 53; also see his "We Must Work with Russia," *New York Times Magazine*, January 17, 1943.

2

Political Leadership and "Dirty Hands": Winston Churchill and the City Bombing of Germany

Stephen A. Garrett

One of the perennial issues in the analysis of the moral conduct of political leaders, and perhaps especially so in the realm of international relations, is the concept of "dirty hands." Reduced to its essentials, the notion of dirty hands suggests that political authorities may be required to do things—or to tolerate things—that would be regarded both by them and by others as unacceptable, even as genuinely evil, if the actions took place in their private lives. Some would say that political leaders actually have little choice in the matter; if they *are* to exercise leadership, they must necessarily set aside their standards of personal morality in those cases where insisting on such standards may be obstructive in advancing the broader public interest. Stated in its most direct form, the political leader has no other alternative, and moreover, *should* have no other alternative.

Two assertions are typically advanced to spare top officials from the burden of moral judgment, to allow them a realm of "freedom from morality" that is supposedly their special preserve and even right. The first has to do with their identity as representatives of the "collective." The idea is that a social unit, especially a nation, has needs and demands that perforce require the leader to set aside any personal moral doubts he may have about either these needs themselves or the means necessary to attain them. In this sense the foreign policy leader is not a creature of free choice, but rather the servant of the primordial demands of his constituency, whether they be for territorial security, economic advantage, religious or ideological influence, or whatever. If he feels uneasy with what is necessary to achieve these, or with the goals themselves, his only legitimate recourse is to stand down from leadership of the nation and pass authority on to someone with less delicate sensitivities.[1]

There is also the argument that advances the special nature of the international system. It asserts that international relations is a peculiarly brutal and anarchic enterprise. Considerations of justice, fairness, or moderation that might be appropriate in dealing with domestic affairs have little if any place in confronting the realities of the world beyond one's shores. Machiavelli offered the basic point: "a man who wishes to make a profession of goodness in every-thing must necessarily come to grief among so many who are not good. Therefore it is necessary for a prince, who wishes to maintain himself, to learn how not to be good, and to use this knowledge and not use it, according to the necessity of the case."[2]

The implications of such an argument convey a rather melancholy judgment. They suggest that even the most well-meaning of individuals neces-sarily must set aside personal moral convictions in dealing with the grim real-ities of the world on behalf of the nation. Would that the world were a better place so that saints could direct the affairs of state. Since the world is not a better place, and indeed is a worse place than any but the most vivid imagina-tion could conceive, the effective leader has to accept the essential tragedy of his position, which is that political power essentially *equates* with dirty hands. Such assertions as these cannot be easily set aside, and there is no claim here that they are not important aspects of the world of statecraft. Yet the essential argument of this chapter is that they represent only a partial truth about the duties, and even more the opportunities, of statesmen. No reasonable person would claim that the leader of a nation can apply exactly the same moral standards to his activities as public servant as he does to his own private life. Yet the legitimate gap between the two can be overstated. The public and pri-vate realms are indeed different, but that does not mean they are totally unconnected. It is simply to say that there is a necessity for reflection on what special moral principles may rightly be applied to public life in contrast with more intimate circumstances. In examining this issue, I propose to offer here a case study in applied ethics that involves the problem of political leadership and dirty hands in its most acute form, that is to say, during wartime itself. It has to do with Winston Churchill's role in the British bombing of German cities during World War II.

BACKGROUND

During the first few months of the war, British long-range bombers did little more than make occasional forays over the Ruhr valley dropping propaganda leaflets, although there were a few strikes against German naval facilities on the Baltic. British restraint during this period may be accounted for in part by its relatively limited technical capability for massive air strikes against Germany. There was also concern about German retaliation in kind if the informal proscription against large-scale city strikes was abandoned. Also important, however, was the principle that civilized states were bound even in wartime to observe the crucial distinction between combatant and noncombatant. This standard had been emphasized by the so-called Hague Draft Rules drawn up in 1923, which denounced the indiscriminate bombing of civilian populations and was reaffirmed as reflecting British policy by British Prime Minister Neville Chamberlain on the outbreak of war.[3]

Having considered the initial British stance on strategic bombing against Germany, it is instructive to consider the events of the night of July 27, 1943. That evening, 787 planes from Bomber Command attacked the center of the German city of Hamburg with a combination of explosive and incendiary bombs. It had been a hot and dry summer in northern Germany, and this fact, combined with the unusually tight concentration of the bombs on the working-class districts of the city, produced a firestorm that eventually covered an area of about four square miles. Temperatures at the center of the firestorm reached about 1,800 degrees Fahrenheit, accompanied by winds of hurricane force. One British pilot described the scene: "It was as if I was looking into what I imagined to be an active volcano. . . . Our actual bombing was like putting another shovelful of coal into the furnace." Over 40,000 people died on that evening in Hamburg within a period of about two hours.[4]

The transition in British policy from a rejection of "indiscriminate" or area bombing to an apparent embrace of precisely this concept resulted over the course of the war in the progressive destruction of almost every major city in Germany. Over 500,000 Germans lost their lives as a result; about twice that number suffered serious injury. Some three million dwellings were destroyed. The British decision to adopt an unalloyed strategy of devastating German cities through air attacks seems to have derived from several factors that can only be briefly summarized here, but which nevertheless have their own importance in arriving at a moral judgment on the strategy itself. One supposed "goal" of the policy was to undermine German civilian morale sufficiently to make it impossible for Hitler to continue the war. How this goal was to work itself out in practice, given the totalitarian character of Nazi Germany, and whether German morale would really break under bombing were items that were left basically unexamined. In actuality the move toward area bombing seems to have been dictated by technical factors as much as by any consideration of strategic airpower doctrine. At this stage of the war, daylight strikes by Bomber Command had basically been abandoned because of the prohibitive losses that German air defenses could inflict on the attacking bombers. Moreover, the accuracy with which British aircrews could hit specific military targets even in daytime had been shown to be badly wanting. Under the circumstances, nighttime bombing of large cities seemed the only available alternative for Bomber Command, both in terms of limiting losses of aircraft and in terms of the crude aiming capabilities of these aircraft. Since those in authority were committed to a massive strategic air offensive of some kind against

Germany, indiscriminate bombing of German cities followed almost as a matter of course.[5]

Winston Churchill had been Prime Minister of Britain since the previous May, and the move toward area bombing received his full support. Indeed, he may be regarded as one of the principal sponsors, if not the principal sponsor, of the new strategy. As early as July 8, 1940, he had written to Lord Beaverbrook, Minister for Aircraft Production, that there was only one thing that would bring Hitler down, and that was "an absolutely devastating exterminating attack by very heavy bombers from this country upon the Nazi homeland. We must be able to overwhelm them by this means, without which I do not see a way through."[6] In looking back on his decision to order the area bombing of Germany, Churchill insisted after the war that the adoption of such a strategy was both necessary and just. He commented to a former staff officer of Bomber Command that "we should never allow ourselves to apologize for what we did to Germany."[7]

STANDARDS FOR EVALUATION

Was such an apology necessary? More specifically, what moral judgment can be rendered on Churchill's supervision of the area offensive? Did he have dirty hands, and if so, can we excuse his having them in this particular case? The first part of the question seems almost self-evident. Anyone who presides over the death and injury of thousands, or, in the case of area bombing, more than a million, may hardly be said to be an innocent. It is the second part of the query that is the really important—and relevant—one. In arriving at an assessment of Churchill's role in the area bombing of Germany, it is necessary to set out certain specific criteria for judgment. It may be tempting to argue that any political leader responsible for such destruction as was visited on Germany by area bombing is to be condemned outright. From this perspective, area bombing was inherently a crime and thus quite indefensible. If a weighing of Churchill's moral position with respect to area bombing is to have a more general significance, however, a rather more systematic set of standards has to be established by which an ethical verdict can be rendered both on him and on other leaders and other situations, especially ones somewhat less dramatic than the devastation of German cities.

Intuitive Values

The first of these has to do with what may be called the "intuitive values" of the leader. An intuitive value judgment regards a certain action as invariably wrong (or right) regardless of its effects, and reflects the pure dictates of conscience.[8] Even given the terrible responsibilities of leadership, particularly in wartime, one has the right to suggest that there are inherent differences between different kinds of policies, and that some are inherently more ethical than others. In the case of the practice of war, for example, the slaughter of innocents—that is, of noncombatants—is almost universally regarded as an evil in itself, quite aside from whatever "utilitarian" calculations may be advanced for the necessity of violating this principle. A moral leader in wartime is thus one who constantly has the protection of innocents as a major consideration.

Even more important than this is the general sanctity of life itself: it is an intuitive requirement that leaders conduct military operations in such a way that not only their own troops, but even those of the enemy, suffer the least harm consistent with the search for victory. An enemy in uniform—just as an enemy noncombatant—does not lose all his rights. It cannot be said that he is subject to idle or vengeful slaughter simply because he is the enemy. This principle is indeed widely accepted. It accounts for the standard injunction that enemy prisoners of war are entitled to certain basic protections, even though their murder might actually be of some military utility to their opponent. In passing moral judgment on wartime leaders, therefore, a first test is the degree to which the leader in question displays an appropriate commitment to and awareness of the intuitive values discussed above. Such a test, for example, helps us to assess the ethics of a Napoleon Bonaparte, who is said to have boasted to Metternich that he could afford to "spend" 30,000 men a month. Also relevant was his comment that "I do not care a fig for the lives of a million men."[9] Whatever his other qualities, this virtual moral nihilism disqualifies (or should disqualify) Napoleon from our admiration.

There is nothing in the body of Churchill's public or private pronouncements that comes close to Napoleon's brutal lack of concern with his own men. Indeed, he consistently had the welfare of the average British soldier very much in mind. Ironically, that was one of the reasons he supported the area bombing of Germany. Churchill was a veteran of the trench warfare of World War I, and it seems to have made a profound impression on him. He was virtually obsessed with finding a way of defeating Germany that would avoid the mindless slaughter of the first great struggle, at least insofar as the British armed forces were concerned. He evidently saw area bombing as a way to achieve this goal. Such attacks would hopefully weaken the German power of resistance sufficiently to make the ultimate Allied invasion of Europe a tolerable exercise in terms of casualties. Area bombing also had another related rationale: it was used by Churchill to deflect American and Soviet pressure for a *premature* invasion of the continent that would, in Churchill's view, carry the risk of quite exorbitant losses. The British resources and energy applied to strategic air strikes against Germany were a testament to the fact that Britain was committed to a vigorous prosecution of the war effort even if she balked at an early second front in Europe. This was an important factor in itself in Britain's relationship with its Allies.

In terms of certain other "intuitive" values, Churchill also presented many attractive qualities, including a capacity for generosity, human kindness and loyalty, that we commonly identify as primary virtues. He was particularly noted for his willingness to extend forgiveness to former enemies. He emphasized in the House of Commons in January 1945 that the Allies had no plan to "exterminate or trample on the German people. ... Not at all. We remain bound by our own customs and our own nature."[10] Yet this is hardly the whole story. There was a darker side to the Churchill persona as well, and it has to be considered in any moral evaluation of his role in the area bombing of Germany. An interesting incident in this regard came on October 17, 1940, when a Conservative Member of Parliament for Eccles (Robert Cary) confronted him in the smoking-room of the House of Commons and demanded that the Prime Minister authorize full-scale city bombing of Germany in retaliation for German attacks on Britain. Churchill's reply: "My dear sir, this is a military and not a civilian war. You and others may desire to kill women and children. We desire (and have succeeded in our desire) to destroy German military objectives." This was an admirable defense of standards of discrimination in wartime, and Churchill appears admirable for having offered it.

Unfortunately, he did not stop there. He went on to say to Cary that "I quite appreciate your point. But my motto is 'Business before Pleasure.' "[11] The coarseness of this remark was reflected in other comments that Churchill sometimes offered about the "character" of the German people, which seemed to suggest that all their suffering was not only militarily appropriate, but even deserved in the bargain because of flaws in their personality. At one point he maintained that one of the purposes of area bombing was to make "the German people taste and gulp each month a sharper dose of the miseries they have showered upon mankind."[12] In April 1941, he offered the sociological observation that "there are less than seventy million malignant Huns—some of whom are curable and others killable."[13] When confronted with the fact that the indiscriminate bombing of cities seemed to represent a significant rejection of previous restraints in the conduct of war, and especially British standards in this regard, he cavalierly remarked that "it is absurd to consider morality on this topic. ... In the last war the bombing of open cities was regarded as forbidden. Now everybody does it as a matter of course. It is simply a question of fashion changing as she does between long and short skirts for women."[14]

In assessing this sort of language, it is important to accept that it was offered during a period of extremely high stress and in some cases during a phase of the war in which the prospects of a German victory—with all that implied for the future of British democracy—were seen not just as a theoretical threat, but as a very real one. Under the circumstances, as one of his close aides and unalloyed admirers argues, it may have been hardly surprising that "as time went on, and the accumulated horrors of the war hardened all our hearts, he grew indifferent to the sufferings of the German cities."[15] Some allowance also has to be made for Churchill's occasional affinity for hyperbole, a tendency with which those around him were quite familiar and which they took pains to minimize in the actual conduct of affairs. All the same, the above comments (as well as others that could be presented in the same vein) are troubling evidence that in certain key respects, Churchill was quite unnecessarily and inappropriately callous about the consequences for German civilians of Bomber Command's nightly forays over their country. Even if he saw area bombing as a crucial component of a strategy for defeating the Nazis, our admiration of his wartime leadership can not help but be diluted by his frequent dismissal of the idea that the suffering of enemy noncombatants was even a relevant item for consideration.

Consequentialism

But did Churchill really feel that area bombing was critical to the successful prosecution of the war effort? There is a second test of the ethics of leaders, and it may be broadly regarded as utilitarian or consequentialist rather than intuitive. We have a right to expect that our leaders will examine all possible alternatives in dealing with a policy problem, and, more than this, make a careful assessment of the likely positive outcomes of certain actions balanced against their negative side effects. As one study puts it, "Awareness of the consequences of one's actions seems a necessary if not sufficient condition for moral conduct. . . . The principle seems [especially] beyond dispute for public officials deciding important policy issues. Officials have a duty to anticipate the important consequences of policies they advocate or implement."[16]

In some ways this may seem like a fairly commonplace injunction. Certainly most, if not all, leaders do consider different ways of achieving their goals, and pick the course of action that seems best calculated to contribute to the desired end. In the case of international relations, however, and particularly during wartime, the consequentialist principle has a special application. Decisions taken in this realm are often going to result not just in grumbles from some dissatisfied interest group, but in considerable human suffering, even (during wartime) in death and destruction. It is thus that the principle of proportionality intrudes itself. Simply put, this requires that for any given action taken in a (presumably) just cause, the positive returns from that action must outweigh the evil side effects that it may produce. To be sure, this is often a difficult concept to apply in practice. How *much* of a contribution does a specific action have to make to counterbalance certain evil side effects?

How do we define what *are* "evil side effects"? In the case of war, however, the second question is perhaps more easily answered. On an intuitive basis, *all* human death or suffering is *ipso facto* an evil effect. The issue thus becomes how one can choose actions that are productive or necessary in the search for victory, while at the same time limiting such death or suffering as much as possible. From a somewhat different perspective, the standards of utility require that if the latter is to be great, the value of the former must be pronounced and unmistakable.

What is striking about Churchill's role in the area bombing of Germany is the apparent *inconsistency* in his analysis as to the practical effects of such a strategy. Before the war began, he was on record as being quite skeptical on the matter. He went out of his way to denounce the concept of "terror" bombing in an article for the American magazine *Collier's* in June 1939, on both moral and practical grounds. These doubts seemed to be washed away, however, once he became Prime Minister. We have already recounted how in the grim days following the fall of France, when Britain stood alone against the might of the German war machine, Churchill seemed to feel that there was only one possibility of reversing the fortunes of war. His minute to Lord Beaverbrook on July 8, 1940, referred to the massive bombing of Germany as the "one sure path" for the defeat of the Nazi menace.[17] In the succeeding months, the Prime Minister was perhaps the principal voice arguing for the importance of Bomber Command as the key to victory.

By the fall of 1941, however, Churchill's views on the strategic bombing offensive seemed to take yet another turn. On October 7, he wrote to Sir Charles Portal, Chief of the Air Staff, along the following lines: "We all hope that the air offensive against Germany will realize the expectations of the Air Staff. . . . I deprecate however placing unbounded confidence in this means of attack. . . . The Air Staff would make a mistake to put their claim too high."[18] Some nine months later (in July 1942), with the United States now in the war, Churchill put the point even more directly:

> In the days when we were fighting alone, we answered the question: "How are you going to win the war?" by saying: "We will shatter Germany by bombing." Since then the enormous injuries inflicted on the German Army and manpower by the Russians, and the accession of the manpower and munitions of the United States, have rendered other possibilities open.[19]

These other possibilities included diverting the aircrews of the Royal Air Force from attacking Germany to direct support of the ground campaign in North Africa, and subsequently in Sicily and Italy, as well as to the destruction of the German U-boat threat in the North Atlantic. Moreover, considerable resources could have been redirected away from the building of heavy bombers to the expansion of the army and navy (a possibility that many, although few within the Royal Air Force, strongly supported).

All of this seems to admit of only one interpretation. In the most desperate days of Britain's struggle with Germany, Churchill supported the area bombing of Germany as the one effort that held out even the smallest hope of preventing German victory. With the United States and the Soviet Union in the war, he saw quite clearly that Germany ultimately would be defeated and that area bombing was now hardly a "military necessity" in any real sense of the term—that is, the only real alternative available to the British war effort. Even assuming that considerable emphasis would continue to be placed on some type of bombing of Germany, moreover, he had in the latter stages of the war an option open to him that was far more attractive in both moral and also in military terms. In his minute of October 7, 1941, the Prime Minister had suggested that Bomber Command might prove to be a truly significant force in the war should the enemy's air defenses be so shattered that what was called precision daylight bombing of arms factories and other targets became a real possibility. In the event, this is precisely what happened during the spring of 1944, particularly with the introduction of long-range fighter escorts such as the Mustang, which made deep-penetration strikes into the Reich against precision targets an inviting strategy. Following the success of the D-Day operation, German air defenses became even more enfeebled. As of this date, Bomber Command had also developed advanced navigational and aiming devices that at last made it possible for British aircrews to undertake precision air strikes in Germany with great accuracy.

The point is that precision bombing promised—and delivered—far more decisive military results than area bombing ever could claim. During the main period of British area bombing of Germany, there was no evidence that German civilian morale had been affected to the degree that it posed a real threat to the continuation of the war effort. Even more significant was the fact that Nazi arms production actually increased rather than decreased. Construction of aircraft of all types went from approximately 15,000 in 1942 to about 40,000 in 1944. The production of tanks increased sixfold. The overall output of weapons and ammunition was almost three times the level achieved at the beginning of 1942.[20] Precision bombing, on the other hand (as mostly practiced by the Americans), had quite opposite and devastating consequences, resulting, for example, in the reduction of German petroleum production to only 10,000 tons in September 1944, barely a fraction of what the German armed forces required for successful operations.

It is only fair to ask whether Churchill had information at the time which suggested the ineffectiveness of area bombing. The answer is almost certainly yes. From sources such as "Ultra," which allowed the British to read secret

German military communications, as well as a number of other photographic and related sources, it was evident to all but the most stubborn eyes that area bombing was not only morally repugnant, but ineffective in the bargain. Churchill himself was an avid consumer of such intelligence. The leading historian of British intelligence states flatly that "no British statesman in modern times has had a more passionate faith in the value of secret intelligence than Winston Churchill." So intense was his interest in the subject that he often demanded to see raw intelligence reports before they had been analyzed by the professionals.[21]

Despite all of the preceding information, in September 1944, Bomber Command was allowed to resume much of its massive area offensive against Germany (after being diverted to support the D-Day invasion) instead of being forced to concentrate on precision daylight strikes against specific military targets such as the German arms industry, petroleum facilities, and the transportation network. It is well to recall in this regard that approximately 80 percent of all the bombs dropped on Germany came in the last 10 months of the war, and cities remained the primary target of Bomber Command until the very end. In terms of the "consequentialist" standard, therefore, Churchill's role in the area bombing of Germany seems even more problematic. Relatively early in the war he had come to have doubts himself about the military utility of such a strategy, and subsequently he had even more information that area attacks were—quite aside from their being morally repugnant—ineffective in the war effort. Moreover, the alternative of precision bombing of German military targets was available to him no later than the summer of 1944. Given these facts, it is hard to explain or to excuse his continued support of, or at least condoning of, the ongoing devastation of German cities and German civilians until virtually the last days of the war. It may be unreasonable to expect wartime leaders to adopt policies simply because they are morally attractive even though they may have harmful military consequences. In this instance there was a compelling congruence between morality and efficiency.

Universalization

There is a third test that may be applied to the moral evaluation of political leaders (even in wartime), although it may be argued that it has somewhat less force than the other two. A standard philosophical principle in establishing moral conduct is the requirement of "universalization." This means that the action undertaken must reflect an appropriate sensitivity to the interests of *all* concerned parties—not just one's own personal interests, or that of the special community one represents.[22] From a somewhat different perspective, what is implicitly involved here is Kant's famous Categorical Imperative, which dictates that one should "act only on that maxim whereby thou canst at the same time will that it should become a universal law." It is evident that there is a prudential as well as an inherent argument behind the concept of universalization. By considering the effects of one's actions in their totality, one may contribute to a more positive or stable collective environment that in itself will benefit the specific community that one represents.

The requirement of universalization, or of the Categorical Imperative, of course presents complications when we consider the conduct of states as opposed to that of individuals. Some would assert the relevance of these concepts to individual life while at the same time doubting whether they really apply to the life of collectives, given the semi-anarchic and self-interested character of international politics. Even if we partially concede the point, however, it seems reasonable to suggest that, by definition, a leader of great moral authority will attempt to go beyond an exclusive focus on the narrow interests of his or her own society and give at least some attention to the broader welfare of the international community as such. This does not mean that the very life and future of one's country has to be mortgaged to the welfare of others; it does imply that there are numerous situations in which a little less for one means a great deal more for others, and there is some considerable moral imperative for recognizing such situations and designing appropriate policies as a result.

In deciding on an "appropriate" British bombing policy in World War II, Churchill was, as it turned out, not totally indifferent to the philosophical requirement of universalization (although it is highly unlikely that he approached the matter in such abstract terms). From the earliest days of his stewardship of the British war effort, he was to insist that due care be given to at least one group of civilians subject to the power of Bomber Command—those living in occupied Western Europe. The fact is that a good deal of British bombing during the war was directed not just at Germany itself, but at a range of targets in France and the Low Countries, and to a lesser extent in Denmark, Norway, and other places as well. In October 1942, the Air Ministry issued a directive to the head of Bomber Command stating that deliberate attacks on the civilian populations in the occupied territories were forbidden, and that all such raids in this area had to be on strictly defined military objectives. More significant was the injunction that aircrews had to take all reasonable measures to insure that "accidental" loss of civilian life was held to an absolute minimum. The same directive added, almost as an aside, that such discrimination was not required in attacks on Germany itself.[23]

This concern with the welfare of others—even if it meant imposing certain restrictions on Bomber Command operations—was reflected most noticeably in the spring of 1944. Under the so-called Transportation Plan, the Allied Chiefs of Staff, at the urging of the Americans, decided to concentrate all

British and American bombing prior to the D-Day invasion on the German rail system in France and Belgium. The theory was that if this system could be shattered, the ability of the Germans to bring reinforcements to the invasion front would be badly compromised, which in turn would increase the likelihood of a successful invasion of the continent. Churchill strongly objected to the Transportation Plan, however, not only on grounds of its possible ineffectiveness, but on moral grounds as well. He even went so far as to appeal to President Roosevelt directly to limit what he called the anticipated "French slaughters" and "the apparently ruthless use of the Air Forces, particularly of the Royal Air Force, on whom the brunt of this kind of work necessarily falls, and the reproaches that would be made upon the inaccuracy of night bombing."[24]

Roosevelt rejected Churchill's appeal, and as it happened, preinvasion bombing in the occupied countries had a less draconian effect on the civilian population than feared. Approximately 12,000 civilians lost their lives. This was a somber enough figure in itself, but what is striking is how Churchill displayed a concern in this instance about civilian suffering that was almost totally absent when it was a question of bombing Germany itself. How to account for the difference? Certainly there was a pragmatic concern in British circles about a very negative political backlash in London's relationship with the de Gaulle Free French government-in-exile if large numbers of Frenchmen were killed in Allied bombing raids. But Churchill asserted a broader moral theory as well when he suggested that the death of French civilians would involve "a friendly people who have committed no crimes against us, and not the German foe, with all their record of cruelty and ruthlessness."[25]

Such an attitude, however understandable, cannot gainsay the fact that even in wartime the enemy population still retains certain rights and interests that require attention. To be sure, it seems reasonable to suggest that these may rightly be regarded as less compelling than the rights and interests of one's own soldiers and civilians, or those of Allied nations. Yet they hardly disappear even in the carnage of war. The idea that the welfare even of the enemy should be a subject of concern inevitably rests (as we have already argued) on the premise that there is no essential difference in the sanctity of life. If, as has been asserted, this applies even in terms of the treatment of enemy soldiers, the principle seems especially important in balancing the welfare of, say, one's own combatants with that of the enemy civilian population who are not combatants. By what moral calculus can we say that the death and injury of enemy civilians is essentially irrelevant as long as there is at least some prospect that such suffering will marginally reduce the danger to one's soldiers? Merely because a state of war exists does not remove the legitimate claims of enemy civilians for a reasonable chance to go on living. In order to protect such rights, it may be necessary for the soldier to accept a *somewhat* higher degree of risk (no one is demanding that they simply sacrifice themselves for the sake of enemy noncombatants).

Air Marshal Arthur Harris, the head of Bomber Command, had no doubt about how to resolve this issue. He observed at one point that "I do not personally regard the whole of the remaining cities of Germany as worth the bones of one British Grenadier."[26] Of many extraordinary statements offered during the war by Harris, this must surely rank among the most extraordinary. Was he really arguing that the killing of indeterminate thousands of additional German civilians was morally counterbalanced by the saving of one British soldier's life? Churchill was relatively more discreet in commenting on this matter, but based on his actions, it does not seem unfair to suggest that implicitly he shared Harris's basic premise. The fact that he allowed Bomber Command to continue its devastation of German cities even up to the last days of the war can only be interpreted as a willingness to set aside whatever marginal concern he may have felt for the German civilian in order to pursue indiscriminate bombing as one way in which to force the Nazi regime into submission.

CHURCHILL'S CONDUCT SUMMARIZED

To reiterate a point made earlier, there is no question but that Churchill did have "dirty hands" in his role as Britain's wartime Prime Minister. Can we go beyond this, however, and argue that Churchill was in some ways a genuinely "wicked" man for whom the dirty hands defense offers an inadequate rebuttal? Such a conclusion is certainly tempting given the fact that he presided over what seems to have been a militarily unnecessary visitation of great calamity on German civilians. The term "wicked," however, is open to various interpretations, and seems to admit of differing forms. Perhaps Churchill's conduct was an example of what S. I. Benn calls "conscientious wickedness."

> Conscientious wickedness is rarely a case of pursuing an end unaware of attendant consequences as evils; it is more often a case of a single-minded pursuit of an objective which . . . can reasonably be seen as good, but at the cost of a callous insensitivity to evil done by the way. It is not that the person believes the incidental evil to be itself good but rather that, having reason to think it evil, he nevertheless systematically disregards it.[27]

The mark of the "non-conscientious" wicked person, Benn continues, is "that such choices are for him neither difficult nor painful since the considerations that would make them so are systematically neutralized."[28]

It would be going too far to say that Churchill was able to put the tribula-
tions of the German civilian population in World War II totally out of mind—
that is, he was not able to totally neutralize his opinion of their sufferings.
On one occasion in June 1943, according to an account by an Australian
representative to the War Cabinet, Churchill was shown some actual bombing films of Germany, which were "very well and dramatically done." He suddenly "sat bolt upright and said to me, 'Are we beasts? Are we taking this too
far?'"[29] Even if such reactions were comparatively rare, there is certainly no
question but that Churchill was devoted to a cause that could "reasonably be
seen as good," i.e., the defeat of the Nazi challenge to civilization itself.
These two circumstances perhaps exculpate Churchill from the grosser charge
that his policy of bombing Germany was an unalloyed wickedness. To be
"non-conscientiously" wicked, moreover, it is necessary that the individual
involved be quite unaware of the fact that any moral issue is presented by
his actions. In a curious sense, the existence of hypocrisy may be an important
standard for judgment here. The hypocrite is at least aware that a moral query
may be presented against his behavior, and thus he attempts to disguise its
actual character. If he were not sensitive to the charge itself, why bother to
engage in the hypocrisy itself? As the French sage la Rochefoucauld put it,
"hypocrisy is the tribute that vice pays to virtue."

In advancing the concept of hypocrisy as a defense of Churchill's moral
standing, we might refer to the memorandum he wrote following the destruction of Dresden. This was probably the most famous (or infamous) application
of Allied bombing during the entire war. On the night of February 13, 1945,
the British attacked Dresden in two waves totaling almost 800 Lancaster
bombers, and a tremendous firestorm of the sort only seen previously at
Hamburg developed. Estimates on casualties from the Dresden raid vary
widely, from a minimal guess of about 35,000 dead to the most drastic estimate
of over 200,000. Throughout the war, spokesmen for the British government
had denied that Bomber Command was simply attacking the center of
German cities, but for a variety of reasons the reality of what had happened
at Dresden became quickly known and widely disseminated. Sharp questioning took place in the House of Commons as to the real nature of Bomber
Command's strategy, and there were widespread doubts expressed in other
quarters as well about the purpose of destroying Dresden. It was against this
background that on March 31, 1945 (some six weeks after the Dresden raid),
Churchill wrote to Sir Charles Portal as follows:

> It seems to me that the moment has come when the question of bombing
> of German cities simply for the sake of increasing the terror, *though under
> other pretexts*, should be reviewed. ... The destruction of Dresden remains
> a serious query against the conduct of Allied bombing. ... The Foreign

Secretary has spoken to me on this subject, and I feel the need for more precise concentration upon military objectives such as oil and communications behind the immediate battle zone, *rather than on mere acts of terror and wanton destruction, however impressive.*[30]

Now it is readily apparent from the historical evidence that Churchill had actually been a prime actor in the decision to attack Dresden, and in this instance even against the doubts of such champions of area bombing as Sir Arthur Harris. Given this fact, his memorandum can only be regarded as an attempt to "cleanse" the historical record. Subsequent histories of British strategic bombing in World War II would record that he had expressed doubts (*ex post facto*) about the destruction of Dresden. As a historian himself, Churchill presumably wanted to have evidence placed in the record about his concern over the effects of area bombing, and specifically its application to Dresden, even though such doubts were noticeably absent in his earlier directives on the devastation of German cities. One may recoil before this example of political dissimulation, yet accept that it represented a belated admission by Churchill that Bomber Command (and he himself) had done wrong, and that he was implicitly saying as much, even though it came at a very late date.

This retroactive acceptance (even indirectly) of guilt may be of some reassurance to those who cherish the memory of the former British Prime Minister and want to continue to do so. For many others, however, a more balanced view would be that Churchill's initiation of, and subsequent support for, the area bombing of Germany remains as a permanent blot on his moral escutcheon. Certainly he was a man of many admirable qualities, and he obviously performed a critical role in vanquishing the Nazi challenge to basic human values. Even so, his part in the destruction of hundreds of thousands of German civilians hardly stands as his finest hour. To accept dirty hands as the price of political leadership, particularly in wartime, is one thing. To excuse a crude indifference (in the case of area bombing) to those very values, to the fundamental requirement that the effects of differing policies be carefully considered, and to the obligation to respect the rights in wartime even of the enemy is quite another. Winston Churchill's role in the ordeal visited on German cities in World War II still stands as a serious indictment of his insensitivity to the enduring moral imperatives that should govern the actions of statesmen.

NOTES

1. These "primordial demands," moreover, are innately selfish and even brutal when compared to the sort of aspirations considered admirable in individual life. See Reinhold Niebuhr's *Moral Man and Immoral Society* (New York: Charles Scribner's Sons, 1932).

2. Niccolò Machiavelli, *The Prince and the Discourses*, Chapter 15 (New York: The Modern Library, 1940), p. 56.

3. John Finnis, Joseph Boyle, and Germain Grisez, eds., *Nuclear Deterrence, Morality, and Realism* (Oxford: Clarendon Press, 1987), p. 39.

4. Gwynne Dyer, *War* (Homewood, IL: Dorsey Press, 1985), p. 93.

5. For a more detailed discussion of the factors leading to the area bombing of Germany, see Stephen A. Garrett, *Ethics and Airpower in World War II* (New York: St. Martin's Press, 1993), pp. 9–14.

6. R. V. Jones, *Most Secret War* (London: Hamish Hamilton, 1978), p. 183.

7. Max Hastings, *Bomber Command* (New York: Simon & Schuster, 1987), p. 107.

8. J. Hare and Carey B. Joynt, *Ethics and International Affairs* (New York: St. Martin's Press, 1982), pp. 4–5.

9. Michael Walzer, *Just and Unjust Wars* (New York: Basic Books, 1977), pp. 29, 136.

10. Sir Harold Nicolson, *The War Years 1939–1945* (New York: Atheneum, 1967), p. 429.

11. Ibid., pp. 121–22.

12. Angus Calder, *The People's War* (New York: Pantheon Books, 1969), p. 491.

13. Robert H. Ahrenfeldt, *Psychiatry in the British Army* (New York: Columbia University Press, 1958), pp. 13–28.

14. Barton Bernstein, "Why We Didn't Use Poison Gas in World War II," *American Heritage* (August–September, 1985), p. 42.

15. Sir John Colville, as quoted in Ronald Lewin's *Churchill as Warlord* (New York: Stein and Day, 1973), p. 7.

16. Mark Moore, "Realms of Obligation and Virtue," in Joel Fleishman et al., eds., *Public Duties: The Moral Obligations of Government Officials* (Cambridge, MA: Harvard University Press, 1981), p. 10.

17. Jones, *Most Secret War*, p. 183.

18. Winston S. Churchill, *The Grand Alliance* (Boston: Houghton Mifflin Company, 1951), pp. 507–9.

19. Winston Churchill, *The Hinge of Fate* (Boston: Houghton Mifflin Company, 1950), p. 770.

20. P. M. S. Blackett, *Political and Military Consequences of Atomic Energy* (London: Turnstile Press, 1948), p. 195.

21. Christopher Andrew, "Churchill and Intelligence," in Michael Handel, ed., *Leaders and Intelligence* (London: Frank Cass, 1989), p. 181.

22. For an interesting discussion of this principle, see G. Elfstrom and N. Fotion, *Military Ethics* (London: Routledge and Kegan Paul, 1986), p. 17.

23. Finnis, Boyle, and Grisez, *Nuclear Deterrence, Morality and Realism*, p. 40.

24. Winston S. Churchill, *Closing the Ring* (Boston: Houghton Mifflin Company, 1951), p. 529.

25. Ibid., pp. 529–30.

26. Dudley Saward, *Bomber Harris* (Garden City, NY: Doubleday, 1985), p. 601.

27. S. I. Benn, "Wickedness," in John Deigh, ed., *Ethics and Personality* (Chicago: University of Chicago Press, 1992), p. 197.

28. Ibid., p. 199.

29. Lord Richard Casey, *Personal Experience 1939–1945* (London: Constable, 1962), p. 171.

30. Noble Frankland and Charles Webster, *The Strategic Air Offensive against Germany 1939–1945*, Vol. 3 (London: Her Majesty's Stationery Office, 1961), p. 112 (emphasis added).

3

No End of a Lesson: Vietnam and the Nature of Moral Choice in Foreign Policy

David Armstrong

It would not be difficult to develop a narrative of American decisions relating to Vietnam that showed, at each crucial turn, successive administrations arriving at a choice of policy that was both morally wrong and, as things transpired, disastrously misguided in other respects, too. In this narrative a clear moral parable would emerge: if statesmen strive to do the right thing according to widely accepted ethical norms, particularly those regarded as having a specific application to statecraft, they will find that they have also served their country's national interests better than if they had followed the injunctions of realists from Machiavelli onward about the necessity to disregard conventional moral principles in the name of the overriding principle of the security and survival of their own state. The supposedly higher value of *raison d'état* will be clearly be seen as no such thing and right and wrong as identical in public and private spheres. If valid, this parable would have profound implications. Although statesmen have frequently invoked "the lesson of Munich" to justify the threat and use of force on many occasions, they have been less inclined than this narrative suggests they should be to use "the lesson of Vietnam" to justify more pacific approaches.[1] More generally, it might give fresh force to Edmund Burke's injunction: "Justice is the great standing policy of civil society; and any eminent departure from it, under any circumstances, lies under the suspicion of being no policy at all."[2] Similarly, the parable gives some support to those who have queried the dominance of realism in the theory of international relations from various critical or postmodern perspectives, which problematize the separation of the observer from the observed and theory from practice.[3] Realism would be revealed not as timeless wisdom, embodying fundamental verities about international politics expressed in scientifically rigorous axioms, characterized by their objectivity and value-neutrality, but as a mere discourse or interpretation that helps to constitute what it is supposedly explaining.

FIVE STEPS TO PERDITION

Such a narrative might begin with the first significant American encounter with Indochina, when, in 1945, the Truman administration decided to ignore several approaches from Ho Chi Minh's Vietminh, the most powerful of the Vietnamese nationalist groups that had been fighting the Japanese. National self-determination had been proclaimed by Truman's predecessor as one of the most important principles for which the United States was fighting,[4] an emphasis repeated by Truman in his first State of the Union address in 1946. Yet for a variety of reasons, ranging from apprehension about the Vietminh's Communist identity to a concern for the impact of losing Vietnam upon French domestic politics, where the Communist Party was enjoying some success, Washington decided to align itself with French attempts to reassert control over Vietnam, albeit through a compliant indigenous government in the South rather than a return to pure colonialism. Although Truman had declared that self-determination should apply equally in Asia, Africa, Europe, and the Western Hemisphere,[5] his administration was able to ignore the principle on this occasion. A Truman biography argues that his specific decisions relating to Vietnam "by no means predetermined all that followed under later, very different Presidents."[6] Truman's own memoirs make it clear, however, that although Indochina was not seen as holding any particular significance, it was already being viewed as one of a number of areas threatened by what was perceived as a monolithic and aggressive communism: the image that dominated American thinking throughout the first two decades of the Cold War.[7] Hence it is not unreasonable to place this, very early, example of America's preparedness to ignore its stated moral principles in the case of Vietnam within the larger context of our parable. Had American policy from 1945 to 1954, when U.S. support for the French war in Indochina grew to a point where it was funding 78 percent of the costs of the French war effort, instead been founded on support for Vietnamese independence, all the damaging consequences of American involvement might have been avoided. These include not only the casualties (58,000 Americans and one million Vietnamese), the financial costs, and the lasting damage to U.S. relations with France, but also more intangible consequences such as the harm to America's reputation.

Reluctance to contemplate self-determination for Vietnam, except on terms agreeable to Washington, continued to characterize U.S. policy; for example, when the United States encouraged the Diem regime in South Vietnam to ignore the 1954 Geneva Conference's requirements for nationwide elections and when it acted against South Vietnamese leaders when they were contemplating a neutralist path for their country in the early 1960s.[8] However, my concern in this section is to identify specific moral norms and illustrate their violation by American decision makers in Vietnam, rather than to write a detailed account of their application or otherwise over the 25 years of the American involvement in the country. In that respect, the second major principle we might consider is the fundamental norm in international law relating to the sanctity of treaties, *pacta sunt servanda* (agreements must be kept), which is an international legal version of the more general admonition to people not to break promises. The agreement in question is the 1954 Geneva Accords, which partitioned the country (on terms less favorable than the North had won in battle) pending the holding of nationwide elections in 1956 and prohibited both sides from forming military alliances with other states and from permitting foreign troops and additional arms and munitions to be introduced.[9] Although the United States refused to sign the Accords, it issued a separate "unilateral declaration of its position" agreeing to "refrain from the threat or use of force" to disturb the Accords, supporting free elections to achieve unity in nations divided against their will, and repeating "its traditional position that peoples are entitled to determine their own future."

There is room to debate the precise legal status of these agreements and of the United States' declaration (as well as a similar declaration by the French-supported "State of Vietnam," which also refused to sign them).[10] It is also true that they were breached by all sides. However, a reasonable case can be advanced that South Vietnam and the United States were the first violators. Only two months after Geneva, the United States formed the Southeast Asia Treaty Organization (SEATO), whose name was clearly designed to imply parallels with NATO. This in itself was something of a provocative gesture, particularly as U.S. Secretary of State John Foster Dulles had wanted South Vietnam to be a member of SEATO—which would have directly violated the Accords. Even the addition of a Protocol to extend the protection of the treaty to Cambodia, Laos, and South Vietnam was, at the very least, against the spirit of the Accords, while the American introduction of a covert military unit in 1954 was equally difficult to reconcile with the principles expressed in its Geneva Declaration.

The third ethical-legal principle ignored by the United States, in this narrative, was the central norm of the Westphalian international order of nonintervention in the domestic affairs of other states. In practice, as the Pentagon Papers' account of the war makes clear, the United States became increasingly involved in South Vietnam's internal affairs from the moment it gave its strong support (against French opposition) to Ngo Dinh Diem's continuing leadership.[11] Insofar as the insurgency in the South was essentially a local affair—something that continues to be debated—America's growing commitment to support Saigon's resistance to it might also be deemed contrary to the nonintervention norm. Out of countless other examples, particular mention might also be made of what was at the very least American connivance in the coup against Diem.[12] A long-standing principle of international law in this context is that no state "shall organize, assist, foment, finance, incite or tolerate subversive, terrorist or armed activities directed towards the violent overthrow of the regime of another State, or interfere in civil strife in another state."[13] By one argument, which perceives the conflict in Vietnam as civil strife rather than externally supported aggression (the position of successive American administrations), the American involvement in its entirety violated this principle, but its toleration of the coup against Diem is a relatively clear-cut violation of it. The United States was later to be specifically criticized on similar grounds by the International Court of Justice in 1986 over its conduct in Nicaragua.[14]

Nonintervention is conventionally regarded as, essentially, a legal rather than an ethical principle because it expresses a corollary of the legal foundation stone of the Westphalian system: the principle of sovereignty. Law and morality are, of course, not identical; although both may be defined as sets of rules, they serve different functions in society, and while a particular law may embody some more general moral principle, it does not necessarily do so.[15] "Thou shalt not kill" is both a moral and a legal rule; "thou shalt drive no faster than 50 miles an hour" is not. In the case of international society, it is, clearly, possible to argue a moral case *for* intervention on humanitarian grounds, and such arguments have been heard with increasing frequency since the end of the Cold War. However, that humanitarian intervention is generally seen as the *exceptional* case, requiring justification on overwhelming moral grounds, suggests that nonintervention continues to be regarded as the higher, or at least more fundamental, norm. Furthermore, it is a norm that in specific cases may itself need moral rather than strictly legal justification: for example, through the argument that an intervention might do more harm than good. Hence, one does not need to agree with Austinian notions of international law as merely "positive morality" to accept that some of the basic principles of international law—and, indeed, of domestic law—derive from or are closely associated with more general moral norms.[16] In this case, nonintervention may be seen as a particular case of the larger moral injunction to respect the freedom of the individual and of such ethical principles as live and let live.

The fourth moral offense of the United States was, at the least, using disproportionate force and, at worst, waging an aggressive war. War is, of course, the most controversial international activity of all so far as general morality is concerned because it may involve conduct that would, if it took place within a national society, be seen as violating several fundamental social values, including the prohibitions against coercion, aggression, cruelty, and killing. For these reasons, pacifists argue that all wars are immoral; states, which see themselves as having to live with the permanent security dilemma imposed by the anarchical nature of the international system, have tried to work out normative justifications for resorting to force in certain circumstances. If anything, international society has become more, rather than less, permissive so far as the use of force is concerned than the relatively restrictive terms of Article 2(4) of the UN Charter seems to imply.[17] However, governments resorting to force in pursuit of their objectives invariably try to ground their conduct in some principle of justice or morality, such as resisting aggression, righting a wrong, or liberating a people from oppression. This suggests that the international community still sees the need for some variant of "just war" criteria to be employed in interstate conflicts. Since the Nuremberg war crimes tribunals, three categories of offenses against these criteria have been distinguished: the act of resorting to force in defiance of international law, or waging an aggressive war; crimes committed in the course of a war; and crimes against humanity. Together with the crime of genocide, these were the main categories adopted by the International Criminal Court set up in the first years of the new century, which the United States has refused to join.

Two points in particular are usually made in relation to the charge that the United States waged aggressive war in Vietnam: the commencement of the bombing campaign in the North in 1964–1965 and the extension of the war to Cambodia in 1970. The famous statistic that the American bombing campaign employed a greater explosive power than all the bombs dropped by all sides in World War II has sometimes been used by critics of the war to charge the United States with violating the just war principle that force used in a war should be proportionate to its objectives. However, "proportionality" is one of the murkiest aspects of just war theory. One authority suggests that "proportionality in coercion constitutes a requirement that responding coercion be limited in intensity and magnitude to what is reasonably necessary promptly to secure the permissible objectives of self-defense."[18] Unfortunately, this begs rather more questions than it answers: clearly the intention of this doctrine is not to impose a criterion of equivalence, one that limited the degree of force used in self-defense to that employed by the enemy, which would simply be a recipe for prolonging a war indefinitely. The key phrases "reasonably necessary" and "permissible objectives" are essentially subjective ones: a military commander would define them in ways that enabled him to ensure the maximum security and minimum casualties for his men; civilian victims—including, in the Vietnamese case, families moved from their homes under the controversial and widely disliked "strategic hamlets" program—would have a different perspective.[19] Moreover, judgments about proportionality depend to a significant degree on prior judgments about the legitimacy of the war as such, in particular whether it might be seen as an aggressive war.

The bombing campaign and the related issues of American use of napalm and defoliants such as Agent Orange are considered in greater detail elsewhere. Here we may briefly note that the American justification for bombing rested on the argument that the United States was assisting South Vietnam to resist aggression; the counterclaim, that it was the United States itself that was committing aggression, is based on arguments that the bombing was a further, and much more serious, violation of the Geneva Accords and that it was undertaken not as a response to aggression, but for a range of lesser reasons including the failure of South Vietnamese forces to deal with their Communist enemies and the need to bring pressure on Hanoi to accept a political solution. The charge of aggressive war in the context of Cambodia rests on more straightforward foundations. Cambodia had sought to maintain its formal neutrality during the war but had been unable to prevent North Vietnam from developing several bases along the eastern border of the country, which it used to supply its forces moving along the Ho Chi Minh Trail from north to south. The new Nixon administration began a secret bombing campaign in Cambodia in 1969 and in April 1970, with its South Vietnamese allies, launched a land attack across the border. Critics of the incursion—who use the less neutral word "invasion"—see it as a clear-cut case of aggression against a neutral state, whose consequences included not only Cambodia's inexorable slide toward the murderous brutality of the Khmer Rouge regime, but the worst moments of the war in the United States itself, when National Guard forces killed students who were protesting against the incursion at Kent State University in Ohio and Jackson State College in Mississippi.[20]

Crimes committed by soldiers during wars (which involve the just war norm of *jus in bello*, as opposed to crimes involved in the initiation of a war, which violate *jus ad bellum*) seem to be inseparable from war, and Vietnam was no exception. All forces on all sides committed such offenses; in this respect, the American troops were hardly more reprehensible than their allies or enemies, notwithstanding the publicity attracted by revelations of American atrocities at the village of My Lai, when more than 400 old men, women, and children were massacred. This is not to exculpate those or any other soldiers involved in such events; their moral guilt is clear enough when the extenuating circumstances usually advanced (heat of battle, ignorance, obeying orders, duress) are dismissed, as they can be in the case of My Lai.[21] But if the issue is whether, to what extent, and in what ways American conduct in Vietnam is particularly morally reprehensible, incidents like My Lai are not central to the specific case that we are constructing in this section. A more serious question in this regard is whether the war as a whole can be viewed as a crime against humanity. Not many, even among the critics of the war, go quite that far, but a few do argue that, taken together, the million deaths in Vietnam alone, the consequences of the Cambodian incursion, the long-term health effects, including continuing birth defects, of the use of

Agent Orange, the use of napalm and other chemical weapons, and, most generally, the nature of the war as a conflict between the world's most powerful state and one of its poorest bring it close to the category of crime against humanity.[22]

The final moral charge against successive American administrations is that of lying—in particular, of lying in contexts that amounted to subverting the U.S. Constitution. When Robert S. McNamara, defense secretary under Kennedy and, for a time, Johnson, decided after years of refusing to write his own account of his controversial period in office, he did so because he had "grown sick at heart witnessing the cynicism and even contempt with which so many people view our political institutions."[23] He was well aware that such reactions had, to a significant degree, been caused by revelations about the various deceptions employed by successive administrations during the Vietnam era, of which one of the most crucial was the use of a report of an attack on two American vessels in the Tonkin Gulf on August 4, 1964 (following an earlier attack on August 2), to secure a near-unanimous vote in Congress giving President Johnson broad powers to take whatever military actions he felt appropriate. McNamara's general verdict on American decisions relating to Vietnam is that "we made an error not of values and intentions but of judgment and capabilities."[24] In the specific case of the Tonkin Gulf Resolution, he continues to maintain, there was no deliberate deception, although he accepts that Johnson abused the power granted to him by the resolution by hugely expanding the American presence in Vietnam far beyond anything Congress would have authorized had it been specifically requested to do so.[25] However, when the President sought the resolution, he was well aware (as was McNamara) of many factors that, at the very least, made the events of August 4 far less than the unambiguous attack against American forces that was being portrayed to Congress: the fact that the administration had been looking for a pretext to increase military pressure on Hanoi for some months, the existence of covert American and South Vietnamese naval operations that would have been seen as provocative by the North, the probability that the American ships were in North Vietnamese territorial waters, and, most of all, the strong possibility that no attack had taken place on August 4, with the reported attack based on mistaken radar readings.[26] A Pentagon source leaked some of this information late on August 4 to one of the two senators who were to oppose the resolution, Wayne Morse; but he was unable to persuade Senator William Fulbright, to whom Johnson had entrusted the task of shepherding the resolution through Congress, especially as McNamara flatly denied one of his assertions, namely, that the American ships were part of covert operations against the North.[27] Similarly, Fulbright (who was later bitterly to regret his part in this affair) was able to dissuade another skeptic, Senator Gaylord Nelson, from proposing an amendment that would have had the effect of limiting the President's powers, on receiving private assurances from Johnson that he had no intention of embarking upon the open-ended land war that Nelson feared.[28] Although the blackest interpretation of these events—that the administration was involved in a conspiracy with the aim of securing the freedom to lead the country into a massive escalation of the war—is almost certainly incorrect, the charge of deception is probably justified.

This, then, is one way of representing the war: as a parable, or moral fable, enjoining leaders to act in accordance with fundamental and well-known values as the best means of serving their country's national interests. There are, however, at least two other ways of interpreting the war (or two alternative narratives), one that depicts American statesmen as acting throughout in accordance with other, equally fundamental, moral principles, the second that sees the war essentially as a tragedy. This chapter considers each of these narratives in turn before indicating problems with all three perspectives and reaching conclusions on ethical statecraft in general.

THE MORALITY OF U.S. DECISIONS

The strongest version of the argument that the United States acted with the noblest of intentions throughout its involvement in Vietnam sees the conflict there as essentially an aspect of a larger battle between good and evil: a battle, moreover, that the United States could have won had it not had its hands tied militarily and had it not faced so many domestic constraints. Unsurprisingly, perhaps, Richard Nixon presents the starkest outline of this narrative in his 1980 book, *The Real War*. At the time he wrote the book, the United States, in his view, was still involved in "World War III," a confrontation, begun as World War II was ending, between a Soviet Union committed to spreading Communist ideology (seen by Nixon as a form of enslavement) around the world and a United States committed to the defense of freedom and democracy. Vietnam had been but one battleground in that struggle, but Nixon's administration had first created the conditions for victory with his Nixon Doctrine of making countries threatened by Communist aggression take primary responsibility for their own defense, then "by following the strategy I initiated in 1969, we and the South Vietnamese were able to win the war militarily by the time of the Paris accords of January 27, 1973. . . . But the public had been so misinformed and misled by unwise government actions and the shallow, inflammatory treatment of events by the media that morale within the United States collapsed just when the North was overwhelmingly defeated on the battlefield. We won a victory after a long hard struggle but then we threw it away . . . when Congress prohibited military operations in or over Indochina and cut back drastically on the aid South Vietnam needed to defend itself."[29]

There is, of course, more than a small element of self-justification in this, but the most striking aspect of this book is its insistence—10 years before the collapse of communism in Europe—on the continuing relevance of the image that had guided U.S. policy since the end of the war, namely, that the United States was involved in a global struggle between good and evil. Repeated American statements—in private as well as in public—were to emphasize the same essential points in support of a portrayal of U.S. foreign policy as a moral crusade. Freedom and democracy were indivisible, and a threat to those values anywhere was a threat to the United States itself: once one domino fell, many more would shortly follow. The "lesson of Munich" should never be forgotten; only firmness and strength in the face of the relentless onward march of totalitarian communism would halt and eventually turn back the tide. In the opinion of one archrealist, Henry Kissinger, it was precisely America's attempt to apply its values to the inappropriate case of Vietnam that was responsible for the disasters that ensued: "America's rejection of national interest as the basis of foreign policy had cast the country adrift on a sea of undifferentiated moralism."[30]

In a narrative that portrays American decision making as based firmly on ethical principles, all five charges against the United States discussed here may be turned on their heads. First, freedom and self-determination were illusory concepts in the context of a world Communist system that was controlled from Moscow and that relied on oppression, thought control, and restrictions on individual liberty to maintain its power. True self-determination could be achieved only within the "free world." This was the image at the heart of the Truman Doctrine, announced in 1947, when he declared an American policy "to support free peoples who are resisting attempted subjugation by armed minorities or by outside pressures."[31] It underpinned the American decision to go to war in Korea and the developing American commitment to Southeast Asia, as exemplified by a speech by John Foster Dulles in March 1954: "The imposition on Southeast Asia of the political system of Communist Russia and its Communist Chinese ally, by whatever means, must be a grave threat to the whole free community."[32] And, in what may also be seen as a brief summary of all American war aims in Vietnam, it remained central to a Joint Chiefs of Staff paper outlining the "Over-all US Concept for Vietnam" on August 27, 1965:

> The RVN (Republic of Vietnam) is a politico/military keystone in Southeast Asia and is symbolic of U.S. determination in Asia—as Berlin is in Europe—to prevent Communist expansion. The United

States is committed to the defense of the RVN in order to assist a free people to remain free. In addition to the freedom of the RVN, U.S. national prestige, credibility and honor with respect to world-wide pledges, and declared national policy are at stake. Further, it is incumbent upon the United States at this stage to invalidate the Communist concept of "wars of national liberation."[33]

As the Joint Chiefs' memorandum suggests, American policy was also strongly influenced by a determination not to be seen as breaking commitments that Washington believed it had undertaken on behalf of South Vietnam: the same *pacta sunt servanda* principle that the United States was accused of violating in the first narrative. Many statements emphasize specific American commitments to Vietnam, such as its SEATO obligations, but a far more frequently expressed concern was with America's reputation as a country that honored its promises to other states. The belief that "abandoning Vietnam" would have repercussions elsewhere in Southeast Asia was an aspect of the domino theory from the time the United States began to take over from France—as, for example, in a 1956 speech by Senator J. F. Kennedy saying that "our prestige in Asia will sink to a new low" if South Vietnam "falls victim to any of the perils that threaten its existence—Communism, political anarchy, poverty and the rest."[34] As the American involvement grew in size, so too did estimates of the potential damage to American prestige and hence to perceptions of the credibility and value of its alliance commitments around the world if it was forced to withdraw. For example, Richard Nixon cites with approval two opinions he received in late 1969: one, from the British counter-insurgency expert Sir Robert Thompson that "the future of Western civilization is at stake in the way you handle yourselves in Vietnam"; the other from Henry Kissinger, that if the antiwar movement in the United States succeeded in forcing an American withdrawal, "the Communists would become totally convinced that they could control our foreign policy through public opinion."[35]

So far as the third of the general principles considered in the first section is concerned, many of the leading American officials who were responsible for the escalating American involvement in Vietnam have since taken the view that the degree of their intervention in South Vietnamese domestic affairs was probably mistaken. This, however, is not because of a late conversion to nonintervention as a moral principle[36] so much as from a realization that nation building to the extent that Washington pursued this goal was not feasible in a state without a deeply entrenched commitment to democratic values among its leaders. The U.S. success in helping to recreate stable democratic societies, through Marshall Aid in Europe and occupation in Japan, was, in other words, not transferable to the completely different circumstances in

Vietnam. At the time, however, the more American military and economic aid to Vietnam increased, the more Washington insisted on political reform, to the point in 1961 when the new Kennedy administration insisted that the price of a huge increase in aid was to be a substantial American role in almost every area of Vietnamese domestic politics.[37] Nonintervention was seen not as a moral principle in itself but, effectively, as the abandonment of morality for a cynical self-interest that disregarded the needs of others. Even the American collusion in changing the Diem regime could be justified on the fundamentally moral grounds that Diem was becoming increasingly autocratic and was clearly not the person to accomplish the high American purposes of building democracy in South Vietnam and holding the line against international communism.[38]

Similarly, the mirror image of the charge that America waged an aggressive war in Vietnam is the argument that the United States was simply defending the South against Communist aggression. Moreover, since the aggression faced by the South was part of a much wider scheme of world domination by the Soviet Union, a firm stand in Vietnam was a contribution to a larger global struggle against a new form of imperialism, one of whose weapons was "wars of national liberation." In this respect, the domino theory may be seen as an aspect of the larger "lesson of Munich" that runs through the thinking of successive American administrations from Truman to Reagan (and which continued during the 1990s with regard to Iraq).[39] Henry Kissinger and others point to the more assertive Soviet policies in Africa and Afghanistan following the American withdrawal from Vietnam as evidence of the validity of the domino theory. A perhaps subtler defense of American policies against the charge of aggression would be that their use of force, certainly when it was increasingly recognized that final military victory could not be achieved, was always designed to achieve the limited objective of forcing Hanoi to accept a negotiated settlement. The significant number of bombing pauses ordered by Johnson demonstrates clearly this essentially political purpose of the bombing. A similar argument may be deployed against charges that the scale of the American bombing campaign, in particular the use of napalm and Agent Orange, amounted to an American crime against humanity. The American strategy was based on the belief that only a war of attrition, in which the enemy became convinced of American determination to continue fighting, could achieve an acceptable political outcome. McNamara argues that in the 1966–1967 period, the Johnson administration was far more concerned about pressure from the right to abandon America's self-imposed restraints in its conduct of the war than about the growing antiwar movement.[40] Air power was a means of deflecting such criticisms at the same time as reassuring South Vietnam of the extent of the American commitment and keeping up the pressure on the North.[41] Even the much-derided faith of the administration's "best and brightest" in the power of modern technology may be interpreted in light of the determination to prevent the war from escalating into a potential conflict with China or the Soviet Union. Given that constraint, and in the absence of significant numbers of military targets for the bombing campaign, napalm, and other weapons designed to hurt and maim rather than kill were seen as the most effective means of bringing the desired pressure to bear on Hanoi. Agent Orange—whose long-term effects on GIs as well as Vietnamese on both sides were not fully appreciated at the time—was seen as a means of denying the enemy the kind of terrain in which he operated most effectively. Similarly, the American incursion into Cambodia was seen as a response to increased aggression there by both indigenous and Vietnamese Communist forces, as well as sending reassuring messages about American will to Saigon at the same time as warning and pressuring Hanoi.[42]

The obvious answer to charges of lying is that the accused was telling the truth—or at least the truth in the light of available intelligence and contemporary understanding of events. Both have been argued strongly by those involved in the decision making relating to Vietnam. Where some degree of deception is acknowledged, as Kissinger (who was not a member of the administration at that time) does with the Tonkin Gulf Resolution, the similar lack of candor with the American people employed by Franklin Roosevelt in pushing his country toward confrontation with Germany is pleaded in mitigation: what most now see as the right policy in terms of larger global considerations excused the element of deception used by Roosevelt.[43] Whether events in Indochina had quite the same global significance as the struggle against Hitler is immaterial; they were seen in a similar light by successive administrations. Others point to the sheer complexity of the policy-making process to excuse the lack of transparency and reliance on spin that sometimes characterizes governmental communications, especially over foreign policy issues. Roger Hilsman, a member of the Kennedy administration, points to three elements in the American policy-making system that sometimes led at the least to an oversimplified presentation of decisions, if not to deliberate obfuscation. The first was that the highly specialized nature of the American bureaucracy meant that "complex problems arising out of [bureaucratic] interaction, as between military and political considerations" tended to end up being considered at the highest level.[44] Inevitably a hard-pressed President, facing numerous domestic and foreign problems and without the benefit of omniscience or the ability to see into the future, would tend to frame a complex but not initially enormously important issue, like Vietnam up to 1965–1966, in black-and-white terms and would present it in that way to the American people. Second, the need to win over a wide constituency in support of policies committing the lives of American forces might lead to "overselling a policy proposal in the sense of claiming too much for it," as Hilsman believes was the case of Kennedy's Vietnam policy. Finally, the same need for wide support might also, at times, create "an incentive *not* to communicate effectively, to be a little fuzzy in articulating policy and its possible outcomes."[45] The peculiarities of foreign policy, where sensitive intelligence sources or delicate aspects of negotiations with foreign powers sometimes need to be concealed, may also tend to lack clarity.

It is clearly possible, using the same facts and even the same moral principles, to argue completely opposite cases so far as the morality of American conduct in Vietnam is concerned. If the lesson of the first narrative was that, had America adhered to the version of moral behavior outlined there, it would have achieved a far more satisfactory outcome in all other respects, the lesson of the second might be that the United States was actually *too* concerned with acting in accordance with its deepest principles, where a colder calculation of its interests might have served it better. This is very much the point of view of Henry Kissinger, who sees American foreign policy since 1945 as based on the principles of resisting aggression and promoting democracy; a policy that fitted the reality in the European context but not in Vietnam, which had no democratic tradition. Kissinger sees Vietnam as "the most ambiguous moral challenge" faced by America since 1945.[46] But because Americans sought moral certainty, they were unable to perceive the ambiguity of the situation in Vietnam and hence opt for more flexible policies there until it was too late.

THE WAR AS TRAGEDY

By far the commonest portrayal of the war is in more value-neutral terms as an unfolding tragedy. In one version of this narrative, "Vietnam is a triumph of the politics of inadvertence. We have achieved our present entanglement, not after due and deliberate considerations, but through a series of small decisions. It is not only idle but unfair to seek out guilty men."[47] Variations on this theme may be found in the later reflections of many of the leading participants, such as Kissinger's analogy with a classical Greek tragedy, "in which the hero is led step by step to his destiny by seemingly random events."[48] Additional subthemes include the wildly exaggerated view of the importance of Vietnam held by several administrations; the fact that the American strategy of fighting a war of attrition was actually far better suited to the Asian Communist doctrines of protracted revolutionary war, allied to the North Vietnamese willingness to accept heavy casualties, than to the imperatives and limitations at work in an open, democratic society; the fact that Hanoi's very clear understanding of American motives and constraints enabled it to ignore or exploit at will the numerous American peace initiatives; the separation between political and military objectives in the United States, as compared with the close harmony between these in Hanoi; lack of co-ordination between administrative departments; a lack of on-the-ground expertise about Indochina of the kind that had guided American decisions relating to the Soviet Union; the inability of the Johnson and Nixon admin-istrations to extricate themselves from a developing entanglement while retaining the degree of honor that a superpower was entitled to expect. Central to the "tragedy" narrative is the thesis that the United States acted throughout its involvement in Vietnam from the best of intentions, seeking first to help to create a thriving democracy, then to preserve it from aggression, and finally to find an exit strategy that would not fundamentally weaken its global standing. The domestic opponents of the war were themselves partici-pants in the tragedy because they too perceived events through a lens of moral absolutism that precluded support for the combination of firmness and willing-ness to negotiate that characterized the Johnson and Nixon administrations. They became, inadvertently, a weapon in the hands of the Communist side and helped, paradoxically, to delay the solution they so desperately sought.

NO END OF A LESSON

Kissinger, McNamara, Nixon, and many others have attempted to draw out the larger lessons of the war, which, in general, they tend to see in terms of the third narrative. To McNamara it seems "beyond understanding, incredible" that he and others did not ask such basic questions as "Was it true that the fall of South Vietnam would trigger the fall of all Southeast Asia? Would that constitute a grave threat to the West's security?"[49] However, he rejects argu-ments such as those advanced at the time by the American socialist Norman Thomas that he "would rather see America save her soul than her face in Southeast Asia" by asking rhetorically, "how do you save your soul? Do you save your soul by pulling out of a situation, or do you save it by fulfilling your commitments?"[50] In other words, he adheres in essence to the moral parable of the second section, which portrays America as sliding deeper into the Vietnamese abyss because of its high moral principles. He also lists 11 causes of the American failure in Vietnam, including misjudgments of adversaries, allies, and risks, and he draws the principal lesson that future American initia-tives should take place within the multilateral framework of the United Nations.[51] In this respect as well, he tends still to be looking for general prin-ciples to guide future policy. Kissinger, in contrast, draws very different con-clusions from the experience. His lessons: before the United States commits itself to combat, America needs to have "a clear understanding of the nature of the threat ... a clear military strategy and an unambiguous definition of what constitutes a successful political outcome." Moreover, "when America commits itself to military action, there can be no alternative to victory [because] prolonged stalemate will sap the endurance and hence the will of the American public."[52] This, in broad terms, also characterizes the American neoconservative response to the "Vietnam syndrome" that, for a time, inhibited American use of force in a number of situations for fear of becoming entangled in another Vietnam.

There may, however, be problems with all three narratives outlined here as well as with the kinds of prescriptions offered by Kissinger and McNamara. The first two narratives, taken together, point to the moral complexities involved in foreign policy decision making. This is especially so in the case of war, which in itself already encapsulates so many moral ambiguities. What this suggests is that moral absolutes can never be a reliable guide to policy making, but does that mean that principles have no part to play in foreign policy? The third narrative shows individuals not in control of events but swept along by a relentless tide of inevitability, which might be taken as evidence for the thesis that most of the time policy makers cannot be held to account for their actions. It might also suggest that there is little point in seeking to act morally in such situations. Cool-headed realism of the kind advocated by Kissinger is more effective as a guide to action.

However, just as McNamara may be making one kind of mistake in trying to cling to the notion that American foreign policy can still be guided by moral principles, so Kissinger may be mistaken in believing that his cold rationality might enable his country to make more effective foreign policy choices. If moralism, as many including Kissinger argue, has been a perennial problem in U.S. thinking about foreign policy, another problem revealed by the Vietnam War was a misguided faith in science, both in its capacity to provide technological solutions to complex political problems and, in its guise as social science, to produce clear, unambiguous policy guidance. One effect of the "Vietnam as tragedy" narrative is help to remove moral responsibility for decisions from those who made them. They might, as in a Greek tragedy, have possessed one fatal flaw in their characters—usually represented by the participants as too much idealism—but once the train of events was underway, they were carried along without any clear means of disembarking. A similar detachment of individual from moral responsibility may be derived from the related notions that the nature of the policy-making process can be clearly understood and deconstructed in "rational choice" and behavioralist terms and that the same application of "science" can lead to "correct" policies. "Rational choice" perspectives create a picture of the enemy—whether it be monolithic communism or a relentlessly power-hungry Middle Eastern dictator—who, removed from constraints such as history, geography, economy, and indeed mortality, simply pursues whatever increments to his power he can lay his hands on because that is the "rational" thing to do.[53] As Anatol Rapoport wrote in 1964, "it was never necessary to inquire what the enemy wants to do, but only what the enemy *can* do. If he can blackmail us, he will. If he can do us in, he will."[54] The task of the American decision maker is thus made simple: presented with a clear threat, he works out the most effective means of dealing with it, guided by the same "rational choice" assumptions about the enemy's probable conduct. If the enemy's behavior appears not to accord with these assumptions about his rationality—as was the case in Vietnam—the realists' response is to improve the science rather than question its underlying assumptions.

But if absolute morality and science are equally flawed, are any general principles available that can both guide decisions more effectively and provide at least some moral underpinning of the kind that public opinion in democracies is wont to insist upon? In fact from an early stage of the Vietnam War, an alternative voice could be heard that was sufficiently well informed about the dilemmas of exercising power not to fall into the counterproductive blanket denunciations of some in the antiwar movement. Because he also identifies a third fundamental problem with American decision making, alongside excess moralism and faith in science, pride of place in this group may be given to Senator Fulbright and his critique of the "arrogance of power." Without a conviction that American military and economic power could overcome all obstacles—indeed, without sufficient power at their disposal to enable "rational choices" to be exercised that would not have been contemplated by a less powerful state—the United States would not have been drawn so deeply into a quagmire of its own making. Certainly, as Fulbright suggests, "power tends to confuse itself with virtue and a great nation is peculiarly susceptible to the idea that its power is a sign of God's favor."[55]

Fulbright explicitly refutes both moralism and behavioralism as ways of understanding international relations, offering instead what he terms "humanism," comprising an attention to human needs, magnanimity, an understanding of cultural differences and an understanding of the irrational elements in human nature.[56] In one of his most powerful passages, he further argues:

> There are two Americas. One is the America of Lincoln and Adlai Stevenson; the other is the America of Teddy Roosevelt and the modern superpatriots. One is generous and humane, the other narrowly egotistical; one is self-critical, the other self-righteous; one is sensible, the other romantic; one is inquiring, the other pontificating; one is moderate, the other filled with passionate intensity; one is judicious and the other arrogant in the use of great power.[57]

Both, he suggests, are characterized "by a kind of moralism, but one is the morality of decent instincts tempered by the knowledge of human imperfection and the other is the morality of absolute self-assurance fired by the crusading spirit."[58] He sees the historical origins of this division as the contrast between the influence of the Puritans—"harsh, ascetic, intolerant, promising salvation for the few but damnation for the many"—and the other English heritage of "tolerance, moderation and experimentalism."[59]

He reaches a clear conclusion about the kind of American foreign policy style he would like to see:

> For my own part, I prefer the America of Lincoln and Adlai Stevenson. I prefer to have my country the friend rather than the enemy of demands for social justice; I prefer to have the communists treated as human beings, with all the human capacity for good and bad, for wisdom and folly, rather than as embodiments of an evil abstraction; and I prefer to see my country in the role of sympathetic friend to humanity rather than its stern and prideful schoolmaster.[60]

Fulbright was far from the only American advancing views of this kind: Under-Secretary of State George W. Ball was similarly urging the need for a more nuanced American policy in Vietnam during 1965.[61]

Many kinds of lessons have been drawn from the Vietnam conflict, ranging from the need for a new American isolationism to the requirement for American interventions to employ overwhelming force. What emerges from the discussion above is that neither interventionist nor noninterventionist policies in themselves necessarily hold a monopoly on morality. Nor, however, can decision makers escape responsibility—including moral responsibility—for their conduct. What Fulbright is calling for, in effect, is a return to the old-fashioned concept of statesmanship, which more clearly encapsulates the need for leaders to have and to exercise certain virtues than the more neutral terms currently in use, such as "decision maker." The classic virtues of statesmanship are wisdom, insight, prudence, common sense, pragmatism, tolerance, willingness to compromise where necessary, a knowledge of history (but not blindly following lessons like the Munich analogy), and an ability to see things from other perspectives. In place of implacable moral or ideological certainties, statesmanship offers common decency, common humanity, and a preference for peace over war. This does not mean, however, that peace will be chosen over war on all occasions: the supreme virtue of statesmanship is judgment. However, in the words of a very young Winston Churchill, "The duty of government is to be first of all practical. I am for makeshifts and expediency. I would like to make the people who live on this world at the same time as I do better fed and happier generally . . . but I would not sacrifice my own generation to a principle however high or a truth however great."[62]

AFTERTHOUGHT: THE MIDDLE EAST IN 2015

I first wrote this chapter for the second edition of *Ethics and Statecraft* in 2003. Inevitably, the controversies aroused by the American-led invasion of Iraq led me to consider relating the discussion of the Vietnam War to the unfolding events in Iraq, but I decided that it was too early to be able to make any informed judgements. Eleven years later, it is still far from clear what will be the outcome of the various conflicts in the Middle East. It is also true that the global historical and geopolitical contexts have been completely transformed since the Cold War era and that the social and political dynamics of the two regions are very different. However, American decisions and actions were a critical variable in both conflicts, so it may be worthwhile making some cautious and tentative comparisons, using the analytical framework developed here.

Taking the first narrative outlined here, if we simply alter the word "Vietnam" in the first sentence of this chapter to "the Middle East," has history repeated itself? Indeed, has it repeated itself as greater tragedy, rather than farce (in the original Marxian version of the quote)? In Vietnam, the United States experienced bitter internal divisions, substantial casualties, and economic damage as well as humiliation in its Cold War struggle—a humiliation that might have been one factor encouraging the Soviet Union to believe it could intervene with impunity in Afghanistan (an intervention whose consequences are still working themselves out today). In the Middle East, while American casualties have been nothing like so great, the Iraqi intervention, arguably, sparked off a chain of events around the region that have led to ever more instability, conflict, and extremism, while leading the current U.S. leadership to back away from too heavy an involvement in any of the current conflicts in the region. While on paper American military might is vastly greater than any competitor today (unlike the more balanced situation in the 1960s), could it be argued that Washington's unwillingness today to act as the world's policeman simply encourages Iranian, Russian, or Chinese adventurism in the same way as the Soviet Union was encouraged in the late 1970s?

Similarly, it would not be difficult to maintain that at least four of the five "steps to perdition" were repeated in Iraq. While national self-determination was not an issue here, the legality of the invasion was disputed from the outset. The U.S. intervention in Afghanistan in 2001 had been supported by two Security Council resolutions and, arguably, met the UN Charter's main exception to its prohibition of the use of force: self-defense. However, evidence of Iraq's support for al Qaeda was virtually nonexistent, although before and after the invasion U.S. officials advanced a different legal formulation in the shape of an extension of an existing legal norm of "anticipatory self-defense." In 1837, British troops had attacked and destroyed a ship, the

Caroline, found in American waters that had been supplying Canadian rebels. In a diplomatic note sent to the British ambassador to Washington in April 1841, U.S. Secretary of State Daniel Webster provided an authoritative definition of anticipatory self-defense. He wrote that such use of force was legal when the necessity is "instant, overwhelming, and leaving no choice of means, and no moment for deliberation." This is taken to mean that anticipatory self-defense is only legal when a state is facing imminent and overpowering attack, necessitating a *preemptive* attack. The U.S. argument after 9/11 was, in essence, that this formula needed to be extended to include *preventive* action, where the threat was not imminent but likely and that terrorism and weapons of mass destruction (WMDs) had created very different circumstances from those that existed in the nineteenth century. This was seen by many as simply offering a legal pretext for the United States to use its overwhelming power wherever it wished. Most legal commentators also dismissed the U.S.-British claim that they were acting in accordance with a Security Council resolution of November 2002 that threatened Iraq with "serious consequences" if it did not comply fully with earlier resolutions requiring it to destroy its existing weapons of mass destruction and long-range missiles. The legal problem was that this resolution (1441) did not stipulate that noncompliance could be met by an invasion without a further specific resolution authorizing such action, and the United States was unable to secure such a resolution.

Similarly, the third ethical-legal principle, of nonintervention in the internal affairs of a state is clearly applicable here, given that the stated purpose of the invasion from the outset was regime change. This could have been achieved in the 1991 war, ordered by the Security Council following Iraq's invasion of Kuwait but, partly because of pressure from other Arab governments, who saw such an outcome as illegal as well as potentially threatening their own positions, the United States backed away from bringing down the Saddam Hussein government. International law also sets out various constraints on what the occupying forces are permitted to do following a military victory, which were clearly ignored by the Coalition Provisional Authority (CPA) that controlled the country from April 2003 to June 2004. This disbanded the dominant political party, the Ba'ath Party, forbidding its members from holding positions in subsequent governments, and it also established a new Human Rights Ministry and set out a highly ambitious program for creating a market economy as well as dissolving the Iraqi army.[63] Inevitably one of the main consequences of these changes was to create a vast disaffected group, most of whom had weapons and military experience. Given that Saddam Hussein's power base was drawn from the minority Sunni population, it was inevitable that their displacement by Shia Muslims would form another basis for conflict.

Moving to the fourth principle—disproportionate force—assessing this is subject to the same general difficulties as outlined in relation to Vietnam. It could easily be argued, however, that, simply by its use of its dominant position to implement the reforms described in the previous paragraph, the coalition was using force to achieve objectives that went far beyond the stated purpose of removing the threat posed by Saddam Hussein. If we broaden the discussion to include consideration of the way in which force was used by the coalition against the local population, while there was no single incident as reprehensible as My Lai, there were many instances of detainee abuse in Abu Ghraib prison and elsewhere. Indeed, on several occasions, the Bush administration came close to arguing that the "war on terror" it claimed to be fighting invalidated existing legal and moral constraints on cruel and inhuman punishment.

Finally, the charge of lying has, of course, been at least as much directed against Bush and Blair (called "Bliar" on numerous posters) as against President Johnson. A 2008 congressional resolution to impeach Bush argued that he had deliberately misled Congress, using "fabricated threats of Iraq weapons of mass destruction to fraudulently obtain support for the authorization of use of force against Iraq" as well as presenting falsehoods that attempted to link Iraq to al Qaeda.[64] These and related charges have been repeated on many occasions, sometimes linked to assertions that the coalition's true motive was seizing control of Iraqi oil.

The alternative narrative put forward the case for seeing U.S. decision making in Vietnam as essentially motivated by moral considerations. In the Iraq context, legal arguments were put by the coalition as well as its opponents, so, strictly speaking, either side might have been correct. Indeed, the very fact that the coalition put so much effort into arguing its legal case is of some ethical significance since this did not happen in the case of Vietnam. An additional part of the legal-moral case might be that the Security Council is hardly the best institution for pursuing justice since its permanent members all have a veto that they can and do apply for purely self-interested rather than legal reasons. So far as nonintervention is concerned, this had already become somewhat diluted by the concept of "responsibility to protect" that has developed since first enunciated by UN Secretary-General Kofi Annan, in 1999. This argues that sovereignty involves responsibilities as well as rights, especially the responsibility for a government to protect its own people. If a government fails in this obligation, rather than the principle of nonintervention prevailing, the international community has the obligation to implement the responsibility to protect principle, including by armed intervention. Although the first formal application of this principle by the Security Council came with the intervention in the Libyan internal conflict in 2011, arguments were advanced by the coalition leaders in 2003 that there was a strong moral case for intervention on what, essentially, were responsibility to protect grounds. Tony Blair, putting the case for intervention to Parliament, concluded with what he refers to in his autobiography as "the moral case for action": ending the brutalities committed by the Saddam regime.[65] A further moral case was advanced by the influential neoconservative group in the United States, who called for a more assertive U.S. foreign policy, including a willingness to promote democratization on the grounds that democracies were likely to be more stable and less extreme and that an American "world policeman" role was necessary in the post–Cold War era. In the case of abuse of prisoners of war, the advocates of the moral case for intervention could at least argue that, unlike My Lai, serious steps were taken to put on trial and punish individuals who had committed abuse, and in some cases the victims were able to bring legal action against the British and American governments. Finally, the charge of lying could be met with the defense that the leaders of the coalition genuinely believed what they were saying about weapons of mass destruction.

If Vietnam was "a triumph of the politics of inadvertence," the Iraq war was doubly so. Indeed, if there is a law of unintended consequences, what followed the invasion can hardly be surpassed as an illustration. In an article in June 2014, Peter Bergen goes so far as to argue that "one of George W. Bush's most toxic legacies is the introduction of al Qaeda into Iraq, which is the ISIS mother ship."[66] In other words, a "war on terror" simply served to produce far greater terror and hostility toward the United States. Even the nonmilitary aspects of U.S. conduct often had disastrous consequences. For example, the pressure toward greater democracy, which was one factor behind the Arab Spring, helped to produce violent internal conflict in Libya, Syria, and Egypt. While the U.S. casualties did not reach Vietnam proportions, more than 4,000 lost their lives and the war cost well over $2 trillion.

There are of course many differences between the two wars. The Vietnam War needs to be seen in the context of U.S. Cold War thinking, the Iraq war in the context of the understandable emotion following 9/11. However Fulbright's "arrogance of power" reflections are at least as applicable today as they were in the 1960s. This book's title places ethics and statecraft together as fundamental principles to be observed in foreign policy decision making. Arguably it is the latter that was lacking in both wars. While it was entirely reasonable for policy makers to perceive that Islamist extremism posed a very different kind of threat from Soviet expansionism, where they were at fault was in their "arrogance of power" belief that overwhelming force could solve extremely complex political problems. It is reasonably clear that while the U.S. intelligence agencies and the State Department all produced extensive studies pointing out many of these complexities, including the probability that the invasion would exacerbate the terrorist problem and the need for careful and sophisticated postwar planning, they were ignored. Indeed the key decision makers, George W. Bush, Dick Cheney, Donald Rumsfeld and Paul Wolfowitz went out of their way to refute such analyses. Iraq, too, offers "no end of a lesson" but, sadly, as George Santayana said more than 100 years ago, "those who cannot remember the past are condemned to repeat it."

NOTES

1. Indeed, for many, including former President Nixon, the "lesson of Vietnam" was precisely the opposite: that force should have been used more effectively or in greater quantities. Richard Nixon, *The Real War* (New York: Warner Books, 1981), pp. 105–36.

2. Edmund Burke, *Reflections on the Revolution in France* (Indianapolis, IN: Bobbs-Merrill, 1959), p. 180, cited in Robert W. Tucker and David C. Hendrickson, *The Imperial Temptation: The New World Order and America's Purpose* (New York: Council on Foreign Relations Press, 1992), p. 133.

3. One of the best works from such a perspective is David Campbell, *Writing Security: United States Foreign Policy and the Politics of Identity* (Manchester: Manchester University Press, 1998).

4. In fact, Roosevelt had already begun to back away from applying this principle to Indochina in the months before his death. Robert Dallek, *Franklin Roosevelt and American Foreign Policy, 1932–1945* (New York: Oxford University Press, 1979), pp. 512–13.

5. *The State of the Union Messages of the Presidents*, Vol. 3 (New York: Chelsea House Publishers, 1967), p. 2908.

6. David McCullough, *Truman* (New York: Simon & Schuster, 1992), p. 990.

7. Harry S. Truman, *Memoirs. Vol. II, 1946–1952: Years of Trial and Hope* (New York: Hodder & Stoughton, 1965), pp. 377, 433, 454.

8. See, for example, the account in George McT. Kahin, *Intervention: How America Became Involved in Vietnam* (New York: Anchor Books, 1986), especially Chapters 7–10.

9. The main agreement—effectively a cessation of hostilities—was, strictly speaking, signed between the French and Communist military leaders, a technicality that gave Diem's government grounds for claiming that it was not bound by the agreement because it had not participated. However, the second main document, a declaration by all participants in the conference except the United States, made it clear that the division of the country was to last no more than two years. For both documents and the U.S. Declaration, see Richard A. Falk, ed., *The Vietnam War and International Law*, Vol. 1 (Princeton, NJ: Princeton University Press, 1968), pp. 543–60.

10. There is a vast literature on the international legal aspects of the war, but several opposing points of view are presented in Falk, *The Vietnam War and International Law*, Vols. 1–2.

11. *The Pentagon Papers*, Senator Gravel, ed., Vol. 1 (Boston: Beacon Press, 1971), pp. 180–84, 213–39.

12. A recent account argues that, notwithstanding conflicting signals from different American decision makers to those planning the coup, "the White House had promoted the attempt by exerting economic pressures on Diem and then assuring his

enemies of help in a successful aftermath." Howard Jones, *Death of a Generation: How the Assassinations of Diem and JFK Prolonged the Vietnam War* (Oxford: Oxford University Press, 2003), p. 405.

13. This has appeared in several documents, including a 1970 UN General Assembly Resolution and the Helsinki Final Act of 1975. James Fawcett, *Law and Power in International Relations* (London: Faber and Faber, 1982), pp. 112–13.

14. Werner Levi, *Contemporary International Law* (Boulder, CO: Westview Press, 1991), pp. 84–88.

15. See, for example, the classic discussion in H. A. L. Hart, *The Concept of Law* (Oxford: Clarendon Press, 1992), pp. 180–207, 221–26.

16. See also Terry Nardin, "Ethical Traditions in International Affairs," and Dorothy V. Jones, "The Declaratory Tradition in Modern International Law," both in Terry Nardin and David R. Mapel, eds., *Traditions of International Ethics* (Cambridge: Cambridge University Press, 1993), pp. 1–22 and 42–61.

17. Anthony Clark Arend and Robert J. Beck, "International Law and the Recourse to Force: A Shift in Paradigms," in Charlotte Ku and Paul F. Diehl, eds., *International Law: Classic and Contemporary Readings* (Boulder, CO: Lynne Rienner, 1998), pp. 327–51.

18. Myres S. McDougal and Florentino P. Feliciano, *Law and Minimum World Public Order* (New Haven, CT: Yale University Press, 1961), pp. 242–43.

19. For a discussion of the proportionality issue in the context of the Vietnam War, see Eliot D. Hawkins, "An Approach to Issues of International Law Raised by the United States Actions in Vietnam," in Falk, *The Vietnam War and International Law*, Vol. 1, pp. 189–93.

20. For the most detailed account of the incursion in these terms, see William Shawcross, *Sideshow: Kissinger, Nixon and the Destruction of Cambodia* (London: Hogarth Press, 1986).

21. For a discussion of this issue in the context of the My Lai killings, see Michael Walzer, *Just and Unjust Wars: A Moral Argument with Historical Illustrations*, 2nd ed. (New York: Basic Books, 1992), pp. 306–16.

22. See, for example, William Blum, *Rogue State* (London: Zed Books, 2002), pp. 51–52, 71, 83–84, 105–6, 135, 228–29.

23. Robert S. McNamara with Brian Van DeMark, *In Retrospect: The Tragedy and Lessons of Vietnam* (New York: Random House, 1995), pp. xv–xvi.

24. Ibid.

25. Ibid., pp. 127–43.

26. Opinions on the administration's response to the Tonkin Gulf incidents range from the straightforward view that Johnson, McNamara, and others were simply lying (for example, Eugene C. Windchy, *Tonkin Gulf* [New York: Doubleday, 1971]), through the similar but more nuanced opinion of David Halberstam that McNamara had been "disingenuous to the point of open dishonesty" about several aspects of the affair (Halberstam, *The Best and the Brightest* [London: Barrie & Jenkins, 1972], p. 419), to a more recent study that concludes that they were essentially mistaken (Edwin E. Moise, *Tonkin Gulf and the Escalation of the Vietnam War* [Chapel Hill: University of North Carolina Press, 1996]).

27. Stanley Karnow, *Vietnam: A History* (New York: Penguin Books, 1984), p. 375.

28. Halberstam, *Best and the Brightest*, pp. 418–19.

29. Nixon, *The Real War*, p. 130.

30. Henry Kissinger, *Diplomacy* (New York: Simon & Schuster, 1994), p. 658.

31. McCullough, *Truman*, p. 548.

32. Speech to the Overseas Press Club, New York City, March 29, 1954, in Marvin E. Gettleman, ed., *Vietnam: History, Documents, and Opinions on a Major World Crisis* (Harmondsworth: Penguin Books, 1965), pp. 96–98.

33. Memorandum from the Joint Chiefs of Staff to Secretary of Defense McNamara, JCSM-652-65, in *Foreign Relations of the United States (FRUS), 1964–1968, Vol. III, Vietnam, June–December 1965* (Washington, DC, 1996), pp. 356–63. Hereafter cited as *FRUS*.

34. Cited in Anthony Short, *The Origins of the Vietnam War* (London: Longman, 1989), p. 209.

35. *The Memoirs of Richard Nixon* (New York: Warner Books, 1978), pp. 501, 504.

36. However, McNamara did later reflect that "we do not have the God-given right to shape every nation in our own image or as we choose." McNamara, *In Retrospect*, p. 323.

37. See, for example, National Security Action Memorandum, 52, May 11, 1961, which stated the American objectives as preventing Communist domination in the South and creating "a viable and increasingly democratic society" by means of military, political, economic, psychological, and covert actions. *Pentagon Papers*, Vol. 2, p. 642.

38. In fact, by 1963, fears that the growth of domestic opposition to Diem would weaken the war effort were predominant in American thinking. Kahin, *Intervention*, pp. 144–48.

39. For a discussion of the Munich lesson in the context of U.S. foreign policy decision making, see Ole R. Holsti and Kames N. Rosenau, *American Leadership in World Affairs: Vietnam and the Breakdown of Consensus* (Boston: Allen & Unwin, 1984), pp. 3–17.

40. McNamara, *In Retrospect*, pp. 252–53.

41. Robert Buzzanco quotes Maxwell Taylor, then American ambassador to Vietnam, to the effect that the air campaign was a means of "producing maximum stress in Hanoi minds." *Masters of War: Military Dissent and Politics in the Vietnam Era* (Cambridge: Cambridge University Press, 1996), p. 192.

42. Henry Kissinger, *The White House Years* (London: Weidenfeld & Nicolson, 1979), pp. 433–521.

43. Kissinger, *Diplomacy*, p. 659. And see Cathal J. Nolan, "Bodyguard of Lies," in this volume.

44. Roger Hilsman, *To Move a Nation: The Politics of Foreign Policy in the Administration of John F. Kennedy* (New York: Delta, 1968), p. 547.

45. Ibid.

46. Kissinger, *Diplomacy*, p. 676.

47. Arthur M. Schlesinger Jr., *The Bitter Heritage: Vietnam and American Democracy, 1941–1966* (London: Sphere Books, 1967), p. 44.

48. Kissinger, *Diplomacy*, p. 645.

49. McNamara, *In Retrospect*, p. 39.

50. Ibid., p. 217.

51. Ibid., pp. 321–26.

52. Kissinger, *Diplomacy*, p. 700.

53. Ron Robin, *The Making of the Cold War Enemy: Culture and Politics in the Military-Intellectual Complex* (Princeton, NJ: Princeton University Press, 2001), provides a powerful critique of the influence of behavioralism.

54. Anatol Rapoport, "Critique of Strategic Thinking," in Roger Fisher, ed., *International Conflict and Behavioral Science* (New York: Basic Books, 1964), p. 234 (cited in Robin, *Making of the Cold War Enemy*, p. 7).

55. J. William Fulbright, *The Arrogance of Power* (Harmondsworth: Penguin Books, 1970), p. 15.

56. Ibid., pp. 157–72.

57. Ibid., p. 235.

58. Ibid.

59. Ibid., p. 239.

60. Ibid., p. 246.

61. For example, *FRUS*, pp. 16–21, 55–57, 62–66, 106–13.

62. Schlesinger, *Bitter Heritage*, p. 100.

63. Wayne Sandholtz, "The Iraq War and International Law," in David Armstrong, ed., *Routledge Handbook of International Law* (Milton Park, UK: Routledge, 2011), p. 231.

64. *Text of Impeaching George W. Bush, President of the United States, of High Crimes and Misdemeanors*, GovTrack.us, https://www.govtrack.us/congress/bills/110/hres1345/text.

65. Tony Blair, *A Journey* (London: Hutchinson, 2010), p. 439.

66. Peter Bergen, "Bush's Toxic Legacy in Iraq," CNN.com, http://edition.cnn.com/2014/06/13/opinion/bergen-iraq-isis-bush/.

4

Noncombatant Immunity and Civilian Liability in Contemporary Asymmetric Warfare

Michael L. Gross

Scenarios like the following are common in contemporary asymmetric warfare:

- "I took everything I needed with me on a motorbike," said one Hezbollah activist. "Another activist rode pillion ... We carried the rocket in a large cloth. The Israeli army used to bomb all the motorbikes, so [we] covered ourselves [with] a large white flag, while we were carrying the rocket."[1]
- "For a guy fighting in Eyta a-Sha'ab, 'withdrawal' means going home, putting your AK-47 under the bed and changing your clothes."[2]
- "The deliberate strategy of Hamas to blend in with the civilian population made it difficult for the IDF (Israel Defense Forces) to achieve the objective of the Gaza Operation—reducing the threat of deliberate attacks against Israeli civilians—while also avoiding harm to Palestinian civilians."[3]
- Facing Taliban forces in Marjah, Afghanistan, in February 2010, one officer complained how "a few crafty, determined insurgents can keep a larger force engaged for hours with some degree of impunity. 'The inability to stop people who don't have weapons is the main hindrance right now ... They know how to use our ROE [rules of engagement] against us.' "[4]
- "[F]ixed launching positions ... had been built mostly in the orchards of local farmers who were paid for their assistance by Hezbollah ... The farmers who operated the systems received their instructions by mobile phones."[5]

As asymmetric conflicts between states and guerrillas, freedom fighters, or rebels replace conventional wars between nation-states, state armies face a number of interrelated challenges. By far, the greatest problem is the inability to distinguish between combatants and noncombatants. For more than 100 years, the law of war was very clear: combatants wear uniforms or insignia, carry their arms openly, submit to a rigid, institutional rank and command structure to distinguish them from criminals, and are bound to obey international law. Everyone else who does not wear a uniform is a civilian noncombatant and is prohibited from carrying weapons or engaging in armed conflict. Within this framework each actor enjoys particular rights and duties. Combatants may bear arms and kill other combatants but must refrain from harming noncombatants directly. Noncombatants must refrain from combat but, in turn, enjoy protection from any kind of direct harm and from disproportionate or excessive collateral harm.

With decades of colonial warfare in the postwar period, uniforms and insignia began to lose their force. By 1977, the Additional Protocols to Geneva Convention confirmed in law what was common in practice:

> Combatants are obliged to distinguish themselves from the civilian population ... Recognizing, however, that there are situations in armed conflicts where, owing to the nature of the hostilities an armed combatant cannot so distinguish himself [he] shall retain his status as a combatant, provided he carries his arms openly during each military engagement.[6]

Two things are important about this permission. One, it is an exception to the general rule that requires uniforms and two, the rule as well as the Protocols in general apply to guerrillas fighting wars of national liberation against colonial, racist, and alien regimes. In due course, however, the exception morphed from an exception into a rule and applied to guerrillas and militants fighting a state army for any number of reasons.

In this environment, state armies will find it very difficult if not impossible to distinguish between combatants and noncombatants by sight alone. To satisfy the demands of distinction now requires state armies to develop intelligence-based tactics such as target killing. Rather than depend upon uniforms, state agencies collect detailed information to determine military affiliation. Once a state is reasonably certain a particular individual is, in fact, a militant liable to deadly disabling harm, Special Forces or drone operators can then mount an attack. There is no question, however, that lack of uniforms make operations risky and often place noncombatants in danger. This situation is complicated by a blurring of combatant and noncombatant roles in warfare. Not only are combatants and noncombatants outwardly indistinguishable, they no longer perform discrete functions. Because guerrilla armies are often numerically small (Hamas and Hezbollah numbered no more than 10,000 fighters and the Taliban about 25,000) they often depend upon a well-developed political wing to provide support.[7] Members of the political wing provide financial, legal, diplomatic, logistical, and other forms of aid.

The crucial questions, then, that emerge from asymmetric war are twofold. First, who merits protection from harm during war? The answer is "noncombatants." But who are the noncombatants and what happens, for example, when they appear on the battlefield as human shields? Second, who among civilians do not enjoy protection? This list includes a large number of civilians who take a direct or indirect part in the fighting. While some of these civilians enjoy protection from any kind of harm, others are liable to various degrees of lethal and nonlethal force during asymmetric war.

NONCOMBATANT IMMUNITY IN MODERN WARFARE

Noncombatant immunity protects noncombatants from direct harm and from unnecessary and disproportionate collateral harm. These are two different but often confused notions. The moral basis for prohibiting direct harm against noncombatants is clear: noncombatants have done nothing to forfeit their right to life. One may therefore not fire upon a civilian with the intent to injure or kill. To do so is a war crime of the first degree. The term "intent," however, is somewhat misleading. Think about a pilot who attacks a military target nested among civilians. In this instance, there is no way to say that he does not "intend" to harm civilians. He knows full well that civilians will die after he drops his bombs. Nevertheless, this is not necessarily a case of direct harm because civilians are not the object of the attack; attacking and killing them has no military value. After the fact, therefore, one may test for intent by looking for any benefit a mission might have gained from harming noncombatants. Any hint that civilian deaths enhanced deterrence, increased political instability, or brought pressure to bear on policy makers to cease fighting points to an express benefit. Such civilian deaths are not incidental or collateral but direct and intentional. There is, then, far more nuance to the prohibition on direct harm than simply proscribing cold-blooded murder, rape, or torture. The ban on direct harm also prohibits any military action that benefits from noncombatant casualties. Understanding the ban on direct harm in this way provides additional protection for noncombatants.

While civilians enjoy protection from direct harm, they enjoy no such protection from proportionate death and collateral injury during war. The word "proportionality" does not appear in the 1977 Additional Protocol I (API) to the Geneva Conventions. Instead, API refers to "incidental loss of life" which is "excessive." In this context, "incidental" loss of life means necessary but unintentional, that is, "collateral," harm:

[Those who plan an attack shall] refrain from launching any attack which may be expected to cause incidental loss of civilian life ... which would be excessive in relation to the concrete and military advantage anticipated.[8]

The principle of proportionality enshrined by this paragraph is shrouded in ambiguity. Contrary to popular opinion, proportionality does not compare the number of civilian casualties each side suffers and then declares a war or battle disproportionate when one side experiences few losses and the other side very many. Rather, the principle of proportionality governs the relationship between military advantage and enemy civilian deaths (and, to a lesser extent, injuries and property damage). Military advantage may mean saving compatriot lives and/or protecting territory or some military asset. Civilian deaths (and sometimes injuries) are, perhaps, easy to count but difficult to compare to military advantage. There is no common currency to compare the two. Moreover, it can be very difficult to count civilian casualties because the definition of civilian, as we will see further below, is open to conflicting interpretations.

In Operation Cast Lead (Gaza, 2008–2009), for example, Israelis and Palestinians counted approximately the same number of Palestinian dead and, in fact, their names were posted in no time. Competing assessments of who among the dead were civilians, however, varied widely from 25 percent to 75 percent of the casualties.[9] The dead, moreover, are only one cost. There is no obvious reason to exclude other harms from the proportionality calculation: the injured, diseased, and displaced together with the short and long damage to transportation, energy, water, or agricultural infrastructures. But fixing these numbers is only part of the problem. Assuming one can quantify military advantage and civilian casualties, what then does "excessive" mean? How many civilian deaths and injuries are proportionate and how many are not? There is no easy answer to this question. Over time, international law has simply taken the advice of Justice Potter Stewart to heart: "one knows it [disproportionate force] when one sees it." The call is largely subjective.

While subjectivity renders the proportionality principle extremely elastic in practice it is not entirely vacuous. There is a limit beyond which civilian casualties are entirely disproportionate. But whether this can be quantified by any neat algorithm or is nothing but a gut feeling is never clear. The Geneva Conventions can only offer advice of questionable utility: " 'Some cases [of excessive harm],' opines the Geneva Convention commentary 'will be clear-cut and the decision easy to take. For example, the presence of a soldier on leave obviously cannot justify the destruction of a village.' "[10]

This admonishment, however, is so "obvious" that any order to destroy a village to disable one soldier on leave is manifestly unlawful. Proportionality, it seems, comes into play only at the extremes, when disproportionate harm is synonymous with flagrantly unlawful death and destruction. As a result, charges of disproportionate harm, so easy for some observers to sometimes press, are also easy for belligerents to refute. The disparity between observers' and participants' perceptions draws from both incommensurable definitions of "excessive" and conflicting understandings of the equally amorphous "concrete and military advantage anticipated." While outside, after-the-fact assessments are valuable (by UN Commissions, for example), greater weight will always be given to the "real-time" evaluation of those whose military advantages are at stake. Under these circumstances, the best one might expect is a reasonable and, more importantly, defensible judgment that articulates a mission's important objectives, its anticipated civilian casualties, an indication that alternative means were not available and that the civilian deaths could not be avoided or further minimized without great cost to a commander and his soldiers.

Beyond this, state armies might do better to concentrate on avoiding direct and unnecessary harm in the course of modern warfare. I already noted how expanding the notion of direct harm can provide additional protection for noncombatants. Unnecessary harm is similarly overlooked. It should be remembered that the principle of proportionality applies only to necessary military operations that aim for a significant military advantage. But what happens when they do not? What happens when civilians lose their lives in unnecessary military operations? The requirement to avoid unnecessary harm is often ignored and refers to any casualty that does not accompany a military advantage. Casualties are unnecessary when they (1) occur *after* legitimate war aims are achieved, (2) occur when *illegitimate* war aims are pursued, and (3) are not required to achieve legitimate war aims. Consider the Second Lebanon War (2006). Here civilians in Israel and Lebanon suffered unnecessary casualties of all three types.

First, there are good reasons to think that Israel's legitimate war aims—restoration of calm to the northern border, displacement of Hezbollah forces to the north, and their replacement with Lebanese forces—were largely achieved with the G/8 declaration of July 7, 2006, 10 days after the war started and certainly once the first UN resolutions were drafted on August 2, 2006, roughly 10 days before the war ended. At the very least, Israel achieved these aims when the UN adopted its final resolution two days before the fighting ended. If, indeed, Israel's war aims were achieved before the end of the fighting, then any casualties incurred after this date were unnecessary and superfluous rather than disproportionate. These would include both Israeli and Lebanese military and civilian casualties.

Second, there is room to distinguish between legitimate and illegitimate war aims. Pursuit of the latter also renders casualties unnecessary rather than disproportionate. At the very least, legitimate war aims must be feasible and attainable. If early Israeli aims included return of the captured soldiers and/or the complete destruction of the Hezbollah or, at a later date, simply disarming Hezbollah forces and it soon became clear that these aims could not be attained, then casualties incurred trying to achieve them are, likewise, unnecessary rather than disproportionate.

Finally, civilian casualties are excessive when not required to accomplish a military goal or if they might have been avoided while successfully pursuing the same goal. Civilians were killed in Lebanon during (1) attacks on Hezbollah bunkers and strongholds in the countryside, (2) attacks on missile dumps and missile launcher sites, (3) attacks on Hezbollah military headquarters in Beirut, and (4) attacks on Lebanese infrastructures. In the first two cases, one must ask, "Was it necessary to harm civilians to destroy bunkers, strongholds, missile dumps, and launcher sites?" With many military targets nested deeply within and scattered among civilian population centers it was not feasible to destroy them without taking civilian lives.[11] Only in these cases, when it is not possible to destroy legitimate military targets without causing widespread collateral damage, is there room to consider whether civilians suffer disproportionate harm. This is not true of the third case, which raises the question of feasibility rather than proportionality. Before any consideration of civilian harm comes the logically prior question: Was it possible to destroy Hezbollah military headquarters in Beirut? If the answer is no, given the limits of the "bunker busting" bombs Israel chose to use, then any casualties are unnecessary. The last case, the destruction of Lebanese infrastructures, raises still a different issue. While the destruction of Hezbollah military and command targets was necessary to achieve Israel's legitimate military goals, it is not clear that the destruction of Lebanese infrastructures was also necessary to achieve these same goals. If not, the resulting casualties are unnecessary and superfluous.

Vigilantly avoiding unnecessary and direct harm as well as injury inflicted in error go a long way toward protecting the lives and property of the civilian population.[12] Droves of noncombatants lose their lives through operational errors, faulty intelligence, or futile military missions. When artillery shells go awry, the wrong targets bombed, or missions end without any discernible benefit, every civilian who lost his or her life along the way died unnecessarily. Civilians only warrant protection, however, when they steer clear of belligerent behavior. If they join the fighting in any way, they may find themselves permissible targets. Other civilians, who scrupulously avoid combat-related activities and enjoy immunity, may find themselves conscripted as human shields. Each of these phenomena, civilian participation and human shields, presents difficult challenges to state armies fighting asymmetric wars. I consider each of these, beginning with human shields.

ASYMMETRIC WAR, NONCOMBATANT IMMUNITY, AND THE PROBLEM OF HUMAN SHIELDS

Human shields drive state armies to distraction. Bound by international law and their own military ethos, state armies find themselves hamstrung when confronting guerrilla armies willing to draw their own civilians into battle. From the viewpoint of state armies, human shields represent a gross violation of the laws of armed conflict. From the perspective of guerrilla organizations, human shields are anything but, and they offer a rational strategy to offset their organization's military weakness.

Clips aired by Israel during the 2008–2009 war in Gaza show how Hamas brought civilians to the rooftops to protect buildings suspected of housing arms or used children to shield militants from attack. In each case, Israel held back and, indeed, each clip is entitled: "Preventing Harm to Civilian Bystanders."[13] However, the clips also make it perfectly clear that human shields are remarkably effective and offer guerrillas a very low-cost tool to deter conventional attacks.

Shielding works because some state armies respect the immunity of non-combatants. We must remember, however, that noncombatant immunity does not protect civilians from all harm. During war, civilians suffer from collateral harm when an army attacks a legitimate military target and cannot avoid civilian casualties. Think about an army attacking an arms depot, the subject of one of the video clips. Civilians living nearby may die when an arms depot is attacked. How many civilians may permissibly lose their lives is the crucial question of proportionality. The answer is probably "not many," considering that this arms depot was not a military target of decisive importance. So to protect such a site, guerrillas will need to send a large number of civilians to the roof of the targeted building. The goal is for guerrillas to now make destroying the target impossible without causing disproportionate harm so that a norm-compliant state will desist rather than kill or injure so many civilians.

Although human shielding can be extremely effective, several points are worth noting. First, only involuntary shields enjoy noncombatant immunity. Any person who willingly serves as a shield takes a direct role in the fighting and loses his or her immunity. The challenge is for a state army to distinguish voluntary from involuntary shielding. This cannot be easy. How is a state army to know why a civilian ascended to the roof of a targeted building? Perhaps he or she was forced at gunpoint or, perhaps, threatened with disciplinary action or simply subject to peer pressure as the occupants of a building took to the roof to defend their cause? In the absence of hard proof, an attacking state army must assume the shields acted involuntarily. Nevertheless, states may warn shielding civilians of an impending attack while assuming that those who remain behind are, indeed, shielding voluntarily. This, too, is a tricky business because failing to heed warnings or flee the battlefield is not necessarily indicative of aggressive intent. Civilians fail to flee for many reasons. Some are old or infirm; others do not wish to abandon their property while others simply lack the means. In the final analysis, attackers must usually assume that shields are civilians immune from direct harm.

But civilians are not protected from collateral harm and here successful shielding bumps up against its limits. Attacking armies may inflict far-ranging collateral harm if it is not excessive relative to the military advantage they seek. So imagine a building housing the high command of a guerrilla movement or missiles primed and ready to launch at a civilian population center. Given the significant military advantage of destroying these facilities, the resulting proportionate harm to enemy civilians might be very great. In other words, 20 or 30 civilians on the rooftop of a building might protect an arms depot but will not deter a strike against high-value targets. If guerrillas cannot bring more civilians to shield, then shielding will fail. It is for this reason that shields seem to work best when targets are of relatively low value, such as a supply center. Here, shielding works because both sides immediately recognize that any attack on the shielded site will cause disproportionate civilian casualties.

It is also noteworthy that the international community is divided about how to advise state armies facing human shields. At one end is Amitai Etzioni: "The onus for avoiding collateral damage altogether is on the terrorists," writes Etzioni. "They have to stop exploiting their status as civilians, stop using civilians as human shields, and homes—as headquarters, as locations to store ammunition and for snipers to ply their deadly trade."[14] This perspective shifts responsibility entirely to the guerrilla side and is echoed in a minority legal opinion that "urges that involuntary shields should be ignored in the proportionality and precautions-in-attack analyses because an enemy violating the law should not be allowed to benefit from its malfeasance."[15] On this view, the attacker has no obligation to protect shields. While such a view would render shielding useless because an attacker has no duty to protect the lives of shields, it suffers from a glaring defect. Malfeasance on the part of guerrillas should not affect the protections due noncombatants. While guerrillas that coerce enemy civilians or foreigners shoulder responsibility for their actions, noncombatants retain their immunity. This should compel attacking armies to refrain from disproportionate harm.

Nonetheless, guidelines for assessing disproportionate harm when attacking shielded facilities are controversial. In a hypothetical example, Avishai Margalit and Michael Walzer describe how Hezbollah seized an Israeli kibbutz and drafted civilians as human shields to prevent an Israeli attack.[16] The identity of the civilians varies from case to case to include Israelis, Lebanese, or foreigners. Regardless, Margalit and Walzer argue that calculations of proportionality and the rules of engagement remain unchanged. Alternatively, other commentators are prepared to discount the lives of human shields and allow the attacker more leeway. "Even if the principle [of proportionality] endures," writes Yoram Dinstein, "the test of what amounts to 'excessive' injury to civilians must be relaxed in the exceptional circumstances of 'human shields' ... [and] must make allowances for the fact that—by dint of the presence (albeit involuntary) of civilians at the site of the military objective—the number of civilian casualties can be foreseen to be higher than usual."[17] Given the elasticity of the proportionality principle, it is hard to see how this discount works in practice. The important point is as follows: attackers are responsible only for the disproportionate harm they cause when attacking a target protected by human shields.

Human shielding, therefore, is neither decisive nor effective in all situations. Fears that state armies are unable to fight shields are unfounded. Human shields are only effective when guerrillas can bring large numbers of civilians to shield targets of less than overwhelming military significance. Shields will not protect high-value targets. Arms depots, midlevel command headquarters, and communication sites, on the other hand, are all amenable to effective shielding that provides guerrillas with a low-cost and effective tactic to counter the military might of their adversaries.

Human shields sometimes work because the shields are noncombatants who enjoy protection from direct harm and from disproportionate collateral harm. During conventional warfare, all civilians enjoy this protection. In asymmetric war, however, there are large numbers of civilians who participate in the hostilities. While civilians taking a direct part in the hostilities were once a marginal phenomenon, it is widespread in asymmetric war as enemy civilians, particularly those belonging to a guerilla organization's political wing, take on essential war-supporting roles. In this environment state armies will often ask who among these civilians is a legitimate target and who among them is liable to deadly force.

CIVILIAN PARTICIPATION IN ASYMMETRIC WAR

Civilians have always supported their nation's war effort by buying war bonds, working in armaments factories, ensuring supplies of basic goods, or otherwise cheering on their troops. Following World War II and the near universal acceptance of the Geneva Conventions, these civilians enjoyed immunity from the worst horrors of war. Since World War II, however, these norms are tested constantly. Civilians provide aid of increasing value to military organizations while states look for ways to disable what can be called "participating civilians." To meet this challenge, international law distinguishes between indirect and direct participation in hostilities; the former providing "war-sustaining" aid while the latter offers "war-fighting" aid. Clear definitions and examples, however, are not so easy to come by. Red Cross guidelines suggest that direct participation signifies acts "likely to adversely affect military operations" and "specifically designed to directly cause ... death, injury or destruction."[18] Indirect participants, on the other hand, embrace the class of participating civilians whose aid is not likely to adversely affect military operations and is not specifically designed to directly cause significant harm. For the ICRC Interpretive Guidelines, indirect participation includes financial and economic services, recruitment and training activities, non-tactical intelligence gathering, propagandizing and diplomacy, assembly and storage of improvised explosive devices (IED), and scientific research and design of weapons and equipment.[19] Other candidates for indirect participation include civilians who provide legal, media, health, telecommunication, transportation, and police services. While these functionaries do not participate directly in "military operations," they do participate directly in and sustain "the conflict in general."[20]

Imagine then the following case. Prior to planning an attack on government forces, members of a guerrilla organization's political wing work assiduously to raise money at home and abroad to buy weapons. During hostilities civilians offer logistical support to guerrillas (food, transportation, medical care), maintain computers and telecommunications facilities, and even house weapons in homes and barns. After a battle ends, the organization's "diplomatic corps" swings into action disseminating gruesome images (some perhaps doctored) of civilian casualties, buttonholing international politicians and preparing lawsuits against state soldiers and politicians for violations of international law.[21]

These civilians, formally protected by the principle of noncombatant immunity, provide war-sustaining services. They take no active part in military operations but deliver the necessary support that makes it possible for insurgents to fight. Unlike noncombatants caught in the cross fire when un-uniformed militants go on the prowl, civilians who provide war-sustaining aid are not innocent and pose a threat of varying intensity. Nevertheless, the ICRC's Interpretive Guidelines' understanding of indirect participation reflects a wide range of belligerent activities that civilians may undertake *without* losing their immunity. One many ask, however, why this is so. After all, it is clear that civilians providing war-sustaining services bear no small measure of responsibility for maintaining a war-making capability. If, as Michael Schmitt claims, direct participation turns on a "clear link between the act and the ensuing harm" and, therefore, warrants liability, then a clear link between an act and a lesser harm also warrants liability.[22] Participating civilians are neither idle nor passive participants; they report for work, draw a paycheck, and collaborate with their colleagues. And while the military advantage of disabling a war-sustaining facility does not justify killing or seriously injuring civilian employees, there are no grounds to grant participating civilians absolute immunity. Nor are there any grounds to push them into the category of direct participation and the liability to lethal harm this entails. The trick is to assign participating civilians appropriate liability and respond with appropriate force. The principle of participatory liability speaks to the first task and nonlethal warfare speaks to the second.

PARTICIPATORY LIABILITY

Support for assigning liability to some civilians is gaining ground. The United States, for example, permits attacks on economic objects of the enemy that indirectly but effectively support and sustain the enemy's warfighting capability.[23] The Bush administration, in turn, targeted "al Qaeda leaders responsible for propaganda, recruitment, [and] religious affairs."[24] In its 2006 war with Lebanon and its recurrent battles with the Palestinians, Israel often exhausts its bank of military targets very early in the fighting and then turns to what Human Rights Watch calls "associated targets." Associated targets are those war-sustaining facilities of the sort just described that are affiliated (associated) with Hezbollah's and Hamas's political wing. American and Israeli policies recognize that civilian aid is integral to modern warfare and that it will be impossible to prevail without disabling war-sustaining infrastructures and those who operate them. The underlying principle that justifies such attacks is participatory liability.[25]

Participatory liability reflects a sliding scale that links participation with liability to harm. The more one participates and contributes to armed conflict, the greater force an enemy may utilize when necessary to disable a participant. Participation reflects both a civilian's function within the organization and the magnitude of the threat the civilian poses. Each aspect of participation is usually observable, marked by a person's occupation and the product or service he or she provides. At one end of the scale are *noncombatants* who assume no role in any war-related activity. They are not responsible for any threat and, therefore, may suffer no direct harm. At the other end are full-fledged *combatants* who conduct armed campaigns against enemy forces and are liable to lethal (but not inhuman) harm when necessary to disable their person and disrupt their activities. In the vast middle ground are participating civilians, analogous to those civilians working for a guerrilla organization's political wing and who provide war-sustaining services.

The principle of participatory liability is, in practice, broader than some envisage. Jeff McMahan suggests, for example, that "only *unjust* civilians can be liable to attack in war" and thereby links liability to moral culpability alone.[26] While theoretically sound, moral culpability can be difficult to ferret out in practice. It is not easy to assign just cause to states when they fight conventional wars. While in asymmetric wars, guerrillas fighting for national self-determination are on the right side of just cause, their adversaries do not necessarily lose their right of self-defense. This happens, for example, when guerrillas overextend their right to fight, as they may when pushing for independence when autonomy is a viable and legitimate option, or when guerrillas fight by impermissible means and resort to terrorism. In these instances, participating civilians on each side are liable to disabling force.

In general, however, the liability of participating civilians is material, not moral. In asymmetric war, guerrillas do not target participating civilians because they present an unjust threat, but because they sustain a force that wages a deadly conflict. Ironically, state armies facing un-uniformed guerrillas have little choice but to apply the principle of participatory liability. In fact, participatory liability guides targeted killing as uniformed soldiers (or drone operators) take deadly aim at those they deem materially responsible for an impending threat while endeavoring to arrest others who pose lesser threats. There are, then, two components to participatory liability: liability and force. Liability is a function of participation and permissible force is function of liability. While state armies in the United States and Israel, for example, grasp the significance of liability, they often fail to modulate the use of force appropriately. As a result, American and Israeli troops attack many of these targets with high explosives and while the Israelis made some attempts to distinguish between physical infrastructures and those who worked there (by targeting empty buildings), causalities remained high. Exact casualties remain difficult to determine and not always because the victims cannot be identified. As noted above, Israel and Hamas agree that approximately 1,300 Palestinians died in the 2008–2009 Gaza War. Of these, the sides also agree that roughly 25 percent of these casualties were militants and 25 percent noncombatants.[27] The controversy centers upon the large middle ground who were affiliated with Hamas in some way (as either law enforcement personnel or those working for its political wing). Israel classifies these as combatants while the Palestinians classify them as noncombatants. It is more reasonable to classify most as participating civilians. Providing war-sustaining aid, they are legitimate targets but are not liable to deadly harm and therefore immune from destructive attacks. To preserve the important moral distinction between combatants, noncombatants, and participating civilians and to disable war-sustaining facilities without causing appreciable injury to participating civilians, there is good reason to consider the place of nonlethal weapons.

NONLETHAL WEAPONS

Nonlethal weapons include a range of technologies that disable and temporarily incapacitate individuals rather than cause loss of life or severe injury. Consider, for example, four possible nonlethal means to disable a financial institution, telecommunications facility, or media outlet that provides war-sustaining aid: calmative chemical agents, electromagnetic technologies, kinetic force, or cyber operations. Calmative agents are fentanyl-based substances similar to those used by the Russians in 2002. They would be delivered to the facility, perhaps by shells or aerosol, with the result of "knocking out" the staff. Using calmative agents in this example requires ground troops both to administer antidotes if necessary and to detain the staff. Participating civilians might then be incarcerated until the end of hostilities or deported. Electromagnetic technologies, such as the U.S. active denial system (ADS), emit very low levels of directed energy that causes sufficient transient pain that causes individuals to flee the beam. While such technologies are well developed, deployment has been constantly delayed due to fears that some would perceive these as weapons of torture. Nevertheless, models designed for urban use offer a means to prevent civilians from entering facilities or removing them once at work without bodily harm.[28] Here, too, participating civilians might face detention and/or deportation.

Tactics that destroy facilities or disrupt their operations may also be nonlethal. Some of these are very conventional and consist of simply destroying facilities with high explosives. This requires warning to evacuate so participating civilians are not present. Although time tested and a tactic of Israel in its recent wars with Hamas and Hezbollah, the strategy faces two significant drawbacks. First, there is always a substantial chance of bodily injury. Warnings are not always effective. The warnings do not always arrive on time, individuals sometimes fail to flee in time, and those who do might find roads impassable. Caught in the cross fire, many may lose their lives. Second, destroying a physical infrastructure is not always effective. Attempts to silence television stations in Belgrade, Baghdad, Beirut, Libya, and Syria proved fruitless while in many other cases, civilian employees can just take their computers and go elsewhere.[29] Clouds have no home.

This raises the specter of cyber-attack, digital viruses, and malware that disable computer networks and erase or steal proprietary information. As states become increasingly sophisticated and gain a technological edge over nonstate organizations, cyber-attacks will become an option of choice to disable their facilities and disrupt their activities. If effective, employees cannot just take their computers and go elsewhere. One must be careful, however, of placing too much stock in cyber warfare as a nonlethal tactic of war. First, many cyber scenarios, though yet unrealized, hold the potential of significant downstream harm and suffering as critical infrastructures crash. Such scenarios describe the dire consequences when dams burst, water supplies are polluted, airplanes crash, trains derail, and medical services fail.[30] These scenarios violate noncombatant immunity in many ways. In some cases, noncombatants are the direct targets of attack, while in others, collateral harm is disproportionate and excessive. Second and in contrast to catastrophic cyber assaults, one may confine cyber-attacks to attacks on social networks, financial institutions, and telecommunications infrastructures. Here, however, noncombatants may suffer more than inconvenience. Depending upon their reliance on social media, ordinary people may suffer severe stress and hardship as their daily lives unravel and their private affairs are laid bare. While these harms are not lethal, they may be sufficiently devastating as to also violate the principle of noncombatant immunity.[31]

CONCLUSION: NONCOMBATANT IMMUNITY AND CIVILIAN LIABILITY IN ASYMMETRIC WAR

Asymmetric war threatens noncombatants in ways not anticipated by the Geneva Conventions and international humanitarian law. First, the lack of uniforms puts civilians in harm's way directly as states do not find it easy to distinguish between combatants and noncombatants and nonstates often turn to human shields as their first line of defense. To help overcome this difficulty states turn to targeted killings and precision weapons, but these are not without problems of their own. Targeted killing often smacks of vengeance and extrajudicial execution, while precision weapons may sometimes cause disproportionate civilian casualties. These dangers are exacerbated when guerrillas turn to human shields leaving law-compliant nations to either abandon their attacks or risk disproportionate harm and the ensuing media storm they may bring. The answer for some states is to respect the rights of shields except in those instances where the military advantage of destroying the site they protect is overwhelming. Under such circumstances, the collateral harm may, indeed, be proportionate.

Second, civilians assume a growing role in asymmetric fighting as numerically inferior guerrilla military forces must turn to the civilian population for war-sustaining and war-fighting aid. Once a marginal phenomenon in conventional war, it is now clear that guerrillas cannot maintain an armed struggle without significant civilian support. Nor can states ever prevail without targeting the same civilian population. Saddled with responsibility for harm, participating civilians face the prospect of disabling force. However, states do not entirely appreciate the fact that force must be proportionate, and here nonlethal weapons offer a viable alternative to overwhelming kinetic force.

As states adapt to the exigencies of asymmetric war, so must international law. By its nature, international humanitarian law is conservative and not amenable to changes that seem to degrade the rights of combatants and non-combatants. Targeting killing, therefore, is often condemned harshly as assassination, human shields are afforded immunity with no discounts for proportionality, and nonlethal weapons, particularly those that utilize chemical agents or electromagnetic technologies, are roundly criticized for causing superfluous injury and unnecessary suffering. These are not idle concerns. Nevertheless, the changing nature of warfare together with the changing role played by civilians should compel lawyers and philosophers to consider new tactics and technologies carefully.

NOTES

1. Amos Harel and Avi Issacharoff, *34 Days: Israel, Hezbollah and the War in Lebanon* (New York: Palgrave Macmillan, 2008), p. 129.

2. Ibid., p. 131.

3. Israel Ministry of Foreign Affairs, *Gaza Operation Investigations: An Update* (Jerusalem: Israel Ministry of Foreign Affairs, January 2010), p. 26.

4. Associated Press, "U.S. Rockets Slam into Afghanistan Home, Killing 12," http://www.foxnews.com/story/2010/02/14/us-rockets-slam-into-afghanistan-home-killing-12/.

5. Uri bar Joseph, "Israel's Military Intelligence Performance in the Second Lebanon War," *International Journal of Intelligence and Counterintelligence*, Vol. 20, No. 4 (December 2007), p. 589.

6. *Protocol I to the Geneva Conventions of 12 August 1949, and Relating to the Protection of Victims of International Armed Conflict* (Protocol I), June 8, 1977, Article 44 (3).

7. Michael L. Gross, *The Ethics of Insurgency: A Critical Guide to Just Guerrilla Warfare* (Cambridge: Cambridge University Press, 2015), pp. 51–52.

8. Protocol I, 1977, Article 57 (2) (iii).

9. Avi Issacharoff, "Rights Group: Most Gazans Killed in War Were Civilians," *Ha'aretz*, September 9, 2009, http://www.haaretz.com/hasen/spages/1113402.html; Y. Lappin, "IDF Releases Cast Lead Casualty Numbers," *Jerusalem Post*, March 26, 2009, http://www.jpost.com/Israel/Article.aspx?id=137286; Palestinian Centre for Human Rights (PCHR), "The Dead in the Course of the Israeli Recent Military Offensive on the Gaza Strip between 27 December 2008 and 18 January 2009," March 19, 2009, http://www.scribd.com/doc/22883962/The-Dead-in-the-course-of-the-Israeli-Military-offensive-on-the-Gaza-Strip-between-27-Dec-2008-and-18-Jan-2009.

10. *Protocol Additional to the Geneva Conventions of 12 August 1949, and relating to the Protection of Victims of International Armed Conflicts (Protocol I), 8 June 1977.* Commentary, Article 57, §2213.

11. Human Rights Watch, "Why They Died: Civilian Casualties in Lebanon during the 2006 War," *Human Rights Watch*, Vol. 19, No. 5(E) (September 2007), pp. 42–57.

12. Michael L. Gross, "The Second Lebanon War: The Question of Proportionality and the Prospect of Nonlethal Warfare," *Journal of Military Ethics*, Vol. 7, No. 1 (2008), pp. 1–22.

13. "IDF Avoids Civilians Casualties in Gaza, Hamas Increases Them," https://www.youtube.com/watch?v=VTArVIHDelg.

14. Amitai Etzioni, "The Case for Drones." E-mail posting from *Communitarian International Relations*, March 31, 2010.

15. Michael N. Schmitt, "Human shields in International Humanitarian Law," *Israel Yearbook on Human Rights*, Vol. 38 (2008), p. 49.

16. Avishai Margalit and Michael Walzer, "Israel: Civilians and Combatants," *New York Review of Books*, Vol. 56, No. 8 (2009), pp. 21–22.

17. Yoram Dinstein, *The Conduct of Hostilities under the Law of International Armed Conflict*, 2nd ed. (Cambridge: Cambridge University Press), p. 155.

18. N. Melzer, *Interpretive Guidance on the Notion of Direct Participation in Hostilities under International Humanitarian Law* (Geneva: International Committee of the Red Cross, 2009), p. 46.

19. Ibid., pp. 35, 53–54.

20. D. Akande, "Clearing the Fog of War? The ICRC's Interpretive Guidance on Direct Participation in Hostilities," *International and Comparative Law Quarterly*, Vol. 59 (2010), p. 188.

21. Gross, *The Ethics of Insurgency*, chap. 3.

22. Michael N. Schmitt, "Interpretive Guidance on the Notion of Direct Participation in Hostilities: A Critical Analysis," *The Harvard National Security Journal*, Vol. 1 (2010), p. 30.

23. Department of the Army, Field Manual FM 3–24, MCWP 3–33.5, *Counterinsurgency* (Washington, DC: Department of the Army, 2006); Dinstein, *The Conduct of Hostilities*, pp. 95–96; Michael N. Schmitt, "Deconstructing Direct Participation in Hostilities: The Constitutive Elements," *New York University Journal of International Law and Politics*, Vol. 42 (2010), pp. 697–739.

24. George W. Bush, *Decision Points* (New York: Random House, 2010), p. 218.

25. Gross, *The Ethics of Insurgency*, chap. 3.

26. Jeff McMahan, *Killing in War* (Oxford: Oxford University Press, 2009), p. 233 (emphasis added).

27. Issacharoff, "Rights Group: Most Gazans Killed in War Were Civilians"; Lappin, "IDF Releases Cast Lead Casualty Numbers"; PCHR, "The Dead in the Course of the Israeli Recent Military Offensive."

28. For a review of nonlethal weapons see Michael L. Gross, *Moral Dilemmas of Modern War* (Cambridge: Cambridge University Press, 2010), pp. 77–99.

29. C. Cordone and A. Gidron, "Was the Serbian TV Station Really a Legitimate Target?" *Le Monde Diplomatique* (2000), http://mondediplo.com/2000/07/03kosovo; M. Gebauer, "Hezbollah's Al-Manar: Broadcasting from the Bunker," *Spiegel Online*, August 10, 2006, http://www.spiegel.de/international/spiegel/hezbollah-s-al-manar

-broadcasting-from-the-bunker-a-430905.html; R. Mackey, "Attack on Pro-Assad Television Studio Raises Questions on Rules of War," *New York Times*, June 27, 2012, http://thelede.blogs.nytimes.com/2012/06/27/attack-on-pro-assad-television -studio-raises-questions-on-rules-of-war/; R. Norton-Taylor, "TV Station Attack Could Be Illegal," *The Guardian*, March 26, 2003, http://www.theguardian.com/ media/2003/mar/26/Iraqandthemedia.iraq2; M. Ryan and D. Brunnstrom, "Libyan TV Still in Air Despite NATO Bombing," *Reuters*, July 30, 2011, http://www .reuters.com/article/2011/07/30/us-libya-nato-idUSTRE76T0KE20110730.

30. J. Anderson and J. Connolly, "Cyber attacks likely to increase," *PEW Research, Internet Project* (October 29, 2014), http://www.pewinternet.org/2014/10/29/cyber -attacks-likely-to-increase.

31. Daphna Canetti, Michael L. Gross, and Israel Waismel-Manor, "Immune from Cyber-Fire? The Psychological and Physiological Effects of Cyberwar," in Fritz Allhoff, Adam Henschke, and Bradley Jay Strawser, eds., *Binary Bullets: The Ethics of Cyberwarfare* (Oxford: Oxford University Press).

Part II

Peacemaking

5

Power and Principle: The Statecraft of Theodore Roosevelt

William N. Tilchin

In light of the discussion of the relationship between ethics and statecraft presented in the Foreword and in the opening two chapters of the second edition of this book, the diplomacy of President Theodore Roosevelt is a natural topic for investigation. Joel Rosenthal's contention that "decision-making always involves reconciling the desirable with the possible" would please Roosevelt, who consistently perceived himself as a "practical idealist" pursuing "realizable ideals."[1] Cathal Nolan's claim that "the most profound realist writers were always aware of the moral realm" applies as well to profound realist *actors*—of whom Roosevelt provides an illuminating example.[2] And by Robert Jackson's eminently fair standard—that the "conduct of state leaders" should be evaluated "in relation to what could reasonably be expected of a person of sound mind and good character in the circumstances"[3]—Roosevelt stands tall, far surpassing "reasonable expectations" both in the way he employed American power and influence and in the ethical component of his diplomacy. TR's foreign policy demonstrates the entire "constellation of political virtues"—prudence, judgment, vision, good faith, courage, and the others—identified by Jackson.[4]

Roosevelt understood keenly the centrality of the factor of power in international relations and was an adroit practitioner of power politics. At the same time, he believed deeply—and continually acted on the belief—that a proper American foreign policy must be firmly grounded in ethical precepts. What Frederick Marks has termed "the moral quotient" was an integral element in the assertive, dynamic statecraft of President Theodore Roosevelt.[5]

THE ROOSEVELTIAN WORLDVIEW[6]

By the time he assumed the presidency upon the assassination of William McKinley in September 1901, Theodore Roosevelt had already developed many of the major elements of the worldview that would guide his presidential

statecraft. Born into a wealthy New York family in 1858, Roosevelt had traveled widely. Moreover, since his youth, Roosevelt had been a voracious and
remarkably retentive reader, enabling him to acquire a great breadth and
depth of knowledge about many subjects, history and international affairs
prominent among them. In the 1880s and 1890s, he had also become a prolific
and accomplished author; and the work he had done researching and writing
his many books—notably including *The Naval War of 1812* (1882) and
The Winning of the West (four volumes, 1889–1896)—naturally had broadened and deepened his knowledge. In these same decades—toward the end
of which he had served with boldness and distinction as Assistant Secretary
of the Navy—Roosevelt had taken his place as a conspicuous figure within
the coterie of leading American expansionist thinkers, an influential group
of big-navy advocates who interacted frequently and who shared many ideas
about strategy, American power, American political and cultural superiority,
and American beneficence. Simultaneously Roosevelt had been building
friendships and corresponding regularly with a number of Britons whose perspectives on the need for Anglo-American cooperation and on other matters
were compatible with his own. All these factors had contributed to the shaping of the new President's outlook on international relations and on
America's role in the world in the century then just beginning.

President Roosevelt believed in the superiority of Western, and particularly
Anglo-American, civilization. He viewed imperialism, at least its U.S. and
British varieties, primarily as a force for the advancement of this superior civilization and the betterment of the human condition, *not* as a vehicle for economic exploitation. Roosevelt closely monitored the United States'
experience in the Philippines, finding in it unambiguous evidence of the
high-minded character of American imperialism.

Roosevelt also believed in the necessity of active U.S. engagement with the
world. As one of the Great Powers, the United States was affected by important events occurring around the globe; hence, Roosevelt considered it not
only fruitless but also harmful to U.S. interests to try to shield the country
from major overseas developments. And the United States needed not only
to engage, but to take initiative; it needed to seek to influence and to shape
important overseas events to its advantage rather than simply observing them
passively and reacting to them later. Considering the deeply entrenched and
potent legacy of President George Washington's farewell address of 1796 urging Americans to "steer clear" of foreign entanglements, TR's belief in active
U.S. internationalism stands among the most radical departures of his
presidency.

Although the President defined U.S. interests in a global context, he did so
very thoughtfully and discriminatingly. In Roosevelt's scheme, the Western
Hemisphere—particularly the Caribbean region, where he saw U.S.

hegemony as a self-evident strategic imperative—and the western Pacific were the two areas of the world most vital to the United States. In other areas Roosevelt was especially attentive to situations where there was conflict or the potential for conflict among two or more of the Great Powers. While a steadfast proponent of the "just war" doctrine, Roosevelt harbored no illusions about the horrors and the unpredictable consequences of war and considered it his moral obligation to do all that he realistically could to prevent or to stop unnecessary Great Power wars. Therefore, he always kept an especially close watch on Europe. In contrast, in Africa and on the mainland of Asia (unless, as in the cases of the Russo-Japanese War and the Moroccan crisis, a Great Power contest was looming or playing out in those areas), TR was usually reluctant to engage the United States directly, perceiving U.S. interests on those continents to be peripheral. Moreover, in defining vital interests, Roosevelt accorded a much lower priority to economic concerns than to strategic ones. Thus, maintaining the Open Door policy throughout China was not a vital American interest in Roosevelt's eyes; amicable U.S.-Japanese relations were far more important to TR and always took precedence.

Roosevelt looked upon arbitration as a useful device for resolving international disagreements, but only if they did not involve questions of vital interests, territorial integrity, or national honor. When a dispute did fall into one or more of these three excluded categories, he was adamant that the United States must be free to act as it saw fit. And not only free but sufficiently strong militarily—for ultimately, TR clearly recognized, it was power more than any other factor that determined the course of international affairs.

Consistent with this perspective, Roosevelt adhered to the doctrine of peace through strength, according to which the most civilized and most righteous nations (as Roosevelt defined these terms) should always be well armed and should take particular care to build up and preserve a preponderance of naval power in order to be able to deter aggression and defend their interests.[7] He considered the United States and Great Britain—which shared, in TR's view, a duty to extend civilization and an attachment to the principles of freedom and self-government—to be the two most civilized and most righteous nations. Moreover, he realized, the two countries' strategic interests tended to coincide. Britain, therefore, was an essential friend for America.

Indeed, the cornerstone of Rooseveltian statecraft was the cultivation and solidification of a special relationship between the United States and the British Empire. TR was both a proud American nationalist and, in important respects, an internationalist. But as his presidency moved along, and as his devotion to U.S.-British unity was continually reinforced by events, he became in a sense an *Anglo*-American nationalist as well.[8] Without reservation, therefore, Roosevelt considered the unrivaled power of the Royal Navy to be an asset to the United States, and in his private correspondence he frequently proclaimed his support for the maintenance by Britain of its over-whelming naval superiority.[9]

The one other power President Roosevelt came to view as highly civilized was France. Roosevelt's concerns over the Franco-Russian alliance and over the long history of unfriendly relations between France and Britain (an unfriendliness exacerbated by their confrontation over the Sudan in 1898) were largely mitigated by the establishment in April 1904 of the Anglo-French *entente cordiale*, which he very quickly came to perceive as a crucially important bulwark against German military adventurism. From 1905 on, TR had a very positive outlook on French diplomacy, considering it entirely unthreatening and looking upon it as an extremely useful asset to the Anglo-American special relationship he was so diligently working to construct.

In contrast, Roosevelt perceived Germany, Russia, and Japan to be poten-tial enemies of the United States. Not only did their interests often clash with those of the United States, but they had not yet attained America's (or Britain's or France's) level of civilization.

TR viewed Germany as aggressive and militaristic and as having respect for the United States only insofar "as it believes that our navy is efficient and that if sufficiently wronged or insulted we would fight."[10] By the closing years of his presidency, his long-standing doubts about the emotional stability and ration-ality of Kaiser Wilhelm II and suspicions about the nature of German society in general had hardened. "The German attitude toward war," Roosevelt lamented in a letter of February 1907 to the British editor John St. Loe Strachey, "is one that in the progress of civilization England and America have outgrown."[11]

Regarding tsarist Russia—viewed by TR more as a long-term than as a short-term menace—Roosevelt foresaw "nothing of permanent good . . . , either for herself or for the rest of the world, until her people begin to tread the path of orderly freedom, of civil liberty, and of a measure of self-government."[12] In its diplomacy, Russia was guilty of "appalling, . . . well-nigh incredible mendacity"; and a Russian victory over Japan in their war of 1904–1905 "would have been a blow to civilization."[13]

As the foregoing quotation suggests, the case of Japan was somewhat more complex in Roosevelt's perception. In a letter of June 1905, TR admiringly called the Japanese "a wonderful and civilized people, . . . who are entitled to stand on an absolute equality with all the other peoples of the civilized world."[14] Moreover, Roosevelt heartily approved of (and informally linked America to) the Anglo-Japanese alliance. Yet even while he was pursuing a cooperative and friendly U.S.-Japanese relationship, the President was uncer-tain about Japan's motives and ultimate intentions. Thus, as he wrote to Whitelaw Reid, his ambassador to Great Britain, in June 1906, "my policy with Japan is to be scrupulously polite, to show a genuine good will toward her, but to keep our navy in such shape that the risk will be great for Japan if it undertakes any aggression upon us."[15]

Roosevelt's disparate assessments of the six Great Powers were reflected in his thinking about the balance of power. It would be inaccurate to assert that he saw "balance" as the key to stabilizing all areas of possible Great Power conflict. He did indeed desire such balance between Russia and Japan in Manchuria. But when Great Britain or the United States was a party to a dispute with another power, balance was the President's minimum objective. A better guarantee of peace—and therefore desirable from the standpoint of international morality as well as U.S. interests—was an *im*balance decidedly favorable to Britain or America or the two of them combined. As the world's most civilized countries, England and the United States would not abuse a position of military supremacy; and such supremacy would ensure against miscalculation on the part of a more selfish, less civilized, less mature power. Thus, Roosevelt was convinced, a preponderance of British or American strength in any region of the globe constituted a safeguard, not a danger.

Although Roosevelt was an ambitious statesman—as reflected in his fast-paced naval building program, in his many bold actions in the foreign policy arena, and in his expansive ideas about the international role the United States could and should play during and beyond his era—he possessed a keen sense of limits as well. "Practical idealism" was among TR's most important working principles, and—just as in his dealings with domestic affairs—he constantly endeavored to mesh realism and ethics in his foreign policy. TR's well-reasoned distinctions between vital and peripheral U.S. interests have already been pointed out. Where there was war or the potential for war (either involving the United States or otherwise), he was adept at evaluating power balances and at anticipating consequences and figuring out whether and how undesirable ones might be avoided. Roosevelt looked at the world through clear lenses (literally as well as figuratively) even while striving to better it: "We can only accomplish good at all," he wrote to the trusted diplomat Henry White in 1906, "by not trying to accomplish the impossible good."[16]

Military, cultural, geographical, international political, and domestic political realities combined to define the limits of the possible in Roosevelt's mind. The greater the stakes, however, the more willing the President was to test those limits by taking political, diplomatic, and military risks in an effort to attain his objectives. For example, he went out on a political and diplomatic limb in what turned out to be a highly successful effort to settle the Franco-German crisis over Morocco in 1905 and 1906 because he saw that situation as extremely dangerous. As Roosevelt wrote to Ambassador Reid shortly after the conclusion of the crisis, "it really did look as if there might be a war," which might "literally" turn into "a world conflagration," and Roosevelt "felt in honor bound to try to prevent the war if I could."[17]

A well-informed, carefully constructed, well-integrated, complex, sophisticated Rooseveltian worldview provided the conceptual foundation for a coherent, dynamic, successful presidential foreign policy. But such an outcome naturally would also require a high level of proficiency in the area of execution. There too, Roosevelt would prove equal to the challenge.

STATECRAFT ROOSEVELTIAN STYLE

The style in which President Theodore Roosevelt practiced the art of statecraft suited his personality and facilitated the attainment of his foreign policy objectives. At the core of Rooseveltian statecraft were presidential domination, personal diplomacy, and the quintessentially Rooseveltian (and often misunderstood and caricatured) "big stick" diplomacy.

As is true of most successful leaders, Roosevelt was skillful both in selecting capable subordinates and in managing them. In many areas of domestic policy, he gave his top appointees substantial leeway in making decisions and in setting administration policy. In the arena of diplomacy, however, the self-confident and singularly knowledgeable 26th President for the most part held strong, well-defined views and was less willing to share authority. And when dealing with the foreign policy matters he saw as most important, Roosevelt charted the broad course of American diplomacy and attended personally to the significant details of its execution.

Two excellent secretaries of state, John Hay (inherited from McKinley) and Elihu Root (appointed following Hay's death in 1905), worked under Roosevelt, and time and again the President availed himself of their services. He did so because he had confidence in their abilities and because their ideas about foreign policy largely coincided with his own. Root, formerly Roosevelt's Secretary of War and in the President's view an upgrade over Hay, functioned as a steady and clear-thinking presidential counselor, a superb administrator, and an extremely loyal, reliable, and effective diplomatic representative.

President Roosevelt developed a network of foreign policy advisers and operatives that extended well beyond his secretaries of state. Prominent figures in this Rooseveltian network included Senator Henry Cabot Lodge of Massachusetts (a very close friend since the 1880s), Secretary of War William Howard Taft, Ambassador to Russia George von Lengerke Meyer, Ambassador to Britain Whitelaw Reid, and the accomplished and versatile diplomat Henry White. A number of foreigners were also sometimes brought into this network, most notably the Britons Cecil Spring Rice and Arthur Lee and France's ambassador to the United States, Jean Jules Jusserand.

This sizable and varying network facilitated the informal, personal diplomacy conducted by the President, which in turn facilitated presidential domination of foreign policy. The trusted Root and Taft became Roosevelt's most intimate foreign policy associates, but TR really had no set inner circle of foreign policy advisers in the usual sense of that concept. Instead he would solicit the counsel of and assign diplomatic missions to different individuals at different times, as it suited his needs. And he generally would interact with them informally; even with the small number of overseas U.S. diplomats in whom Roosevelt had great confidence—particularly Meyer, Reid, and White—important communications tended to be in the form of private letters dispatched outside the established channels. Fundamentally, TR liked to "move with secrecy and quiet to shape events, letting only a few close friends know even a portion of the larger picture."[18] Indeed, often when Roosevelt appeared to be seeking advice, he was really looking for a stamp of approval for decisions he had already made. He intended to and did in fact maintain a tight grip on the reins of American diplomacy throughout his presidency.

Not only did informal, personal diplomacy facilitate presidential control of foreign policy, it offered Roosevelt a couple of other advantages as well. The President sometimes took diplomatic initiatives for which he believed it would be difficult to win domestic political backing; in such cases he could proceed quietly and without publicity in pursuit of his goals. (Conversely, when TR anticipated a favorable public reaction—to his acquisition of the Panama Canal Zone, for example—he would methodically orchestrate publicity for his diplomatic activities.[19]) And informal, personal diplomacy enabled Roosevelt to achieve important foreign policy victories without humiliating the losing side, a key tenet of big stick diplomacy.

As practiced by its architect, big stick diplomacy had at its foundation five central principles. The first was the possession of a formidable military capability, which during the opening decade of the twentieth century meant, especially, a large, well-equipped, well-trained U.S. Navy. "Diplomacy," Roosevelt declared before a Naval War College audience on July 22, 1908, "rests on the substantial basis of potential force."[20] The second principle was to act justly toward other nations. The third was never to bluff, and the fourth was to strike only if prepared to strike hard. Fifth and finally, as just mentioned, big stick diplomacy required its practitioner to allow an honorable adversary to save face in defeat. In a letter to Ambassador Reid of December 1908, President Roosevelt discussed big stick diplomacy in these words: "The foreign policy in which I believe is in very fact the policy of speaking softly and carrying a big stick. I want to make it evident to every foreign nation that I intend to do justice; and neither to wrong them nor to hurt their self-respect; but that on the other hand, I am both entirely ready and entirely able to see that our rights are maintained in their turn."[21]

The two-phase Moroccan crisis of 1905 and 1906 offers perhaps the most extraordinary example of Rooseveltian personal diplomacy in action. During the spring and summer of 1905, Roosevelt stayed completely out of the public eye as he stealthily worked through Secretary of War Taft, German Ambassador to the U.S. Speck von Sternburg, Ambassador Reid, and, with an astonishing degree of intimacy, Ambassador Jusserand—along with Spring Rice, Lodge, and others—to arrange a conference that headed off a Franco-German war. While willing to risk public exposure of an involvement for which only a tiny minority of Americans would have seen any justification, the President naturally preferred to avoid—and adroitly succeeded in avoiding—such exposure. During the second and somewhat less dangerous phase of the crisis, the Algeciras conference of January–April 1906 (at which U.S. participation was public knowledge but was downplayed by the administration), Roosevelt once again operated masterfully behind the scenes. Having appointed Henry White—considered by TR "the most useful man in the entire diplomatic service"[22]—as chief American delegate at Algeciras, the President then employed the thoroughly dependable Secretary of State Root as his agent for communicating with White. Meanwhile, Roosevelt was more directly in contact with the French and German governments through frequent personal interactions with Jusserand and Sternburg in Washington.

While in the end Roosevelt prevailed on behalf of France and Britain and to the dismay of Germany, and while the President leaned heavily on Germany to reach this outcome, the Moroccan crisis was not a classic case of Rooseveltian big stick diplomacy. For at no time during either phase of the crisis did the President even consider using, much less threaten to use, U.S. military force against Germany. "I did not intend to take any position," he explained to Reid in the aftermath of the crisis, "which I would not be willing at all costs to maintain."[23] Still, elements of big stick diplomacy were very much in evidence here. For one, the foregoing quotation affirms the no-bluffing principle. Moreover, judging correctly that Germany had willfully provoked the crisis, Roosevelt believed he was acting justly in upholding the position of France. And the face-saving principle was vividly in play. After deftly engineering Germany's capitulation (largely through invoking at just the right time Germany's June 1905 pledge to defer to the U.S. President in the event of a deadlock at the conference), TR did his best to persuade Germany that the outcome was actually a German victory; and he lavished public praise on the vain kaiser for Wilhelm's "brilliant" statesmanship.

The episode routinely cited as the epitome of Rooseveltian big stick diplomacy—the U.S. acquisition of the Panama Canal Zone—is in reality a very imperfect example. For TR's success in this instance was as much a product of exasperation and opportunism as it was of calculation and initiative.

In addition, the President did not extend himself to shield Colombia, the big loser in the affair, from humiliation.

By September 1903, after many fruitless months of endeavoring in good faith to reach an agreement with the government of the backward-looking and obstructive "authoritarian ideologue" José Marroquín,[24] Roosevelt had lost patience with what he confidentially termed "the foolish and homicidal corruptionists in Bogota."[25] Hence, well aware of the strong and rising secessionist ferment in Colombian-ruled Panama, TR and Secretary of State Hay encouraged this revolutionary movement—but only in private, and even then only by indirection.[26] Beginning on October 17, the President ordered U.S. naval vessels to sail toward Panama—not to take an active part in the revolution, but, as stipulated in a U.S.-Colombian treaty of 1846, "to 'maintain free and uninterrupted transit' across the isthmus and to prevent the landing of any armed force, whether Colombian or Panamanian."[27] The bloodless Panamanian rebellion was carried out in less than three days, ending on November 6. Richard Collin accurately apportions responsibility as follows: "Although Roosevelt and the Americans were hardly innocent, Panama was the most active agent of its own revolution."[28]

The United States promptly granted recognition to the new Panamanian government and beefed up its naval presence in the area to prevent Colombia from overturning Panama's separation; there would be no further pretense of American neutrality. The Hay-Bunau-Varilla Treaty, granting the United States sovereignty "in perpetuity" over a 10-mile-wide canal zone and making Panama a virtual protectorate of the United States, was signed on November 18, 1903, and ratified by the Senate on February 23, 1904. The construction of the Panama Canal, a mammoth undertaking in which President Roosevelt was deeply interested and became heavily involved, soon commenced.

Roosevelt was extremely proud of his statesmanship relating to the acquisition of the Panama Canal Zone, believing that he had absolutely nothing to hide, and that he not only had advanced the interests of the United States but also had thwarted Colombia's attempt to impede the progress of humanity. He would never cease to defend his actions vigorously, most notably in the autobiography he published in 1913.[29]

As for Colombia, TR did meet personally on December 6, 1903, with Rafael Reyes—the head of a Colombian mission seeking to regain control of Panama and soon afterward Colombia's President—and did reply to a confidential letter from President Reyes with a reasonably cordial confidential letter of his own in February 1905. But Roosevelt never made any serious effort to mitigate Colombia's embarrassment, thereby appearing to violate an important principle of big stick diplomacy. Perhaps, in light of Colombia's highly objectionable behavior in 1903 and its military weakness, Roosevelt believed that such an effort was both unwarranted and unnecessary. Or perhaps, as his letter to Reyes suggests, he simply could figure out no way to implement the principle in this unique instance.[30]

There were, on the other hand, three truly classic displays of Rooseveltian big stick diplomacy. In chronological order, they were directed at Germany, Great Britain, and Japan.

Joint Anglo-German military action against Venezuela for the purpose of debt collection beginning in December 1902 led to a German-American confrontation. Blaming Germany for the expedition, and seeing the expedition as a challenge to the Monroe Doctrine, President Roosevelt dispatched a battleship squadron to the waters near Venezuela, insisted on arbitration (for which the Venezuelan government was calling), and privately issued in mid-December and in early February two timely and stern ultimatums to the German government.[31] By the middle of February 1903, Germany had agreed to Roosevelt's demand for arbitration, and the crisis had ended. Adhering to all the tenets of big stick diplomacy, TR had found Germany's conduct unjust and unacceptable, had readied the necessary military forces, had personally issued unambiguous warnings, and by keeping those warnings private had made it possible for Germany to back down without losing face.

Right from the beginning of (and even before) his presidency, TR looked upon the Canadian interpretation of the Alaskan–British Columbian border as "an outrage pure and simple."[32] Thus, he saw the boundary question as an issue of national honor and was adamantly opposed to abandoning any essential elements of the American claim. Yet the Anglo-American friendship he had been cultivating was also immensely important to Roosevelt. The reconciliation of these conflicting imperatives would require statecraft of the highest order. The President measured up to the test.

The story of the resolution of the Alaskan boundary quarrel reveals a determined American statesman adroitly employing personal diplomacy and big stick diplomacy to attain the result at which he was aiming. Having "quietly and unostentatiously" dispatched troops to the disputed region in 1902,[33] Roosevelt agreed early in 1903 to the establishment of an "impartial" six-person tribunal, including three Americans appointed by himself, to settle the boundary question. However, TR's selections—Secretary of War Root, Senator Lodge, and former senator George Turner, upon all of whom Roosevelt could depend to sustain the U.S. claim—made it apparent that he looked upon the tribunal, in Charles Campbell's words, merely as "a device to help a friendly country, which had blundered through deference to an obstreperous colony, climb down from an untenable position."[34] The President then launched a multipronged diplomatic offensive, utilizing a number of personal agents—particularly Root, Lodge, Turner, Hay, Henry White, Ambassador to Britain Joseph Choate, and U.S. Supreme Court Justice Oliver Wendell Holmes—to drive home two crucial messages to British Colonial Secretary Joseph Chamberlain, Foreign Secretary Lord Lansdowne, Prime Minister Arthur Balfour, and Lord Chief Justice Alverstone, the lone Briton on the tribunal. First, in the absence of a settlement affirming all the essential aspects of the American stance, TR would deploy sufficient numbers of U.S. troops to "take possession of the disputed territory" and would ask Congress for "an appropriation which will enable me to run the boundary on my own hook."[35] But, second, there were "two or three lesser points on which there is doubt," and on these he was prepared to countenance U.S. concessions in order to provide England with a dignified way out.[36] The key American and British participants picked up Roosevelt's signals, and an agreement—supported by the one British and three American tribunal members but not by the two Canadians—was reached in October 1903.[37]

Just as impressive was Roosevelt's handling of the crisis in U.S.-Japanese relations that was sparked by the San Francisco school board's passage in October 1906 of a resolution segregating Asian schoolchildren and was stoked by the continuing immigration to the United States of substantial numbers of Japanese laborers. TR's well-conceived, multifaceted approach entailed pressuring the Californians to end the blatant discrimination (and accompanying violence) while emphasizing to Japan his disapproval of Californian behavior; working with Japanese officials to find an amicable way to halt the flow of Japanese workers to the American mainland; and strengthening and exhibiting the U.S. Navy both to deter Japan and to prepare for war should it prove unavoidable. Behind the scenes he engaged the services of Arthur Lee and Canada's commissioner of labor and immigration, William L. Mackenzie King, among others, in an attempt—only partially successful—to draw Great Britain, Japan's ally, into his diplomatic enterprise. In Roosevelt's single most illustrious act of big stick diplomacy, he sent the American battleship fleet (the "Great White Fleet") on a 14-month world cruise beginning in December 1907. Not a threatening word was spoken—indeed, Japan invited the fleet to its shores and extended it a grand welcome in October 1908— but the warning that America was strong and ready was unmistakable. Meanwhile, a "Gentlemen's Agreement"—structured in such a way as to spare Japan humiliation—finally brought the immigration problem under control by the middle of 1908. Then, in November of that year, the signing of the Root-Takahira Agreement, demonstrating to the world the achievement of respectful and friendly relations between the United States and Japan, marked a climactic triumph for the President's Japanese policy. Roosevelt immodestly but very accurately summed up his accomplishment in a letter to Lee of December 20, 1908: "My policy of constant friendliness and courtesy toward Japan, *coupled with sending the fleet around the world*, has borne good results!"[38]

THE DIPLOMATIC RECORD

President Roosevelt's foreign policy aspirations were extremely ambitious. Although TR pursued these aspirations simultaneously, seeing them as overlapping and mutually dependent parts of a whole, it may be useful to single out the following five as particularly important: (1) building and solidifying a singularly special relationship between the British Empire and the United States; (2) establishing U.S. hegemony in the Western Hemisphere, especially in the Caribbean region; (3) sharply expanding the international role played by the United States; (4) contributing to peaceful and stable relations among the Great Powers of the world; and (5) contributing to the progress of civilization.

Essential to the pursuit of this far-reaching foreign policy agenda, the President fully understood, was a powerful U.S. Navy. The author of *The Naval War of 1812* and former Assistant Secretary of the Navy was an exceptionally well-informed, attentive, enthusiastic navalist, who both knew what he wanted for the navy and possessed the political and managerial attributes needed to realize most of those desires. Between 1901 and 1905, Roosevelt pushed Congress into authorizing the construction of 10 battleships among more than 30 total warships. Then, after slowing down temporarily, TR responded to the dreadnought revolution (marked by larger battleships carrying uniform batteries of big guns, of which the Royal Navy's HMS *Dreadnought*, completed in December 1906, was the prototype) and to increasing tension in U.S.-Japanese relations by calling for a stepped-up pace of naval building, with an emphasis on adding dreadnoughts to the battleship fleet. The world cruise of the Great White Fleet not only waved a big stick at Japan, but also functioned as a magnificent public relations spectacle that extracted from an antagonistic Congress in 1908 an authorization for two dreadnoughts (Roosevelt had astutely demanded four) and a commitment to fund two per year in the future. By 1907, the U.S. Navy, the world's sixth in size in 1901, had grown into the second largest. Moreover, by aggressively overseeing the implementation of a radical program of naval reform, President Roosevelt had greatly improved training (especially in gunnery), readiness, and overall efficiency. The proud outgoing President, as Stephen Howarth observes, "was fully aware that he personally could take the main credit for placing the United States' fighting ships in their new high position."[39]

Building and strengthening an Anglo-American special relationship was, as noted earlier, the cornerstone of Rooseveltian statecraft. Although relations between the United States and Great Britain were in reasonably good condition when Roosevelt assumed the presidency in September 1901 (owing especially to Britain's decidedly pro-American neutrality during the Spanish-American War of 1898 and to the United States' equally pro-British neutrality during the ongoing Boer War), the young Anglo-American rapprochement was still quite fragile, its future uncertain. Over the next seven and one-half years, with determination, lucidity, and a steady hand, President Roosevelt would take the lead in transforming this fragile rapprochement into a seasoned friendship and a deep-rooted informal partnership.

During the period 1901–1903, the President furthered the cause of Anglo-American amity in several ways. He began by continuing unchanged through the end of the Boer War in the spring of 1902 the McKinley administration's unpopular, but politically sustainable, pro-British neutrality policy.[40] In dealing with the crisis of December 1902–February 1903 over the joint Anglo-German attack on Venezuela, Roosevelt assessed British behavior as merely foolish and thus dealt harshly only with Germany, whose conduct he considered genuinely threatening. In the immediate aftermath of this crisis, TR did speak pointedly to Ambassador Michael Herbert, thereby making sure that the British government grasped the mistake of being "roped in as an appendage to Germany" and would never repeat it.[41] Most significant was the well-considered, hands-on presidential diplomacy, previously examined, that achieved a resolution in October 1903 to the very sensitive and complicated Alaskan boundary dispute. As he continued throughout his presidency to pursue his goal of building a strong special relationship between England and the United States, TR would encounter no more hurdles of such magnitude. As he claimed retrospectively in 1911, the agreement on the Alaskan border "settled the last serious trouble between the British Empire and ourselves."[42]

Advances in Anglo-American relations during the early years of Roosevelt's presidency paralleled and contributed to his progress in asserting U.S. hegemony in and around the Caribbean. First, the U.S.-British Hay-Pauncefote Treaty of November 1901 cleared the way for the United States to build, control, and fortify a trans-isthmian canal. Then, as discussed in the preceding section, Roosevelt opportunistically acquired the Panama Canal Zone from newly independent Panama in November 1903; the digging of the canal, of which the U.S. Navy would be a primary beneficiary, could now proceed. And the President aggressively pushed forward the development of Guantanamo, Cuba, as the United States' "main naval base ... in the Caribbean Sea and the principal guard of the Atlantic entrance of the Panama Canal." Similarly, he began the development of Pearl Harbor,

Hawaii, "the key to the Pacific Ocean," as the U.S. Navy's most important Pacific base; its many functions also would include defending the canal.[43]

Meanwhile, recovering quickly from its Venezuelan misadventure, in 1903 the British government began encouraging the United States to play a more active part in the affairs of Latin America. The following year, spurred by chaotic conditions in the Dominican Republic, TR issued the Roosevelt Corollary to the Monroe Doctrine, proclaiming the obligation of the United States to counteract "gross wrongdoing" in the hemisphere: "If we intend to say 'Hands off' to the powers of Europe, . . . we must keep order ourselves."[44]

Roosevelt was actually very reluctant to exercise this new international policing authority, and he initially resisted the Dominican government's overtures for U.S. intervention. By the beginning of 1905, however, the President believed it was imperative to act, and he arranged to establish a U.S. customs receivership in the Dominican Republic. And when partisan politics impeded Senate ratification of the Dillingham-Sanchez Protocol, the President fell back on his broad constructionist principles and, through an executive agreement with the Dominican government, instituted a modus vivendi embodying the terms of the protocol. In the Dominican Republic the U.S. customs receivership was kept limited by Roosevelt and functioned very well, enabling the Caribbean nation to repay debts owed to foreigners and to finance government operations. Finally, early in 1907, the Senate ratified a slightly modified U.S.-Dominican treaty.

For their part, Britain's leaders provided tangible evidence of their support for the greatly expanded U.S. role by almost completely withdrawing British naval forces from the Caribbean region, leaving the protection of British colonial and other interests there in American hands. "South of us," TR could write with conviction to King Edward VII in March 1905, "our interests are identical with yours."[45]

TR's Dominican intervention was one of only two he undertook under the terms of the Roosevelt Corollary. The second was in Cuba, for whose benefit (and the validation of America's good faith) Roosevelt had won ratification of a tariff reciprocity treaty back in December 1903 after a long struggle with Congress. Roosevelt's Cuban intervention, lasting from September 1906 until January 1909, was undertaken with particularly strong reluctance. Even with both the Cuban government and the leaders of an armed uprising against it requesting U.S. military intervention, Roosevelt exhausted the possibilities for diplomatic mediation before ordering forces ashore and setting up a provisional government. Roosevelt certainly had no imperial designs on Cuba; he privately told Secretary of War Taft in January 1907, "Our business is to establish peace and order on a satisfactory basis, start the new government, and then leave the Island."[46] And, in essence, the U.S. intervention adhered to the President's prescription.[47]

As is suggested by both the infrequency and the restraint with which he intervened under his corollary, Roosevelt considered it a priority to try to minimize Latin American resentment and suspicion of the United States. His most proactive initiative in this regard was Secretary of State Root's goodwill tour of seven Latin American countries during the summer and early fall of 1906. The highlight of this journey occurred July 31 in Brazil at the Third International American Conference, where Root declared: "We wish no victories but those of peace; for no territory except our own; for no sovereignty except the sovereignty over ourselves."[48] The President was delighted with his trusted secretary's "wonderful trip,"[49] following which Root continued to work hard and effectively on behalf of better U.S.–Latin American relations. By 1909, "Root had substantially improved the nation's ties with Latin America."[50]

In light of President Roosevelt's admirable record in the area of Latin American policy, it seems worthwhile to ask why the image of a heavy-handed and widespread interventionism persists in the popular mind and continues to be sustained even by some scholars. Part of the explanation is the controversy still surrounding the U.S. acquisition of the Panama Canal Zone. But, as has been explained, the Panamanian revolution of November 1903 was authentic, and the successful policy of TR, who unquestionably had become very frustrated by Colombia's obstructive behavior, was actually more reactive and opportunistic than calculated.[51]

Another, and probably more important, part of the explanation springs from the Roosevelt Corollary to the Monroe Doctrine. It is true that the Roosevelt Corollary provided theoretical cover for the rampant U.S. interventionism in Latin America of the 1910s and 1920s. But this was decidedly not its purpose, and it seems inappropriate to fault Roosevelt for the subsequent misuse by others of his prescription for encouraging orderly development in the hemisphere and persuading outside powers to steer clear. Roosevelt's concept was based on combining, as Richard Collin puts it, "power, responsibility, and especially altruism," and the President's actions validated his intentions.[52] The interventionist dollar diplomacy of William Howard Taft (and of Warren Harding and Calvin Coolidge) departed sharply from the approach of TR, who, while naturally desiring a level international playing field for U.S. business, conducted a foreign policy that elevated U.S. strategic interests and the "progress of civilization" (which required respect for and upright conduct toward weaker nations) far above the promotion of American economic advantage.[53] Likewise, the "moral interventionism" practiced in Latin America by Woodrow Wilson deviated markedly from the less ambitious, less intrusive, more respectful policy carried out by Roosevelt and Root. Yes, Roosevelt's Latin American policy was paternalistic (albeit quite beneficently so), but charges of graver misdeeds are historically inaccurate and should, at long last, be put to rest.

Roosevelt's goals of greatly expanding the international role played by the United States and of contributing to peaceful and stable relations among the Great Powers were advanced most notably by his extraordinary mediation of the Russo-Japanese War and of the Moroccan crisis. Although he was a close and keenly interested observer of the Russo-Japanese contest right from its onset in February 1904, and although by December of that year he was already thinking seriously about trying his hand as a mediator, he did not step forward until an opportunity arose in the spring of 1905 in the wake of major Japanese military successes. After plenty of discreet preliminary work by the President, the door was opened in May when Japan—financially strapped and militarily overextended despite its victories—requested that Roosevelt offer mediation to Russia "on his own initiative." Then, through the intensive and extremely adept application of personal diplomacy involving British, French, and German as well as Russian and Japanese officials—using the summer White House in Oyster Bay, New York, as his base of operations—Roosevelt arranged for the convening in early August of a Russo-Japanese peace conference in Portsmouth, New Hampshire, and proceeded to overcome formidable obstacles as he shepherded it to the triumphant conclusion of the Treaty of Portsmouth of September 5. This treaty, which restored an Asian balance of power, earned TR the Nobel Peace Prize for 1906 and may have been his foremost single achievement as a statesman. If so, Roosevelt's equally remarkable mediation of the two-phase Franco-German dispute over Morocco in 1905 and 1906, outlined earlier, would have to rank a close second. For this highly flammable crisis very conceivably could have brought on World War I nine years before it actually began.

Theodore Roosevelt's work as a mediator par excellence during the two gravest international crises of his presidency also contributed to the strengthening of the Anglo-American special relationship on which he was so intent. In both instances, he bolstered the Anglo-American connection by his resolute preservation of the Anglo-French *entente cordiale*. Because England was allied with Japan while France was allied with Russia, the Russo-Japanese War imperiled the young entente, a threat exacerbated by wartime German diplomatic activity aimed at undermining the French-British link. And for its part, the Moroccan crisis represented a frontal German assault on the entente. So Roosevelt was motivated to become involved not only by the lofty goal of restoring or preserving peace among the powers and by the desire to wield American influence on the world stage, but also by a determination to protect the Anglo-French entente, which he considered a vital element in an international balance of power favorable to the defense and promotion of Anglo-American interests.

The manner in which President Roosevelt dealt with the Newfoundland fisheries problem—"the longest dispute in the history of American foreign policy"[54]—spotlights the depth of his commitment to Anglo-American unity. When this on-and-off dispute was renewed by Newfoundland in 1905 in retaliation for the U.S. Senate's unfriendly treatment of a U.S.-Newfoundland reciprocity (bilateral tariff reduction) treaty, Roosevelt did not react hastily. Indeed, he considered his own country to be primarily to blame. America's course, he explained to Henry Cabot Lodge, "has given deep offense to Newfoundland, and most naturally. If the circumstances had been reversed, this country in its turn would have been deeply angered." The United States, he continued, should "try to show such patience and forbearance as possible until the exasperation caused by our very unfortunate action has worn off."[55] When Newfoundland placed additional restrictions on American fishermen in 1906, Ambassador Reid, representing the President, worked out a temporary modus vivendi with the British government. And when negotiations reached an impasse in the summer of 1907, Roosevelt proposed to resolve the fisheries issue through binding arbitration by the Hague Tribunal. Britain agreed; formal arrangements were set early in 1909; the following year (after Roosevelt had left the presidency), the tribunal rendered a compromise verdict. TR's sense of proportion and fairness, along with his creativity and his thoughtful prioritization of U.S. interests, had brought to a satisfactory conclusion this previously intractable dispute with the best and most important friend of the United States. It was another impressive triumph for Rooseveltian statecraft.

In light of Roosevelt's highly partisan stance on the Anglo-German rivalry and his excellent record in building an Anglo-American bond, his success in maintaining amicable U.S.-German relations throughout his presidency is noteworthy—and praiseworthy. Good relations with Germany were naturally preferable to hostile ones, and, importantly, they gave TR a degree of influence over German foreign policy that he otherwise would not have wielded. Thus, the German government actively supported TR in his mediation of the Russo-Japanese War and, as already noted, ultimately acceded to the President's pro-French prescription for ending the Moroccan crisis. Crucial to his effectiveness with Germany was Roosevelt's adeptness at handling the mercurial Kaiser Wilhelm II. Aware of Wilhelm's "intense egoism," TR endeavored to be friendly to the kaiser and was careful to avoid giving him "legitimate offense." Even "where I have forced him to give way," the President explained confidentially to Henry White in August 1906, "I have been sedulously anxious to build a bridge of gold for him, and to give him the satisfaction of feeling that his dignity and reputation ... were safe."[56]

For Roosevelt, the most difficult foreign power with which to manage U.S. relations was Russia. The government of Tsar Nicholas II, Roosevelt clearly recognized, was brutal toward its own citizens and habitually mendacious in its foreign relations. In 1903, TR considered, but upon reflection decided against, actively resisting Russian encroachments in Manchuria; alongside his awareness of the serious impediment posed by domestic political realities, he concluded that no vital U.S. interests were at stake on the Asian mainland. Also in 1903, the President defied the Russian government's wishes by forwarding to Russia a U.S. citizens petition expressing outrage and calling for justice in the wake of large-scale government-sponsored anti-Jewish atrocities in Kishinev. This action accomplished three purposes: it conveyed to the Russian government Roosevelt's genuine feelings of repulsion; it strengthened support for the administration among Jewish Americans; and it intensified the pressure on Russia to moderate its policy in Manchuria.

Roosevelt's frustrating interactions with Russian officials during the Russo-Japanese peace negotiations in August 1905 did not improve his perspective on Russia. Nonetheless, thinking strategically, TR believed that Russian power in East Asia served the important function of balancing Japanese power. Similarly, he indicated cautious approval in 1907 when, to bolster its defensive posture against Germany, Great Britain added a rapprochement with Russia to its 1904 entente with France. "I was glad to see your agreement with Russia," he informed Cecil Spring Rice, "but of course we are all perfectly ignorant of what Russia's future will be."[57]

In the area of U.S.-Japan relations, Rooseveltian statecraft was by any standard strikingly successful. As mentioned previously, TR's mediation of the Russo-Japanese War occurred in response to a private Japanese request. In addition, the secret Taft-Katsura agreement of July 1905 provides incontestable evidence that Roosevelt unequivocally approved of and informally linked the United States to the Anglo-Japanese alliance.[58] And (again as pointed out previously) Roosevelt not only defused the hot-and-cold U.S.-Japanese immigration-racism crisis of 1906–1909; through a multifaceted policy highlighted by the 14-month world cruise of the Great White Fleet, he carried U.S.-Japanese relations to new heights of friendship, affirmed by the Root-Takahira Agreement of November 1908. In this accord, while giving lip service to "the independence and integrity of China," the governments of Japan and the United States "firmly" resolved "reciprocally to respect the territorial possessions belonging to each other" and to uphold "the existing status quo" in East Asia and the Pacific[59]: Japan would continue to stay away from the Philippines; the United States would continue to support Japanese control of Korea; and it was transparently implied that where Japan's predominant position in southern Manchuria clashed with America's Open Door policy in China, the former would take precedence. (TR's successors as President— beginning with Taft, despite Roosevelt's protests—would undo his fine handiwork in building friendly U.S.-Japanese relations.)

Nearly all the accomplishments so far presented—particularly TR's success in forging an Anglo-American special relationship—furthered in some measure Roosevelt's strong, idealistic desire to contribute to the progress of civilization. Policies specifically aimed at this objective were his work on behalf of the principle of arbitration, his efforts to prepare the people of the Philippines for self-government, and his encouragement of British leaders similarly to continue to pursue with confidence a wise and generous imperial policy focused on uplifting the native peoples in the dependent colonies of the British Empire.

As is suggested by his recourse to the Hague Tribunal to settle the Newfoundland fisheries problem, Roosevelt firmly believed in arbitration as a proper, civilized means of resolving non-vital international disagreements. In June 1905, he expressed his outlook in these words in a letter to Lyman Abbott: "It is neither possible nor desirable in the present stage of the world's progress to agree to arbitrate all questions that may come up between different nations. But it is entirely possible and exceedingly desirable to limit the classes of cases which it is not possible definitely to promise beforehand to arbitrate, and to provide not only that all other questions shall be arbitrated, but so far as possible the manner and method of proceeding to such arbitration."[60] On this issue, however, TR was blocked by the Senate from fully implementing his ideas.[61]

Roosevelt approached the question of U.S. rule in the Philippines with a genuine sense of a civilizing mission and a paternalistic determination to act in the interest of the indigenous population. After completing in 1902 the very harsh suppression of the insurrection against the American takeover, the President pushed hard for, but failed to obtain from Congress, a large-scale tariff relief bill for the Philippines; he did succeed, however, in sharply reducing the influence and privileges of the Catholic parish priests in the Philippines, thereby redressing an important grievance of the people of the archipelago. Roosevelt paid close attention to all aspects of governance in the Philippines. In 1907, he sent Secretary Taft there "to open the new Filipino assembly, the first major instrument of self-government for the Islands."[62] Where the United States had made mistakes, TR told the British writer and editor Sydney Brooks in 1908, "I am steadily trying to advance and perfect remedies."[63] As he prepared to leave the presidency early in 1909, Roosevelt was very proud of what had been achieved under his watch, confidently asserting in an important speech that "we are constantly giving to the people of the Philippines an increasing share in, an increasing opportunity to learn by practice, the difficult art of self-government. ... We are leading them forward steadily in the right direction."[64]

Although at times critical of Britain's imperial performance in some of its colonies, Malaya in particular, on the whole Roosevelt was immensely impressed with the size of the British Empire, generally approved of the way it was run, and viewed it as a potent force for the maintenance of world peace and for the advancement of civilization. For the most part he expressed his admiration and offered his encouragement privately, as when he proclaimed in a letter of December 1908 to John Morley, Secretary of State for India, that "English rule in India has marked one of the signal triumphs of civilization."[65] Soon afterward, on January 18, 1909, in response to a little prodding (only a little was necessary) from Brooks and other Britons, the President publicly addressed the same subject. His unambiguously laudatory, even celebratory remarks on this occasion not only enunciated Roosevelt's genuine sentiments but also served his diplomatic agenda in two ways. First, TR's unstinting open praise shored up British self-confidence during a difficult period for British rule in India. And second, it brought to the leaders and citizens of Great Britain a new level of awareness of and appreciation for the Anglo-American special relationship and the excellent work Roosevelt had been doing for more than seven years to advance it.[66]

As he proceeded over the course of his presidency to build an outstanding record of accomplishment as a statesman, the politically astute 26th president had to deal with the realities of a public tending to be ignorant of and apathetic toward foreign policy issues and a Congress tending to be narrow and unsupportive, even obstructive. Therefore, while he explained to the public as much as he thought was politically feasible, he often intentionally oversimplified when presenting his objectives and motives. As for Congress, where the approval of two-thirds of the Senate was needed to ratify treaties, and where majorities in both houses were required to enact legislation and to fund naval-building and other programs, TR employed a combination of reliance on friends, reasoned persuasion, cajolery, and political gamesmanship—along with resorting to the "bully pulpit" and staging public relations spectacles (most notably the world cruise of the Great White Fleet)—in order to extract as much as possible of what he was seeking. Naturally he was sometimes unsuccessful, but his political skills and intelligence and persistence and savvy usually enabled him to prevail. Moreover, there were some initiatives (most importantly Roosevelt's involvement during the first phase of the Moroccan crisis in 1905) that could be carried out in complete secrecy, and there were others (most importantly the administering through an executive agreement of the Dominican Republic's customs houses during 1905–1907) where the President found a way to circumvent congressional obstruction.

Criticisms of Roosevelt for failing to educate the public more fully and for his broad constructionist approach to foreign policy are not very convincing. In the successful pursuit of an expansive, sophisticated, farsighted foreign policy agenda that both enhanced the United States' position in the world and actively contributed to international stability and peace, TR did his best to educate without undermining his various diplomatic endeavors, and he operated according to a constitutionally legitimate, if controversial, theory of presidential authority. His record as a statesman would have been extraordinary even had he enjoyed a more congenial political climate. Without that climate, it was all the more extraordinary.

"The strength of will, reasoning power, and other mental dispositions and disciplines to do what is morally required in the circumstances" (Robert Jackson's words)[67] were exhibited in abundance in Rooseveltian diplomacy. Even more, in his conduct of foreign policy, America's 26th President displayed a degree of perspicacity that transcended his era. It would take the disastrous failure of isolationism and appeasement and the terrible experience of World War II to revive TR's way of thinking about U.S. foreign relations and to bring his guiding precepts—formidable and credible deterrent power, broadly conceived U.S. interests, and Anglo-American solidarity and preeminence—into the mainstream, where they have been ever since.[68] In the final analysis, the statecraft of Theodore Roosevelt, featuring an exemplary blend of power and principle, produced great short-term and long-term benefits for the United States and the world.

NOTES

1. Joel H. Rosenthal, "Foreword: Biography, Ethics, and Statecraft," in Cathal J. Nolan, ed., *Ethics and Statecraft: The Moral Dimension of International Affairs*, 2nd ed. (Westport, CT: Praeger, 2004), p. xvii; William N. Tilchin, "Morality and the Presidency of Theodore Roosevelt," *The Long Term View*, Vol. 3, No. 3 (Fall 1996), pp. 57–58.

2. Cathal J. Nolan, "Introduction," in Nolan, *Ethics and Statecraft*, p. 11.

3. Robert H. Jackson, "The Situational Ethics of Statecraft," in Nolan, *Ethics and Statecraft*, p. 19.

4. Ibid., pp. 27–28.

5. Frederick W. Marks III, *Velvet on Iron: The Diplomacy of Theodore Roosevelt* (Lincoln: University of Nebraska Press, 1979), pp. 89–128.

6. For a similar but somewhat more fully developed discussion of the Rooseveltian worldview, see William N. Tilchin, "For the Present and the Future: The Well-Conceived, Successful, and Farsighted Statecraft of President Theodore Roosevelt," *Diplomacy & Statecraft*, Vol. 19, No. 4 (December 2008), pp. 658–70.

7. "I believe in peace," TR wrote to Andrew Carnegie in 1906, "but I believe that as things are at present, the course not only of peace but of what is greater than peace, justice, is favored by having those nations which really stand at the head of civilization show . . . that they ask peace in the name of justice and not from any weakness." TR to Carnegie, August 6, 1906, Elting E. Morison, John M. Blum, and Alfred D. Chandler, eds., *The Letters of Theodore Roosevelt* (8 vols., Cambridge, MA: Harvard University Press, 1951–1954), Vol. 5, p. 346. *The Letters of Theodore Roosevelt* is hereafter cited as *Letters of TR*.

8. See, in particular, William N. Tilchin, *Theodore Roosevelt and the British Empire: A Study in Presidential Statecraft* (New York: St. Martin's Press, 1997), pp. 227–28. Hereafter cited as Tilchin, *TR and the British Empire*.

9. See, for example, TR to Arthur Lee, June 6, 1905, *Letters of TR*, Vol. 4, p. 1207; and TR to Lee, August 7, 1908, *Letters of TR*, Vol. 6, p. 1159.

10. TR to Oscar Straus, February 27, 1906, *Letters of TR*, Vol. 5, p. 168.

11. TR to John St. Loe Strachey, February 22, 1907, *Letters of TR*, Vol. 5, p. 596.

12. TR to Cecil Spring Rice, June 13, 1904, *Letters of TR*, Vol. 4, p. 829.

13. TR to John Hay, May 22, 1903, *Letters of TR*, Vol. 3, p. 478; TR to Albert Shaw, June 22, 1903, *Letters of TR*, Vol. 3, p. 497; TR to Henry Cabot Lodge, June 16, 1905, *Letters of TR*, Vol. 4, p. 1230.

14. TR to David Bowman Schneder, June 19, 1905, *Letters of TR*, Vol. 4, pp. 1240–41.

15. TR to Whitelaw Reid, June 27, 1906, *Letters of TR*, Vol. 5, p. 320.

16. TR to Henry White, August 14, 1906, *Letters of TR*, Vol. 5, p. 359.

17. TR to Reid, April 28, 1906, *Letters of TR*, Vol. 5, p. 236.

18. Lewis L. Gould, *The Presidency of Theodore Roosevelt* (Lawrence: University Press of Kansas, 1991), p. 174. Hereafter cited as Gould, *Presidency of TR*.

19. See Serge Ricard, *Théodore Roosevelt: principes et pratique d'une politique étrangère* [Theodore Roosevelt: Principles and Practice of a Foreign Policy] (Aix-en-Provence, France: Université de Provence, 1991), p. 253. Hereafter cited as Ricard, *TR: principes et pratique*.

20. Quoted in Morison et al., *Letters of TR*, Vol. 6, p. 1108n.

21. TR to Reid, December 4, 1908, *Letters of TR*, Vol. 6, p. 1410.

22. Raymond A. Esthus, *Theodore Roosevelt and the International Rivalries* (1970; reprint, Claremont, CA: Regina Books, 1982), p. 17.

23. TR to Reid, April 28, 1906, *Letters of TR*, Vol. 5, p. 234.

24. See Richard H. Collin, *Theodore Roosevelt's Caribbean: The Panama Canal, the Monroe Doctrine, and the Latin American Context* (Baton Rouge: Louisiana State University Press, 1990), especially p. 312. Hereafter cited as Collin, *TR's Caribbean*.

25. TR to Hay, September 15, 1903, *Letters of TR*, Vol. 3, p. 599.

26. Apparently right after his first meeting with Philippe Bunau-Varilla, the leading figure in the Panamanian revolutionary drama, Roosevelt wrote these words to his friend Albert Shaw: "Privately, I freely say to you that I should be delighted if Panama were an independent State . . .; but for me to say so publicly would amount to an instigation of a revolt, and therefore I cannot say it." TR to Shaw, October 10, 1903, *Letters of TR*, Vol. 3, p. 628.

27. Gould, *Presidency of TR*, p. 96. Actually, these orders reached Commander John Hubbard of the *Nashville* on November 3, the day the revolution began, only after Hubbard had permitted Colombia to land over 400 troops, nearly wrecking the revolution. See Collin, *TR's Caribbean*, pp. 262–66.

28. Collin, *TR's Caribbean*, p. 245.

29. Theodore Roosevelt, *Theodore Roosevelt: An Autobiography* (1913; reprint, New York: Da Capo Press, 1985), pp. 526–46.

30. TR to Rafael Reyes, February 20, 1905, *Letters of TR*, Vol. 4, p. 1124.

31. See especially Edmund Morris, " 'A Few Pregnant Days': Theodore Roosevelt and the Venezuelan Crisis of 1902," *Theodore Roosevelt Association Journal*, Vol. 15, No. 1 (Winter 1989), pp. 2–13; and Ricard, *TR: principes et pratique*, pp. 279–294.

32. TR to Hay, July 10, 1902, *Letters of TR*, Vol. 3, p. 287.

33. TR to Elihu Root, March 29, 1902, quoted in Richard H. Collin, *Theodore Roosevelt, Culture, Diplomacy, and Expansion: A New View of American Imperialism* (Baton Rouge: Louisiana State University Press, 1985), p. 178.

34. Charles S. Campbell Jr., *Anglo-American Understanding, 1898–1903* (Baltimore: Johns Hopkins University Press, 1957), p. 311.

35. TR to George Turner, August 8, 1903, quoted in Campbell, *Anglo-American Understanding*, p. 327; TR to Oliver Wendell Holmes, July 25, 1903, *Letters of TR*, Vol. 3, p. 529.

36. TR to Holmes, July 25, 1903, *Letters of TR*, Vol. 3, p. 529.

37. For a much fuller discussion of Roosevelt's masterful management of the diplomacy of the Alaskan boundary dispute, see Tilchin, *TR and the British Empire*, pp. 36–48.

38. TR to Lee, December 20, 1908, *Letters of TR*, Vol. 6, p. 1432 (emphasis in original).

39. Stephen Howarth, *To Shining Sea: A History of the United States Navy, 1775–1991* (New York: Random House, 1991), p. 288.

40. See William N. Tilchin, "The United States and the Boer War," in Keith Wilson, ed., *The International Impact of the Boer War* (Chesham, UK: Acumen Publishing, 2001), pp. 107–22.

41. Tilchin, *TR and the British Empire*, p. 34.

42. TR to Alfred Thayer Mahan, June 8, 1911, quoted in Campbell, *Anglo-American Understanding*, p. 347.

43. TR to Charles Warren Fairbanks, February 21, 1908, *Letters of TR*, Vol. 6, p. 951.

44. TR to Root, June 7, 1904, *Letters of TR*, Vol. 4, pp. 821–22.

45. TR to King Edward VII, March 9, 1905, *Letters of TR*, Vol. 4, p. 1136. The co-operative Anglo-American handling of the troublesome Jamaica incident of 1907 underlined the fundamental accuracy of Roosevelt's observation. This incident and its diplomatic aftermath are recounted in detail in Tilchin, *TR and the British Empire*, pp. 115–68. A briefer version is provided in Tilchin, "Theodore Roosevelt, Anglo-American Relations, and the Jamaica Incident of 1907," *Diplomatic History*, Vol. 19, No. 3 (Summer 1995), pp. 385–405.

46. TR to William Howard Taft, January 22, 1907, *Letters of TR*, Vol. 5, p. 560.

47. See especially Collin, *TR's Caribbean*, pp. 529–42.

48. Quoted in ibid., p. 491. Along with the Dominican and Cuban episodes, evidence of the sincerity and veracity of Root's statement can be found in the benign, well-reasoned circumspection with which, in partnership with Mexico, the Roosevelt administration attempted (with mixed results) to help resolve Central American conflicts involving Guatemala, El Salvador, Nicaragua, and Honduras in 1906 and 1907.

49. TR to Lodge, October 2, 1906, *Letters of TR*, Vol. 5, p. 440.

50. Gould, *Presidency of TR*, pp. 251–52.

51. Roosevelt's critics (and, for that matter, defenders) long assumed that he boasted in a speech delivered in California two years after leaving the presidency: "I took the Canal Zone." But a careful analysis presented by James F. Vivian in 1980 strongly suggests that TR made no such public statement. Instead, Vivian demonstrates,

Roosevelt more likely claimed rather innocuously that he "took a trip to the Isthmus" and that he "started the canal." Vivian, "The 'Taking' of the Panama Canal Zone: Myth and Reality," *Diplomatic History*, Vol. 4, No. 1 (Winter 1980), pp. 95–100.

52. Collin, *TR's Caribbean*, p. 547.

53. In a well-researched essay focused on the Dominican intervention, Cyrus Veeser argues that "Roosevelt's Corollary . . ., an interventionist manifesto, provided a rationale for [Dollar Diplomacy]." But Veeser simultaneously—and revealingly— makes clear the failure of the corrupt, self-serving Santo Domingo Improvement Company and its devoted and talented agent, John Bassett Moore, to manipulate Roosevelt: "By the spring of 1905, Moore and the Improvement Company realized that the special status they had long enjoyed in Washington was being overwhelmed by Roosevelt's commitment to harmony among the Great Powers and stability in the Dominican Republic." Veeser, "Inventing Dollar Diplomacy: The Gilded-Age Origins of the Roosevelt Corollary to the Monroe Doctrine," *Diplomatic History*, Vol. 27, No. 3 (June 2003), pp. 301, 321.

54. Alexander DeConde, *A History of American Foreign Policy*, 3rd ed. (2 vols., New York: Charles Scribner's Sons, 1978), Vol. 1, p. 365.

55. TR to Lodge, August 19, 1905, *Letters of TR*, Vol. 4, pp. 1305–6.

56. TR to White, August 14, 1906, *Letters of TR*, Vol. 5, p. 358.

57. TR to Spring Rice, December 21, 1907, *Letters of TR*, Vol. 6, p. 871.

58. On behalf of the President, Secretary of War Taft informed the Japanese that "the Government of the United States . . . could be counted on by [Japan and Great Britain] quite as confidently as if the United States were under treaty obligations." Taft to Root, telegram, July 29, 1905, quoted in Howard K. Beale, *Theodore Roosevelt and the Rise of America to World Power* (1956; reprint, Baltimore: Johns Hopkins University Press, 1984), p. 157.

59. Quoted in Henry Steele Commager, ed., *Documents of American History*, 9th ed. (2 vols., Englewood Cliffs, NJ: Prentice-Hall, 1973), Vol. 2, p. 53.

60. TR to Lyman Abbott, June 8, 1905, *Letters of TR*, Vol. 4, p. 1208.

61. See Tilchin, *TR and the British Empire*, p. 260, n. 8.

62. Morison et al., *Letters of TR*, Vol. 5, p. 742n.

63. TR to Sydney Brooks, November 20, 1908, *Letters of TR*, Vol. 6, p. 1370.

64. TR, "Address of the President at the celebration [sic] of the African Diamond Jubilee of the Methodist Episcopal Church, Washington, D.C., January 18, 1909," pp. 28–29, Theodore Roosevelt Collection, Harvard College Library, Cambridge, MA.

65. TR to John Morley, December 1, 1908, *Letters of TR*, Vol. 6, p. 1402.

66. See TR, "Address to Methodist Episcopal Church," pp. 17–24; Reid to TR, January 22, 1909, Theodore Roosevelt Papers, reel 87, Library of Congress, Washington, D.C., and Harvard College Library, Cambridge, MA; and Lee to TR, January 29, 1909, TR Papers, reel 88.

67. Jackson, "Situational Ethics of Statecraft," p. 26.

68. See William N. Tilchin, "Then and Since: The Remarkable and Enduring Foreign Policy of Theodore Roosevelt," *Theodore Roosevelt Association Journal*, Vol. 35, Nos. 1 & 2 (Winter–Spring 2014), pp. 45–51.

6

The Higher Realism of Woodrow Wilson[*]

Arthur S. Link

On March 4, 1913, a gaunt man walked to the stands outside the east front of the Capitol in Washington to take the oath of office as twenty-eighth President of the United States. Although his face was somber with a sense of high seriousness, it radiated strength and determination, and there was thrilling power in his voice as he summoned the American people to the tasks of national reconstruction. Eight years later, in 1921, he assisted in the rituals inaugurating his successor, Warren G. Harding. Now he was broken in body, and his drawn face reflected the pain that came from his recent repudiation at the hands of the people during the election of 1920.

He was Woodrow Wilson, born in Staunton, Virginia, on December 29, 1856, reared in Presbyterian manses in Georgia and the Carolinas, educated at Davidson College in North Carolina and Princeton University, trained in the study of law at the University of Virginia, and prepared for a career in teaching and scholarship at the Johns Hopkins University. He had taught successively from 1885 to 1902 at Bryn Mawr College in Pennsylvania, Wesleyan University in Connecticut, and Princeton, and had served as president of the latter institution from 1902 to 1910. Plunging into the sea of politics in 1910, he had won the governorship of New Jersey and had gone on with almost irresistible power to capture the presidency in 1912. Then he had guided the destinies of the American people from 1913 to 1921 and helped to direct the destinies of the world during eight of the most critical years of the modern epoch.

I am happy to come before this particular audience in this venerable city to talk about the man who has been the subject of my main thought and work for twenty years. I must confess at the outset that I have prepared this paper with a definite purpose in mind. It is neither to praise Woodrow Wilson nor to bury

---

*This chapter was the Founder's Day address to the Presbyterian Historical Society in Philadelphia on October 12, 1962. It appeared in *Journal of Presbyterian History*, Vol. 41, No. 1 (March 1963), pp. 1–13, and is reprinted by permission.

him. The record of his contribution has its own integrity, and what little I could say would neither add to nor detract from it. It is not to bring you any new view of President Wilson, for I doubt that I could say anything really new about him at this point. My purpose is, rather, to attempt to pull together a number of thoughts and convictions that have been coursing through my mind during the past few years, in brief, to clarify my own conclusions about the subject of my life's work.

I have felt impelled to this undertaking in part by many conversations with English and German historians which have challenged my own emerging view of President Wilson. My experiences during a year abroad in 1958–59 have brought home the fact that Europeans on the whole still view Wilson very much as many of them viewed him forty years ago at the end of the Paris Peace Conference and the great struggle in the United States over ratification of the Treaty of Versailles. This European image is, I think it is fair to say, one of a well-intentioned idealist, a man good by Christian standards, but essentially a destructive force in modern history because he was visionary, unrealistic, provincial, and ignorant of European problems, zealous and messianic in conceit, but devoid of either practical knowledge or the humility to follow others better informed than he. I do not think that this is an essentially unfair statement of the European point of view. It was, of course, the image propagated by John Maynard Keynes, Georges Clemenceau, and many persons among the thoughtful European public at the end of the Peace Conference. It is the view still largely held by English, French, and German scholars alike, if for different reasons.

I have felt impelled to my subject not only by recent forceful reminders of the strong survival of the old European image of President Wilson, but also by the emergence in our own country during the past few years of a new school of historical critics, and by their work in constructing an image of President Wilson that is remarkably like the older European one. Calling themselves realists, and drawing their inspiration from the distinguished diplomat-historian, George Kennan, and the Austrian-trained authority in international relations, Hans J. Morgenthau, now at the University of Chicago, these new American critics have found Wilson wanting because he did not think in terms of strategy, bases, and armed power, but dwelt too much in ethereal realms.

Are the old European and new American critics right, I have asked myself over and over during the past few years: is this the image that I also see, the Wilson that I know? Were the Austrians right in thinking that his irresponsible preaching of a slogan, "self-determination," was primarily responsible for the destruction of the Habsburg Empire? Were the Germans right in holding him responsible for what they regarded as the monstrous betrayal of Versailles? Were the French right in thinking that he prevented the imposition of the only kind of peace settlement upon Germany that could endure? Were the English and new American critics near the truth when they portrayed him as a tragic figure irrelevant in the modern world?

I must confess that I have sometimes been tempted to agree. No one who has ever given any serious attention to President Wilson's life could fail to agree that he was *primarily* a Christian idealist. By this I mean a man who almost always tended to judge policies on a basis of whether they were right by Christian standards, not whether they brought material or strategic advantages. I mean also a man whose foreign policies were motivated by the assumption that a nation as much as an individual should live according to Judeo-Christian ethics, and by a positive repudiation of the assumptions of the classical "realists" about international behavior.

No one who has given serious study to Wilson's career, moreover, could fail to agree that there is at least an appearance of reality about the old European and new American image. Wilson was not merely an idealist, but a crusading idealist. An orator of enormous eloquence and power, he was also a phrasemaker who more than once fell victim to the magic of his own words. In international relations, he did not give undue weight to material forces or base his policies upon the assumption that nations must always act selfishly. At times, he did seem to give the appearance of believing that he was a kind of messiah divinely appointed to deliver Europe from the tyranny of history.

I have myself made all these criticisms and others more elaborately in my own writings. But they have never really satisfied me and do not satisfy me now. I do not think that they add up to a historical image that is accurate. Indeed, I cannot escape the conclusion that they altogether miss the main point and meaning of President Wilson's career. The point, in my opinion, and the theme of this paper, is that, among all the major statesmen and thoughtful critics of his age, President Wilson was in fact the supreme realist, and that because this is true, what he stood for and fought to accomplish has significant meaning for our own generation.

This is, to be sure, a very broad, perhaps even an audacious statement, one that does not mean very much unless we are careful to define our terms. A realist, I take it, is one who faces life and its situation without illusions, in short, one who can see realities or truth through the fog of delusion that normally shrouds the earth-bound individual. If the European and American critics of President Wilson who thought mainly in strategic and material terms, who measured national power by army divisions, naval bases, and the like, if *they* were realists, then President Wilson was a realist of a different sort. Sheerly for purposes of convenience, let us call his view of the way individuals and nations should cope in dealing with situations a "higher realism," higher because more perceptive, more in accord with ultimate reality, more likely to win the long-run moral approval of societies professing allegiance to the common western, humane, Judeo-Christian traditions.

We still have not passed beyond the statement of a thesis and a definition of elementary terminology. There now remains the much more important task of seeing to what degree the evidence of Wilson's career supports my generalization. We obviously do not have time to review all the important events of Wilson's long and active career in a brief essay. On the other hand, we cannot concentrate our attention on one aspect without running the risks of distortion. President Wilson actually had three separate public careers: as university president and educational statesman, as a domestic leader concerned with problems of political and economic reconstruction in the United States, and, finally, as a world statesman who attempted to give leadership to a movement for the reconstruction of the international community. He made large and seemingly different contributions in each field. And yet we must try to view his career and labors as a whole, for he was fundamentally the same man throughout. His "higher realism" was no less a force in his leadership at home than abroad.

It was evident in a striking way in the first contributions that he made as a public leader, as president of Princeton University from 1902 to 1910. There were, first, the things that he did and tried to do for Princeton: his introduction of a systematic and meaningful course of undergraduate study, and his positive repudiation of a chaotic free-elective system; his creation of the preceptorial, or conference, method of instruction to supplement the lecture system; and his proposal for the reorganization of undergraduate social life in order to elevate the intellectual life of the university. By such plans and by his own inspiration, he not only transformed Princeton, but also helped to transform higher education in the United States.

And yet Wilson made his greatest contributions in the field of education more by the things that he stood for than by what he did. For one thing, he stood for standards and academic integrity. For another, he had an exalted concept of the university and college and the role that they play in preparing men and women for the nation's service because they were dedicated to the cause of truth and the intellectual enrichment of mankind. Finally during an era of increasing specialization and degradation of undergraduate curricula by the introduction of all sorts of so-called useful programs of study, Wilson never ceased to remind fellow teachers and administrators that their first job was to help to perpetuate the cultural traditions upon which western civilization rested, not to teach students how to make money.

Who, we are entitled to ask, were the true "realists" in educational policy? Were they the alleged realists of Wilson's time, the sincere devotees of the new so-called progressive concepts and faddists, who were then beginning their long attack upon traditional studies and destroying the unity of university curricula? To ask the question is almost to answer it. The entire drive in American higher education during the past twenty years toward recovery of standards and unity in curricula and against the vulgarization that followed the widespread introduction of so-called useful courses of study—this entire movement, so full of promise, is testimony to the higher realism of Wilson's leadership in the academic world.

It was the same, I would suggest, with Wilson's leadership during his second career as governor of New Jersey from 1911 to 1913 and President of the United States from 1913 to 1921. He came to political leadership at one of the most critical junctures in American history, at the high tide of what American historians call the progressive movement. For more than a quarter of a century, the American people had been in revolt in city, state, and nation against corruption and venality among officeholders, irresponsibility on all levels of government, and, above all, the emergence and spread of great aggregations of economic power among railroads, banks, corporations, and so on, which were uncontrolled and often repudiated any responsibility to the people as a whole. This revolt was at the point of culmination at the very time Wilson was catapulted into political life in 1910. And because this was true the American people were now confronted with certain choices that would determine their future political system and the role that government would hereafter play in making fundamental economic decisions.

There was, first, the choice concerning the reconstruction of the American political system. Some so-called realists of the time argued cogently from the facts that the very concept and structure of representative government were fatally defective, and that the answer lay either in direct democracy or in concentration of political power in fewer hands. "Realists" on the other side, eager to preserve a status quo that benefited their own economic interests, argued just as convincingly that the American constitutional system, with its diffusion and separation of powers, was the most nearly perfect form of government on earth.

There was, second, the choice concerning the role that government should play in economic life. At the one extreme were the "realists" who, talking in terms of immutable economic law, defended traditional American policies of laissez faire in an effort to protect their privileged position. At the other extreme were "realists" with a greater popular appeal—men who demanded a sweeping extension of the power of government to bridle all hitherto uncontrolled economic interests. Some of these were socialists, ready to abandon capitalism in the major sectors of the economy altogether. Others were progressives who believed in capitalism but argued that it had reached a permanent phase of semi-monopolistic maturity in the United States and could be saved only by instituting sweeping and rigorous public controls over all important areas of national economic life.

It was Woodrow Wilson's privilege to play a decisive role in the determination of these choices. To the "realists" who had despaired of representative government in the cities and states, he replied more by example than by precept—by giving a spectacular example of responsible leadership in action as governor of New Jersey. By making representative government work on the local level, he, along with the company of other leaders at the time, guaranteed its survival. To the "realists" (and he had earlier been among them) who had proclaimed the incapacity of the presidential-congressional system to cope with the great problems of national administration, Wilson responded both by reasoned word and striking deed, by transforming the office of President from that of an aloof presiding official into incomparably the most powerful force in the American constitutional system—the force that gave unity and direction not only to the other branches of the federal government but to public opinion as well. This, we can now see, was the "higher realism" of a man who well understood the weaknesses of the American institutional structure but who knew the fundamental strength of the American democracy far better than most so-called realists of his time.

I think that it is fair to say that President Wilson demonstrated the same kind of long-run wisdom, or "higher realism," in leading the American people to adoption of new policies for the regulation of economic life. He rejected the arguments both of defenders of the status quo and of proponents of violent change as being unsound in principle and unacceptable to the majority of the people. And he (along with his supporters in Congress) instituted a series of measures to impose increased public direction and control, but also to balance private initiative with public regulation in order to stimulate the enormous latent competitive energies of the people. In short, he laid the solid foundations of the present mixed American system of political economy, which, to the amazement and bafflement of many Europeans, works so curiously and so well. Viewing the subsequent development of the American economy within the framework erected by President Wilson and his colleagues, I think that we would have to conclude that Wilson's solution was the only "realistic" one that could have been adopted. It saved American capitalism by making it socially responsible and hence acceptable to the people, without, however, impeding the forces that are essential for growth in the capitalistic system.

I am sure that in talking about Wilson's "higher realism" in meeting domestic challenges, I have simply been saying things and making judgments with which virtually every historian of the United States would readily agree. It is precisely this "higher realism" that has entitled Wilson to rank, by the agreement of American historians, among the four or five most successful presidents in our history. In talking about Wilson's policies and contributions in the realm of foreign affairs, I am, I know, on more controversial ground.

Wilson was magnificently prepared for leadership in internal affairs by long study of American history and institutions. He had little if any preparation for leadership in the world at large; indeed, at the outset of his tenure in the White House he had no serious interest in foreign affairs. At the outset and later he made mistakes that still seriously impair his record. Even so, I cannot but conclude that President Wilson on the whole showed the same kind of wisdom and long-range vision and understanding—in short, "higher realism"—in his third career as international statesman as he had already revealed in his first two careers at home. This, I know, is a big statement, and I would like to preface it with a few generalizations about Wilson's thought and character as a diplomatist in order to lay foundations for some later observations.

The first is the most obvious and the one with which most historians would agree, namely, that President Wilson was, as I have already said, above all an idealist in the conduct of foreign affairs, one who subordinated immediate goals and material interests to what he considered to be superior ethical standards and moral purposes. His idealism was perhaps best revealed in his thinking about the purposes that the United States should serve in the world. The mission of America, he said over and over and sincerely believed, was not a mission of aggrandizement of material power but one of service to mankind. It was a mission of peace, of sacrifice, of leading the nations into a new international community organized to achieve right ends. Second, all of Wilson's thinking about international relations was conditioned, in general, by a loathing for war and, in particular, by a conviction that physical force should never be used to achieve selfish and material aims. Third, Wilson was actually in many ways "realistic," even by conventional standards, in his thinking about and methods in the conduct of foreign relations. For example, he used armed force in the classic way to achieve certain diplomatic objectives in Mexico and the Caribbean. He understood the meaning of the term "balance of power." He was keenly aware of the relevance of material interests and had few illusions about the fundamental bases of international behavior. It is, one must say, the sheerest nonsense to talk about him as an impractical idealist and visionary. Fourth, while admitting that there were times when a nation has no recourse but to use armed force in international disputes, and while using force himself on behalf of the American government on certain occasions, President Wilson never permitted war's neuroses and fascinations either to derange his reason or to obscure the political objectives for which force was being used. Hence he was never the victim of that greatest twentieth-century delusion, that it is necessary to win wars even at the risk of losing everything for which wars are fought.

This is a very imperfect characterization of the thought and character of Wilson the diplomatist, but it may help us to understand his policies during the greatest tragedy of the modern epoch and the event that raised the gravest challenges to his leadership—the First World War. It was for Wilson a period with three distinct stages: the period of American neutrality, from August 1914 to April 1917; the period of American belligerency, from April 1917 to November 1918; and the period of peacemaking, from November 1918 to June 1919. The challenges of each period were different, but he met them all, on the whole, with the same "higher realism" that had characterized his leadership at home.

His policies during the first period can best be briefly described by saying that, from the outbreak of the war in Europe to the beginning of the German unlimited submarine campaign in early 1917, President Wilson tried as hard as any person could have done to be neutral, to make the necessary accommodations to the exercise of belligerent power, and to engage in stern defense of American rights only when they could not, because fundamental human principles were involved, be compromised.

Some of the recent American "realists" have joined the older English and French critics in charging Wilson with impractical idealism precisely because he did follow such a course—because he did not rally the American people to preparation for what they have said was an inevitable participation; because he conducted long and patient negotiations to avoid a break with Germany; because he did not undertake large and early measures of assistance to the Allies and thus help to shorten the duration of Europe's agony; because he refused throughout the period of American neutrality even to align the American people and their government morally on the Allied side.

Looking back upon the final outcome, as we are entitled to do, we well might wonder who the true realists were during this period: so-called realists, or President Wilson, who in an almost uncanny way kept himself immune from the emotional hysterias and passions that seized other men; who believed that the causes of the war were so complex and remote that is was impossible to assess the blame for it; who, overborne by the tragedy of the event, fought desperately to preserve American neutrality so that he could perform the healing task of reconciliation once the nations of Europe had come to some sense; who believed that an enduring peace could come only through a "peace without victory," a "peace between equals"? Who were the deluded men who had lost sight of reality? The European leaders who thought that they could win decisive victories on the battlefields and on or under the seas, and who thought they could impose their nations' wills upon other great peoples? Or Wilson, who thought that they were momentarily mad?

The climactic confrontation, the supreme reckoning between so-called realists and the alleged impractical idealist, came once the United States had been forced into the conflict and Germany was defeated. It did not occur earlier, because the British and French leaders had refused to permit it to occur before the Armistice was safely signed. But it could not then be long postponed, for the Allied leaders had matured their plans, and President Wilson had meanwhile formed a peace program of his own and announced it to the world in the Fourteen Points address and other speeches.

There is no need to review the turbulent events of the Paris Peace Conference here. They are familiar enough, to begin with; but a detailed account of them now would obscure my larger purpose—to look back upon the Paris settlement and, while looking back, to attempt to see who the true realists were. The supreme task of the victors at Paris in 1919 was, obviously, to work out a peace settlement and reconstruct an international order that could endure. It had to be a peace that could survive the ebbing of passions and hatreds that consumed Europe in 1919. It had to be a peace that could survive because it could command the approval of the German people. Above all, it had to be the kind of settlement that would endure because it could retain the long-run support of the American and English peoples, even the French people. The necessity of constructing this kind of settlement was, as we can now see clearly, the supreme reality of peacemaking in 1919. We must, therefore, judge men and measures at the Paris Conference according to whether they met this test or not.

By this criterion I do not see how any fair historian can but conclude that the so-called realists at Paris—the dedicated if cynical Clemenceau, concerned only about the future security of France; the well-intentioned Lloyd George, who had given so many hostages to war passions at home and to the Commonwealth that he was no longer a free man; and the Italians, Sonnino and Orlando, eager only for spoils—how could they be called anything other than sublime irrationalists and dreamers? Theirs was a dream, a nightmare, of unreality. Given the task of reconstructing Europe and preventing a future war, they would have responded by attempting to perpetuate the division of Europe and by making a new war almost inevitable.

On the other side and standing usually in solitary if splendid isolation was the alleged impractical idealist fighting for the only kind of settlement that had any chance of survival—for a peace of reconciliation, for disarmament by victors as well as vanquished, against annexations and indemnities, and for a new international organization that would include former enemy states as active members from the beginning. Over and over he warned that this was the only kind of peace that would prove acceptable to the American people in the short run and to the moral opinion of the world in the long run, in short, the only kind of settlement that could endure. It should require little reference to events that followed the Paris Conference to demonstrate the "higher realism" of President Wilson's views.

If proof is needed on specific points, one could cite, for example, Wilson's point of view on the problem of reparations. Over and over he insisted, and with a steadfast consistency, that reparations should be compensation for specific willful damage only, not indemnity; that the Germans should not be saddled with a debt that was heavier than they could carry; and that there should be a time limit to the obligation that the German nation should be forced to assume. What the Allied leaders demanded and finally obtained is well known to this audience. What the realistic solution of this problem was is now too obvious for comment. Or, as a second example, one might cite Wilson's attitude toward the Russian Revolution—how he saw the deeply rooted causes of that cataclysm and the futility of any western effort to suppress it by military force; and how the realism of his attitude contrasted with the egregious folly of so-called realists who thought that it lay within their power to change the course of Russian history.

The result of the clash between European so-called realism and Wilsonian so-called idealism was of course the Treaty of Versailles, that compromise that violated some of the terms of the agreement by which the Germans had stopped fighting and made a mockery of some of the principal planks in the American President's peace program. Why, it is fair to ask, did President Wilson permit such a peace to be made and sign the treaty embodying it? The answer, I submit, is that it was "higher realism" that drove him to this difficult decision. Having won many of the things for which he had been fighting, he had to give as well as to take, for he could not impose his will upon his colleagues. He signed the Versailles Treaty in the conviction that the passage of time and the Treaty's new creation, the League of Nations, would almost certainly operate to rectify what he knew were the mistakes of the peacemakers. He signed the Versailles Treaty, in short, because he believed that it was the best settlement possible in the circumstances of 1919.

What President Wilson hoped would occur did of course in large part take place during the 1920s and early 1930s, even though alleged realists in the United States combined with authentic visionaries to repudiate Wilson's work and prevent their government from playing the role of mediating leadership within the League of Nations of which Wilson had dreamed. The great tragedy of the postwar period was not that the Versailles Treaty was imperfect. It was that the forces of reconciliation could not operate rapidly enough without American leadership in the League, that France and Great Britain lacked the will to defend the treaty alone during the 1930s and, above all, that the German people submitted to demonic forces that promised a speedy rectification of all the alleged injustices of Versailles. But this is precisely what President Wilson, in another flash of "higher realism," predicted would occur if the so-called realists, both in the United States and in Europe, continued to have their way.

That is the age-old question, whether the so-called realists or the higher realists shall have their way in determination of national and international policies. President Wilson survives as a more powerful force in history than when he lived because he gave us the supreme demonstration in the twentieth century of higher realism in statesmanship. This, obviously, was no accident. Woodrow Wilson's "higher realism" was the product of insight and wisdom informed by active Christian faith. He was not, fundamentally, a moralizer, as he so often seemed to be, but a man who lived in faith, trying to be guided by the Holy Spirit in meeting the complex problems of a changing nation and world. Using one of his own metaphors, we can say that the light of Heaven gleamed upon his sword. His precepts and ideals will be relevant so long as democracy endures and so long as men seek after a new international community organized for peace and the advancement of mankind.

AFTERWORD

After twenty-five years of additional research on Wilson and his time, I have concluded that this chapter still stands as a fair evaluation and that I have no desire to revise it, except to make a few mainly stylistic changes. A number of fine monographs and biographical studies since 1970 have, it seems to me, elaborated and confirmed the interpretation of Wilson set forth in "The Higher Realism." This is true of such books (to mention only a few) as John Milton Cooper, Jr., *The Warrior and the Priest: Woodrow Wilson and Theodore Roosevelt* (1983); the essays by eminent Wilson scholars in Arthur S. Link, *Woodrow Wilson and a Revolutionary World, 1913–1921* (1982), to which I contributed only a foreword; Arthur S. Link, with the assistance of Manfred F. Boemeke, translator and editor, *The Deliberations of the Council of Four (March 24–June 28, 1919): Notes of the Official Interpreter, Paul Mantoux*, 2 vols. (1992); Antony Lentin, *Lloyd George, Woodrow Wilson and the Guilt of Germany: An Essay in the Pre-History of Appeasement* (1984); Betty Miller Unterberger, *The United States, Revolutionary Russia, and the Rise of Czechoslovakia* (1989); David R. Woodward, *Trial by Friendship: Anglo-American Relations, 1917–1918* (1993); Thomas J. Knock, *To End All Wars: Woodrow Wilson and the Quest for a New World Order* (1992); and August Heckscher, *Woodrow Wilson: A Biography* (1991). If anyone wants a good illustration of Wilson's higher realism in dealing with Central Europe and Russia, let him or her read Professor Unterberger's book. Also, cautionary for those who still believe that Wilson was a naive idealist are two books by Frederick S. Calhoun: *Power and Principle: Armed Intervention in Wilsonian Foreign Policy* (1986) and *Uses of Force and Wilsonian Foreign Policy* (1993).

This historiographical tidal wave has, if I may say so, expanded and complemented what I said in "The Higher Realism of Woodrow Wilson." But most gratifying to me are the recent words by George F. Kennan, one of the early "realist" critics of Wilson:

I now view Wilson . . . as a man who like so many other people of broad vision and acute sensitivities, was ahead of his time, and did not live long enough to know that great and commanding relevance many of his ideas would acquire before this century was out. In this sense, I have to correct or modify, at this stage of my own life, many of the impressions I had about him at an earlier stage. In his vision of the future needs of world society, I now see Wilson as ahead of any other statesman of his time.[1]

As we enter the post–Cold War era, when international leaders are struggling to establish a new and better world order, even Wilson's critics agree that he set the agenda for future foreign policy initiatives. That agenda is undergirded and motivated by the following Wilsonian assumptions:

- Aggressive war cannot be tolerated and has to be met and forcefully overcome by the collective action of peace loving nations through the United Nations.
- Every people with a common history, language, geographical identity, etc., enjoy the inherent right to self-determination, that is, independence and the right to govern themselves without the threat of intimidation, subjugation, or of being bartered about (in Wilson's words) in the now discredited game of the balance of power.
- As for the United States, its foreign policy should be devoted to the advancement of democracy and human rights and the cooperation of nations and the preservation of peace through the United Nations.
- Most important, nations, and the men and women who lead them, are subject to the rule of law and high ethical standards just as individuals are.

This incomplete list of assumptions does not encapsulate Wilson's "higher realism" in statecraft and foreign affairs. But their acceptance by right-minded people makes it clear that the main elements of Wilson's "higher realism" are still standards by which we judge the relations of nations one to another.

NOTE

1. Comments on the paper entitled "Kennan versus Wilson by Professor Thomas J. Knock," in J. M. Cooper, Jr., and Charles E. Neu, eds., *The Wilson Era: Essays in Honor of Arthur S. Link* (Arlington Heights, IL: Harlan Davidson, 1991), p. 330.

7

Responsibility to Protect: Preventing Genocide and Mass Atrocities

Alex J. Bellamy

Although the phrase "responsibility to protect" was first coined only in 2001, the principle is the product of long-standing efforts to identify and define crimes that have "shocked the conscience of mankind" and to protect populations from them. The story of its emergence starts in the shadow of the Holocaust when the call of "Never Again" galvanized efforts to ensure that these horrors were never repeated. Advocates, such as Raphael Lemkin, a Jewish lawyer who campaigned tirelessly on the cause, and some state leaders hoped to build a new international community based on the United Nations that would criminalize and prevent the unspeakable crimes committed by the Nazis and their allies.

In 1947, the newly established UN General Assembly approved the Genocide Convention, which prohibited the crime of genocide, awarded all states a responsibility to prevent it, and demanded that they punish the perpetrators of these crimes—as the wartime allies had done through the Nuremberg and Tokyo trials.[1] Genocide refers to one subset of atrocity crimes—those committed with the intent to destroy a whole group. Recently, the International Court of Justice (ICJ) judged that as a result of this convention, all states have a legal responsibility to do what they can, within existing law, to prevent genocide. Specifically, the court found that states had a responsibility to take positive action to prevent genocide when they have prior knowledge about its likely commission and the capacity to influence the suspected would-be perpetrators.

Two years after the Genocide Convention, the four Geneva Conventions (1949) codified the laws of war and identified deliberate attacks on civilians and prisoners as "war crimes." The subsequent Protocols (1977) to the Geneva Convention established the immunity of all noncombatants, whether in international or noninternational armed conflicts, from the intentional use of armed force against them and required that parties cooperate with one another to prevent violations of the law. More recently, the Rome Statute of the International Criminal Court (ICC) (1998) extended some of these provisions to contexts outside of armed conflict under the rubric of "crimes against humanity," while the International Criminal Tribunal for Yugoslavia (ICTY) confirmed that the practice of "ethnic cleansing" constituted one such crime.

However, international practice has seldom lived up to the demands of international law. With concern for human dignity trumped by the global struggle for geopolitical supremacy during the Cold War, mass atrocities remained quite common and, despite these advances in international law, the perpetrators often acted with impunity. Communist regimes used mass violence against civilian populations to eradicate "bad elements," impose their authority, and radically transform societies in breathtakingly short periods of time. At various times, Stalin, Mao and Pol Pot, Communist leaders in the Soviet Union, China, and Cambodia, respectively, all used mass violence to achieve their goals, resulting in the premature deaths of tens of millions of people. Historians argue about whether Stalin killed more people than Hitler, but whichever was the bloodiest, it is a relatively close run thing. New research on the scale of mass killing in Maoist China, which accounted for several million people before the end of the Cold War, might prompt us to the conclusion that no people have been killed in larger number than the Chinese at the hands of their own government. While smaller in absolute numbers, the lunacy of Khmer Rouge rule in Cambodia led to the death of more than one-quarter of that country's population in just three and a half years. When Vietnam invaded and put an end to the slaughter, it was lambasted for violating Cambodia's sovereignty and subjected to economic sanctions—a clear signal of how low a priority stopping genocide and mass killing was until quite recently. Other Communist regimes, including that in North Korea and several former regimes in Eastern Europe, were, in some periods, equally brutal.

But it was not just Communist regimes that used extreme violence against civilian populations to prosecute their own political agendas. On the eve of the Korean War, South Korea's military regime rounded up and executed suspected Communists and their families. Precisely how many were killed will never be known, but estimates suggest that at the very least, some 100,000 people were killed. The massacres were barely reported at the time. A decade later, nationalist extremists in Indonesia and their allies massacred approximately 600,000 suspected and actual Communists during a six-month spree in 1965–1966, raising barely a ripple of international press coverage, let alone condemnation. Similar stories could be told of right-wing regimes in Argentina, Chile, El Salvador, and Guatemala, though the sheer scale of killing was significantly less; and by the 1980s, these governments started to come under intense pressure to mend their ways. Nationalism and bloody self-interest, too, was a cause of mass killing—as with Pakistan's bloody suppression and potential genocide in East Pakistan (Bangladesh), Idi Amin's reign of terror in Uganda, recurrent ethnic massacres in Burundi and Rwanda, and the Biafran war in Nigeria.

Despite the advance of international laws prohibiting these crimes, very little was done to stop them—in part because Cold War politics trumped concern for human rights, with the result that perpetrators were often protected by one or other of the superpowers; and in part because sovereignty was judged to be a more important value than human rights.[2] It was hoped by some that the end of the Cold War would reverse these priorities and usher in a "New World Order," but these hopes were soon dashed.

During the 1990s, the gap between these international legal responsibilities in relation to the protection of populations from grave abuses and actual lived experience became more obvious. Genocide in Rwanda and Srebrenica; mass killing and ethnic cleansing in Angola, Bosnia, Burundi, Croatia, East Timor, Kosovo, Liberia, Sierra Leone, and Zaire/Congo; state repression in northern and southern Iraq; and acute state fragility and civil war leading to mass human suffering in Somalia exposed the hollowness of legal responsibilities in the face of armed groups willing and able to generate and use mass civilian suffering for their own ends. The international community was initially ill prepared to respond. UN peacekeepers recoiled in the face of the *genocidaires* in Rwanda, where 800,000 people were massacred in 100 days, and stood aside as Security Council–mandated "safe areas" collapsed in Bosnia—in Srebrenica in 1995, 7,000 men and boys were taken from a UN-guarded safe area and massacred; U.S. forces were hounded out of Mogadishu in Somalia, taking with them UN peacekeepers and any hope of delivering humanitarian aid to civilians; and political and diplomatic efforts were insufficient to stop Angola's slide back into war or the widely predicted mass violence that greeted East Timor's vote for independence. In addition to the immediate death tolls, these and other crises also created a global crisis of internal displacement, as up to 20 million people were forced from their homes but left unable to claim the protections afforded by international refugee law because they had not crossed international borders. Why, though, were governments so reluctant to act to fulfill their pledge of "Never Again"?

NEVER AGAIN ALL OVER AGAIN: RELUCTANT STATE ACTORS

There were at least three reasons why the pledge of "Never Again" was seldom matched with determined action. The first was the lingering power of state sovereignty. The international community is comprised of sovereign states that pursue their own interests (however defined), privilege domestic over foreign concerns, and generally cherish their legal right to determine their own affairs. Any account of contemporary world politics has to take this reality as a starting point. In the foreseeable future, most states are not likely to support limits on their sovereignty: sovereignty, which in many parts of the world was hard won from colonial powers, is not likely to be given away easily. Nor are most states going to become cosmopolitans overnight or prove able to reconcile their different interests and perspectives in every situation.

This has several ramifications. First, states—especially those experiencing genocide and mass atrocities—are protective of their own sovereignty and can impose limitations on international action. Of course, the UN Security Council has the authority to override these limits and enforce its decisions, but it has seldom chosen to do so for a range of practical, political, and prin-cipled reasons. It is worth observing that when the Council has extended its authority to its farthest reach by establishing transitional governments under its own authority, it has always done so with the express consent—indeed, at the invitation of—the relevant parties. Transitional administrations in Eastern Slavonia, Bosnia, Kosovo, and East Timor were all established with the consent of the parties involved.

During NATO's intervention in Libya, the UN began planning for a post-conflict reconstruction mission. The plans were leaked, and Libya's new government declared that it would not accept an international peacekeeping mission. While that might certainly have suited Western governments eager to avoid long-term entanglements in Libya, it bears mentioning that the ini-tial blockage to an international mission came from the Libyan authorities and not from international society.

Second, it is common to read that failures of protection are failures of political will. But what is political will, and why does it "fail"? Political will works in at least two ways to inhibit international action to protect people from mass atrocities. The first, and least discussed, is not about "failure" at all. It has to do with the *presence* of countervailing interest. In other words, we fail to protect civilians not just because those with the capacity to do so are reluctant to incur the costs, but also because they sometimes believe that sup-porting or shielding the perpetrators of mass atrocities serves their own best interests. For example, the link between China's interest in Sudanese oil and arms sales and its obstinate refusal to impose sanctions or other measures on that country's government despite its clear responsibility for war crimes, crimes against humanity, and possibly even genocide in Darfur is well known. More recently, Russia's decisions to repeatedly block UN action on Syria were prompted by its interest in protecting a friendly regime, preventing the spread of radical Islamism, and supporting its arms export business. The West has also put its own interests ahead of protection needs from time to time. During the long Cold War against communism, it supplied arms to the Indonesian government just as that government slaughtered Communists and brutally suppressed East Timor. In the early 1980s, the United States supported, funded, and armed the genocidal regime in Guatemala and prevented international efforts to end the conflict there as well as in El Salvador. Motivated mainly by its interest in preserving Francophone influence in Africa, France funded and armed the Hutu government in Rwanda and sup-plied a substantial proportion of the machetes used for genocide. At the very least, France's position muddied the Council's waters when it came to responding to the Rwandan genocide in 1994.

Sometimes, therefore, political will prompts states to protect or assist the perpetrators of mass atrocities. When those states are permanent veto-wielding members of the UN Security Council, the interests of one can make it impossible for all the others to marshal effective responses to mass atrocities.

The second, and more commonly discussed, aspect of political will relates to the fact that states are primarily responsible for the well-being of their own citizens. As such, they are likely to prove reluctant to spend precious tax income and risk soldiers' lives in order to save foreigners from mass atroc-ities in faraway places. The costs of decisive action to end mass atrocities are rarely small—a particular problem in an age of austerity. The NATO-led intervention in Libya, for example, cost British taxpayers between £300 mil-lion and £400 million—the equivalent of servicing nearly 3,000 hospital beds for a year. Both France and Britain came close to exhausting their stockpiles of very expensive precision-guided munitions, and the cost of replacing those munitions places a heavy burden on already stretched national budgets. And while public opinion in democratic countries might tolerate the deployment of military forces to protect people in other counties from grave inhumanity, it does not look kindly on more than very modest casualties in these opera-tions because they are seen as "wars of choice" and not necessity. The large cost in life incurred by NATO's intervention in Afghanistan without a defini-tive success in either military or humanitarian outcomes is likely only to exac-erbate this tendency.

However understandable it may be from the perspective of domestic poli-tics, the lack of willingness to commit resources to the protection of people from mass atrocities can have devastating effects. Some were detailed by the Report of the Independent Inquiry into the UN's failure to prevent or halt the Rwandan genocide in 1994. The inquiry found that this abject failure was caused by "the lack of resources and political commitment devoted to developments in Rwanda ... There was a persistent lack of political will by Member States to act, or to act with enough assertiveness." The absence of will affected the UN's own response and "was also evident in the recurrent dif-ficulties to get the necessary troops" for the UN's peacekeeping mission in Rwanda.[3] The "overriding failure" of will in Rwanda resulted in the deployment of international forces on the ground that lacked the resources they needed to protect people from genocide. The UN's mission there was smaller than had been recommended, slow to deploy owing to the reluctance of states to contribute effective troops, and debilitated by administrative difficulties. When troops did arrive to join the UN mission, they were often inadequately trained and equipped. Both the UN and RAND found that a properly mandated and configured force numbering around 2,500 would have been sufficient to stop the genocide in its tracks. But the world could not muster these resources when it mattered most.

The UN's failure in Rwanda was a failure of political will. For largely political reasons, its mission to Rwanda was conceived as a small, cheap, and consent-dependent one despite advice at the time that this would prove sorely inadequate. It was a tragic coincidence of history that the UN's mandate for Rwanda was decided upon just one week after the killing of American peacekeepers in Somalia in the now famous "Black Hawk Down" incident. At that time, the U.S. administration and probably the public as well was understandably in no mood to support or pay for the dispatch of more peacekeepers to Africa.

There is much debate about the capacity of public opinion to influence political will and push governments toward greater activism in response to mass atrocities. The crisis in Darfur, for example, gave cause for the emergence of a major global campaign (the "Save Darfur Coalition"), which tried to persuade Western governments, and the United States especially, to take action. To be fair, the campaign succeeded in putting and keeping the issue on the international agenda for longer than it otherwise might have been. Although slow and inadequate, the world did eventually muster the will to deploy peacekeepers, refer the matter to the International Criminal Court, sponsor a series of major peace initiatives, and organize one of the largest-ever humanitarian operations. These efforts, the latter especially, undoubtedly saved lives and might not have happened without determined public agitation in the West.

However, the capacity of public opinion to influence foreign policy and generate will where there is none is limited. The so-called "CNN effect" has never pushed a democratic government to do something it did not want to do. The simple and brutal reason for this is that very few, if any, voters change the way they vote over a government's record of responding or not responding to foreign atrocities. How many American Democratic Party voters voted Republican *because* of the failure to intervene in Rwanda? Or Syria? The truth is that atrocities in foreign places do not rank highly on any national list of political priorities. As a result, governments—especially democratic ones— are understandably risk averse. In most cases, as in Kosovo, governments themselves lead public opinion on foreign affairs. In others, such as Darfur, public pressure might push governments to take diplomatic or other forms of action that do not incur material or diplomatic costs, but there are real limits to the costs they will be prepared to incur. One simple rule of thumb is that political activism and public opinion have greater effect where the political, financial, and material costs associated with the desired policy are low. As expected costs increase, so the capacity of activists to persuade governments to shoulder them diminishes.

The third source of limitation is prudential considerations. Even when states have genuine moral concerns about mass atrocities in distant lands, prudential considerations may counsel against the adoption of some of the policies that might be proposed in response. Sometimes, leaders judge that a proposed policy will do more harm than good, for instance by provoking a wider conflict, jeopardizing the support of groups thought necessary for the delivery of vital humanitarian assistance, or creating false hopes of a military victory that encourage the parties to avoid good-faith negotiations. Other times, states might simply prioritize other humanitarian concerns. Alternatively, they might calculate that they lack the capacity to intervene effectively. These considerations are evident in most debates about how best to respond to protection emergencies.

When the UN Security Council debated what to do about Kosovo, in 1999, prudential considerations were at least as important as principled ones. A few days after NATO began its bombing campaign over Yugoslavia, Russia introduced a draft resolution to the Security Council condemning the intervention. Russia's criticisms of NATO centered on two points. The first was that NATO did not have the authority to use force without authorization from the Security Council. Russia's second argument was that the intervention was likely to make the situation worse and hinder attempts to broker a settlement.

In relation to Darfur, where some 100,000 civilians were killed between 2003 and 2005 by militia aligned with the government of Sudan, those who preferred a cautious international approach argued that trying to coerce the Sudanese government would do more harm than good by provoking a wider crisis. It would also, they thought, jeopardize the pursuit of other goals such as a negotiated peace agreement to end the decades-long civil war between the government and the Sudanese People's Liberation Army (SPLA) in the south, a war that had claimed more than two million lives. Moreover, with ongoing commitments in Iraq, Afghanistan, and the Balkans, the West lacked the military capacity to intervene effectively, and few thought that Western intervention in another Arab-led country seemed like a good idea. No other group of states came forward to take up the mantle, even though regional responsibility is both a principle of the modern United Nations and the African Union, which also proved ineffective in its response to the crisis.

TOWARD R2P

As failures of protection mounted and the gap between "Never Again" and practices of protection turned into a chasm, states and international organizations began to learn the lessons of these failures and to develop new concepts such as the "protection of civilians" and "sovereignty as responsibility." Developments included the emergence of the concept of sovereignty as responsibility. Initial ideas about sovereignty as responsibility were developed by UN official Francis Deng and Roberta Cohen, an expert based at the Brookings Institution in Washington, D.C., in the context of the crisis of displacement in the mid-1990s. Deng was appointed as the UN Secretary-General's Special Representative on Internally Displaced Persons (IDPs) in 1993. IDPs faced dramatically increased rates of mortality, poverty, and human rights abuse, yet remained at the mercy of the state that had failed to protect them. Deng and Cohen developed the concept of sovereignty as responsibility as a diplomatic and moral tool to persuade states to allow IDPs access to humanitarian assistance and enjoyment of their human rights.[4] Simply put, the concept rested on the idea that sovereignty carried responsibilities as well as rights and that chief among those responsibilities was the state's duty to protect populations in its care. When states are unable to exercise this duty, they should request international assistance. If they do not, then they should be held accountable.[5]

From this, R2P derived its focus on "responsibility," the notion that the primary responsibility to protect rests with the sovereign states, and that the purpose of external action should be to assist the state to fulfill its obligations and, failing that, to provide protection to vulnerable populations where possible.

At the same time, a number of regional organizations adopted their own initiatives that contributed to the emergence of R2P. Most notably, the Constitutive Act of the African Union (AU), adopted in 2000, gave the organization a right to intervene in the affairs of its member states in matters relating to genocide and crimes against humanity. The AU also developed its own peacekeeping capacities and adopted a protection mandate in Darfur (2003). It deployed a small peacekeeping operation in Darfur (AMIS), which, while too overstretched and underresourced to provide comprehensive protection, nevertheless made it more difficult for the parties to get away with large-scale and systematic attacks on civilians. The EU established and deployed high readiness brigades in response to protection crises, and in the mid-1990s, the OSCE established its High Commissioner for National Minorities to assist states under stress. NATO also incorporated the protection of civilians into its crisis management work.[6]

Often caught on the front line of emergencies caused by armed conflict, natural disasters, and poverty, humanitarian relief agencies increasingly recognized the limits of traditional approaches to humanitarian action that distributed aid on the basis of need and neutrality without regard for the underlying politics. Sometimes, this approach created the phenomenon of the "well fed dead"—civilians given food, housing, and medical relief by humanitarians only to be killed or displaced again by armed conflicts. Sometimes, humanitarians inadvertently made matters worse by aiding *genocidaires* and unwittingly providing bases for armed groups, as happened in eastern Democratic Republic of the Congo after the Rwandan genocide.[7] In response, many humanitarian organizations, including Oxfam and CARE, adopted "protection" as one of their core goals, promoting the idea that the protection of people from egregious crimes ought to be part of the international community's core business.[8]

High-profile peacekeeping failures in Rwanda, Bosnia, and elsewhere prompted fresh thinking about the protection roles and responsibilities of peacekeepers. In 2000, the UN's Panel on Peace Operations (the so-called "Brahimi Report") argued that peacekeepers who witnessed violence against civilians should be "presumed to be authorized to stop it, within their means." Starting in 1999, with the UN Mission in Sierra Leone (UNAMSIL), the Security Council has, with increasing regularity, employed Chapter VII of the UN Charter to authorize peacekeepers to use "all necessary means" to protect civilians. Today, most UN peacekeeping operations have a protection mandate.[9]

All these developments pushed the UN Security Council to think more seriously about the protection of people from atrocities. In 1998, at the request of Canada, the Council requested a report from the Secretary-General on how the UN might improve the protection of civilians in armed conflict. The following year, it adopted Resolution 1265 expressing its "willingness" to consider "appropriate measures" in response to "situations of armed conflict where civilians are being targeted or where humanitarian assistance to civilians is being deliberately obstructed." Periodic reports of the Secretary-General on the protection of civilians in armed conflict have become a recurrent feature of the Council's work, and through this it has, among other things, pledged to work towards an end to impunity, requested that member states ratify key human rights treaties, adopted an aide memoire on protection, and demanded humanitarian access.

These and other initiatives allowed the then UN Secretary-General, Kofi Annan, to declare in 1999 that "state sovereignty, in its most basic sense, is being redefined ... States are now widely understood to be the servants of their people, not vice versa."[10] This emerging conception of sovereignty as entailing responsibilities clashed, however, with more traditional ways of understanding it. Since 1648 at least, sovereignty was commonly understood as entailing a right to noninterference, a traditional plank of international law that was reaffirmed in Article 2(7) of the UN Charter. This raised the difficult question of how the international community should respond to situations in which the state failed to protect its own population from conscience-shocking crimes or when the state itself was among the principal perpetrators of such crimes. These questions were brought into sharp focus by the crisis in Kosovo in 1998–1999. When international negotiations, sanctions, and observers failed to stem the tide of violence, which included the systematic ethnic cleansing of Kosovar Albanians by Yugoslav government forces, NATO decided to intervene militarily despite not having a UN Security Council mandate to do so. The intervention triggered a major debate on the circumstances in which the use of force for human protection purposes might be justifiable, the intricacies of which were reflected in the findings of an international commission on the issue, which found that NATO's actions in Kosovo were "illegal but legitimate."[11]

At issue was the relationship between the state and its own population, the credibility of the international community's commitment to very basic standards of human rights, and the role of both regional security organizations and the UN in the twenty-first century. The dilemmas involved were set out most succinctly by Kofi Annan in his 1999 Address to the General Assembly:

> To those for whom the greatest threat to the future of international order is the use of force in the absence of a Security Council mandate, one might ask ... in the context of Rwanda: If, in those dark days and hours leading up to the genocide, a coalition of States had been prepared to act in defence of the Tutsi population, but did not receive prompt Council authorization, should such a coalition have stood aside and allowed the horror to unfold?
>
> To those for whom the Kosovo action heralded a new era when States and groups of States can take military action outside the established mechanisms for enforcing international law, one might ask: Is there not a danger of such interventions undermining the imperfect, yet resilient, security system created after the Second World War, and of setting dangerous precedents for future interventions without a clear criterion to decide who might invoke these precedents and in what circumstances?[12]

It was in part to find answers to these questions that Canada decided to establish an International Commission on Intervention and State Sovereignty (ICISS) in 2000. The ICISS was chaired by former Australian foreign minister Gareth Evans and Mohammed Sahnoun, a former Algerian diplomat who served the UN as special adviser on the Horn of Africa and special representative in Somalia and the Great Lakes of Africa. The commission's report, entitled *Responsibility to Protect*, was released in December 2001 and endorsed by Annan, who described it as "the most comprehensive and carefully thought-out response we have seen to date."[13] The ICISS insisted that states had a responsibility to protect their citizens from genocide, mass killing, and ethnic cleansing, and that when they proved either unwilling or unable to fulfill this duty, that responsibility was transferred to the international community. From this perspective, R2P comprised three interrelated sets of responsibilities: to prevent, react, and rebuild.[14] The commission identified proposals designed to strengthen the international community's effectiveness in each of these, including the articulation of a prevention toolkit, decision-making criteria for the use of force, and a hierarchy of international authority in situations where the Security Council was divided.

R2P would not have enjoyed such a rapid rise without the endorsement of Annan and his decision, taken in the wake of the oil-for-food scandal that rocked the credibility of both his own office and the UN more generally, to summon a world summit to consider proposals for reform of the UN. In preparation for the summit, Annan commissioned a high-level panel to examine the challenges confronting the organization and make recommendations as to how it might meet them. In its final report, the panel endorsed "the emerging norm that there is a responsibility to protect," supported the ICISS proposal for the establishment of criteria to guide decisions about the use of force, and called for the permanent members of the Security Council to exercise restraint in their use of veto in situations involving large-scale violence against civilians.[15] Annan adopted most of these recommendations in his own blueprint for reform, *In Larger Freedom*.[16] This put the concept squarely on the international agenda at the 2005 World Summit.

To summarize, R2P emerged out of the failure of international efforts to respond to episodes of genocide and mass atrocities in the 1990s. Developments in a range of fields—including peacekeeping, refugee and displacement work, humanitarian relief, international diplomacy, and regional action—in response to the widely felt failures to protect people from great harm in a number of different places, focused international attention on the protection of human life in situations of conscience-shocking inhumanity. The crises in Rwanda and Kosovo exposed two critical challenges related to the political will to act (Rwanda) and the authority on which action may be taken (Kosovo). The ICISS was established in response to these challenges, and its landmark report coined the phrase "responsibility to protect" and further developed earlier ideas about the state's primary responsibility to protect its own population and the role of the international community when it failed to do so.

RESPONSIBILITY TO PROTECT

R2P was unanimously endorsed by the 2005 World Summit, the largest ever gathering of heads of state and government. The summit's outcome document was later adopted as a General Assembly resolution. After several months of detailed consultation and negotiation carried out at the highest levels of government and the UN, world leaders unanimously adopted R2P at the UN World Summit. Under the heading "responsibility to protect," Paragraphs 138–140 of the Summit's Outcome Document declared that:

> 138. Each individual state has the responsibility to protect its populations from genocide, war crimes, ethnic cleansing and crimes against humanity. This responsibility entails the prevention of such crimes, including their incitement, through appropriate and necessary means. We accept that responsibility and will act in accordance with it. The international community should, as appropriate, encourage and help States to exercise this responsibility and support the United Nations in establishing an early warning capability.
>
> 139. The international community, through the United Nations, also has the responsibility to use appropriate diplomatic, humanitarian and other peaceful means, in accordance with Chapters VI and VIII of the Charter of the United Nations, to help protect populations from war crimes, ethnic cleansing and crimes against humanity. In this context, we are prepared to take collective action, in a timely and decisive manner, through the Security Council, in accordance with the Charter, including Chapter VII, on a case-by-case basis and in cooperation with relevant regional organizations as appropriate, should peaceful means be inadequate and national authorities manifestly fail to protect their populations from genocide, war crimes, ethnic cleansing and crimes against humanity. We stress the need for the General Assembly to continue consideration of the responsibility to protect populations from genocide, war crimes, ethnic cleansing and crimes against humanity and its implications, bearing in mind the principles of the Charter and international law. We also intend to commit ourselves, as necessary and appropriate, to helping States build capacity to protect their populations from genocide, war crimes, ethnic cleansing and crimes against humanity before crises and conflicts break out.
>
> 140. We fully support the mission of the Special Adviser of the Secretary-General on the Prevention of Genocide.

This commitment has been reaffirmed several times by the UN Security Council (Resolutions 1674 [2006], 1894 [2009], and 2150 [2014]), and the

General Assembly has committed itself to ongoing consideration of its implementation (A/RES/63/308). To understand precisely what states committed themselves to, it is important to bear six key points in mind in this regard

First, R2P is narrow in scope, but universal and enduring in its coverage. The principle applies everywhere, all the time. In other words, all states have a permanent responsibility to protect their populations from the four crimes. As UN Secretary-General Ban Ki-moon pointed out in 2012, the question is never one of whether or not R2P "applies"—because this wrongly implies that there are situations in which states do not have a responsibility to protect their populations—but of how best to realize its goals in any given situation. The concept is narrow, though, in that it relates only to the four crimes identified in the 2005 World Summit Outcome Document—genocide, war crimes, ethnic cleansing and crimes against humanity—and to their prevention. The concept does not relate to threats to human life stemming from natural disasters, diseases, armed conflict in general, or nondemocratic forms of government.[17]

Second, states have a responsibility to protect all populations under their care, not just citizens. Paragraphs 138 and 139 specifically refer to populations and not citizens. This can be significant in situations where states fail to protect sections of a population because they are not judged to be citizens, as in the case of the Muslim Rohingya in Myanmar.

Third, R2P is based on well-established principles of existing international law. The atrocity crimes to which it relates are enumerated in international law. As was noted at the beginning of the chapter, states already have obligations to: prevent and punish genocide, war crimes, and crimes against humanity; assist states to fulfill their obligations under international humanitarian law; and promote compliance with the law. In addition, the World Summit Outcome Document is clear in stating that R2P is to be implemented through the UN Charter. Nothing in the R2P principle permits states or regional organizations to violate the Charter, for example by intervening without a Security Council mandate.

Fourth, the World Summit Outcome Document calls explicitly for the prevention of the four crimes and their incitement. As such, prevention is at the core of R2P, with other measures contemplated only when prevention fails or (in line with Article 42 of the UN Charter) is thought likely to fail by the UN Security Council.

Fifth, reaffirming a principle of Security Council primacy since 1945, force may be used only when authorized by the UN Security Council and when other, peaceful, measures adopted under Chapters VI and VIII of the UN Charter are thought unlikely to succeed.

Sixth, member states declared their support for the mandate of the Special Adviser for the Prevention of Genocide and promised to support strengthening the UN's capacity for early warning. The Mandate of the Special Adviser for the Prevention of Genocide, appointed in 2004, included tasks directly related to early warning and assessment: (1) to collect existing information, in particular from within the UN system, relating to violations of human rights that could give rise, if nothing were done, to genocide; (2) to bring situations of concern to the Secretary-General and, through him, to the Security Council; (3) to make recommendations to the Security Council, through the Secretary-General, on actions to prevent or halt genocide; (4) to liaise with the UN system on activities for the prevention of genocide and to enhance the capacity of the UN system to analyze and manage relevant information.

Since its adoption in 2005, R2P has become part of the diplomatic language used, albeit unevenly and with patchy results, to prevent and respond to atrocity crimes. The practical use of R2P got off to a slow and discouraging start. In the almost five years between Security Council Resolution 1674 (2006) and Resolution 1970 on Libya (2009), the Council referred to the concept only once (though it did refer to R2P prior to Resolution 1674, in Resolution 1653 [2006] on the Great Lakes Region of Africa). This came in a highly contentious preambular paragraph in Resolution 1706 (2006) on the situation in Darfur, where Sudanese government forces and their notorious allies the "Janjaweed" militia had let rip a reign of terror resulting in the deaths of some 100,000 people and forced displacement of over two million more. Several Council members were cautious about the inclusion of R2P in the resolution (China abstained in the vote) and about the diplomatic pressure that was brought to bear to secure it. The diplomatic victory on Resolution 1706 proved to be pyrrhic. The resolution has gone down in history as one of the Council's worst ever because it mandated a peacekeeping operation that was never likely to be deployed.[18] What is more, the wounds of the diplomatic battle that preceded it ran so deep that the Council stayed well away from using R2P in the context of Darfur, or any other crisis for that matter. Perhaps a little unfairly, since the crisis preceded R2P, Darfur quickly became a "test case" for R2P. It was a test that the UN and international community were widely judged to have failed.

Although the Security Council backed away from R2P, there were signs that others remained committed to its goals. In late 2007, a dispute about the result of the presidential election spiraled into ethnic and tribal violence in Kenya, resulting in the killing of some 1,500 people and the forced displacement 300,000 more. The international community responded with a coordinated diplomatic effort. Kofi Annan was appointed mediator by the African Union. Approaching the situation "in the R2P prism," as he put it,

Annan persuaded the country's President, Mwai Kibaki, and main opponent, Raila Odinga, to conclude a power-sharing agreement and rein in the mobs. This diplomatic effort, couched squarely in R2P terms, pulled Kenya back from the brink of a terrible fate. It also provided a tangible demonstration of R2P's capacity to facilitate atrocity prevention through peaceful means.

Worse was to come in Sri Lanka in 2008–2009. In late 2008, Sri Lankan government forces launched a major offensive to eliminate the Tamil Tigers (LTTE), a terrorist organization proscribed in many Western countries. Amidst reports of mounting civilian casualties and indiscriminate force, the UN withdrew its staff from the region and, with only a few exceptions, failed to raise or condemn the violation of international human rights and humanitarian law by government forces. The Security Council could not muster the will even to meet formally on the crisis. Approximately 40,000 civilians were killed, the great majority as a result of government actions. A UN Panel of Inquiry later found that "events in Sri Lanka mark a grave failure of the UN to adequately respond to early warnings . . . to the detriment of hundreds of thousands of civilians and in contradiction with the principles and responsibilities of the UN."[19] This is a case I will return to later, hoping to better understand why the world failed so badly and how we might do better next time.

With the UN and its member states so hesitant to implement their 2005 commitment to R2P, few—if any—anticipated the role that the principle would play in the dramatic events of 2011. On December 17, 2010, Mohamed Bouazizi, a Tunisian street vendor, set himself alight in protest at repeated harassment by state authorities. This single act of protest sparked a region-wide revolution that came to be known as the "Arab Spring." In February 2011, the "Arab Spring" reached Libya. Protests there quickly turned into a major uprising that threatened to topple the dictator Muammar Gadhafi, who had ruled with an iron fist for over 40 years. Gadhafi's forces responded to the challenge with typical brutality, and the Libyan leader issued chilling threats of retribution reminiscent of the terms used to incite the Rwandan genocide nearly 20 years earlier.

The following month, in March 2011, the Security Council responded to the unfolding crisis by throwing almost its entire portfolio of preventive measures at the situation in Libya. Resolution 1970, which was adopted unanimously, referred specifically to R2P, demanded an immediate cessation of violence, established a political process aimed at finding a negotiated settlement, imposed targeted financial sanctions on the regime and an arms embargo, and referred the matter to the International Criminal Court for investigation. In sharp contrast to the bitterness of debates about R2P just five years earlier, the inclusion of R2P in Resolution 1970 was utterly uncontroversial.

When the Gadhafi regime failed to comply with the Council's demands and looked likely to topple the rebel stronghold of Benghazi and commit a massacre there, the Council took the unprecedented step of authorizing the use of force against a state to protect civilians from imminent danger, enforce a no-fly zone, and enforce an arms embargo (Resolution 1973). NATO and its allies hastily arranged a "coalition of the willing," which prevented the fall of Benghazi and the widely anticipated massacre there. The coalition then proceeded to intervene, with air power alone, in the ongoing struggle for control of the apparatus of the Libyan state. The conflict dragged on until the regime collapsed and Gadhafi was himself killed, provoking a new storm of controversy over the sanctioned use of forceful international intervention.

Libya marked the first time in its history that the Council had authorized the use of force for human protection purposes without the consent of the recognized government concerned. Although the Council had come close in the past, it had never before crossed the line.

A few days after the adoption of its landmark resolution on Libya, the Security Council unanimously adopted Resolution 1975 on Côte d'Ivoire. Having lost an election, the country's now former President, Laurent Gbagbo, refused to stand down. Following the advice of international election monitors, the Council declared Alassane Ouattarra to be the country's President and authorized the use of force to protect the civilian population. UN forces already stationed in Côte d'Ivoire as part of the UNOCI operation deployed to oversee an end to the country's civil war and transition to a new, democratic government acted alongside French forces to stop the escalating violence, remove Gbagbo, and allow the elected President to take his place at the head of the new government.

The Council's responses to the crises in Libya and Côte d'Ivoire, achieved without a single negative vote, were groundbreaking. They clearly demonstrated a newly found determination to act on the responsibility to protect populations from atrocity crimes, including through the use of force when necessary. But the responses proved highly controversial. Critics complained that NATO and the UN had overstepped their mandates by contributing to regime change; that they had used disproportionate force, which increased civilian casualties; and that they had ignored or outright rejected opportunities for further political dialogue. Russia in particular argued that the Libyan experience colored its thinking on the subsequent crisis in Syria, pushing it to resist Western pressure on the al-Assad regime on the grounds that it might open the door to forced regime change.

Although the Council has indeed been deadlocked on Syria and has failed to respond adequately to a crisis that has resulted in the deaths of more than 100,000 people and forced in excess of four million people from their homes, controversies about the implementation of protection mandates in Libya and Côte d'Ivoire did not inhibit the constructive use of R2P in other contexts. Resolution 1996, adopted in July 2011, established a UN peace operation for

South Sudan and called upon the international community to provide assistance to help the new government there to fulfill its responsibility to protect. Resolution 2014, adopted in October 2011, reminded the government of Yemen of its primary responsibility to protect its population. In its September 2011 Presidential Statement on preventive diplomacy, the Council again recalled its commitment to R2P. More recently, Resolution 2085 (2012) on Mali authorized an international mission to assist the government there in fulfilling its responsibility to protect, among other things, Resolution 2117 (2013) on small arms and light weapons recognized their capacity to result in the commission of R2P crimes, and Resolution 2121 (2013) on the Central African Republic underscored the government's responsibility to protect its own population.

In a remarkably short space of time, therefore, R2P has been transformed from a concept proposed by an international commission into an international principle unanimously endorsed by the world's governments and usefully employed in more than a dozen real-life situations. It is a principle that frames how the world thinks about the prevention of genocide and mass atrocities and responds to the outbreak of these crimes.

CONCLUSION

R2P can be understood as an attempt to realize the promise of "Never Again." In its first 10 years, R2P has emerged as an international norm that tries to find a balance between sovereignty and the defense of human rights and to establish a framework that makes it more difficult for perpetrators to "get away" with committing mass atrocities and more likely that the international community will protect the intended victims. With only a tiny handful of exceptions, states accept that they have made a commitment to R2P and agree on its fundamental components. Thus, as far as almost all the world's governments are concerned, the key debates about R2P are not ones about whether to accept the principle or about its meaning and scope, but rather are focused on its implementation in practice. But while R2P is not just a "convenient vocabulary" employed when powerful states find it useful, its practical implementation remains challenged by the three factors that have always inhibited decisive action to stop atrocities: sovereignty, interests, and prudence. However, R2P has established itself as a norm associated with profound underlying changes to the way in which international society responds to the problem of genocide and mass atrocities. Notably, international society is now more likely to respond to these situations than it was prior to 2005 and, significantly, is much more likely to prioritize protection. If the first 10 years were primarily about establishing the norm, therefore, the next 10 should be about its implementation since repeated failures to fulfill R2P or the norm's association with controversial practices could undermine the very consensus that underpins it. This will involve concerted action to address the accountability and effectiveness issues associated with the Security Council in order to reassure member states concerned about coercive interference and improve the Council's performance, tangible work aimed at fostering comprehensive responses to genocide and mass atrocities that draw on all the available levers, and efforts to create realistic expectations about what can be achieved in the decade to come.

NOTES

1. The story behind the Genocide Convention is conveyed by Samantha Power, *A Problem from Hell: America and the Age of Genocide* (New York: Basic Books, 2002).

2. For the best account of this, see Nicholas J. Wheeler, *Saving Strangers: Humanitarian Intervention in International Society* (Oxford: Oxford University Press, 2000).

3. Independent Commission, *Report of the Independent Inquiry into the Actions of the United Nations during the 1994 Genocide in Rwanda*, December 12, 1999, p. 1.

4. See Roberta Cohen and Francis M. Deng, *Masses in Flight: The Global Crisis of Internal Displacement* (Washington, DC: Brookings Institution Press, 1998).

5. Francis M. Deng et al., *Sovereignty as Responsibility: Conflict Management in Africa* (Washington, DC: Brookings Institution Press, 1996), p. 1.

6. S. Neil MacFarlane and Yuen Foong, *Human Security and the UN: A Critical History* (Bloomington: Indiana University Press, 2006), p. 174.

7. Fiona Terry, *Condemned to Repeat? The Paradoxes of Humanitarian Aid* (Ithaca, NY: Cornell University Press, 2002).

8. For example, Sorcha O'Callaghan and Sara Pantuliano, *Protective Action: Incorporating Civilian Protection into Humanitarian Response*, HPG Report 26 (London: Humanitarian Policy Group, December 2007); Oxfam International, *Beyond the Headlines: An Agenda for Action to Protect Civilians in Neglected Conflicts* (Oxford: Oxfam GB for Oxfam International, 2003); OCHA, *Special Report: Civilian Protection in Armed Conflict* (New York: OCHA Integrated Regional Information Network, 2003).

9. See Victoria K. Holt and Tobias C. Berkman, *The Impossible Mandate? Military Preparedness, the Responsibility to Protect and Modern Peace Operations* (Washington, DC: The Henry L. Stimson Center, 2006).

10. Kofi Annan, "Two Concepts of Sovereignty," *The Economist*, Vol. 352, No. 137 (September 18, 1999).

11. Independent International Commission on Kosovo, *The Kosovo Report* (Oxford: Oxford University Press, 2000).

12. Kofi Annan, "Annual Report to the UN General Assembly," September 20, 1999.

13. Kofi Annan, "The Responsibility to Protect," Address to the International Peace Academy, UN press release SG/SM/8125 (February 15, 2002).

14. International Commission on Intervention and State Sovereignty, *The Responsibility to Protect* (Ottawa: International Development Research Centre, 2001).

15. UN High Level Panel on Threats, Challenges and Change, *A More Secure World: Our Shared Responsibility*, A/59/565, December 2, 2004, para. 203. On the issue of veto restraint, see Ariela Blatter and Paul D. Williams, "The Responsibility Not to Veto," *Global Responsibility to Protect*, Vol. 3, No. 3 (2011).

16. Kofi Annan, "In Larger Freedom: Towards Development, Security and Human Rights for All," A/59/2005 (March 21, 2005).

17. Contrary to what some academics have claimed. See, for example, Robert Pape, "When Duty Calls: A Pragmatic Standard of Humanitarian Intervention," *International Security*, Vol. 37, No. 1 (Summer 2012).

18. Colum Lynch, "The 10 Worst UN Security Council Resolutions Ever," *Foreign Policy* (March 21, 2010), http://turtlebay.foreignpolicy.com/posts/2010/05/21/the_10 _worst_un_security_council_resolutions_ever

19. Report of the Internal Review Panel on the UN's Actions in Sri Lanka, November 2012, para. 80.

Part III

Transformation

8

Realism and Idealism in Historical Perspective: Otto von Bismarck

Otto Pflanze

A few years ago I attended a conference of historians, political scientists, and foreign policy experts on the subject "The Realist Tradition in U.S. Foreign Policy" that focused on three presumed "realists": Hans Morgenthau, Reinhold Niebuhr, and George Kennan. In the course of the afternoon, the speakers came to the conclusion, with some disappointment (or so it seemed to me), that there was an undercurrent of idealism to be found in the writings of all three. On reflection, I could think of no historical figure with a reputation for realism of whom the same is not true. Was there ever a realist so pure as to be untouched by ethico-ideological concerns? And is not the opposite question also valid: was there ever an idealist unconcerned about power and its uses?

To arrive at a conclusive answer to these questions within the scope of a chapter would, of course, be impossible. What can be done is to sketch out in broad strokes the relevant early history of European diplomacy and then examine in greater detail the thought and practice of one of its most gifted practitioners.

First, it is necessary to clarify the terms being used here. In this essay "realism" and "idealism" identify models or ideal types derived from common political usage rather than from philosophical definitions. Realism concerns the actual or real; idealism, the abstract or speculative. The realist focuses on what is; the idealist, on what ought to be. To the realist, governments are primarily motivated by self-interest or the "interests of state"; to the idealist, governments should focus on the interests of mankind as a whole, whose welfare is best served by the application of absolute values and standards. In political life, realists and idealists alike wrestle with the problem of power, its use and misuse. The realist accepts both the legitimacy of force and its practical limitations for the actualization of political goals; the idealist may decry coercion and violence and yet recognize its necessity for the achievement of ideal ends.

Idealism can also take the form of fanaticism, in which case any means can be justified to achieve the desired end.

UNIVERSAL MONARCHY OR BALANCE OF POWER?

Historically these models are seldom to be found in their pure state, whether in the form of theory or conduct. Consider, first, the case of Niccolò Machiavelli, often regarded as the prototypical realist. Machiavelli was long misunderstood because his readers judged him on the basis of the amoral political tactics that he recommended in *The Prince*, but ignored his views about the conditions that seemed to make such tactics necessary: namely, the moral depravity of Renaissance rulers, the disunity and weakness of Italy under the city-state system, and the desirability of creating order out of chaos. His other works, furthermore, show that Machiavelli was a convinced republican dedicated to the principle of individual liberty. Realism and idealism coexisted in his political thought, but not always at the same place in his writings.[1]

Machiavelli's greatest contribution to the development of political realism was to divorce the study of politics from theology. That was possible in the largely secular society of fifteenth-century Renaissance Italy, whose city-states developed foreign policies based upon reasoned self-interest and the balance of power in a largely self-contained peninsular state system.[2] As a model for all Europe, however, the Italian system was premature.

The growth of large territorial states in France, Spain, and Austria in the sixteenth century ended Italy's self-containment. After 1494, the peninsula became a sideshow of European politics, in which the main event was a long duel between the Habsburg and Valois-Bourbon dynasties for supremacy in Europe. That conflict, which continued intermittently for nearly two centuries, had a power-political character. The Habsburgs of Spain and Austria sought to consolidate their hold on Italy, Germany, and the Netherlands in the quest for a "universal monarchy" like those of Charlemagne and the Roman Empire. At the court of Charles V and Philip II, universal monarchy was not only a dynastic, but also an ideal goal; it was the first step toward restoration of the unity of Christendom, driven since 1517 by the Protestant Reformation. In the religious wars of the sixteenth and seventeenth centuries, realism and idealism, the simultaneous quests for universal power and universal faith, were again joined. When Habsburg Spain declined in the late sixteenth century, the Austrian Habsburgs took up the cause. In 1629, the goal seemed attainable, when at a climactic moment of the Thirty Years' War, Catholic armies under Habsburg leadership conquered northern Germany and Jutland.

The response of the Valois and Bourbon kings of France from Francis I onward was to support any power willing to oppose the Habsburgs, whether Catholic, Protestant, or Muslim. When Gustavus Adolphus of Sweden assumed leadership of the Protestant cause by entering the Thirty Years' War in 1630, he was assisted financially by France. Under the leadership of Cardinal Richelieu, France remained out of the conflict until a compromise peace, signed at Prague in 1635, threatened to end the war before France had achieved its objectives against the Habsburgs. Catholic France, in alliance with Sweden and the Protestant princes of the Holy Roman Empire, went to war against Catholic Austria. Hitherto a struggle for both power and religion, the Thirty Years' War now lost its religious component.

As the statesman most responsible for this consequence, Richelieu is often regarded as the progenitor of a new age of political realism, of undisguised power politics divorced from all ideological concerns. William Church has shown that this image is simplistic by tracing the connections between Catholic faith and *raison d'état* in Richelieu's thought. His belief in the divine right of the Bourbon dynasty led naturally to the suppression of internal opposition, the quest for defensible frontiers, and the liquidation of Habsburg encirclement. Religious conviction and reason of state were inseparable in the cardinal's mind; the Protestant heresy was of secondary importance.[3]

By the time Louis XIV launched his bid for universal monarchy at the end of the seventeenth century, the European state system had reached a stage of development that made this goal much more difficult to achieve, at least with the means then available. Although Louis XIV ruled the wealthiest, most populous country in Europe, the wars he launched from 1667 to 1713 ended largely in failure, for they triggered the formation of defensive alliances among the threatened states that ultimately frustrated the French attack. Out of these struggles came the European balance of power.[4]

THE "CLASSICAL SCHOOL" AND ITS ETHOS

In the history of politics, whether internal or international, reality tends to be validated by theory. The idea of universal monarchy was derived from the realities of the Roman Empire, universal church, and *res publica Christiania* of medieval Europe. Out of the struggles against universal monarchy came, first, the reality of the balance of power and, then, its idea or principle in political thought. In 1648, the Treaty of Westphalia confirmed in law the sovereignty of individual states, a development that had matured over the course of two centuries, and in 1714, the Treaty of Utrecht declared that the lasting "peace and tranquility of Christendom" was to rest on "an equal balance of power."[5]

The balance of power had become the regulative principle of the European states system.

The problems of war and peace engaged the active minds of the Enlightenment, to whom the discovery of nature's laws constituted an intellectual endeavor of the highest priority. Among "enlightened" rulers and statesmen the conviction grew that the balance of power was not only a natural phenomenon of political life, but also a desirable bulwark against tyranny. By its means European powers, great and small, could prevent any one power from destroying the liberty and sovereignty of others. It appeared to provide the only practical assurance of safety in a politically divided continent. But it was also seen as a guarantee that rulers would pursue rational foreign policies. They would abandon the unbridled pursuit of personal and dynastic aggrandizement typical of the past. Instead, they would pursue the calculated "interest of state" within the restraints imposed by the European equilibrium. Greed would be restrained by reason as well as by the threat of retaliation.

But most *philosophes* were subjects, not rulers, and they concerned themselves primarily with issues of human freedom, social equality, the social contract, and international peace. *Philosophes* of this orientation rejected the doctrines of *raison d'état* and balance of power, which sanctioned war as an instrument of state policy. Why, they asked, should relations between states not be governed by the same moral principles expected of relations between individuals?[6] "Foreign affairs," wrote Felix Gilbert, "showed most clearly the ills of a world not yet ruled by reason."[7]

The balance of power was the prevailing system of European politics from 1714 to 1792, yet this era of "cabinet politics" was hardly tranquil. In fact, it was marked by frequent tensions, as rulers calculated, ministers plotted, and generals planned. Increasingly, diplomacy was professionalized[8]—and likewise armies. Among the Great Powers, standing armies became common; the soldiers were uniformed, drilled, and disciplined; the weaponry improved and standardized. The ranks were mostly filled with mercenaries without patriotic attachment to the governments and countries they served. Frederick the Great thought that his subjects should take no notice when the King went to war; the affair was his, not theirs.[9] At peace conferences, territories were bartered away with little or no attention to the wishes of the inhabitants. What has been dubbed the era of "classical diplomacy" could only prosper in a society dominated by absolute monarchies served by an aristocratic elite common to all Europe and motivated by the same social mores, values, and interests.[10]

The careers of Frederick the Great, King of Prussia, and Prince Wenzel Anton von Kaunitz, Chancellor and Foreign Minister of Austria under Empress Maria Theresa, exemplify the classical school of foreign policy. Frederick—ruler, general, and *philosophe*—embodied both the realistic and idealistic sides of the Enlightenment. His studies of recent European history and politics had convinced him that *raison d'état* and balance of power required Prussia's expansion. On assuming the throne in 1740, he launched an attack on Austria to acquire the province of Silesia. He succeeded, but only after two long, exhausting wars that brought Prussia to the brink of disaster. As a realist Frederick focused on state power (both internal and external); as an idealist he felt obliged to promote the welfare of his subjects. He was well aware of the contradiction between these interests. Their competing obligations presented Frederick with an ethical dilemma that he could never resolve.[11]

The Prussian challenge compelled Maria Theresa to reorganize and centralize the government of the Habsburg Empire. In 1755, Kaunitz plotted what became known as "the diplomatic revolution." He effected an alliance of Austria, France, and Russia against Prussia, whose defeat was, by his "political algebra," certain even before the first shot was fired. But Prussia survived the Seven Years' War and kept Silesia. Kaunitz's algebra could not accommodate such incalculable factors as Frederick's generalship and the mortality and whims of Russian rulers. On the verge of defeat in 1762, Frederick was rescued by the death of Tsarina Elizabeth and the succession of Peter III, who idolized the Prussian "philosopher king" and withdrew Russia from the anti-Prussian alliance.[12]

The balance of power ended the quest for universal monarchy, and yet it induced wars at least as often as it prevented them. Furthermore, the balance functioned to bring about the peaceful dissolution of one of Europe's largest states. Huge in size but politically and militarily impotent, Poland was liquidated by Russia, Prussia, and Austria in three partitions (1772, 1793, and 1795). Each of the participating powers feared that one or both of its eventual partners might gain a significant advantage by acting alone; hence they agreed to act in concert. This use of the balance of power as an instrument for mutual aggression shocked the Western world. To a contemporary German historian, Arnold Heeren, the partitions began the dismantlement of the European state system ultimately completed by Napoleon. "The potentates themselves began its subversion! ... What dismemberment could be illegal, if this should be regarded as lawful?"[13] Thomas Jefferson judged the liquidation of Poland to be an event no less significant than the French Revolution.[14]

Philosophers of the Age of Reason had the problem of reconciling the actuality of war and conflict with the ideals of peace and harmony. Perhaps, they speculated, the former was but a necessary stage toward the latter; the advance of reason would create an era of "perpetual peace."[15] In Immanuel Kant's famous essay on this subject, realism and idealism are necessary to each other; the progress of reason in the species, driven by conflicts between opposing interests, must lead within states to republican governments and between states to a federation of peoples (*Völkerbund*). In each case the evolving rule of law would compel men and nations to curb their baser instincts. The "mechanism of nature" would lead mankind from the real to the ideal—or, put another way, the ideal is ever in the process of becoming real in accordance with "nature's hidden plan." This philosophy of history enabled Kant to reconcile the spheres of phenomenal experience and noumenal values that were the two pillars of his philosophical system.[16]

Even as Kant composed his "philosophical sketch" in 1795, Europe was involved in what became a war for and against universal monarchy in a new form, that of a universal empire based on revolutionary reform, popular patriotism, and military dictatorship. Napoleon's conquests liquidated many sovereignties great and small, and nearly swept away the balance of power system itself. And yet the statesmen who assembled at Vienna in 1814–1815 to draft the peace that ended this great war belonged to the same aristocratic elite of the age of classical diplomacy. Metternich, Castlereagh, Hardenberg, and Talleyrand were all born, educated, and experienced in the old tradition. They thought in terms of *raison d'état* and the balance of power. The treaty they drafted largely maintained the peace of Europe for 40 years—until the Crimean War and the wars for Italian and German national unity.[17] And yet the relative stability of the Vienna system was owed not only to the balance of power, but also to the reestablished authority of a ruling elite, whose economic and social power base had not yet been eroded by the Industrial Revolution.

But there were differences. Their predecessors in the eighteenth century had believed that the balance of power was a natural mechanism governing the political process. The ease with which Napoleon exploited the divisions of Europe for the expansion of France's frontiers and sphere of influence had proven them wrong. The peacemakers at Vienna were faced with the task of creating a new and hence artificial balance of power through the reallocation of territories and spheres of influence in Germany and Italy to frustrate a future attack either by France in the west or by Russia in the east. This reallocation made a mockery of the doctrine of "legitimacy" introduced at the congress by Talleyrand and designed to prevent a punitive loss of territory to France, now ruled by a restored Bourbon dynasty.

Until its legitimacy was challenged by the French Revolution, Europe's traditional ruling class of the *ancien régime* had wielded power without the need for a defensive ideology (other than divine right); but now in the early stages of the romantic era and the religious revival that accompanied it, organic or historical law provided a new idealism with which to consolidate and perpetuate the Vienna settlement and the endangered social elite of the "classical school." Out of the Congress of Vienna came the reactionary "Holy Alliance" and, more substantially, an agreement by the peacemakers to hold future congresses for the suppression of revolutionary movements. Four congresses were held between 1818 and 1822, but Great Britain would not cooperate and the congress system collapsed.[18]

The congress system, although doomed by its reactionary purpose, did not disappear without a trace. The tradition lingered that Europe possessed a common states system, that the balance of power was its regulative principle, and that congresses and conferences for the settlement of differences were acceptable substitutes for war. As the nineteenth century progressed, that system was generally termed the "Concert of Europe."[19] On occasion, the concert took steps to mitigate the use of violence in settling international conflicts (at Paris in 1856 and at The Hague in 1899 and 1907). By the centennial of his death in 1804, Kant's confidence in the progress of reason—and the mechanism of its propulsion—appeared to have, at least, some justification. Here it suffices to note that the linkage between realism and idealism in Western thought about international relations is again confirmed.

BISMARCK: A "CLASSICAL DIPLOMATIST?"

In the 1950s, Bismarck was regarded by important German historians as having been the last great master of the art of "cabinet diplomacy" as practiced by the classical school of the eighteenth century. Born in 1815, he came to power in 1862 in an age increasingly dominated by national passions and crusading ideologies. And yet one prominent German historian of the post–World War II era asserted that Bismarck was "the last great cabinet statesman in European history . . . a spiritual successor of Frederick the Great in a completely changed world." He had "nothing to do with the nationalism of the nineteenth and twentieth centuries and its blind fanaticism. One cannot possibly stress that fact sharply enough."[20] A second German historian of the same era was equally emphatic, maintaining that Bismarck "had nothing in common with the dictators of the nationalistic era" and was completely devoid of that *moderne Vaterländerei* typical of the new national patriotism.[21] And a third testified that "Bismarck was not at all a man of national or popular ideas"; instead he was "a man of state and the reason of state . . . a man of pure *raison d'état*."[22] If these statements are true, Bismarck was an anachronism, a practitioner of eighteenth-century statecraft in the nineteenth century, untouched by the "age of ideology" in which he lived and acted.

The judgment of these historians is obviously suspect. They were scholars born and educated in imperial Germany, whose professorial careers dated from the era of the Weimar Republic and who were eager to establish after the defeat of the Nazi regime that Germany's recent catastrophe was owed to the triumph in 1933 of an unsavory band of adventurers who came to power under the republic and were not representative of the German social and political tradition of the imperial age. They wanted to protect Bismarck against the charge of having been a precursor of Hitler. What better way than to find in him a latter-day Frederick the Great? But let us examine their case on its own merits, quite apart from their motives. Was Bismarck a man of pure *raison d'état*? Was he a realist unaffected by idealism in the emerging "age of ideology"?

During the 1850s, Bismarck, not yet 40 years old, was appointed Prussian delegate to the Diet of the German Confederation in Frankfurt am Main, at that time the most important diplomatic post of the Prussian government. From that post he strove to change Prussian foreign policy, which since 1815 had concentrated on preserving the Holy Alliance with Austria and Russia as the bulwark of the conservative order in Europe. He was convinced of the need for Prussia to expand in Germany "within the geographical area made dependent upon us by nature,"[23] achieving at least a role of equality with Austria in the leadership of the Confederation. What Prussia required, he concluded, was a new source of power capable of forcing Austria and its allies among the German small states either to bend or buckle. To this end Prussia must "hold open every door and every turning."[24] Isolated within Germany, Berlin must seek alliances in Europe capable of threatening Austria's security and terrorizing the lesser states. "Fear and fear again—that is the only thing which has any effect in the palaces from Munich to Bückeburg."[25] Prussia's logical partner for this purpose was France, which in Bismarck's opinion was no longer a danger to the stability of Europe.

Although affected by the argument, King Friedrich Wilhelm IV of Prussia could not be brought to take any step that might lead to a breach with Austria. The traditions of Austrian leadership in the German Confederation and solidarity with Austria and Russia in the Holy Alliance were too deeply embedded in the King's thinking. One of the King's close advisers, Leopold von Gerlach, was deeply shocked by the radical proposals of the man he had considered to be his "pupil" in political affairs. The two men exchanged a series of letters, which illustrate the differences between realistic and idealistic views on foreign policy in this era.[26] Basically the dispute was one of relatives, not absolutes. While the interest of state and the struggle against revolution were important to both men, Bismarck gave precedence to the former, Gerlach to the latter.

Gerlach opposed *rapprochement* with Napoleon III on the ground that the Napoleonic dynasty, having been founded on revolution, had no claim to legitimacy. It did not belong to the respectable family of European monarchs. Self-interest would compel Napoleon, he argued, to ally himself with the popular forces of liberal and national revolution. Using Bismarck's own words, he wrote that *this* was the "reality" that it was folly to "ignore."

Bismarck's interviews with Napoleon in 1855 and 1857 had convinced him that the emperor was of a far different caliber than the first Napoleon. Where Napoleon Bonaparte had been bold, aggressive, and calculating, his nephew was sly, limited, and sentimental. There was no danger of a resurgence of French imperialism on a revolutionary scale; the founder of the second empire had neither the instincts of a conqueror nor the talents of a field commander. Nor was he impelled by the necessity of propagating revolution. On the contrary, liberalism was as great a threat to his own power as to that of any other European monarch. His imperial ambitions were centered on Italy rather than on the Rhine, where French expansion would certainly recreate the coalition that had crushed the first Napoleon.

Bismarck also attacked Gerlach's concept of "legitimacy," which he dismissed as historically untenable. All of the so-called legitimate dynasties of Europe, including the Hohenzollern, had revolutionary origins. The Napoleonic regime had as good a claim to legitimacy as any other.[27] "As a romanticist I can shed a tear for his fate," he wrote of King Louis Philippe of France, deposed in the revolution of 1848. "As a diplomat I would be his servant, were I a Frenchman. Being what I am, however, I count France only as a piece and to be sure an unavoidable one in the chess game of politics, no matter who happens to be her ruler. In this game it is my business to serve only my king and my country."[28]

Gerlach was a deeply religious man whose theology was inseparable from his politics. By contrast, Bismarck reached adulthood without religious convictions. In 1846, he underwent a conversion under the influence of German pietists, and thereafter prayer and Bible reading became daily habits. Unlike his pietistic friends, however, he did not find in religion a doctrinal basis for his politics. He concluded that the usefulness of prayer lay in its implied "submission to a stronger power." What he received from God, he believed, was the obligation to follow the dictates of his reason and conscience. Religion gave to his natural self-confidence a moral underpinning, and added to the certitude with which he asserted his will in the political process. But it did not otherwise affect his political conduct. In short, Bismarck could not share Gerlach's belief in the "Christian state" and his conviction that religious faith must inform state policy.[29]

Bismarck was a royalist, as one would expect given his Junker origins. Hence he preferred the vocabulary of feudalism to that of the modern state: "subject" instead of "citizen," "royal servant" instead of "state servant." In later years he often referred to himself as the "vassal" of his "liege lord," the King. And yet that was mere rhetoric. He rejected the views of romantic conservatives like Gerlach, who argued for the restoration in Prussia of a modernized version of the medieval *Ständestaat*. With a frequency that carries conviction,

Bismarck maintained that the Hohenzollern dynasty reigned by divine right ("by the grace of God"). From this it cannot be assumed that he had any over-riding reverence for the institution of monarchy as such.[30] Under the stress of war in 1866, he was capable of supporting ethnic rebellions against the Habsburg Empire and of liquidating traditional sovereignties in Germany. That he favored monarchical alliances after 1871 and accordingly built and rebuilt the Three Emperors League (Germany-Austria-Russia) was more a matter of geopolitical expediency than of doctrine or principle. Had Russia deserted the alliance, he would have sought a replacement in Great Britain.[31]

Bismarck's attitude toward the state was pragmatic, not theological. What impressed him was not its divine, legal, idealistic, or cultural nature, but its power. During his political career he saw himself as "the man of state and the king," standing above the chaos of social and political life and seeking without fear or favor, prejudice or partisanship, the ideal line of conduct in a foreign and domestic policy dictated by *raison d'état*. "I am," he once said, "a disciplined statesman who subordinates himself to the total needs and require-ments of the state in the interest of peace and the welfare of my country."[32]

BISMARCK: A NATIONALIST?

Because he unified Germany, Bismarck is often assumed to have been a German nationalist, an assumption that would seem to place him in the cat-egory of an idealist. As already has been shown, Bismarck's primary motiva-tion was the expansion of Prussia and its equality of power and status with Austria within the German Confederation; what we call "German unifica-tion" came out of that effort. Furthermore, the word "nation" has had more than one definition, and it is necessary to identify what it meant to Bismarck. In his early years he used the terms "Prussian nation" and "Prussian nationality." During 1866–1867, he is said to have often remarked, "My highest ambition is to make the Germans into a nation." The "establish-ment of the German nationality" is how he sometimes described his life's work. By the "German nation," a term that Bismarck used after 1871, he clearly meant the German Reich, not the German-speaking people of Europe. For him nations had concrete existence only when united under a sovereign state. Clearly he thought in terms of the "state-nation," not the "nation-state."[33]

The distinction is important for our purpose here. The frontiers of the Reich of 1871 excluded millions of German-speaking peoples in central and eastern Europe. To the end of his life Bismarck insisted that the ethnic Germans of Austria and Russia should remain subjects of the Habsburg and Romanov dynasties. The German Reich had no *irredenta* to be recovered. To attempt the union of all German-speaking peoples under a single political roof would have destroyed the balance-of-power system as the regulative principle of European international politics. It is safe to say that Bismarck never entertained such a revolutionary thought.

In the eighteenth-century tradition, he looked upon the balance of power as a shelter for the protection and consolidation of what he had created in 1864–1871. Diplomatic finesse enabled him to isolate the battlefields of the wars he fought. The foes of Prussia-Germany fought against it without supporting intervention by any outside power. During his last two decades as Chancellor, Bismarck's skill in keeping the German Reich "one of *three* on the European chess-board," shielded his "revolution from above" from the uncertainties of a major European war. "All politics," he declared in a statement reminiscent of Kaunitz, "reduces itself to this formula: to try to be one of three, so long as the world is governed by the unstable equilibrium of five Great Powers."[34] Despite grave crises in 1876–1878 and 1885–1887, his management of the equilibrium preserved the peace of Europe—because in Bismarck's judgment, it was in the rational self-interest of Germany to do so. The same can be said of his resolute refusal to countenance a preventive war against France, an action repeatedly urged upon him by Prussian generals during diplomatic crises after 1871.[35]

Here we have positive support for the claim that Bismarck was a diplomatist of the classical school in the eighteenth-century tradition, which believed that foreign and military policy must be dictated by the reasoned interest of state and pursued within the limits of the balance-of-power system. His success at this would seem to place him in Robert Jackson's category of a "situational ethicist."

BISMARCK: AN ANACHRONISM?

If this were his entire story, we would have to conclude that Bismarck was indeed an anachronism, a nineteenth-century statesman in the eighteenth-century tradition, a committed realist in an age of increasing idealistic commitment.

A candid, long overlooked statement by Bismarck himself, buried in an address of 1869 to the Prussian parliament, reveals the fallacy in such a conclusion. "In Europe's present situation, in the present state of civilization, it is impossible to undertake great political and perhaps warlike actions for secret reasons of cabinet diplomacy that may be unraveled later by historians. Now one can only conduct war out of national motives, from motives that are national to the degree that their compelling nature is recognized by the great majority of the population."[36] As noted, Frederick the Great went to war against Austria in 1740 to expand Prussia, an act of *Realpolitik* that required no idealistic explanation. One hundred and twenty-six years later, Bismarck repeated the deed, but felt compelled to explain and justify the act before the bar of public opinion.[37]

The three wars that Prussia fought under Bismarck's leadership show in themselves the progression from the old diplomacy to the new. The occasion for war against Denmark in 1864 was the Danish attempt to incorporate Schleswig, which was inhabited by Germans except for a few districts on its northern frontier, into the Danish state. The Schleswig cause was considered in Germany to be a national one, but Bismarck fought the war in alliance with Austria and in defiance of German public opinion. The conflict of 1866 was a civil war within the German Confederation: Austria was backed by many Confederate states; Prussia, by none. The war became popular in Prussia only as it progressed. Bismarck's effort to depict the conflict as a war for German national unity was greeted initially with scorn. Prussia's outright annexation of Schleswig-Holstein, Hannover, Hesse-Cassel, and Frankfurt was accepted only in combination with the establishment of a North German Confederation under a constitution with many liberal features, including a parliament chosen by universal and secret male suffrage.[38]

Only the war against France in 1870–1871 can be considered a truly national war of modern character. In the preceding four years, Bismarck's hope for a voluntary and evolutionary union of northern and southern Germany under the Hohenzollern crown had been dashed. Nothing was more likely to regalvanize national sentiment than a war against Germany's traditional foe. For that matter the war was popular on both sides of the Rhine. Continued French resistance under popular leadership after the defeat and capture of Napoleon III at Sedan in September 1870 aroused Bismarck himself to private utterances of ferocity toward the French. To bring the war to an end, he urged the generals to hasten the bombardment of Paris. And yet even under these circumstances he insisted, as he had in 1866, that the war be contained, that political objectives take precedence over military expediency. The peace imposed on Austria in 1866 cost the Habsburg Empire no territory, because Bismarck wished to hold open the possibility of future reconciliation. Yet in 1870–1871, he insisted on the annexation of Alsace and Lorraine from France. He had concluded that the French would neither forgive nor forget their humiliation at German hands; hence the gate to the Rhine valley, France's traditional route for the invasion of Germany, had to be closed. Bismarck's third and final war was fought as a war of peoples as well as of governments.[39]

By word and deed Bismarck never ceased after 1866 to convey the impression that the new Germany was not just an extension of the Prussian *Machtstaat*, to which the citizenry owed mere formal obedience, but also an organic national state requiring their patriotic allegiance. He deliberately exploited German national patriotism for the expansion of Prussia's territory, population, and power. The stress he placed on the national character of the German Reich helped to consolidate it by overcoming particularistic loyalties among Germans, but it also served to estrange further the ethnic minorities living within the Reich's borders. The ethnic conception that helped to reconcile Hanoverians, Saxons, Bavarians, Swabians, and other German *Stämme* to the rule of Berlin could only heighten the sense of alienation felt by the Reich's Polish, Danish, and French citizens, who demanded for themselves the same right of ethnic self-determination claimed by Germans. Bismarck's tactical use of German nationalism as a moral reinforcement for a Reich created by Prussian power politics blocked the political assimilation of the empire's ethnic minorities and thereby endangered the security of its frontiers. Bismarck concluded that the only practical escape from this dilemma was Germanization. Greater ethnic homogeneity, it seemed, was a precondition for the final consolidation of the German Reich. And yet the government's attacks on their cultural identity only served to estrange further the Reich's ethnic minorities and alarm their ethnic brethren residing beyond its frontiers.[40]

Furthermore, the tactic had an effect upon the German-speaking people of the Habsburg Empire that went beyond Bismarck's intentions. In negotiating the Dual Alliance between Germany and Austria-Hungary in 1879, he reckoned that such an alliance would be popular with ethnic Germans in both countries. But the result exceeded his expectations—to the point of embarrassment.

In 1892, two years after his dismissal as Reichskanzler by Wilhelm II, Bismarck traveled through Prague to Vienna and back through Munich. He went to attend the marriage of his eldest son to an Austrian countess, and the trip, undertaken despite his continuing feud with the German Kaiser, turned into a triumphal journey such as would have pleased a Roman emperor. In both countries he was received by thousands upon thousands of citizens, who gathered wherever he appeared in public—at hotels where he stopped, at railway stations where he arrived or departed, and even along the railway tracks where his train passed. In Austria he was hailed by pan-German demonstrators, singing *Die Wacht am Rhein* and other German patriotic tunes. Bismarck responded by insisting, as he did on all similar occasions from 1866 to the end of his life in 1898, that ethnic Germans residing in the Habsburg and Russian empires were subjects of their respective rulers and should not expect inclusion in a united Germany. On his trip to Vienna he sought to discourage pan-German demonstrations, but with little success. His deeds and charisma spoke louder than his cautionary words, and echoed on into the future.[41]

Bismarck was not out of step with his own time. He lived and acted in an age of transition from an older society in which landowning magnates of a traditional ruling class still had a major voice in public policy in central and eastern Europe. The balance-of-power system, as reestablished in 1815, was still the primary mechanism of international politics in a divided Europe. War was still an accepted instrument of state policy. The wars he initiated and fought remained within the limits of the balance-of-power system, despite the territorial rearrangements of 1864, 1866, and 1870–1871. But, as we have seen, he recognized that warfare could no longer be conducted "for secret reasons of cabinet diplomacy" but only out of "national motives ... whose compelling nature is recognized by the great majority of the population." For the same reason he also recognized that in this age an internal "revolution from above" could only be executed and consolidated through the exploitation of national sentiment, and with the help of a national parliament based on universal suffrage.

CONCLUSION

This chapter suggests that there was a persistent linkage between the politics of realism and idealism in European affairs during the approximately four centuries discussed here. The linkage can even be found during the era of "classical politics" in the eighteenth century, when it is often presumed to have been absent, and likewise in the nineteenth-century career of Bismarck, of whom the same presumption has been made. That the linkage existed in the Middle Ages is obvious (consider the Crusades). And it is equally apparent that the linkage has been a central feature of twentieth-century international politics (consider the Cold War).

In conclusion, it may be rewarding to speculate briefly on some of the reasons for this phenomenon. The politics of realism has a twofold character. On the one hand, it demands that the statesman have a cool, rational intellect, uncorrupted by ethical or ideological bias, and be capable of analyzing and understanding the characteristics of the power structure within which he or she functions. On the other hand, it requires that intellect to evaluate with the same detachment the tactics needed for success in executing those functions in view of the observed realities. These calculations require that the person weigh both the possibilities and limits of state power. What contingencies may develop as a consequence of any contemplated action? What reactions are likely to follow, and how are they to be coped with? The answers to these questions call for the exercise of judgment. In the crucible of judgment are many ingredients other than reason: hopes, fears, prejudices, presumptions, errors of fact and logic, and, yes, personal and societal values.

This explains the persistent linkage between the politics of realism and the politics of idealism; i.e., the existence of a spectrum ranging from the objective calculation of power and possibility to the subjective influence of personal emotions, predispositions, and value systems. Idealism, because of its focus on what ought to be, can skew a statesman's sense of the real, and realism, because of its concentration on the power of coercion, can neglect the power of moral idealism, of human sentiments and values. The normal relationship between realism and idealism, then, is more dialectical than polar. What ought logically to be irreconcilable opposites have historically been joined in an uneasy, indeed unavoidable embrace.

NOTES

1. The most recent major study of Machiavelli assesses him chiefly as a moralist and moral philosopher, the inventor of a "new moral reasoning." Sebastian de Grazia, *Machiavelli in Hell* (Princeton, NJ: Princeton University Press, 1989).

2. Garrett Mattingly, *Renaissance Diplomacy* (London: Cape, 1955).

3. William F. Church, *Richelieu and Reason of State* (Princeton, NJ: Princeton University Press, 1972), pp. 372–415.

4. John B. Wolf, *Toward a European Balance of Power, 1620–1715* (Chicago: Rand McNally, 1970) and *The Emergence of the Great Powers, 1685–1715* (New York: Harper and Row, 1951).

5. Maurice Keens-Soper, "The Practice of a States-System," in Michael J. Donelan, ed., *The Reason of States: a Study in International Political Theory* (London: Allen and Unwin, 1978), pp. 25–44; Edward V. Gulick, *Europe's Classical Balance of Power: A Case History of the Theory and Practice of One of the Great Concepts of European Statecraft* (New York: Norton, 1955), pp. 3–89; and Moorhead Wright, ed., *Theory and Practice of the Balance of Power, 1486–1914: Selected European Writings* (Totowa, NJ: Rowman and Littlefield, 1975).

6. Felix Gilbert, *To the Farewell Address: Ideas of Early American Foreign Policy* (Princeton, NJ: Princeton University Press, 1961), p. 65. See also Gulick, *Classical Balance of Power*, pp. 30–51, and Donelan, ed., *The Reason of States*.

7. Gilbert, *Farewell Address*, p. 61.

8. See François de Callières, *De la Manièrede Negocier avec les Souverains* [first published in 1716; probably written two decades earlier], translated as H. M. A. Keens-Soper and Karl W. Schweizer, eds., *The Art of Diplomacy* (London: Leicester University Press, 1983). Harold Nicolson called Callières's work "the best manual of diplomatic method ever written." See his *The Evolution of Diplomatic Method* (New York: Macmillan, 1954), p. 62.

9. Peter R. Rohden, *Die Klassische Diplomatie von Kaunitz bis Metternich* (Leipzig: Koehler and Amelang, 1939), p. 24.

10. "The balance-of-power theory . . . can be shown to be, at best, a theory of the general good, a theory of self-discipline, a theory of survival for the group, and a theory of moderation." Gulick, *Classical Balance of Power*, p. 45. See also Rohden, *Klassische Diplomatie*, pp. 1–30, and Georges Livet, *L'équilibre européen de la fin du XVe à la fin du XVIIIe siècle* (Vendome: Presses Universitaire, 1976).

11. On Frederick the Great, see the classic work by Friedrich Meinecke, *Die Idee der Staatsräson in der neueren Geschichte* (Munich and Berlin: Oldenbourg, 1924),

pp. 340–424; also the biographies of Gerhard Ritter, *Friedrich der Grosse, Ein Historisches Profil*, 3rd ed. (Heidelberg: Quelle and Meyer, 1954), and Theodor Schieder, *Friedrich der Grosse: ein Königtum der Widersprüche* (Frankfurt a. M.: Propyläen, 1983); and "Die Idee des Gleichgewichts bei Friedrich dem Grossen," in Klaus Hildebrand and Reiner Pommerin, eds., *Deutsche Frage und europäisches Gleichgewicht* (Cologne: Böhlau, 1985), pp. 1–14.

12. Walter Dorn, *Competition for Empire, 1740–1763* (New York: Harper, 1940), pp. 292–386; Rohden, *Klassische Diplomatie*, pp. 16–30.

13. Quoted by Henry L. Roberts in the foreword to Herbert H. Kaplan, *The First Partition of Poland* (New York: Columbia University Press, 1962), p. ix.

14. Hajo Holborn, *The Political Collapse of Europe* (New York: Knopf, 1951), p. 16.

15. Gilbert, *Farewell Address*, pp. 60–66.

16. *Zum ewigen Frieden, Ein philosophischer Entwurf. Akademie Ausgabe, Kants Werke*, Vol. 8 (Berlin: W. de Gruyter, 1912); Lewis White Beck, ed., *Immanuel Kant: Perpetual Peace* (Indianapolis, IN: Bobbs-Merrill, 1957), and *Immanuel Kant: On History* (Indianapolis, IN: Bobbs-Merrill, 1963).

17. After World War II, the comparative durability of the equilibrium established among the great powers at Vienna attracted the attention of historians and political scientists, who wanted to know why it had succeeded so well in contrast to the Versailles settlement a century later. For example, Harold Nicolson, *The Congress of Vienna: A Study in Allied Unity, 1812–1822* (New York: Viking Press, 1946); and Henry Kissinger, *A World Restored: Metternich, Castlereagh and the Problems of Peace, 1812–1822* (Boston: Houghton Mifflin, 1957).

18. See Walter Alison Phillips, *The Confederation of Europe: A Study of the European Alliance, 1813–1823, as an Experiment in the International Organization of Peace* (London: Longmans, 1914; 2nd ed., 1920).

19. Carsten Holbraad, *The Concert of Europe: A Study in German and British International Theory, 1815–1914* (New York: Barnes and Noble, 1971); and Keens-Soper, "Practice of a States-System."

20. Gerhard Ritter, *Europa und die deutsche Frage* (Munich: Münchener Verlag, 1948), pp. 77–108, "Das Bismarckproblem," *Merkur*, Vol. 4 (1950), p. 673, *Staatskunst und Kriegshandwerk, Das Problem des "Militarismus" in Deutschland* (Munich: Oldenbourg, 1954), Vol. 1, pp. 302–29.

21. Franz Schnabel, "Bismarck und die Klassische Diplomatie," *Aussenpolitik*, Vol. 3 (1952), pp. 635–42, and "Das Problem Bismarck," *Hochland*, Vol. 42 (1949), pp. 8–9.

22. Wilhelm Schüssler, *Um das Geschichtsbild* (Gladbeck: Freizeiten, 1953), pp. 120–21. Hans Rothfels, another prominent historian of the time, took a similar position, denying that Bismarck's German Reich could validly be called a "national state" because of its eastern frontiers, which included a few million Poles and excluded millions of Germans in Austria and Russia. See his *Bismarck und der Osten* (Leipzig: Hinrichs, 1934), and "Bismarck und das neunzehnte Jahrhundert," in Walther Hubatsch, ed., *Schicksalswege deutscher Vergangenheit* (Düsseldorf: Droste, 1950), pp. 233–48.

23. Herman von Petersdorff and others, eds., Bismarck: *Die gesammelten Werke*, 15 vols. (Berlin: Verlags-Gesellschaft, 1923–1933), Vol. 1, p. 17. Hereafter cited as

Bismarck, *Werke*. For a full discussion of Bismarck's philosophy of politics, aims, and tactical methods, see Otto Pflanze, "Bismarck's 'Realpolitik,'" *The Review of Politics*, Vol. 20 (October 1958), pp. 492–514, and *Bismarck and the Development of Germany*, 3 vols. (Princeton, NJ: Princeton University Press, 1990), Vol. 1, pp. 80–99.

24. Bismarck, *Werke*, Vol. 14, p. 473; see also Vol. 2, pp. 150, 223.

25. Bismarck, *Werke*, Vol. 14, p. 372.

26. For the entire exchange, see *Briefwechsel des Generals Leopold von Gerlach mit dem Bundestagsgesandten Otto von Bismarck*, 3rd ed. (Berlin: W. Hertz, 1893); also Bismarck, *Werke*, Vol. 14, pp. 460ff., Vol. 15, pp. 110ff.

27. Bismarck, *Werke*, Vol. 2, pp. 226ff., and Vol. 14, pp. 470ff.

28. Bismarck, *Werke*, Vol. 14, p. 465.

29. On Bismarck's religious views, see Pflanze, *Bismarck and the Development of Germany*, Vol. 1, pp. 48–53 (the references in footnotes 48–55 are important for discussion of the long controversy over the character, genuineness, and depth of Bismarck's conversion). See also Arnold Oskar Meyer, *Bismarcks Glaube nach neuen Quellen aus dem Familienarchiv* (Munich: Beck, 1936); and Hajo Holborn, "Bismarck's Realpolitik," *Journal of the History of Ideas*, Vol. 21 (1960), pp. 85–90.

30. For Bismarck's conception of the state and its relationship to civil society see Pflanze, *Bismarck and the Development of Germany*, Vol. 1, pp. 53–62.

31. Pflanze, *Bismarck and the Development of Germany*, Vol. 2, pp. 246–78, 415–41, 490–510, and Vol. 3, pp. 78–97, 218–59, 443.

32. To the Prussian chamber of deputies, December 17, 1873. Horst Kohl, ed., *Die politischen Reden des Fürsten Bismarck* (Stuttgart: Cotta, 1892–1905), Vol. 6, p. 131. This was, of course, a political statement intended to counteract the blood-and-iron public image Bismarck had acquired in Europe during the events of 1862–1871. But it can also be accepted, I believe, as Bismarck's image of himself.

33. For Bismarck's views on the nation and nationalism, see Pflanze, *Bismarck and the Development of Germany*, Vol. 1, pp. 66–70; also "Bismarck and German Nationalism," *American Historical Review*, Vol. 60 (1955), pp. 548–66.

34. To Alexandrovitch Saburov, January 20, 1880. J. Y. Simpson, ed., *The Saburov Memoirs, or Bismarck and Russia* (New York: Macmillan, 1929), p. 111.

35. Gerhard Ritter, *Staatskunst and Kriegshandwerk* (Munich: Oldenbourg, 1954), Vol. 1, pp. 238–329; Gordon A. Craig, *The Politics of the Prussian Army, 1640–1945* (Oxford: Clarendon, 1955), pp. 255, 268–70.

36. To the Reichstag of the North German Confederation, April 22, 1869. Bismarck, *Werke*, Vol. 11, p. 50.

37. A German liberal publicist is credited with inventing the term *Realpolitik*. See August Ludwig von Rochau, *Grundsätze der Realpolitik, angewendet auf die staatlichen Zustände Deutschlands* (Stuttgart: Cotta, 1853). Rochau believed that their idealism itself had been responsible for the failure of liberal-nationalists to unite Germany in 1848, and he urged a more realistic approach in the future—striking evidence of the linkage between idealism and realism in German political attitudes during this era.

38. At the time Bismarck was regarded by liberal nationalists as a black reactionary because of his quarrel, called the "constitutional conflict," with the Prussian Landtag. His hidden agenda in the Schleswig-Holstein affair was to annex the duchies to

Prussia; nationalist opinion in Germany called for an independent principality under the rule of Prince Friedrich of Augustenburg. See Pflanze, *Bismarck and the Development of Germany*, Vol. I, pp. 257–316.

39. Pflanze, *Bismarck and the Development of Germany*, Vol. 1, pp. 392–409, 470–506.

40. Pflanze, *Bismarck and the Development of Germany*, Vol. 2, pp. 93–126, 247–51, Vol. 3, pp. 198–209, 234–39, 434–36.

41. See Pflanze, *Bismarck and the Development of Germany*, Vol. 3, pp. 395–99, 444–57.

9

Konrad Adenauer, Arms, and the Redemption of Germany

Carl C. Hodge

Among other evils which being unarmed brings you, it causes you to be despised.

—Niccolò Machiavelli, *The Prince*

The rearmament of Germany, whose armies had only recently lost the most ambitious and destructive campaign of conquest in history, represented the greatest controversy of West European politics after 1945. From the time of national unification in 1871, the German officer corps had constituted a reactionary state-unto-itself. Under Hitler, the *Wehrmacht* became the principal weapon of the Third Reich's war against the geopolitical status quo and modern civilization itself. Defeated Germany was despised because of its arms rather than in spite of them. "After the experience of 1914, of the interwar years and of 1939," asked a British weekly in November 1949, "can there be salvation in any course save that of seeing the Germans have no army at all, large or small?"[1]

Yet Konrad Adenauer, the first Chancellor of the Federal Republic of Germany founded in May of that year, judged the arming of Germany's second democracy to be critical to its very survival. German rearmament was in part the product of changing international circumstance and the conviction in Washington that the containment of Soviet power in Europe would require a multilateral diplomatic, economic, and military effort in which defeated Germany had an important role to play. But equally, the terms of German military revival bore the stamp of Adenauer's personal commitment to democratic government and the redemption of his country's claim to a place among civilized states. At the core of Adenauer's campaign for German rearmament lay the apparent contradiction that a man with military enthusiasms, who needed only to survey Germany's urban landscape to appreciate the price of its martial tradition, should pursue aggressively the constitution of a new German army. It becomes less surprising when one recalls the choices confronting Adenauer between 1949 and 1955, along with the particular political and diplomatic ends that rearmament was to serve.

For some time into the history of the Bonn Republic, Adenauer had few assets, apart from his own reading of the fears and ambitions of Germany's wartime enemies and future allies, to mobilize on behalf of the Federal Republic's interests. His diplomacy depended preponderantly on acquired political instincts and a fairly coherent interpretation of his country's past. Adenauer believed that from 1871 to 1945, Germany had been consistently remiss in a task considered by Bismarck to be critical to successful foreign relations over the long term, the establishment of friendship with other states. The maxim of nineteenth-century *Realpolitik*, that between nations there could be no friendship but only a convergence or divergence of interests, was an intellectual fashion of its time, the realism of which was profoundly overrated by its avowed practitioners. Its impact on Germany had been devastating. Since Bismarck, the Reich had all too often relied on clever diplomacy at the expense of a more sober calculation of national interest. It had made itself powerful yet isolated. Only through membership in and commitment to an international political community, Adenauer reasoned, could Germany have escaped isolation, gained greater insight into the motivations of other nations, recognized good faith when it was on offer, and avoided the disastrous miscalculations that hubris brought in its train.[2] Adenauer also believed that the experience of the Third Reich had a more immediate relevance to postwar Europe. During the 1930s, the appeasement of Germany by the major Western powers had itself fed the appetite of Nazi geopolitical ambitions. As Chancellor of the Federal Republic at the onset of the Cold War, he reasoned that a similar failure to make a determined and multilateral stand against the gambits of Moscow's diplomacy would produce much the same result. Like the Third Reich, the Soviet state recognized no law beyond the application of power—its own power for the extension of Soviet influence or the power of its opponents to thwart the same.[3] A policy of strength and resolve alone would impress Moscow. If Germans, exhausted and demoralized by war, could be brought to recognize that revived military strength was essential yet possible only in concert with the Western democracies, they could in time be shown that a higher *Realpolitik* incorporated amity and trust among like-minded governments into the diplomatic equation.

The notion of a political community was itself related to Adenauer's conviction that economic and technological change in the first half of the twentieth century had made it impossible to administer the domestic affairs of any state without constant reference to factors beyond its borders. As mayor of Cologne during the early Weimar Republic, he had had to acquire foreign credit for a debt-ridden city. It was in part the damage done to the local economy by the crises of international diplomacy and shocks to the world economy that made him an early advocate of some form of European economic integration. In this he thought that Europe should take instruction from the United States, whose integrated continental market had provided the solid economic foundations of its democratic constitution.[4] Along with leaders such as Robert Schuman and Jean Monnet in France and Alcide de Gasperi in Italy, Adenauer is a founding father both of European Christian democracy and of the European Community. The Christian Democratic Union (CDU), the party Adenauer built into the dynamic electoral force of postwar German politics, was an offspring of the Weimar-era Catholic Center Party remodeled into a broad-based non-confessional force of the center-right.[5] In August 1949, the CDU ran on a platform of federalism, a socially responsible market economy, European unity, and militant anticommunism that elected Adenauer to the head of a three-party coalition government.

Adenauer approached democratic governance as a call to political trusteeship. Adopting a Weberian ethic of responsibility, he assumed a mandate to interpret for himself the best interests of the German people and to seek public approval at the end of his term for the consequences of his actions rather than the intentions of his policies.[6] Adenauer's personal definition of politics spoke of "the art of realizing that which is recognized as ethically responsible." This required above all courage, consistency, and determination to resist the ever-present temptation of convenient duplicity. "Don't lie, even in politics," he once told a junior colleague, "a politician cannot always speak openly, but when he does he should be sincere."[7] For Adenauer, sound political engagement was based on principles that one could defend in the best and worst of times. Political deeds of enduring significance came only from a sense of the continuity of ultimate purpose, without which even well-intentioned policy all too easily went awry under the conflicting pressures and shifting circumstance of public affairs.

And yet Adenauer understood like few European democrats of his generation that success in the public arena often depended on a measure of opportunism, the ability to pounce at any chance to further a worthwhile policy. A worthwhile policy for the Federal Republic, indeed its very *raison d'être*, was to change the whole course of German history. Given the trajectory of that history from 1914 to 1945, it was a task daunting enough to require from its architect a measure of opportunism embedded in a purpose noble enough to excuse one or two outright falsehoods in the realization.

THE HIGHER REALISM OF A WESTERN ALLIANCE

For five years after World War II, the question of reestablishing Germany's armed forces was taboo in official debate concerning the future of Western Europe. Yet even with the establishment of the Brussels Pact in March 1948 and the North Atlantic Treaty Organization (NATO) in April 1949, plans for the defense of Western Europe against potential Soviet aggression were woefully inadequate. When in November 1949, American Secretary of State Dean Acheson informed British and French officials that the Truman administration considered West Germany an ally, he formalized Washington's position that additional strength should be tapped and that their former foe should provide it.[8]

Adenauer was personally unenthused at the prospect of a new German army, but he came to regard rearmament as a military necessity in itself, as well as a political issue instrumental to the acquisition of diplomatic influence. The government of a provisional state such as the Federal Republic had to take into the account both the threat of Soviet military aggression and the implications of indirect political pressure for domestic stability. Rearmament also held out the promise that the Bonn Republic's status under the Potsdam Agreement could be revised through the investment in national sovereignty and self-determination that the establishment of an armed service symbolized. For Adenauer security and sovereignty were very much coincident, since a credible military barrier to Soviet expansion in Europe seemed critical to the prospects of West German democratic consolidation.[9]

The collateral benefits were possibly even greater, especially if a German contribution to military security were to be associated with the larger project of West European integration. In such a connection Adenauer saw the chance to make a clean break with discredited tradition. In the past Germany had insisted on too many diplomatic options in Europe. From Bismarck's alliance strategies to the Treaty of Rapallo in 1922 and the 1939 Molotov-Ribbentrop Pact, this insistence had resulted in a tendency to play off Russia against France, East against West. While *Schaukelpolitik* (see-saw policy) won foreign recognition of the Reich's power, at its core was a tendency toward equivocation and artifice that undermined any sense of German integrity in those Western capitals where it was needed most: Paris, London, and Washington.[10]

By virtue of culture alone, Adenauer the Rhinelander instinctively looked to France as Germany's natural partner for European economic reconstruction and viewed provincial politics from a broader European perspective; as mayor of Cologne in the 1920s, he had even pondered the merits of Rhenish separatism involving a special economic relationship with France and a confederate arrangement with Germany. In the 1950s, economics and diplomacy were linked even more closely. A German democracy committed to Franco-German partnership within a Western alliance would ensure its neighbors against the specter of recidivism, and simultaneously give them a stake in German economic revival. From this perspective, the polarities of the Cold War produced a unique opportunity, in so far as they forced the Federal Republic to choose between two fundamentally different political and economic systems and their concomitant strategic alignments.[11] *Schaukelpolitik* was to be abandoned in favor of *Westpolitik*, and democratic Germany was to become a West European polity as never before.

Because Adenauer could not rely on a liberal democratic tradition among his countrymen to make the choice easy, he was doubly concerned to establish a credible Western security regime to appeal to their sense of security. Germans who could not love the Bonn Republic for its democratic constitution could still be brought to appreciate the advantages of protection from Russian revanchism and Soviet communism. A December 1949 interview with the American daily, the *Cleveland Plain Dealer*, gave the Chancellor the opportunity for some calculated newsmaking with this in mind. In it Adenauer asserted that the Allied powers who had defeated and disarmed Germany now had an obvious moral obligation to provide for its defense; that such provisions that existed were unimpressive; and that the addition of German forces under European command might help to improve the situation. Controversy triggered by the interview on both sides of the Atlantic prompted Adenauer to temper his remarks almost immediately. But the cat was out of the bag. Adenauer's remarks caught Washington's foreign policy thinking at a point where it tended in the direction of a much more assertive stance toward Moscow. He prodded American insecurities, encouraged the new Cold War militancy of the Truman administration, and looked to enhance the benefits for the Federal Republic of the new resolve in its commitment to containing Soviet power. Soviet restraint could be had only through respect for Western arms. Strategic logic, Adenauer knew, ran well ahead of diplomacy and pointed to one conclusion:

> But if the Federal Republic was to be defended, it was clear that other western countries should not have to do the whole job. It was only fair that West Germany contribute to her own defense. Without German troops it was hard to see how even Europe west of the Rhine could be defended, but if West German territory were included in the area to be defended, even more troops would be required, and no one but Germany could supply them. Officially in late 1949 the western powers still opposed German rearmament in any form, but in military circles in all three of the major western countries, it was taken for granted that German troops would be needed.[12]

Undeniably, the outbreak of the Korean conflict improved the Bonn government's bargaining position. But Adenauer also worried that where Korea
encouraged policy makers in the United States to view the contest with
communism in *global* terms, it could also undermine the American commitment to Europe as the *primary* theater of struggle. Moreover, Adenauer considered the Communist menace in Western Europe to be real and imminent.
He was never among that coterie of European politicians who thought the
invocation of Cold War themes as simply a convenient instrument for turning
Washington's head. His sincerity in this matter came through in correspondence with Dannie Heineman, a longtime friend and director of the Sofina
Konzern in Brussels, wherein the Chancellor maintained that every feature
of the Soviet presence in Eastern Europe attested to Moscow's ambition to
establish an imperial status over the entire continent.

A Soviet ideological invasion of the West was already underway in the
form of strong Communist parties in France and Italy, whose potential
Washington did not, in Adenauer's view, appreciate fully. In Germany,
Soviet power confronted a demoralized populace loath to accept that it might
yet have to make military sacrifices for its own freedom, and skeptical that the
United States, Britain, or France would defend them. Worse still, many
Germans of the occupied Federal Republic did not consider themselves free
in any sovereign sense. Popular defeatism could be overcome only by a dramatic improvement of the West's military strength and a fundamental change
in the official status of the West German state.[13] Adenauer's biographer inter-
prets the Heineman letter as a *cri du coeur* to a personal confidant to do what
he could on behalf of a Chancellor fearful for the political viability of the
Federal Republic. Heineman forwarded Adenauer's concerns verbatim to the
desk of General Eisenhower, then Supreme Allied Commander for Europe
(SACEUR). By December 1950, copies had been passed on to U.S.
Secretary of Defense George Marshall and every other upper-echelon official
responsible for American policy in Europe.[14]

Into the newly intensified debate on European security the French
government tossed the Pleven Plan for a European Defense Community
(EDC). The plan was a makeshift alternative to France's nightmare, the establishment of a West German national army and an independent general staff,
and was designed to spin out rather than speed up official discussion of the
security problem. But in retrospect this, too, had its advantages. Because the
EDC idea resonated so well with the theme of West European integration, it
was hard to oppose in principle. For Adenauer, the lengthy debate over the
EDC turned out to be an important phase in the effort first to formulate, and
then to legitimate, his foreign policy at home and abroad.

The EDC had a good many enemies in Germany. The venerable German
Social Democratic Party (SPD) campaigned against it with considerable

success in local and state elections in 1950–1951, and drew support from the Protestant church, most notably from the popular neutralist pastor Martin Niemöller. The SPD leader, Kurt Schumacher, argued that the Federal Republic's membership in a security arrangement directed against the Soviet Union would scupper indefinitely the chances for what was surely the supreme ambition of any Bonn government, the reunification of West Germany with the eastern zone of occupation. He charged further that the EDC proposal would impose too many obligations on the Federal Republic in exchange for too few commitments from the Western powers for the defense of German soil, in effect that it would make West Germany the battlefield in the defense of other countries. Adenauer countered that the Federal Republic was at this juncture in no position to make demands of the Western allies. And though he would never admit it publicly, national reunification was not at all uppermost among the Chancellor's priorities. Any arrangement for a reunified Germany acceptable to Moscow, he believed, would lead to de facto neutrality and save *Schaukelpolitik* from the grave.[15]

Especially galling were pacifist claims to the moral high ground of the rearmament debate. In the face of Soviet policy and military might, West German pacifism seemed to Adenauer either the child of breathtaking credulity or a philosophical veneer for appeasement. He labeled Niemöller an enemy of the West German state and accepted the resignation of Gustav Heinemann, a cabinet minister openly sympathetic to Niemöller, with undisguised contempt for the minister's views. In protest the Chancellor's most devoted critics named him "The Hammer" and wove the Heinemann episode into the folklore of the pacifist cause. For years they never tired of citing it as proof of his cold, authoritarian character.[16]

But Adenauer also had outspoken allies of considerable prestige. Korea, proclaimed Charles de Gaulle, made German rearmament inevitable, and Winston Churchill proposed to the European Council in Strasbourg the immediate creation of an integrated European army. Cardinal Frings of Cologne invoked the traditional Catholic notion of just war and denounced neutrality as moral abdication.[17] Sensing that there existed in Germany no popular majority for rearmament on any blueprint, Adenauer rejected a referendum on the issue and instead channeled his energies toward securing the kind of American defense commitment to Europe that might eventually turn the domestic debate in his favor.

His memorandum to U.S. High Commissioner John McCloy in June 1951, in which he touched upon the principal aspects of Germany's current position on the continent and its meaning to other European states, is a case in point. Adenauer played down any immediate danger of war but stressed the strategic importance of Europe to American policy with his own variation on domino theory. "For if Soviet Russia gains control of the manpower and resources of the Federal Republic," he warned, "its war-making potential and economic power will increase enormously. France, Italy and the Benelux states will then fall quickly to communism."[18] Adenauer then turned to the Federal Republic's occupied status and argued that Germans needed to see a political dividend in voluntary self-defense—in other words, that there could be no defense of Europe without Germany, and no meaningful German commitment without sovereignty. "In my opinion," he wrote, "the German people have, despite the experience of past decades, more than any other European people the qualities required to build a dike against the Soviet Union."[19] The words themselves were not especially forceful, but their logic was potent indeed. They told McCloy that the United States had a good deal to lose in Europe and that, like it or not, Germany was the key to American success there. In informal exchanges with the German press corps, Adenauer intimated that he thought stealth and discretion utterly essential to Bonn's diplomacy, but he also employed the term *Grossmacht* (great power) in characterizing the sovereignty he sought for the Federal Republic relative to Britain and France.[20] The Chancellor thought his government should drive a hard bargain with whatever it had to offer, and he was prepared to conjure for any ally, including the United States, the image of a demoralized German populace embracing neutrality if it were denied full recognition in a Western alliance.[21]

In mid-July 1950, McCloy confided to Secretary of State Acheson that the price of denying Germans the right to fight in a military emergency, even if that were to mean inducting Germans into the U.S. Army, would be "that we should probably lose Germany politically as well as militarily without hope of regain."[22] Expressed so dramatically, concerns such as these were critical in bringing Washington around to a European formula for German rearmament, despite its complications, in the hope that it would expedite the task of establishing a credible defense for Western Europe by removing French resistance to some form of German contribution.

Adenauer meanwhile assigned a panel of former *Wehrmacht* generals the task of drafting Bonn's own proposals for West European security. The resulting Himmeroder Memorandum envisaged the inclusion of a German force of 250,000 men in 12 armored and mobile divisions, supported by an air force of 825 planes and a navy of some 200 ships. It also called for a forward defense of Western Europe such as would make the Elbe River, rather than the Rhine, the front line of engagement with Soviet forces. The plan was more ambitious than any security package then under serious consideration in Paris, London, or Washington, or anything Adenauer himself was willing to acknowledge publicly in Germany. It bore the signature of the *Wehrmacht*'s experience in Russia, and its vision of a "forward" defense of the Federal Republic flew in the face of the original NATO concept of placing the bulk of Western forces well to the west of the East German frontier.[23]

At the Petersberg talks of January 1951, during which the American, British, and French deputy high commissioners heard German ideas for rearmament, Adenauer's military advisers used the Himmeroder document as the basis for a set of comprehensive proposals. It was an impressive presentation that complemented Adenauer's dialogue with McCloy by connecting the administrative aspects of defense to German sovereignty. At its core was the technical argument that military practicality required nationally homogeneous German armored divisions under German command. To this the German delegation added a proposal for the creation of a German Ministry of Defense, arguing that the democratic constitution of the Federal Republic perforce required that its military be answerable to the Bonn parliament.[24] Finally, they pointed out that their recommendations on the overall organization of Western forces were based on experience acquired in four years of war against the Soviet Union and were entirely compatible with American military doctrine recorded in the U.S. Army Field Manual. Obviously taken aback by the thoroughness of the German presentation, U.S. representative General George Hayes wired Washington for advice "as to the position to be taken" regarding alternative forms of organization within the Brussels formula.[25]

In 1950–1951, Adenauer doubted that Washington could be relied upon to maintain a large American military presence in Europe over the long term unless it could be moved to see the United States as irrevocably tied to the old continent. If the possibility of such a presence depended on Bonn's official endorsement of a supranational European force—because of Washington's concerns about burden-sharing and its desire to placate France—then he was determined to demonstrate Bonn's good intentions on European security *above all to the United States*. The content of the Himmeroder Memorandum demonstrates that he nonetheless never accepted that the substance of a European force would have to conform to the Pleven Plan. One had to board the train, then change its destination. The Chancellor understood and identified with the American concept of double-containment in Europe: containing Soviet influence within its present frontiers and containing German revival within a Western political constellation. Whereas Washington wanted to transform Germany into a West European democracy, Adenauer wanted to make the United States a West European power.[26]

With this in mind, he listed a number of outstanding grievances against France that collectively, he argued, could only benefit the nationalist rhetoric of the SPD in the Federal Republic. From McCloy he asked that Washington be reminded that only when sufficient American pressure was brought to bear on Paris would French policy toward Germany be compatible with the larger

goals of U.S. diplomacy in Europe.[27] When McCloy pushed the case with
Paris for German sovereignty and rearmament, the American press ventured
that McCloy was in the Chancellor's pocket. But the best evidence is that
Adenauer and McCloy collaborated closely on rearmament above all because
their personal views of the security problem genuinely converged. Reporting
on an interview with Adenauer in March 1951, McCloy noted how the
Chancellor went out of his way to express his distrust of British and French
intentions relative to American policy. He then observed that German officials were "not above sowing a little dissension between Allies" and that it
might therefore be wise to take the Chancellor's praise of the United States
"with a grain of salt."[28]

Inevitably, the EDC was the target of Soviet gambits in sabotage.
In March 1952, Stalin's note to the Western powers on the issue of a
German peace treaty held out the prospect of German reunification, with a
mind to driving a wedge between Bonn and its allies.[29] But by 1952, West
Germany had turned its foreign trade deficit into a modest surplus, aided in
part by a global demand for investment goods fueled by the Korean War.
The benefits in jobs and wages increased popular support for Adenauer's policy of West European integration and a German military contribution to a
European army. Stalin's *démarche* was too late. The economic boom strengthened structural ties between the Federal Republic and Western markets, and
gave its populace reason to consider with skepticism the alleged alternatives
to Adenauer's Cold War diplomacy.[30]

On May 26, 1952, German sovereignty came a step closer. On that date
Bonn signed with Britain, France, and the United States a Convention on
Relations with the Federal Republic of Germany, which terminated the
Occupation Statute in return for Bonn's commitment to raise German forces
as prescribed under the Contractual Agreement of the EDC.[31] Of course,
none of this meant that the EDC was home and free. Its implementation
awaited ratification in the national parliaments. The newly elected
Eisenhower administration supported with increasing vigor German rearmament through the EDC as a credible collective security regime for Europe,
not least of all because Eisenhower's military expertise recognized the need
for a German defense contribution, while his experience as SACEUR told
him that the Bonn Republic was a reliable ally while in Adenauer's hands.[32]

THE FEDERAL REPUBLIC, SOVEREIGN AND ATLANTICIST

Eisenhower launched an immediate diplomatic offensive on the EDC's
behalf, with a view to speeding up ratification in France and Germany.
His Secretary of State, John Foster Dulles, in fact applied considerable pressure
on both Paris and Bonn throughout 1953, with repeated warnings that

Washington was losing its patience.[33] For Adenauer, these cautions included a strong recommendation that his government reach agreement with Paris on the status of the Saar region, before 1939 a German province but considered by France a semiautonomous region since 1945. Faced with a general election in September 1953, Adenauer needed to accommodate Paris to an extent that would convince Washington of German reasonableness, while avoiding concessions that could weaken his position with a German electorate poised to pass judgment on his first term as Chancellor.[34]

When France declared in January 1953 that its ratification of the EDC would depend upon a resolution of the Saar dispute, Adenauer committed his government somewhat vaguely to the "continued organic development" of the treaty. When Paris announced the following May a Franco-Saar convention that would give the Saar government the right to make international agreements, he again refused to be drawn. After a formal protest of the convention, he temporized on counterinitiatives and allowed the Saar issue to drift until after the elections. He then assured Secretary Dulles that "Germany would make a serious attempt to solve the Saar problem" and blamed the delays on changes in the French government.[35] The Chancellor was aware of Eisenhower's growing annoyance at French linkage diplomacy and saw some advantages in France's growing self-isolation over the EDC. It was a regrettable but possibly necessary price for real progress on a security arrangement acceptable to Bonn. Simple geography meant that there would be another time and opportunity to collaborate with Paris on the work of the New Europe. France could play at obstructionism, but French isolationism was not a serious option over the long haul.

Precisely how the maneuvers of 1953 were viewed by the West German voters is guesswork, but the electoral dividend was considerable. In the September election, the CDU popular vote jumped from 31 percent in 1949 to 45.2 percent, while that of the SPD atrophied to 28.8 percent. Adenauer entered a new term in a vastly strengthened domestic position. The victory left his governing coalition in possession of two-thirds of the seats in the upper and lower houses of the Bonn parliament, and in a position to amend the Federal Republic's constitution, if necessary, in order to permit the Federal Republic to undertake whatever was required to meet its obligations under the EDC blueprint. As Adenauer saw it, this approach had two important virtues: it would deliver to Washington proof of German readiness to contribute to Western security, and it would make more difficult French efforts to add further amendments to the EDC.[36]

On the second calculation he was wrong. The French government of Pierre Mendès-France piled on new preconditions for French ratification, before the French parliament voted down the EDC outright in August 1954.[37] The disappointment was the bitterest of Adenauer's chancellorship. Yet, as depressed as he was that four years of painstaking statesmanship were now apparently wreckage, he had no difficulty in almost immediately adapting the priorities of his government to a new situation. Similarly, the Eisenhower administration switched rather smoothly to the NATO alternative for German rearmament. Two things helped to make the United States an enthusiast of this solution: the consistency of Adenauer's diplomacy over the preceding four years, now capped by Bonn's EDC ratification against France's veto; and the personal trust Adenauer had earned in Washington.

The first consequence of the EDC's demise was to make Adenauer into the most important man in Europe, in so far as the Chancellor's reaction "suddenly became the most immediate and critical factor in the European security situation."[38] Fully cognizant of the stronger position in which France had unintentionally placed him, Adenauer's initial gesture was to stress that proposed alternatives to the EDC would have to deliver full sovereignty to the Federal Republic. He was also concerned to make the most of Germany's image abroad, when he lamented publicly how France had isolated itself from Europe and the United States, and then he emphasized that Bonn's diplomacy would nonetheless continue to stress reconciliation and cooperation with Paris.[39]

The substantive initiative now shifted to London and Washington, and it was to fresh Anglo-American overtures that the newly empowered Adenauer had to find the appropriate response. British Foreign Minister Anthony Eden made the first move, with Dulles's consent and advice, by touring continental capitals to win support for a security conference in London. Meanwhile, Dulles asked the other Western allies to surrender most of their powers of occupation in Germany and accept the Federal Republic as a member of NATO under the Brussels Treaty. In the autumn of 1954, he pressed the agenda on German admission to NATO, discreetly yet firmly, buttressed by a resolute belief in the imperative of a West German security contribution and his faith in Adenauer's integrity.

In London, Adenauer made the most of the pressure Washington was applying to its European allies for a successful resolution to the security crisis. The conference's turning point arrived with Adenauer's assurance that the Federal Republic would forswear the production of atomic, biological, or chemical weapons. Because Mendès-France could make no such commitment on behalf of France, Adenauer was effectively saying that the Federal Republic would in principle agree to French military superiority. He accepted in addition the principle that German troops would come fully under NATO command, along with other limitations on sovereignty that for the time being would make the Federal Republic less than a perfectly equal partner. At that point in security debate when Germany's position was at its strongest, in other words, Adenauer calmly removed any intellectually respectable rationale for a

French veto of German membership in NATO. Dulles hailed Adenauer's concession as an act of great statesmanship made by "a true European who made real sacrifices to European principles."[40] The Chancellor's commitments also prompted Mendès-France to drop the demand that a definitive solution to the Saar issue precede French acquiescence.

The London conference thus essentially ended the first stage of the debate on the Bonn Republic's place in Western Europe. According to the Paris agreements of October 1954, the Federal Republic was freed from the authority of the Allied High Commission, and was to have its own national armed forces, enrolled simultaneously in NATO and the Western European Union (WEU). At the same time, Bonn's allies recognized the Federal Republic as the only state legitimately constituted to speak for the German people. Ever conscious of the havoc wrought by nationalism in Germany's history, Adenauer never openly admitted that for him, democracy in one part of a divided Germany was a greater good than reunification of the whole. As Chancellor, he would not defer to the attachments of fellow Germans whose political judgment had been refuted by history, but neither would he abdicate in what he saw as his deeper obligation to them. The drawn-out nature of the EDC debate itself enabled Adenauer to bring sufficient numbers of Germans to view postwar Europe from his perspective, and to accept that Western assurances on reunification were "the only reliable guarantee that the two parts of Germany would ever be rejoined."[41]

The double talk periodically employed in defending his policies to German voters was largely absent from Adenauer's dialogue with Bonn's Western allies, especially the United States. Indeed, the Chancellor's remarkable courage in standing up for what he considered the just claims of the Bonn government on behalf of its citizens was complemented by a frank revelation of his very real concern at the prospects of European security and democracy. His ever-present willingness to color Washington's view of Cold War Europe arose above all from a genuine fear of Soviet intentions, and equally honest doubts that Washington grasped the gravity of the situation. However often he argued Bonn's cause to a point that tested the patience of the American superpower, he nonetheless strengthened the Federal Republic's weak diplomatic position with the example of his personal reliability.

This point merits special emphasis. For all its guile, Adenauer's diplomacy was hardly Florentine in inspiration or intent. The great irony is that someone of his background and disposition understood so well that rearming a nation infamous for its misadventures in war should be vital to the respect the Bonn Republic needed from its friends and foes. Adenauer used the rearmament issue to break with the past and reconstitute German diplomacy with a set of principles that eventually earned the Federal Republic a place of leadership in the European Community. In a unified German state whose options are no longer subject to the polarities of Cold War, the foundations he laid are now being tested as never before. If, in the end, the Federal Republic is not equal to the burden of European leadership, scholars might yet look for some flaw in Adenauer's design. But they cannot charge him with moral irresponsibility. At a time when the Bonn Republic was not yet 10 years old, the American historian Gordon Craig observed that "the nation whose unity was first forged by Bismarck, he [Adenauer] wished to submerge in a greater unity. Even failure should not be allowed to dim the grandeur of the attempt."[42]

NOTES

1. *The Economist* (November 26, 1949), p. 1.

2. Anneliese Poppinga, *Konrad Adenauer: Geschichtsverständnis, Weltanschauung und politische Praxis* (Stuttgart: Deutsche Verlags-Anstalt, 1975), pp. 47–48, 119–214. See also Hans-Peter Schwarz, *Adenauer,* 2 vols. (Stuttgart: Deutsche Verlags-Anstalt, 1986).

3. Poppinga, *Konrad Adenauer,* p. 46.

4. Ibid., pp. 58–61; Schwarz, *Adenauer,* Vol. 1, pp. 301–4; Werner Weidenfeld, *Konrad Adenauer und Europa* (Bonn: Europa Union Verlag, 1976).

5. Rudolf Morsey, "Der politische Aufstieg Konrad Adenauers, 1945–1949," in Rudolf Morsey and Konrad Repgen, eds., *Adenauer Studien* I (Mainz: Matthias-Grünewald-Verlag, 1971), pp. 20–57. On Christian Democracy, see Michael Fogarty, *Christian Democracy in Western Europe, 1820–1953* (London: Routledge and Kegan Paul, 1957), pp. 27–40; Arnold J. Heidenheimer, *Adenauer and the CDU* (The Hague: Martinus Nijhoff, 1960); Dorothee Buchhaas, *Die Volkspartei* (Düsseldorf: Droste, 1981).

6. See Max Weber, "Politics as a Vocation," in H. H. Gerth and C. Wright Mills, eds., *From Max Weber: Essays in Sociology* (New York: Oxford University Press, 1958), pp. 120–28; Raymond Aron, "Max Weber and Modern Social Science," in Franciszek Draus, ed., *History, Truth, Liberty: Selected Writings of Raymond Aron* (Chicago: University of Chicago Press, 1985), pp. 348–50.

7. Quoted in Poppinga, *Konrad Adenauer,* p. 27.

8. Dean Acheson, *Present at the Creation* (New York: W. W. Norton, 1969), pp. 435–37; Christian Greiner, "The Defense of Western Europe and the Rearmament of Western Germany," in Olav Riste, ed., *Western Security: The Formative Years* (Oslo: Norwegian University Press, 1985), pp. 150–57; Theo Sommer, "Wiederbewaffnung und Verteidigungspolitik," in Hans-Peter Schwarz and Richard Löwenthal, eds., *Die zweite Republik: 25 Jahre Bundesrepublik Deutschland, Eine Bilanz* (Stuttgart: Seewald, 1974), pp. 580–81.

9. Schwarz, *Adenauer,* Vol. 1, pp. 763–65.

10. Hans-Peter Schwarz, "Das aussenpolitische Konzept Konrad Adenauers," in Rudolf Morsey and Konrad Repgen, eds., *Adenauer Studien* I (Mainz: Matthias-Grünewald-Verlag, 1971), pp. 83–85; Michael Stürmer, *Die Grenzen der Macht* (Berlin: Siedler, 1990), pp. 106–7.

11. Zara Steiner, *The Lights That Failed: European International History, 1919–1933* (New York: Oxford University Press, 2005), pp. 234–35; Wolfram F. Hanrieder, *Germany, America, Europe: Forty Years of German Foreign Policy* (New Haven, CT: Yale University Press, 1989), pp. 148–49; Werner Link, "Die aussenpolitische Staatsräson der Bundesrepublik Deutschland," in Manfred Funke et al., eds., *Demokratie und Diktatur: Geist und Gestalt Politischer Herrschaft in Deutschland und Europa* (Düsseldorf: Droste, 1987), pp. 400–416; Edwina S. Campbell, *Germany's Past and Europe's Future: The Challenges of West German Foreign Policy* (Washington, DC: Pergamon-Brassey's, 1989), pp. 15–16.

12. Quoted in Marc Trachtenberg, *A Constructed Peace: The Making of the European Settlement, 1945–1963* (Princeton, NJ: Princeton University Press, 1999), p. 102. See also Konrad Adenauer, *Erinnerungen, 1945–53* (Stuttgart: Deutsche Verlags-Anstalt, 1965), pp. 245–46; Schwarz, *Adenauer*, Vol. 1, pp. 735–36; Thomas Allen Schwartz, *America's Germany: John J. McCloy and the Federal Republic of Germany* (Cambridge, MA: Harvard University Press, 1991), pp. 116–18; R. G. Foerster, "Innenpolitische Aspekte der Sicherheit Westdeutschlands, 1947–1950," in R. G. Foerster et al., eds., *Anfänge westdeutscher Sicherheitspolitik, 1945–1956*, 2 vols. (Munich: R. Oldenbourg, 1982), Vol. 1, pp. 451–52.

13. Nr. 348, November 15, 1950 (Bonn): An Dannie Heineman, in Peter Mensing, ed., *Adenauer Briefe, 1949–1951* (Berlin: Siedler, 1985), pp. 305–8.

14. Schwarz, *Adenauer*, Vol. 1, pp. 837–38. Heineman also wrote to John McCloy, U.S. high commissioner to the Federal Republic, with a character sketch of Adenauer. He drew attention both to the Chancellor's periodic "dictatorial tendencies" and his moral courage, and he speculated that Adenauer probably failed to appreciate how strong was Western skepticism about Germany's good intentions no matter what kind of government was in power.

15. F. Roy Willis, *France, Germany and the New Europe, 1945–1967* (New York: Oxford University Press, 1969), pp. 151–53; G. D. Drummond, *The German Social Democrats in Opposition, 1949–1960: The Case against Rearmament* (Norman: University of Oklahoma Press, 1982), pp. 34–37; Karl Barr, ed., *Deutsche Verteidigungspolitik, 1947–1967: Dokumente and Kommentare* (Boppard am Rhein: Harald Boldt, 1968), p. 80; Hanrieder, *Germany, America, Europe*, pp. 155–56; Kurt Sontheimer, *Die Adenauer-Ära: Grundlegung der Bundesrepublik* (Munich: DTV, 1991), p. 43.

16. Johanna Vogel, *Kirche und Wiederbewaffnung* (Göttingen: Vandenhoeck und Ruprecht, 1978) pp. 130–40; Schwarz, *Adenauer*, Vol. 1, pp. 771–74.

17. A. Doering-Manteuffel, *Katholizismus und Wiederbewaffnung* (Mainz: Grünewald, 1981), p. 85.

18. Nr. 44, June 7, 1951 (Bonn): An den Hohen Kommissar der Vereinigten Staaten von Amerika, John J. McCloy, Frankfurt/Main, *Adenauer Briefe, 1951–1953*, p. 67.

19. Ibid., pp. 69–70.

20. Nr. 15, June 1, 1951, in Hans Jürgen Küsters, ed., *Adenauer Teegespräche, 1950–1954* (Berlin: Siedler, 1984), p. 93.

21. Nr. 17, July 13, 1951, *Adenauer Teegespräche, 1950–1954*, pp. 101–3. See also Anne Deighton, "Arming the Key Battleground: German Rearmament, 1950–1955," *Diplomacy and Statecraft*, Vol. 3, No. 2 (July 1992), p. 351.

22. Quoted in Schwartz, *America's Germany*, p. 128; Acheson, *Present at the Creation*, p. 436.

23. Hans-Peter Schwarz, *Die Ära Adenauer* (Stuttgart: Deutsche Verlags-Anstalt, 1981), p. 137.

24. Gerhard Wettig, *Entmilitarisierung und Wiederbewaffnung in Deutschland, 1943–1955* (Munich: Oldenbourg, 1967), pp. 407–8; U.S. Department of State, *Foreign Relations of the United States* (hereafter *FRUS*), 1951, Vol. 3, p. 995; Schwartz, *America's Germany*, pp. 211–13.

25. *FRUS*, 1951, Vol. 3, pp. 998–99, 1001.

26. Hans-Jürgen Schröder, "Kanzler der Alliierten? Die Bedeutung der USA für die Außenpolitik Adenauers," in Joseph Foschepoth, ed., *Adenauer und die deutsche Frage* (Göttingen: Vandenhoeck und Ruprecht, 1988), pp. 118–45; Hanrieder, *Germany, America, Europe*, pp. 6–11, 156–57.

27. Nr. 44, June 7, 1951 (Bonn): An den Hohen Kommissar der Vereinigten Staaten von Amerika, John J. McCloy, Frankfurt/Main, *Adenauer Briefe, 1951–1953*, p. 65.

28. Schwarz, *Adenauer*, Vol. 1, p. 840; *FRUS*, 1951, III, pp. 1026–27; Irwin Wall, *The United States and the Making of Postwar France, 1945–1954* (New York: Cambridge University Press, 1991), p. 192; John Gillingham, *Coal, Steel and the Rebirth of Europe, 1945–1955* (New York: Cambridge University Press, 1991), pp. 260–62.

29. Nr. 26, April 2, 1952, *Adenauer Teegespräche*, 1950–1954, pp. 231–33; Hanrieder, *Germany, America, Europe*, pp. 153–54, 155–58; Rolf Steininger, *Eine vertane Chance: Die Stalin-Note vom 10. März 1952* (Bonn: Dietz, 1985); Hermann Graml, "Die Legende von der verpassten Gelegenheit," *Vierteljahreschefte für Zeitgeschichte*, Vol. 29 (1981), pp. 307–41; Joseph Foschepoth, "Wesintegration statt Wiedervereinigung: Adenauers Deutschlandpolitik 1949–1965," in Foschepoth, *Adenauer und die deutsche Frage* (Göttingen: Vandenhoeck und Ruprecht, 1988), pp. 29–60.

30. Wilfried Loth, "The Korean War and the Reorganization of the European Security System, 1948–1955," in R. Ahmann, A. M. Birke, and M. Howard, eds., *The Quest for Stability: Problems of West European Security, 1918–1957* (London: Oxford University Press, 1993), pp. 481–84; F. H. Tenbruck, "Alltagsnormen und Lebensgefühlen der Bundesrepublik," in Schwarz and Löwenthal, *Die zweite Republik*, pp. 289–310.

31. The agreement provided for a West German ground force of 500,000 men, a tactical air force, and a coastal defense. In other words, it moved significantly in the direction of the Himmeroder proposals and was bound to be displeasing to France. Willis, *France, Germany, and the New Europe*, p. 138.

32. Dwight D. Eisenhower, *The White House Years, 1953–1956: Mandate for Change* (Garden City, NY: Doubleday, 1963), pp. 396–99.

33. The Eisenhower administration simultaneously undertook to forward the case for a restoration of German sovereignty on the grounds of the proven political maturity of the Adenauer government. A special effort was made to coordinate U.S. and

British policy and to indicate to Bonn that, in the event of a French veto of the EDC, the United States and Britain were prepared to admit the Federal Republic to NATO even over France's protests. Wettig, *Entmilitarisierung und Wiederbewaffnung in Deutschland*, pp. 566–67; Frederick W. Marks III, *Power and Peace: The Diplomacy of John Foster Dulles* (Westport, CT: Praeger, 1993), pp. 55–58; B. R. Duchin, "The 'Agonizing Reappraisal': Eisenhower, Dulles and the EDC," *Diplomatic History*, Vol. 19, No. 2 (1992), pp. 201–21.

34. Trachtenberg, *A Constructed Peace*, pp. 121–122; James G. Hershberg, " 'Explosion in the Offing': German Rearmament and American Diplomacy," *Diplomatic History*, Vol. 16, No. 4 (1992), p. 541. On the background to France's claims on the Saar, see F. Roy Willis, *The French in Germany, 1945–1949* (Stanford, CA: Stanford University Press, 1962), pp. 15–16, 34–35, 141–43.

35. Willis, *France, Germany and the New Europe*, p. 201; Schwarz, *Adenauer*, Vol. 2, p. 59; *FRUS, 1952–1954*, Vol. 7, p. 431.

36. Wettig, *Entmilitarisierung und Wiederbewaffnung in Deutschland*, pp. 599–60, 546.

37. Raymond Aron and Daniel Lerner, *France Defeats the EDC* (New York: Praeger, 1957); Paul Noack, *Das Scheitern der Europäischen Verteidigungsgemeinschaft: Entscheidungsprozesse vor und nach dem 30. August 1954* (Düsseldorf: Droste, 1977).

38. Edward Fursdon, *The European Defense Community: A History* (London: Macmillan, 1980), p. 309.

39. Fursdon, *The European Defense Community*, pp. 309–10; Konrad Adenauer, *Erinnerungen, 1953–1955*, Vol. 2 (Stuttgart: Deutsche Verlags-Anstalt, 1965), pp. 302–4.

40. Schwarz, *Adenauer*, Vol. 1, pp. 153–57; Marks, *Power and Peace*, pp. 57–60; Hans-Jürgen Grabbe, "Konrad Adenauer, John Foster Dulles, and West German-American Relations," in R. H. Immerman, ed., *John Foster Dulles and the Diplomacy of the Cold War* (Princeton, NJ: Princeton University Press, 1990), pp. 114–20; Rolf Steininger, "Das Scheitern der EVG und der Beitritt der Bundesrepublik zur NATO," *Aus Politik und Zeitgeschichte*, B 17/85 (1985), pp. 3–18; G. Ziebura, *Die deutsch-französischen Beziehungen seit 1945* (Stuttgart: Neske, 1970), pp. 65–81.

41. A. James McAdams, *Germany Divided: From the Wall to Reunification* (Princeton, NJ: Princeton University Press, 1993), p. 20; Hanrieder, *Germany, America, Europe*, pp. 157–58; Hans Peter Schwarz, "Die Politik der Westbindung oder die Staatsraison der Bundesrepublik Deutschland," *Zeitschrift für Politik*, Vol. 22, No. 4 (1975), pp. 307–37.

42. Gordon Craig, *From Bismarck to Adenauer: Aspects of German Statecraft* (Baltimore: Johns Hopkins University Press, 1958), p. 148; Heinrich August Winkler, *Der lange Weg nach Westen*, 2 vols. (Munich: C. H. Beck, 2000), Vol. 2, pp. 636–639.

10

Eduard Shevardnadze and the End of the Soviet System: Necessity and Choice

Paul Marantz

> We have to face up to the issue of politics and morality, of morality in politics, of bringing the ideals of society in line with its practice.[1]
>
> —Shevardnadze (1988)

> "Chernobyl Day" tore the blindfold from our eyes and persuaded us that politics and morals could not diverge. We had to gauge our politics constantly by moral criteria. Lest I be thought too sancti-monious, I shall say that moral politics is the credo of the pragma-tist, a person whom life has taught that immoral politics go nowhere.[2]
>
> —Shevardnadze (1991)

Communist *apparatchiks*, the officials who spend their careers toiling away within the Party bureaucracy, are not usually thought of as individuals with strong principles and well-developed moral codes. For the most part, they have proven to be opportunists, careerists, or worse. Yet Eduard Shevardnadze may well be a striking exception. Even though his ambitions and well-developed political skills brought him to the highest levels of the Communist Party and government of the Soviet Union, it appears that he somehow retained a strong sense of personal morality and a belief that principles must play an important role in guiding policy. As Soviet Foreign Minister from July 1985 to early 1991, he was able to put some of his beliefs into practice. He played a crucial role in trans-forming Soviet foreign policy, accommodating the Soviet Union to its declining position in world affairs, and bringing about an unexpectedly rapid and peaceful end to decades of Cold War and confrontation.

Shevardnadze was a very unlikely choice for the post of Foreign Minister. He spent most of his career far from Moscow in his native republic of Georgia. Unlike his immediate predecessor, Andrei Gromyko, who had labored for almost two decades in the diplomatic service and had been an ambassador to the United States and Great Britain as well as Permanent Representative to the United Nations prior to being selected as Foreign Minister, Shevardnadze had virtually no background in foreign policy. His only vaguely related experience was the various brief trips he had made abroad as a party official, a short period of service as a member of the Soviet Committee for Solidarity with Asian and African countries, and his participation in Politburo meetings as a Candidate Member from 1978 to 1985.[3]

The son of a schoolteacher, Shevardnadze was born in 1928 in a small village in Georgia. At the age of 20, he joined the Communist Party. Like so many other aspiring politicians of his generation, Shevardnadze advanced his career by moving up through the ranks of the *Komsomol* (Communist Youth League). By 1957, he had become First Secretary of the Georgian *Komsomol*. In 1965, after holding various other *Komsomol* and Party posts, he became head of the Georgian Ministry for the Maintenance of Public Order, a position he occupied for the next seven years. As the top police official in the republic, he was responsible for combatting crime and corruption as well as dissent. In 1972, he was promoted to the most powerful post in the republic, the First Secretary of the Georgian Communist Party. He occupied this position until he was selected by Gorbachev in 1985 to come to Moscow to become Foreign Minister. During Brezhnev's domination of Soviet politics, which lasted from 1964 until 1982, only an astute, hard-headed, determined, and flexible politician could have survived in these demanding positions.[4]

Although Shevardnadze's career followed the path of a typical successful official at the republic level, he was not an ordinary Party hack. He was highly intelligent, hard-working, energetic in his fight against corruption, modest, and approachable.[5] Despite the conservatism of the Brezhnev period, he was able to take some modest initiatives to promote market-oriented reform in agriculture and industry, to defend the Georgian language and culture, to encourage greater openness, and to give more attention to public opinion.[6] At the same time, he was politically astute and willing to make the compromises that the system required of all ambitious politicians. In 1976, for example, he was not above pandering to the Party leadership in Moscow by proclaiming at a meeting that "for us Georgians the sun rises not in the east but in the north, in Russia."[7]

Shevardnadze owed his appointment as Foreign Minister to his long-standing friendship with Mikhail Gorbachev. By 1985, they had known each other for some 25 years. Their careers had followed a similar trajectory. Like Shevardnadze, Gorbachev was also a *Komsomol* official in the 1950s and early 1960s, serving in a nearby region of southern Russia. Both were promoted to the position of Candidate Member of the Politburo of the Communist Party of the Soviet Union in the late 1970s. They met often, became good friends, and frequently vacationed together. Gradually, they came to trust one another and to be ever franker in their conversations about the Soviet Union's many problems. According to Shevardnadze, by the late 1970s, "we no longer held anything back."[8] In the winter of 1984–1985, a few months before Gorbachev became General Secretary, Shevardnadze was especially frank in his indictment of the Soviet system. He evidently told Gorbachev: "Everything is rotten. It has to be changed."[9]

Shevardnadze's appointment as Foreign Minister came as a great surprise to Shevardnadze himself and to most observers in the Soviet Union and the West. In a moment of angry candor, Anatoly Dobrynin, the long-time Soviet Ambassador to the United States, who evidently hoped that he would become Foreign Minister, remarked to the American Secretary of State George Shultz: "Our foreign policy is going down the drain. They have named an agricultural type."[10]

Shevardnadze initially tried to decline the appointment, citing his lack of experience, but Gorbachev insisted that he wanted his good friend in this key position. Western observers took the appointment of the inexperienced Shevardnadze as a sign that Gorbachev would take personal charge of Soviet foreign policy. There was some truth in this, and Gorbachev remained heavily involved in the formulation and conduct of Soviet foreign policy throughout his term in office. But it was a mistake to underestimate Shevardnadze. He threw himself into his job with great energy, working brutally long hours until he completely mastered his portfolio. Shevardnadze became a key player in the transformation of Soviet foreign policy, changing Moscow's adversarial relationship with the capitalist world to one of active cooperation and partnership.

Shevardnadze embodies an unusual combination of traits. He is a man of conviction who also values moderation and pragmatic compromise.[11] Though he was a beneficiary of the Communist system, having risen from humble origins to a position of great power and privilege, he was acutely aware of the system's failures and was willing to change them. He was a very skilled politician and policy maker but was modest about his attainments, frank about his shortcomings, and genuinely interested in encouraging his subordinates to be candid in their criticism of the Foreign Ministry's actions.

When Gorbachev's policies veered away from reform in the autumn of 1990, Shevardnadze felt that he could no longer support his long-time friend. On a number of previous occasions he had warned that he would resign rather than compromise strongly held positions.[12] This time he followed through on his threat.

On December 20, 1990, he stunned the Soviet people and heightened anxiety throughout the world by unexpectedly announcing his resignation as Foreign Minister. He complained that his foreign policy of conciliation with

the West had been unfairly attacked and warned that the danger of dictatorship loomed before the Soviet Union.[13] His resignation speech was a protest
against the trend toward authoritarianism and an attempt to get the reformers
to stop their fratricidal bickering with one another and unite against the old
guard. When Shevardnadze's prophecy of approaching dictatorship came to
pass with the attempted coup of August 1991, he quickly joined the crowds
outside Boris Yeltsin's headquarters and courageously helped to rally the
opposition to the seizure of power.

With the disintegration of the Soviet Union in December 1991,
Shevardnadze's career took a new turn. At age 64, he could have chosen a
comfortable retirement. Ensconced in a Moscow foreign policy think tank
that he had helped found, he could have assumed the role of elder statesman,
lecturing to appreciative Western audiences, writing his memoirs, and
enjoying a comfortable standard of living based upon hard currency earnings
from lecture fees and royalties.

Instead, in early 1992, he returned to strife-torn Georgia as the newly
elected head of the government to take up the daunting task of trying to unify
this newly independent country, which was being ripped apart by secessionist
movements, by a smoldering civil war waged by the supporters of his ousted
predecessor, Zviad Gamsakhurdia, by the rise of various armed militias, by
the breakdown of law and order, and by economic collapse. His life has been
repeatedly threatened, and on several occasions he has narrowly escaped assassination attempts.[14]

Shevardnadze's personal odyssey had not ended. In November 1992, he
revealed that he had abandoned atheism and had been baptized in the
Georgian Orthodox Church. His journey has been a long one. As he put it,
"I have an icon in my office now, though there was a time when I had
Stalin's portrait on the wall."[15]

During his five and one-half years as Foreign Minister, Shevardnadze presided over a remarkable transformation of Soviet foreign policy. It is true, of
course, that a string of failures—which included the costly stalemate in
Afghanistan, the crushing burden of the arms race, the fall of the Berlin
Wall, and the collapse of communism in Eastern Europe—compelled the
Soviet leadership to reconsider past policies. But the particular response they
made to these setbacks, and the fact that the Soviet Union accommodated
itself to its sharply reduced international status so quickly and with so little
violence, is in significant measure a result of the creative leadership of
Shevardnadze.

Shevardnadze was certainly not alone in articulating the basic principles of
what came to be called the "new political thinking." Gorbachev was very
active in espousing these principles, and many scholars and policy advisers
played a pivotal role in persuading the leadership of the need for a new

approach to foreign policy.[16] Nonetheless, Shevardnadze was especially important in advocating and implementing these new principles because of his key roles as Foreign Minister, member of the Politburo, and close associate of Gorbachev.

Moreover, unlike many veterans of the Soviet foreign policy establishment, for him the new thinking was not just another political line that had to be mouthed because it was decreed by the leadership. He spoke with apparent conviction and evident passion on behalf of a major reversal of past policy. While some of the principles he espoused (such as establishing mutual trust) might seem to be no more than empty clichés or meaningless platitudes, in the context of traditional Soviet policy—which was often based upon confrontation, mistrust of the "class enemy," and a short-sighted view of what the Soviet national interest was—these principles were nothing less than revolutionary.

Three main themes recur again and again in Shevardnadze's speeches and writings. These concern the need for the Soviet Union to overcome its isolation from the international community by showing other nations that it could be trusted, the necessity of forging a new conception of Soviet national security, and the vital importance of bringing greater openness to the formulation and debate of Soviet foreign policy. In an attempt to convey the unusual combination of pragmatism and moral force that Shevardnadze brought to the analysis of Soviet foreign policy, his statements are quoted at some length in the discussion here.

Throughout much of Russian history, there has been a sharp conflict between two different outlooks, that of the Westernizers and that of the Slavophiles. The Westernizers have argued that Russia could best overcome its lamentable backwardness by emulating the more advanced West, by borrowing from it, and by associating with it as closely as possible. In contrast, the Slavophiles have stressed Russia's distinctiveness, its need to find its own path, and the necessity of rejecting the corrupt and alien ways of the West.[17]

Paradoxically, the official Soviet ideology of Marxism-Leninism had a great deal in common with the Slavophile rejection of the West, despite the lip service that was paid to Marx and his supposedly universal model of social development. Soviet ideology and foreign policy were built on the premise that there existed two separate and deeply antagonistic worlds—the capitalist world and the socialist world—which were totally incompatible. Scorn was heaped upon "bourgeois" institutions, conceptions of human rights, and foreign policy.

Despite Shevardnadze's unimpeachable credentials as a member of the Communist establishment, he is a fervent Westernizer. He believed that the Soviet Union had erred in counterpoising its system and its values to those of the West, that the Soviet Union needed to heal its breach with the outside world. For him, there were not two mutually opposed worlds—the socialist and the capitalist—but one international community from which the Soviet Union had foolishly estranged itself, thereby doing grievous harm to its economy, its political institutions, and its fundamental moral health. The advanced nations of the West were not the class enemy but "the civilized world," which the Soviet Union urgently needed to join.

In the memoirs that he published in 1991, Shevardnadze was scathing in his criticism of past Soviet behavior:

> People did not trust us. How many times before had various statements been made by the political leadership, a certain line of action proclaimed, while everything remained unchanged? . . . [A]greements with the "bour-geoisie" or with the "imperialists" were always regarded in our country as a necessary evil at best, but more often as a means to gain time, a tactical maneuver. . . . An ideological struggle was on, and any means were fair. The main thing was to protect our goalposts. . . . The image of the Soviet Union in the eyes of the world was of little real concern.[18]

In a major statement on Soviet foreign policy, which he delivered on July 25, 1988, at a high-level conference organized by the Ministry of Foreign Affairs, Shevardnadze set out his views at some length, lecturing his more cynical colleagues:

> Here I want to talk about a problem which, as far as I know, is extremely rarely addressed by researchers. The point at issue is the image of a coun-try as an important aspect of its existence in the international commu-nity, in the modern civilized world. . . . We should not pretend, Comrades, that norms and notions of what is proper, of what is called civilized conduct in the world community do not concern us. If you want to be accepted in it you must observe them.[19]

In reply to his critics, he stated:

> Sometimes one hears the view that we pay too much attention to what the outside world will say about us. In this connection I would like the stress the following. . . . [W]e cannot exhibit indifference to what others are saying and thinking about us. For our self-respect, our well-being, our position in the world hinge largely on the attitude of others towards us as well.[20]

This unorthodox conception of Soviet relations with the outside world was forcefully expressed in Shevardnadze's discussion of Soviet foreign policy before the Soviet legislature on October 23, 1989. He stated:

The notion that we can ignore the world around us and disregard other people's interests has cost our people and socialism dearly in the past. ... If we want to be part of a civilized world, we must consider how our actions and words are perceived. The diplomatic service can and should provide supreme organs of power with more prompt and precise information about those instances when our positions, approaches, and actions conflict with prevailing international opinions, legal norms, and moral and ethical standards.[21]

In condemning the harm done to Soviet foreign policy by the invasion of Afghanistan, Shevardnadze stated:

When more than 100 UN members kept condemning our action for a number of years, did we need anything else to make us realize: We had placed ourselves in opposition to the world community, had violated norms of behavior and gone against common human interests.[22]

For Shevardnadze, it was vitally important that the Soviet Union become a full member of "the civilized world." This could only be done by admitting past errors, putting new policies in place, winning the trust of other nations, and restoring—as he put it—"the good name of the country."[23]

Another major theme that recurs in Shevardnadze's speeches and writings concerns the need for the Soviet Union to be guided by a new conception of what constitutes its national security. In his view, a redefinition of Soviet security interests was necessary to get rid of the past preoccupation with unlimited military might. He argued that the Soviet arms buildup had done great harm to the country's fundamental interests by causing other nations to be fearful of Soviet intentions, by undermining the domestic economy, and by lowering the people's standard of living.

Shevardnadze strongly attacked the neglect of the people's well-being, which he blamed on a fundamental misunderstanding of what constitutes security and strength in the modern world.

[T]he category of the power and security of the state under modern conditions is something entirely different from what it was during the thirties when we sang: "The Red Army is stronger than all." Can a state be strong and secure when its economy fails, fundamental sciences are in a state of stagnation, agriculture can in no way get on its feet, and the citizens are suffering from a shortage of literally everything?[24]

In his memoirs, Shevardnadze further elaborated on this view:

> We became a superpower largely because of our military might. But the bloated size and unrestrained escalation of this military might was reducing us to the level of a third-rate country, unleashing processes that pushed us to the brink of catastrophe. Our military expenditures as a percentage of gross national product were two and a half times greater that those of the United States. . . . We have captured first place in the world weapons trade (28 percent of the entire sales total), and have made the Kalashnikov submachine gun the hallmark of our advanced technology. But we occupy about sixtieth place in standard of living, thirty-second place in average life expectancy, and fiftieth in infant mortality. What kind of national security is this? It is not just immoral but politically dangerous to equate national security with tanks and warheads, while leaving out such "trivia" as human life and welfare.[25]

In short, he argued that "a country of socially and politically humiliated people cannot gain security."[26]

In opposition to the past preoccupation with military strength, Shevardnadze advanced a few simple propositions: the country should recognize that it possessed limited resources and there were certain things in the foreign sphere which it could not afford; foreign policy should be tailored to domestic priorities rather than vice versa; and in view of the low Soviet standard of living, resources should be found to increase the people's well-being. All of this sounds like self-evident common sense, the kind of elementary considerations that any policy maker would be sure to take into account. But in the closed world of Soviet politics, where a handful of privileged leaders imposed their own narrow conceptions of what was good for the country on a long-suffering and largely powerless population, this represented a frontal challenge to traditional practices.

As Shevardnadze noted during an interview with a Soviet newspaper in the spring of 1989:

> In the times before restructuring "counting kopecks" when making decisions in the political area (I include defense issues here) was regarded as almost disgraceful. Foreign policy was like a thing unto itself. . . . Actually the "residual principle" was in effect with respect to the entire national economy. The domestic civilian economy got what was left over after the foreign economic and defense measures were taken care of. We directly ignored the fact that in the international and defense spheres there could be things which our country simply could not afford.[27]

In an address in June 1987 to a meeting of members of the Soviet foreign policy establishment, Shevardnadze was brutally frank:

> Beyond the borders of the Soviet Union you and I represent a great country which in the last 15 years has been steadily losing its position as one of the leading industrially developed countries. . . . If we are finally honest, we frequently encouraged and at times even induced enormous material investments in hopeless foreign policy projects and tacitly promoted actions which both in the direct and the indirect sense have cost the people dearly even to this day. . . . The fact that the foreign policy service—one of the most important and most sensitive links in the system of state management—carried out its obligation out of touch with the country's fundamental vital interest is on our conscience.[28]

While in the past, domestic needs were subordinated to foreign policy considerations, Shevardnadze argued that now the reverse was vitally necessary. Far-reaching internal reform was absolutely essential, and the key task of Soviet foreign policy was to do everything possible to facilitate and promote domestic development: "[T]he most important function of our foreign policy is to create the optimal conditions for the economic and social development of our country."[29]

Shevardnadze made one of his most important contributions to the reform of Soviet domestic and foreign policy by fighting against the obsessive secrecy that characterized Soviet policy making. He was a leading champion of greater openness and played an important role in securing the release of the anti-Stalin film *Repentance* in late 1986.[30] This powerful film created a sensation and helped unleash an ever-growing stream of historical revelations that provided a powerful impetus to further reform.

By mid-1987, the discussion of Soviet domestic affairs was becoming increasingly open. Day by day and month by month, the bounds of permissible discussion were widened. However, foreign policy questions were almost totally insulated from this process. Scholars and journalists were not allowed to encroach on this sensitive domain.

Shevardnadze took the lead in bringing *glasnost* to the discussion of Soviet foreign policy. He rejected the traditional pretense of infallibility and was remarkably candid about the errors and shortcomings of Soviet foreign policy. He ensured that his speeches were openly published so that they would stimulate discussion and fresh thinking. He attacked the walling off of foreign policy from critical scrutiny. In a speech on October 27, 1987, he stated:

> Bold, interesting, and controversial articles have appeared on many basic questions of domestic life in all its manifestations, party and state

construction, the economy, culture, art, and science. But there is nothing like it in the field of foreign policy. Is it really because everything is
correct with us and variants other than those which are being implemented do not exist?[31]

Shevardnadze backed up his words with decisive action. In early 1988, the
editor of the journal *Mezhdunarodnaya Zhizn'* (published in English as
International Affairs) was replaced. The new editor was Boris Pyadyshev, an
associate of Shevardnadze at the Ministry of Foreign Affairs. His mandate
was to transform the journal so that it would provide a forum for the discussion
of previously restricted questions. Up until that time, *Mezhdunarodnaya Zhizn'*
had been the tame house organ of the Ministry of Foreign Affairs. In wooden
language that was heavily laden with ideological rhetoric, it unimaginatively
toed the official line, avoiding even the slightest hint of controversy or origi-
nality. Under Pyadyshev's editorship, *Mezhdunarodnaya Zhizn'* quickly
advanced to the front ranks of the battle for greater openness, and one by
one many of the taboos that prevented the open discussion of Soviet foreign
policy fell.[32]

Shevardnadze supported greater openness on both principled and pragmatic grounds. If greater democracy was to be promoted and if the Soviet
parliament, which for the first time was gaining genuine powers of oversight,
was to be able to carry out its new responsibilities, then the public discussion
of foreign policy matters had to be elevated to a higher level. Moreover, one
of the most effective ways to break the grip that the military and the Party
bureaucracies had on the formulation of Soviet foreign policy was by high-
lighting the failure of past policies and by supporting demands for greater
openness about the true cost of military spending and foreign aid. Frank discussion in the press and open hearings in the Soviet legislature would
strengthen Shevardnadze's hand as he did battle with those resisting change.

When Gorbachev, Shevardnadze, and other members of the Soviet leadership first began articulating the principles of the "new thinking" in 1986 and
1987, their statements were greeted with skepticism in the West. Many
Western analysts saw this as little more than a propagandistic exercise aimed
at improving the Soviet Union's image without changing the substance of
Soviet foreign policy. The "new thinking" was dismissed as consisting of vacuous clichés and empty slogans. Tough-minded analysts argued that what really
counted were deeds, not words.[33]

Even when Soviet policy began to change quite substantially, and Moscow
agreed to withdraw its troops from Afghanistan, accepted the "zero option" for
the elimination of intermediate-range nuclear forces, and announced sharp
cuts in its conventional forces, some Western analysts remained highly skeptical about the Soviet embrace of "new thinking." They saw the Soviet talk of a

"world community," of a new role for the United Nations, and of "comprehensive security" and "universal human interests" as a smoke screen that was
being used to hide a Soviet defeat behind the verbiage of high principle.[34]
According to this argument, Soviet power was in sharp decline, and Soviet
foreign power was in retreat. Rather than frankly acknowledge these unpleasant facts, Soviet spokesmen attempted to claim that the Soviet Union was in
the forefront of the struggle to elevate international politics to a higher level
and to ensure that the enlightened principles of cooperative security rather
than narrow considerations of unilateral advantage prevailed. The Soviets
were simply attempting to disguise defeat as victory by portraying the changes
that were taking place as the triumph of principles that the Soviet Union had
long championed.

Some analysts further argued that the key explanatory variable accounting
for the alteration in Soviet policy was not changes in the belief system or values of the Soviet leadership but irresistible economic, social, and political
forces, which were largely beyond their control. The Soviet leadership was
compelled by circumstances to modify their policies. Individual preferences
and values mattered little. New realities left the Soviet leadership little choice
but to bend to the powerful forces reshaping the world.[35]

The thesis of this chapter is very different. It argues that for Shevardnadze,
who played such a critical role in Soviet foreign policy, support for "new
thinking" was much more than a propaganda ploy or the forced and grudging
acceptance of declining Soviet power. In his case, it represented nothing less
than a paradigm shift, a fundamental change in how the world was understood. Shevardnadze was breaking with decades of confrontation and class
warfare. He moved away from class perspectives that emphasized division
and antagonism between "the two camps" to a more complex perspective that
stressed the common concerns and interests that all nations shared regardless
of ideological divisions.

In July 1988, Shevardnadze made a deceptively simple statement.
He declared that "the rivalry between the two systems can no longer be
viewed as the leading tendency of the modern age."[36] This statement signified
a fundamental break with the outlook that had previously animated Soviet
foreign policy. It did not come easy to lifelong Communist Party officials.
As Shevardnadze remarked in an earlier interview with Don Oberdorfer of
the *Washington Post*: "Our basic, fundamental position was the position of class
and class values and this is how we were brought up—all of us."[37]
Shevardnadze noted that the shift to new principles of Soviet foreign policy
beginning in 1986 "gave rise to a very stormy reaction" in the Foreign
Ministry and elsewhere.[38] Similarly, Marshall Sergei Akhromeev, Chief of
the General Staff, remarked: "For me personally, to rethink all these things
and to view the situation from a different angle was very painful. . . . Most of

my life I've thought in a different manner."[39] Indeed, for Akhromeev, the change was so painful that when the attempted coup of August 1991 failed, signifying the end of a powerful and cohesive Soviet Union, he committed suicide.

Shevardnadze's statement set off a sharp debate within the Soviet leadership. Yegor Ligachev, the most powerful conservative voice within the Politburo, quickly responded to Shevardnadze. In a speech given on August 5, 1988, Ligachev stated: "We proceed from the class nature of international relations. Any other formulation of the issue only introduces confusion into the thinking of Soviet people and our friends abroad."[40] However, Shevardnadze enjoyed the support of Gorbachev, and his position prevailed. The traditional dichotomous and confrontational view of the world was scrapped. Forms of cooperation with the capitalist world that had previously been unthinkable now became possible.

The question remains, however, whether this change in outlook was compelled by circumstances. Was the Soviet leadership forced to act as they did by domestic economic crisis and the deterioration of Moscow's international position? Did they lack any real room for choice?

By their very nature, questions such as these, which involve speculation about alternative futures, are very difficult to answer. Historians and political scientists lack the intellectual tools to decide conclusively the "iffy" questions of history. However, several observations are in order.

It should be recalled that the very changes in Soviet policy that some observers now see as having been inevitable were viewed during the Cold War as being just about impossible. By the early 1980s, many Western observers recognized that the Soviet system was performing poorly and was beset by a number of serious domestic and foreign problems. But the general consensus was that these problems could be managed for the foreseeable future. The Soviet leadership was seen as being firmly in control and as having both the will and the ability to avoid fundamental change. The Soviet Union had survived many past crises (e.g., collectivization in the 1920s, the purges in the 1930s, World War II in the 1940s, and the transition to a new leadership and partial de-Stalinization in the 1950s), and almost all observers expected that it would successfully weather its current difficulties. To portray the opening up of the Soviet Union in the late 1980s and the disintegration of Communist Party rule in 1991 as having been inevitable betrays a failure of imagination and an unwillingness to recognize that what happened was not mandated by irresistible economic and social forces but was the outcome of conscious choices made between a number of different policy options. Economic problems and foreign policy setbacks framed and influenced the choices that were made, but they did not determine them.

When the Politburo met in March 1985 to choose a successor to Konstantin Chernenko, its members apparently did not believe the country was in crisis. They chose Gorbachev as the new General Secretary, not because they wanted him to transform the Soviet system, but because they expected him to make it work better. Whatever reformist objectives Gorbachev may have had in 1985, he kept well hidden. His main strength was that his Politburo colleagues saw him as a much-needed change from the tired and ill old men who had preceded him as General Secretary. Gorbachev's vast energy, capacity for hard work, intelligence, and apparent political skill helped solidify his support among the members of the Politburo, who had buried three General Secretaries in the past two and one-half years and recognized that the country needed more energetic leadership.

The cautious conservatives who dominated the Soviet leadership thought that Gorbachev was a safe choice. He had demonstrated his ability and reliability during his five years on the Politburo, and he had displayed no overt signs of radicalism. In his speech to the March 11, 1985, crucial meeting of the Politburo, which chose him as General Secretary, he neither sought nor received a mandate for radical change. Gorbachev stated: "Our economy needs more dynamism. This dynamism is needed for the development of our foreign policy."[41] But he also reassuringly said:

> We do not need to change policy. It is correct and it is true. It is genuine Leninist politics. We need, however, to speed up, to move forward, to disclose shortcomings and overcome them and realize our shining future. . . . I assure you I will do everything to justify the trust of the Party.[42]

By the time Boris Yeltsin wrote his memoirs in 1990, he was locked in a bitter power struggle with Gorbachev, and he had few good words to say about his former colleague, who had presided over his expulsion from the Soviet leadership in late 1987. Yet even he acknowledged the critical role that Gorbachev played in initiating reform:

> The chief problem in his launching of *perestroika* was that he was practically alone, surrounded by the authors and impresarios of Brezhnev's "era of stagnation," who were determined to ensure the indestructibility of the old order of things.[43]

Yeltsin also said of Gorbachev:

> He could have gone on just as Brezhnev and Chernenko did before him. I estimate that the country's natural resources and the people's patience

would have outlasted his lifetime, long enough for him to have lived the well-fed and happy life of the leader of a totalitarian state.[44]

The year 1989 was a pivotal period for the Soviet Union. It was then that the leadership lost its control over events. In 1986–1988, Gorbachev presided over a revolution from above. The leadership directed the pace of change and could have reimposed tight controls at any time. However, by mid-1989, this was no longer so. In 1989, the economy began to decline sharply after several years of modest growth, fueling popular discontent.[45] Long suppressed national grievances burst forth, and the republics began to assert themselves. The revelations produced by *glasnost* robbed the Communist Party of its remaining claims to legitimacy. From 1989 on, the Politburo became the prisoner of events rather than their master.

However, in large measure this new situation was a direct result of the course followed in 1988: the misconceived economic reforms, the toleration of greater openness in the media, and the attempt to open up the political system in a controlled fashion by reinvigorating the Supreme Soviet. In March 1988, Yegor Ligachev, who was the number two man in the Politburo, attacked Gorbachev's reformist policies. Ligachev's challenge was repulsed only after a stormy two-day meeting of the Politburo at which Gorbachev used all the power and authority that his position as General Secretary conferred upon him.[46] Gorbachev's victory was by no means preordained. It owed more to his political skill and power than to the merits of his program. Whereas he could count on the support of the two committed reformers in the Politburo, Shevardnadze and Aleksandr Yakovlev, the political loyalties of the other members were much less certain. Had Ligachev prevailed at this critical juncture, the whole course of Soviet development might have turned out very differently.[47]

By the mid-1980s, it was becoming increasingly clear that the rigid and inefficient Soviet economy was unable to match the dynamism and innovativeness of the free market economies of the West. Economic weakness was bound to undermine its international power. But if a Soviet decline was in some sense inevitable, there was nothing inevitable about its timing or the form it would take. The veteran Sovietologist Myron Rush provides the following characterization of the situation that existed in 1985 when Gorbachev came to power:

> The Soviet Union, while manifestly in trouble as many observed, was not posed for a collapse, nor was it even in acute crisis. The Soviet Union was viable and probably could have lasted another decade or two, with good fortune a good bit longer; but deeply flawed, it was vulnerable to adverse chance events.[48]

An economist, Vladimir Kontorovich, shares this perspective. He points out that the Soviet economy did not decline significantly in the immediate pre-Gorbachev period of 1979–1984, and that it may have even grown at the rate of 1–2 percent per year.[49] There also appear to have been alternatives to the destabilizing reforms undertaken by Gorbachev. The economy could have been accelerated by making some quick cuts in military spending, by embracing detente so that the arms race would have been curbed, thus yielding more substantial reductions in the military budget, and by soliciting Western technical assistance and financial aid to develop the Soviet Union's abundant oil and natural gas reserves. This would have created modest economic growth that would have enhanced stability and allowed the Soviet system to muddle along for some time. It would not have enabled the Soviet Union to catch up with the West, and it would not have reversed the Soviet Union's long-term decline, but it would have significantly delayed it.[50]

Paul Kennedy's much-acclaimed work *The Rise and Fall of the Great Powers* called attention to the Soviet Union's economic difficulties and the implications they had for Moscow's international standing. He warned, "[T]here is nothing in the character or tradition of the Russian state to suggest that it could ever accept imperial decline gracefully."[51] A number of other analysts argued either that Soviet foreign policy was incapable of change, for the regime needed the image of a powerful enemy to rationalize its domestic power, or that a declining and pessimistic Soviet leadership might be even more dangerous than an optimistic one because this might lead to risky foreign policy adventures aimed at salvaging Soviet power.[52] The fact that contrary to these expectations Soviet foreign policy did accommodate itself so "gracefully" and with so little violence to a very painful series of defeats, ranging from Afghanistan and the loss of its East European empire to the reunification of Germany and the disintegration of the Soviet Union itself, suggests that individual choice in response to highly dangerous circumstances did make a difference.

Decades of unrelenting striving for power, of ruthless imperial rule, and of amoral geopolitical maneuvering had cost the Soviet Union dearly. The Soviet Union was saddled with a military budget it could not afford, its population was alienated and dispirited, the country was widely feared, it had few genuine friends, and its rigid economy languished in isolation from the stimulating influences of a competitive world economy.

The policies that Shevardnadze supported went right to the heart of the problem. He argued that the Soviet Union needed to be trusted rather than feared, that it had to guide its policies by "universal human values," that it had to respect international human rights agreements, that it should lower military expenditures and look upon the people's well-being as a crucial element of national power, that it should respect "freedom of choice" in

Afghanistan and Eastern Europe, and that it should rejoin "the civilized world."

Needless to say, the rethinking of Soviet foreign policy did not happen in a vacuum. An uncompetitive economy and a collapsing empire compelled a re-examination of past policy. In response to these problems, "new thinking" was embraced by Gorbachev and promoted by Soviet scholars and policy makers. Shevardnadze was not an isolated figure. But at a crucial time in world affairs, he helped the Soviet Union navigate through a very dangerous passage and achieve a safe landing under very difficult circumstances.

Despite the greater openness of Soviet political discourse in the late 1980s, there is much that we still don't know. The memoirs of Shevardnadze and other top Soviet officials are not especially revealing about the leaders' private thoughts or how key decisions were reached. How far did Shevardnadze go in his questioning of the basic features of the Soviet political system? What was he trying to change and what was he trying to save? How much of his seeming moral conviction was genuine and how much was skillful political packaging aimed at selling needed changes to resistant Communist officials at home and skeptical policy makers abroad? Perhaps in the future, if our very limited access to Soviet archives covering the Gorbachev years improves, we may be able to answer some of these questions. For now, we can simply reflect on how skillfully Shevardnadze used the language of moral conviction to reorient Soviet foreign policy away from traditional patterns of behavior and to create the basis for a new relationship between the Soviet Union and the West.

Shevardnadze was very fortunate in that he became Soviet Foreign Minister at a time when a more principled foreign policy was very much in the country's interest. The dictates of morality and self-interest coincided to an unusual extent. But it is to his credit that he very ably made the most of this opportunity. Even though he was unable to preserve the Soviet Union, he has secured a place in history by helping to bring about a remarkably peaceful end to one of the most intractable and dangerous confrontations the world has witnessed.

NOTES

1. Eduard Shevardnadze, Report to the Ministry of Foreign Affairs Conference, July 25, 1988, in *International Affairs*, No. 10 (1988), p. 23.

2. Eduard Shevardnadze, *The Future Belongs to Freedom* (London: Sinclair-Stevenson, 1991), pp. 175–76.

3. The careers of Gromyko and Shevardnadze are detailed in Alexander G. Rahr, ed., *A Biographic Directory of 100 Leading Soviet Officials*, 3rd ed. (Munich: Radio Liberty Research, 1986), pp. 80–82, 186–88.

4. Shevardnadze's praise of Brezhnev and his support for the decision to send Soviet troops into Afghanistan are cited in Yegor Ligachev, *Inside Gorbachev's Kremlin* (New York: Pantheon Books, 1993), pp. 168–69.

5. Carolyn McGiffert Ekedahl and Melvin A. Goodman, *The Wars of Eduard Shevardnadze* (University Park: Pennsylvania State University Press, 1997), pp. 7–28; Elizabeth Fuller, "A Portrait of Eduard Shevardnadze," *Radio Liberty Research Bulletin*, RL 219/85 (July 3, 1985), pp. 1–11.

6. Don Oberdorfer, *The Turn from the Cold War to a New Era: The United States and the Soviet Union, 1983–1990* (New York: Poseidon Press, 1991), pp. 118–20.

7. Fuller, "A Portrait of Eduard Shevardnadze," p. 10. Also see Yegor Ligachev, *Inside Gorbachev's Kremlin* (New York: Pantheon, 1993), pp. 168–69.

8. Shevardnadze, *The Future Belongs to Freedom*, p. 23.

9. Ibid., p. 37. Gorbachev gave a similar version in a speech to cultural leaders on November 28, 1990. Gorbachev's remarks were published in *Pravda* on December 1, 1990, and are translated in Foreign Broadcast Information Service, *Daily Report: Soviet Union*, December 5, 1990, p. 44. (Hereafter cited as FBIS.)

10. George P. Shultz, *Turmoil and Triumph: My Years as Secretary of State* (New York: Charles Scribner's Sons, 1993), p. 572. In his memoirs, Dobrynin was much more diplomatic. Anatoly Dobrynin, *In Confidence* (New York: Random House, 1995), pp. 575–77.

11. The American secretaries of state George P. Shultz and James A. Baker were able to establish a very constructive working relationship with Shevardnadze, and they praised his openness, honesty, pragmatism, and flexibility in hammering out solutions to difficult problems. Shultz, *Turmoil and Triumph*, p. 886; Michael R. Beschloss and Strobe Talbott, *At the Highest Levels: The Inside Story of the End of the Cold War* (Boston: Little, Brown, 1993), pp. 96, 121, 179–82.

12. *Pravda*, October 24, 1989, as translated in FBIS, October 24, 1989, p. 45; Oberdorfer, *Turn from the Cold War*, p. 409.

13. The text of his resignation speech is reprinted in Shevardnadze, *The Future Belongs to Freedom*, pp. 201–4; Pavel Palazchenko, *My Years with Gorbachev and Shevardnadze* (University Park: Pennsylvania State University Press, 1997), pp. 238–43.

14. Georgie Anne Geyer, "Conversations with Eduard Shevardnadze," *The Washington Quarterly*, Vol. 23, No. 2 (Spring 2000), pp. 55, 61, 63.

15. *The Globe and Mail* (Toronto), November 24, 1992, p. A1.

16. Allen Lynch, *Gorbachev's International Outlook: Intellectual Origins and Political Consequences* (New York: Institute for East-West Security Studies, 1989); Jeff Checkel, "Ideas, Institutions, and the Gorbachev Foreign Policy Revolution," *World Politics*, Vol. 45, No. 2 (January 1993), pp. 271–73.

17. Tibor Szamuely, *The Russian Tradition* (London: Fontana Press, 1988), pp. 251–59.

18. Shevardnadze, *The Future Belongs to Freedom*, p. 87.

19. *International Affairs*, No. 10 (October 1988), p. 23.

20. Ibid., p. 24.

21. *Pravda*, October 24, 1989, as translated in FBIS, October 24, 1989, p. 43.

22. Ibid., p. 45.

23. Ibid., p. 24; Shevardnadze, *The Future Belongs to Freedom*, p. 87.

24. *Argumenty i Fakty*, May 6–12, 1989, as translated in FBIS, May 15, 1989, p. 92.

25. Shevardnadze, *The Future Belongs to Freedom*, p. 54.

26. Ibid., p. 55.

27. *Argumenty i Fakty*, May 6–12, 1989, as translated in FBIS, May 15, 1989, p. 93.

28. Vestnik Ministerstva Inostrannykh Del SSSR, No. 2 (1987), as translated in FBIS, October 27, 1989, p. 52.

29. *Vestnik Ministerstva Inostrannykh Del SSSR*, No. 3 (September 1987), as translated in FBIS, November 3, 1987, p. 91.

30. David Remnick, *Lenin's Tomb: The Last Days of the Soviet Empire* (New York: Random House, 1993), pp. 42–46.

31. *Vestnik Ministerstva Inostrannykh Del SSSR*, No. 2 (1987), as translated in FBIS, October 27, 1987, p. 54.

32. For example, see Alexei Izyumov and Andrei Kortunov, "The USSR in a Changing World," *International Affairs*, No. 8 (1988), pp. 46–56. Also see John Van Oudenaren, *The Role of Shevardnadze and the Ministry of Foreign Affairs in the Making of Soviet Defense and Arms Control Policy*, Rand Report R-3898-USDP (July 1990), p. 18.

33. Harry Gelman, "Gorbachev's Dilemmas and His Conflicting Foreign-Policy Goals," *Orbis*, Vol. 30, No. 2 (Summer 1986), pp. 231–47; Thane Gustafson, "Will Soviet Foreign Policy Change under Gorbachev?" *The Washington Quarterly*, Vol. 9, No. 4 (Autumn 1986); Dimitri K. Simes, "Gorbachev: A New Foreign Policy?" *Foreign Affairs*, Vol. 65, No. 3 (1987), pp. 477–500; Abraham Becker et al., *The 27th Congress of the Communist Party of the Soviet Union: A Report from the Airlie House Conference* (Santa Monica, CA: Rand, 1986).

34. Stephen Sestanovich, "Gorbachev's Foreign Policy: A Diplomacy of Decline," *Problems of Communism*, Vol. 37, No. 1 (January–February 1988), pp. 1–15.

35. Daniel Deudney and G. John Ikenberry, "Soviet Reform and the End of the Cold War: Explaining Large-Scale Historical Change," *Review of International Studies*, Vol. 17, No. 3 (July 1991), pp. 225–50.

36. *International Affairs*, No. 10 (October 1988), p. 20; Jack F. Matlock Jr., *Autopsy on an Empire* (New York: Random House, 1995), pp. 143–48.

37. Oberdorfer, *Turn from the Cold War*, p. 161.

38. Ibid.

39. Ibid.

40. *Pravda*, August 6, 1988, as translated in FBIS, August 8, 1988, p. 39.

41. Remnick, *Lenin's Tomb*, p. 520.

42. Ibid.

43. Boris Yeltsin, *Against the Grain: An Autobiography* (New York: Summit Books, 1990), p. 140.

44. Ibid., p. 139.

45. Vladimir Kontorovich, "The Economic Fallacy," *The National Interest*, No. 31 (Spring 1993), pp. 38–41; Peter Rutland, "Sovietology: Notes for a Post-Mortem," *The National Interest*, No. 31 (Spring 1993), p. 121.

46. Remnick, *Lenin's Tomb*, p. 84; Yegor Ligachev, *Inside Gorbachev's Kremlin: The Memoirs of Yegor Ligachev* (New York: Pantheon Books, 1993), pp. 304–11.

47. Christopher Young, "The Strategy of Political Liberalization: A Comparative View of Gorbachev's Reforms," *World Politics*, Vol. 45, No. 1 (October 1992), pp. 57–64.

48. Myron Rush, "Fate and Fortune," *The National Interest*, No. 31 (Spring 1993), p. 19. Also see the excellent discussion in Alexander Dallin, "Causes of the Collapse of the USSR," *Post-Soviet Affairs*, Vol. 8, No. 4 (October–December 1992), pp. 279–302.

49. Kontorovich, "The Economic Fallacy," p. 35.

50. Ibid., p. 44.

51. Paul Kennedy, *The Rise and Fall of the Great Powers* (London: Fontana Press, 1989), p. 664. Also see John Lewis Gaddis, *The Long Peace* (New York: Oxford University Press, 1987), p. 244.

52. Colin S. Gray, "The Most Dangerous Decade: Historic Mission, Legitimacy, and Dynamics of the Soviet Empire in the 1980s," *Orbis*, Vol. 25, No. 1 (Spring 1981), pp. 13–28; Edward N. Luttwak, *The Grand Strategy of the Soviet Union* (New York: St. Martin's Press, 1983); Richard Pipes, *Survival Is Not Enough* (New York: Simon & Schuster, 1984).

Part IV

Emerging Issues

11

"The Lady Doth Protest Too Much": Intervention and the Turn to Ethics in International Law

Martti Koskenniemi

In a famous talk nearly 50 years ago, Professor Martin Wight of the London School of Economics posed the question about why there was no international theory. One of the reasons he found is the fact that it would have to be expressed in the languages of political theory and law. However, these were languages developed in the thinking about the state and about the control of social life in normal conditions:

> Political theory and law are maps of experience or systems of action within the realm of normal relationships and calculable results. They are the theory of the good life. International theory is the theory of survival. What for political theory is the extreme case (as revolution or civil war) is for international theory the regular case.[1]

The distinction between the normal and the exceptional came to be part of the realist explanation of international law's weakness. In the domestic context, situations are routine. Political normality by far outweighs the incidence of the exception—that is, ultimately revolution. By contrast, the international context was idiosyncratic and involved "the ultimate experience of life and death, national existence and national extinction." It was not the realm of the regularized search for happiness or avoidance of displeasure: it was the struggle for survival. Political theories would not apply and legal rules would not work because the need for survival far outweighed the need for compliance.

Lawyers are not, of course, insensitive to the distinction between the normal and the exceptional. "Hard cases make bad law," we say. Few would fail to distinguish between the law regulating the provision of parking tickets to diplomats and the law concerning the use of force. In the *Nuclear Weapons* case (1996), for example, the International Court of Justice came very close to admitting that no law could govern the case of self-defense when the very existence of the state was at stake.[2] During the Cold War, international lawyers largely gave up any attempt to conceive of the balance of power in terms of legal rules or principles. The dark passion of Great Power politics overwhelmed law's rational calculations. Thus, many have understood the post-1989 transformation as a move from an *exceptional* situation to a *normality* where the rules of civilized behavior would finally come to govern international life. The limitation of the scope of law during the Cold War had been an anomaly; now it was possible to restart the project of organizing the administration of the international society by the Rule of Law in the image of the liberal West. Collective enforcement under the UN Charter "would function in a regular and non-selective manner each time that circumstances required it, thus providing an institutional guarantee to the broad core of constitutional principles."[3] Sovereignty would lose its exceptional force as a barrier against the enforcement of human rights, democracy, or the requirements of the global market. The setting up of the International Criminal Court (1998) would imply a rejection of the "culture of impunity" that seemed such a violation of normal legal accountability.[4] It was to continue the constitutionalization of the international order, celebrated as a major implication of the dispute-settlement system under the World Trade Organization.[5] Today, these questions are everywhere in the debates about how to capture within law the fluid processes of globalization.[6] International law may have fragmented into subsystems and special regimes. But surely there is some Archimedean point, some *telos* or value that united the disparate technologies of international rule under some central idea. The tendency in the West to think of that idea in terms of ethics, or morality, did not stop when formal natural law had finally lost its power to economics as the preferred vocabulary for governmental advice. On the contrary, ethics is a natural companion to economics, turning decision makers to examine their consciences when the routine algorithm of optimal utility breaks down.

The effort to complete the international legal order by turning decision makers to examine their consciences when "exceptional" situations arise has taken place through an increasing deformalization of the legal craft. General principles and open-ended standards such as "reasonableness," "good faith," "equity," and so on proliferate, shifting the balance of power from those who make the rules to those who should apply them, lifting powerful executive institutions to the center. The urge to respond to situations defined as "humanitarian crises" is part of this deformalization, as we shall see. It looks beyond formal rules (such as the UN Charter) and appeals directly to the decision maker's conscience and to the conscience of large audiences: "A man's gotta do what a man's gotta do." To appeal to feeling rather than reason has always been a preferred way for those who govern to avoid questions about why *they* should govern in the first place and to restate the absolute necessity of their staying in power to respond to ever-recurring crises, arising from presumed atavistic sentiments, nationalism, religious extremism, or just the plain craziness of others hidden in the fabric of the international world.

Examining the legal argument about humanitarian use of force since the bombing of Serbia in 1999 enables me to provide a focused genealogy of modern international law as it moves, in a familiar succession of argumentative steps, from formalism to ethics, in order to capture within law a great crisis that under the old, "realistic" view would have fallen beyond its scope. But it also allows me to argue that the obsession to extend the law to such crises, while understandable in a historical perspective, enlists political energies to support causes dictated by the hegemonic powers and is unresponsive to the violence and injustice that sustain the global everyday. The "turn to ethics" is profoundly conservative in its implications. Many critics observed the "ideological" character of Kosovo.[7] What I wish to do is to generalize from that incident to the interminable debates on R2P and the state of a discipline as it struggles to find credibility and critical voice in the conditions of increasingly imperial politics.

PRECEDENTS

The bombing of Yugoslavia in the spring of 1999 caused around 500 civilian casualties.[8] From the perspective of the Western Alliance, these deaths were perhaps a tragic but unavoidable collateral damage. For international lawyers, they are an agonizing puzzle: humanity's sacrifice for the gift of the Rule of Law or the consummation of a blatant breach of the UN Charter? Part of the agony stems from the difficulty to think that those are the only alternatives. In some ways, formal law seemed unable to deal with Kosovo. So, many preferred to describe it through the discourse of diplomatic or military strategy: you could not negotiate with the enemy, because the only language he understands is force! Others sought to encompass those deaths within the frame of historical causality: it has always been bad down there, it could not be changed overnight—what is important is the creation of the conditions for a more democratic Yugoslavia, and a more humane international order. But most commentators have envisaged Kosovo as a moral or ethical issue, a matter of rights or principles. It is this perspective that tends to separate Kosovo from the old world of the Cold War. While "then" it was all a calculation of military force and balance of power, "now" it has become a matter of moral ideals, self-determination, democracy, and human rights. When the Secretary-General of NATO announced that the attack on Serbia had commenced, he did this in the following terms: "We must stop the violence and bring an end to the humanitarian catastrophe now taking place in Kosovo. We have a moral duty to do so."[9] This then became the "Annan Doctrine," one that has been read as part of an emerging "humanity law" that would be grounded on all-encompassing feeling of sympathy toward the whole humanity. The "shift of discourse" that took place at the time, traced by Teitel in 2011, was significant inasmuch as "[s]ubsequent interventions, such as Iraq, would be rationalized in ambiguous yet analogous terms—not primarily in terms of state interests but in humanity terms."[10]

What was the relationship between the "moral duty" invoked by the Secretary-General and the question about the lawfulness of the killing of the 500? A simple answer would be to relegate the former into a matter of the private conscience, or describe it as part of the foreign policy debate about the pros and cons of Western involvement. But this would be uncomfortably close to Cold War realism and would counteract the urge to think about the international world, too, in terms of what Wight called the "theory of the good life." Now there have, of course, been activist lawyers who have claimed that there is no reason why the law should not be applicable to *any* international matter, including the high politics of survival, a conclusion sometimes received from the assumed nature of law as a "complete system."[11] NATO was either entitled to bomb Serbia, or it was not. *Tertium non datur*. Surely, it is an essential part of the Rule of Law that society contains no corner of outsidethelaw. And yet, such formalism might not respond to the hearty's desire. Surely "we" cannot just stand aside if atrocities take place, whatever a formal instrument, drafted in another period, with other situations in mind, might appear to say. Surely it is possible to enlist the law on the side of such a moral intuition. "Peace" and "humanity" are themselves legal notions, embedded in law itself.[12] But is natural law still available to us?

After more than a decade of debate, the positions are well known. For some, "Kosovo" was a formal breach of the UN Charter and there was nothing more to say about it. Others read their moral intuitions as part of the law: because the intervention was morally necessary, it was also lawful. However, most lawyers—including myself—took the ambivalent position that it was both formally illegal and morally necessary.[13] Such schizophrenia tears wide open the fragile fabric of diplomatic consensus and exposes the aporia of a normative structure deferring simultaneously to the impossibility of ethical politics in a divided, agnostic, and unjust world and the impossibility not to assess political action in the light of some ethical standpoint. The agony of lawyers that paraded through conferences and symposia on Kosovo and "R2P" manifests itself in the odd view that brings law and ethics together by assuming that the Council "legalized" the NATO action ex post facto,[14] suggesting that whichever conclusion one holds, it remains a rather secondary rationalization in view of the speciality of the events.

To think of Kosovo (or Iraq, or Afghanistan, or Libya, or Mali) as law is to move it from the realm of the exceptional to that of the routine. It becomes a "case" of a "doctrine"—the law of humanitarian intervention, responsibility to protect. To the extent that we then wish to take account of its special aspects, and admit various informal arguments to characterize it, it moves us in the direction of the idiosyncratic, personal—until at the end it becomes the single situation that appeals to us not through the rational rhetoric of the rules but its singular meaning, as it were, through our souls. In this way, I suggest, the debate triggered by Kosovo has invited international lawyers to throw away dry professionalism and imagine themselves as moral agents in a *mission civilicatrice*. I think of this as a particularly shallow and dangerous moralization that forecloses political energies needed for transformation elsewhere. This is why my title picks up the spontaneous cry—"the Lady protests too much, methinks"—that Shakespeare put into Queen Gertrude's mouth. The debates reveal that "Kosovo," or any of the incidents where the same call for action has been voiced, is not only about what happened "out there"—in the play that Hamlet had staged for his mother to watch—but also, and importantly, about what took place "here," in the audience. Reacting to the play, Queen Gertrude was reacting to her own guilt, which, of course, was the *real* subject being dealt with. Analogously, "responsibility to protect" has come to be a debate about ourselves, about what we hold as normal and what as exceptional, and through that fact, about what sort of international law we practice.

LEGAL REASONING

Let me now trace the eight steps through which international lawyers have been transformed into moralists by the logic of the argument from humanitarian intervention, which also traces modern international law's odyssey for "policy-relevance."

Step 1: (Formal law stricto sensu—*law as pure form).* Lawyers who held the bombing illegal based this on the formal breach of Article 2(4) of the UN Charter that was involved. As is well-known, the article admits of only two principal exceptions: authorization by the Security Council and self-defense under Article 51. Neither was present. *Ergo,* the bombing was illegal. Although there is little doubt of the professional correctness of this conclusion, it still seems arrogantly insensitive to the humanitarian dilemmas involved. It resembles a formalism that would require a head of state to refrain from a preemptive strike against a lonely submarine at the North Pole, even if that were the only way to save the population of the capital city from a nuclear attack from that ship—simply because no "armed attack" had yet taken place as required by the language of Article 51. But does the law require the sacrifice of thousands for the altar of the law? Surely the relevant texts should be read so as to produce a "reasonable" result. If it is the *intention* of the self-defense rule to protect the state, surely it should not be applied in a way to bring about the destruction of the state.

But how does one know whether selfdefense is applicable? Clearly, this cannot be determined independently of a definition of the relevant "self." For the North Atlantic Alliance it may not be implausible to think of European security as a matter for its own security. Or perhaps the relevant "self" was the Albanian population in Kosovo—in which case the NATO attack might have been lawful assistance for a people struggling for self-determination under the 1975 Friendly Relations Declaration.[15] To what extent might such considerations offset the requirement of prior armed attack? In order to give sense to the normal meaning of the language of the relevant instruments, and solve hierarchical controversies, it is necessary to move to interpretation, that is beyond the pure form of Articles 2(4) and 51.

Step 2: (Formal law lato sensu—*law as representative for "underlying" social, historical, systemic, or other such "values")*. Although it is difficult (though by no means impossible) to sustain humanitarian intervention as a formal custom,[16] many might receive it from the object and purpose of the UN Charter, supported by a series of General Assembly resolutions plus the residual custom that contains a principle of proportionality and perhaps no longer sustains sovereignty against massive human rights violations. In the case of the Charter, recourse to its object and purpose is "of special significance" due to its constitutional nature and extreme difficulty of carrying out formal revisions.[17] There is no doubt that the violent oppression of ethnic Albanians in Kosovo by the Milošević regime was against the Charter. If the Charter prohibits such oppression, then surely it must also provide the means whereby it is discontinued. Remember the nonrecognition of South Rhodesia by the UN during 1965–1979, the sanctions against South Africa, or the official international community's silence after India's intervention in East Pakistan in 1971. If sovereignty is an expression of communal liberty and self-rule, then surely it cannot be permitted to destroy them.[18] "[A] jurist rooted in the late twentieth century can hardly say that an invasion by outside forces to remove [an usurper of power] and install the elected government is a violation of national sovereignty."[19]

Notice that the argument in the opposite direction occupies the same terrain. Why would it be necessary to stick closely to the formal prohibition of force and the narrow understanding of the exceptions thereto? Well, surely because of the dangers of abuse and selectivity, the fact that "[m]ilitary enforcement raises the spectre of colonialism and war."[20] There is no space of "innocent" literality. If challenged, a restrictive view—even if motivated by bona fide concerns of intellectual rigor—is immediately called upon to produce a substantive defense and will thus reveal its underlying ideology.[21]

At that point we have irrevocably left formalism for hermeneutics. Law is now how it is interpreted. As the "deep-structural" values that the interpretation is expected to reveal do not exist independently of human purposes, we are down the slippery slope of trying to identify those purposes. This might be accomplished in different ways.

Step 3: (Instrumentalism). As human activity, international law is not a mechanic transformation of a piece of textual information into action. It is, rather, activity with a point, oriented toward a human purpose. The point of criminal law is to maintain social peace; the point of contract is to exchange goods. Without such point, the law and the contract would seem utterly meaningless, or aspects of some strange metaphysics. This is how a Martian might feel trying to interpret what parliaments and businessmen do in abstraction of any point: the raising of the hands, the filing of the ballot, and the exchange of pieces of paper—exotic rituals indeed, which we understand as the pointoriented activities of legislation or trade. The same is true of international law, of course. The point of the UN Charter is to attain peace, human rights, economic welfare. We do not appreciate the Charter because of some mystical quality of its text or the aura of its authors. The Charter is not God. We honor it because we believe it leads us to valuable secular purposes.

This is also how many lawyers understand the sacrifice of the 500 Serbs.[22] The sacrifice is justified by the point of the Charter, to prevent aggression, to bring peace to the Balkans, to protect human rights and selfdetermination. Or, conversely, it was mass murder because the Charter seeks to prevent aggression, to protect sovereignty, to channel disputes into UN organs. If human activity is an activity with a point, and the UN is a human activity, then to understand it—and not simply to apply its formal text—we must examine whether the point of the Charter and the point of the sacrifice do or do not coincide. But now a formidable problem emerges.

If law is thoroughly instrumental, we should be able to ascertain what it is an instrument for. However, if we *do* know that, we already have access to an objective moral world of what "we" as UN members want (or what is "good") and no longer need (formal) law at all—except as a practical guide on how to get there. However—and here is the difficulty—if law is just a "practical guide" to reach a point, *then we have no need for it if we already know the point.* We have then silently stepped out of the melancholy agnosticism of legal modernity and entered an earthly paradise in which (1) we can think of ourselves as (again) capable of knowing the good in some interindividually valid way without the necessary intervention of any authority, or mediator; and (2) the things we know are good are coterminous with each other, there is no conflict between them, and consequently no need for rules on conflict resolution. Morgenthau was wrong: human life is not tragic, utopia is available. Morgenthau was right; it does not include a binding, formal law.[23]

The "object and purpose" test is not just a technique; it is a replacement of the legal form by a claim about substantive morality. It thus involves difficulties of philosophical anthropology and epistemology that bring us to the edge of modernity, and maybe beyond. But it also meets with the practical obstacle that people—and states—still do disagree on what is good, and, by extension, how the Charter should be interpreted. Far from resolving the problem of Kosovo, hermeneutics restates that problem in another vocabulary: the sacrifice was necessary for the same reason that it seemed necessary for Abraham to kill Isaac, because that is what God said.[24] Verbal uniformity may sometimes reflect or bring about substantive agreement. However, often it veils disagreement, and when it does, merely to insist on "strict compliance" with the rule is pointless as the disagreement is about what there is to comply with in the first place.[25]

Step 4: (Utilitarianism). Well, you might think, it is true that formal law does not solve the issue, and that God is not available for guidance, but that this is to exaggerate the difficulty. Perhaps, you think, all that is needed is to balance the stakes, to calculate. Is it not the purpose of political action to attain the greatest good for the greatest number? If intervention can save more lives than it might destroy, then it must be carried out. The 500 were sacrificed for the greater good. Many of us often reason this way. Much recent international regulation has refrained from laying down substantive dos and don'ts and instead referred to an *ad hoc* balancing of interests in a contextual, deformalized fashion, in order to attain the greatest overall utility.[26] But many of us are also aware of the problems, familiar as they have been since John Stuart Mill's adjustment of Benthamite "pig-philosophy." Which items are included in the calculation? How are those items weighed against each other? Would massive destruction of nature be part of the package—how might it compare to civilian deaths? What about the formal status of the victims: surely the cost of 10 dead pilots—by flying lower in order to hit only true military targets—might have been a more acceptable offer for the Rule of Law than 500 Serbian civilians? But what is the ratio, and which are the relevant values? What about accepting the death of 1,000 soldiers in a ground campaign to spare 500 civilians as an offshoot of an air war? However, at some point it becomes abominable to count heads in this way. The targeting of old Serbs in order to save young Kosovar Albanians might work as an effective deterrent in which the ratio in terms of saved years would clearly be in favor. However, it would make banal the value of lives, and inculcate an insensitive and dangerous bureaucratization that lowers the threshold toward killing if only that might seem rational under some administrative reason. Besides, it presumes full knowledge of the sacrifice that is going to be required and the consequences of alternative scenarios. But we know now that NATO knew precious little of the actual effects of its bombing on the ground—and had still less of an idea about the political results. As Thomas Nagel put the point:

> Once the door is opened to calculations of utility and national interest, the usual speculations about the future of freedom, peace, and economic prosperity can be brought to bear to ease the consciences of those responsible for a certain number of charred babies.[27]

Step 5: (Rights). Due to such formidable difficulties, many would say that law or morality is not just about head counting: surely they are also about justice, in particular about rights. Rights, in this version, act as "trumps" that prohibit the carrying out of policies that would otherwise seem to provide an aggregate benefit.[28] Indeed, Article 6 of the 1966 UN Covenant on Civil and Political Rights lays down the right to life without provision for exception. As there is no derogation from right to life, the bombing was illegal. But the right to life is, of course, not absolute in this way: the provision prohibits only the "arbitrary" deprivation of life, and what is "arbitrary" is to be defined *in casu*. Killing in war or in selfdefense does not qualify as a breach of Article 6.[29] But the point is larger. Rights are always consequential on a prior definition of some benefit as "right" and on contextual appreciation where rights language is given a meaning (especially in terms of somebody's enforceable duties). Likewise, conflicting rights can only be put to a hierarchy by reference to some policy about the distribution of entitlements under conditions of relative scarcity.[30] In other words, rights depend on their meaning and force on the character of the political community in which they function.[31] This applies also to the right to life. Abortion and euthanasia, for instance, receive normative status only once we know the society that is our reference point. In the practice of international institutions—that is to say, within the "thin" culture of public cosmopolitanism—rights turn into effects of utilitarian calculations. Far from "trumping" policies, rights defer to them. To believe otherwise is to accept some policy about rights as binding in an absolute, nonpolitical way—that is to say, to believe it was given to human society instead of created by it, like God's words.[32]

Step 6: (Legislative discourse). But if humanitarian intervention involves deference to political principles or balancing calculations, then it threatens to degenerate into a pretense for the use of power by those who have the means. After all, Hitler, too, intervened in the *Sudetenland* to protect the German population—and Russia is today all over its former Soviet empire arguing for the need to protect ethnic Russians or to support the self-determination of breakaway regions. To avoid this, many have suggested the establishment of criteria for such intervention that would check against the possibility of political misuse. If those criteria were clear enough, it would be possible to ascertain objectively—automatically—whether an intervention was justified or not.[33]

RESPONSIBILITY TO PROTECT

This suggestion triggered, in 2001, the initiative under the rubric "responsibility to protect." The idea was, among other things, to amend or at least interpret the Charter in such a way as to allow forcible military action when "necessary." The ICISS report spoke passionately about "the urgent needs of the potential beneficiaries of the action."[34] In a kind of hocus-pocus move, using the indeterminacy of the expression "sovereignty," the Commission suggested that the state itself, where atrocity was taking place, had "responsibility" to deal with it—and if it did not (for whatever reason), then it was for the "international community" to act. The language was half codified with the High-Level Panel on Threats and Change in December 2004 and in the "World Summit Outcome" the following year.[35] Since then, the General Assembly has established institutional positions for the matter and keeps discussing it every year, opening an opportunity for world leaders to vent their humanitarian sentiments while simultaneously making sure that no such normative action would to be taken that would actually threaten their states, now or later, or the "stability" of an order that has brought them to power.[36]

"Responsibility to Protect" was launched as an effort to deal with the dilemma of "illegal but justified." Like many other official and unofficial initiatives in the aftermath of Kosovo, it was imagined as a rule-drafting exercise that could finally end the insecurity of decision makers (and populations) about international response. The exact nature of that insecurity is important to understand. On the one hand, it had to do with the precarious situation of vulnerable populations. Will help come when it is needed? Will it be efficient? But at least as important was the other insecurity—namely, whether the novel normative framework will actually only empower those who have the economic and military means, to use force whenever they might feel it is in their interests. As Anne Peters put it, in order to avoid that, it becomes "a Trojan Horse for bad old imperial, colonial and militarist habits," and "it must be construed very narrowly."[37] An absolute standard was needed, one that could not be misinterpreted, accidentally or on purpose, a standard that would allow the "international community" to verify whether an action was or was not lawful.

However, this is to restate the difficulty with rules. However enlightened, peaceful, and rational the appliers are, rules cannot be applied in the automatic fashion that their proponents suppose. This is because any rule or criterion will be both over- and under-inclusive. It will include some cases that we did not wish to include, and it will appear to leave out some cases that we would have wanted to include had we known of them when the criteria were drafted. Say the criterion allows intervention if 500 are killed. From the perspective of a devout Catholic nation, this would allow, perhaps even call for, intervention to prevent the thousands of cases of abortion routinely practiced in the secular West. Surely that would seem over-inclusive. But, it would not apply in a case where only 400 were killed. But would this not be quite arbitrary? Should there really be no difference between the case where the 400 were military men, killed in combat, and the case of newborn babies, charred to death in their cradles because they belonged to an ethnic minority?

A very precise ("automatic") criterion would be undesirable for the reason Julius Stone pointed out in a related context, namely because it would be a "trap for the innocent and a signpost for the guilty."[38] It would compel the well-meaning state to watch the atrocity being committed until some in itself arbitrary level has been attained—and allow the dictator to continue until that very point. A criterion is always also a permission: *This is how far I can go!* It is precisely for this reason that the attempts to define "aggression" have either failed or ended up in parody. When the General Assembly in 1952 started to look for a definition, its concern was to check political misuse by the Security Council of its broad enforcement powers under Chapter VII. A definition was finally adopted by the Assembly in December 1974.[39] In an operative part that contains eight articles and takes a good two sheets of the space of a regular UN document, the definition lists as "aggression" not only "first use of armed force by a State in contravention of the Charter," but also other kinds of "invasion," "bombardment," "blockade," and "sending of armed bands," as well as "substantial involvement" in such actions. After the long—but non-exhaustive—list of examples, the definition then provides that "the Security Council may determine that other acts constitute aggression under the provisions of the Charter." The very point of such an exercise was to limit Security Council discretion, but ended up defining as aggression whatever the Council chose to regard as such!

The new definition of the "crime of aggression" in Article 8 *bis* (1) of the 2010 Kampala revision of the Statute of 2010 of the International Criminal Court fares no better in this respect.[40] It covers an "act of aggression" that "by its character, gravity and scale constitutes a manifest violation of the United Nations Charter." Moreover, the "elements" of the crime of aggression and "other understandings" adopted at Kampala have turned the definition into a weighing standard. To qualify as "aggression," an act must be a "manifest violation of the UN Charter" (Element 5) and its presence should ascertained by taking account of "all circumstances of each particular case, including the gravity of the acts concerned and their consequences, in accordance with the Charter of the United Nations" (Understanding 6).[41] Moreover, the use of force implicated in aggression under Article 8 *bis* (1) ought to take place "against the sovereignty, territorial integrity or political independence of any State, or in any other manner inconsistent with the Charter of the UN." This purposive standard opens up the whole of the Charter as the interpretative ground on which disputes about "the crime of aggression" will be waged. How come the definition ended in a weighing standard that hardly responds to criminal lawyers' cherished principle of legality? Because what is being regulated is not some petty crime that occurs routinely, but hugely important political-military events. All contextual determinants must be taken into account; the hands of the law-applier must be left free. To the extent that the ICC might itself become actually operative (a very unlikely occurrence), the terms of the definition ensure that its verdict can always be labeled as political action against an enemy.

The core of the problem does not lie with the technical difficulty of finding appropriate language. This is merely an index of the substantive issue that *all* war cannot be regarded as illegal—that although the use of force involves killing and destruction, pain and suffering, there are (tragic) situations where a responsible politician will have to acknowledge its necessity. Problems about the definition of aggression are about the difficulty of foreseeing when such necessity might arise. They are, in other words, about the conditions and limits of just war. The problem of "aggression" operates alongside many other ambiguous and open-ended concepts that have to do with legitimate force and is infected by the difficulties of pinning down a clear sense to those *other* concepts. But the problem is ultimately not so much conceptual as material. It is about the way the world is. The ambiguity of the available concepts is merely the other side of the *vagueness of the world itself* and our need not to prejudice our action in the future on the basis of past experience, limited as any such experience is as a guide in a future that it by definition "new."

Little is to be expected of legislation. The more precise the proposed criteria, the more automatic their application, the more arbitrary any exclusion or inclusion would appear. This would be arbitrariness not just in regard to some contested policy, but to the humanitarian point of the rule. This is why it would be a mistake to assume that the definitions of aggression fail due to the scheming malevolence of diplomats. Everyone participated in the exercise with two legitimate aims: (1) whatever you agree, do not end up curtailing the action of your home state when action is needed to defend its essential interests, and (2) try as best you can to prevent action that might be prejudicial to the interests of your state. Now when everyone participates on such instructions, the result could only be meaningless: language that is both absolutely binding and absolutely open-ended.

This is easy to demonstrate by way of an example. As an absolute criterion such as "500" allows the slow torturing to death of 499, flexible terminology is needed. The situation should be such that "fundamental human rights are being or are likely to be seriously violated on a large scale and there is an urgent need for intervention."[42] Like the definition of aggression, this seems both sensible and inconsequential. It is responsive to the humanitarian urge and avoids the danger of absolutism—but only by simultaneously opening the door for military action in dubious cases, and facilitating the tyrant's hypocrisy. We are back in the original situation. As soon as the rule is no longer automatic, but involves discretion, the possibility of abuse that was the point of the rule to eradicate reappears.[43] Why?

The proposal to legislate over responses to massive human rights violations—a proposal at the heart of the debates on "responsibility to protect"—brings forth the very problem that Martin Wight pointed out and with which I opened this essay: namely, that formal rules work well in a domestic normality where situations are routine and the need to honor the formal validity of the law by far outweighs incidental problems in its application. The benefits of exceptionless compliance offset the losses. Think about the organization of the popular vote. Most societies have an absolute rule about the voting age—often 18. Why do they have such a rule? It is because it is thought that only mature people should be entitled to participate in the direction of political order. However, the rule is clearly both over- and under-inclusive. It allows some people to vote who are immature—your middle-aged alcoholic neighbor who gambled his family's savings, for example. It also excludes others that clearly are mature—your 17-year-old daughter who just had a straight A from her social science class is another example. Note again that the problem is not an external distortion: the inclusion and the exclusion appear problematic because they contradict the point of the rule. But we still insist to apply the rule. Why? It is because the only alternative would be to condition voting rights directly on the substantive criterion of "maturity." However, this would allocate the decision on the delimitation of the electorate to those who have been put in the position to assess the "maturity" of the voters. Now, you might think that is all right if it is *you* who sits on the "maturity board"—but it is more likely to be *your neighbor*.

In domestic normality it is possible to live with automatic rules because the alternative is so much worse. The occasional injustice is not too dramatic and will be dispelled: your neighbor falls in love and sobers up; your daughter votes in the next election. No threat to the legal order emerges. Revolution will not take place. But this is otherwise in an international emergency of some gravity. An injustice caused by the law immediately challenges the validity of a legal system that calls for compliance even against self-interest. The point of the rule (that is, the need to prevent serious and large-scale violations of fundamental human rights) is more important than its formal validity. In the domestic situation, the rule is applied perhaps in millions of situations. Automaticity excludes political manipulation, and the connected routine brings about an overall result that is more valuable than any (small) injustice that is being caused. In the international situation, on the other hand, and especially if the situation is defined as a "serious violation of fundamental rights," the need to uphold the formal validity of the law cannot be compared to the weight of the impulse to act now.[44] If the rule does not allow this, so much worse for the rule. Any appeal for passivity in the interests of upholding a general sense of law obedience will ring hollow, even cynical.

Step 7 (Law as Procedure). After all such problems, you might conclude that international law's role lies less in offering substantive rules, whether absolute or flexible, than in providing a decision process that allows a controlled treatment of the situation. It would channel the problem to institutions and bodies— *regimes*, in a word—in which interested parties could agree on the right interpretation, or the correct course of action, if possible under conditions of transparency and accountability.[45] This would be a democratic way to deal with the problem. However, what would the correct procedure be? For some, it was precisely the procedural side-stepping of the Security Council where the illegality of the bombing lay. For others, NATO decision making offered enough "collectiveness" to account for lawfulness. Some would retort, of course, that how can a regional body arrogate to itself the power to decide on a matter entrusted by the Charter to a universal one? To those, however, seasoned observers would respond in the way Morgenthau commented on the UN's first efforts to deal with the crises in Greece, Spain, Indonesia, and Iran. They "provided opportunities for exercises in parliamentary procedure, but in no occasion has even an attempt been made to facing the political issues of which these situations are surface manifestations."[46] One need not share Morgenthau's distaste of liberalism to admit that institutional procedures in the UN and elsewhere often provide more of an excuse for nonaction than a reasoned technique for solving acute crises. However, many political theorists might seek "ideal speech situations" to account for institutional legitimacy, what is "ideal" will remain open for controversy, and empirical evidence of it is largely absent from the international scene. The argument of the Uniting for Peace Resolution in 1950 that justifies overtaking the Security Council if the Council is "unable to act" was then, and remains, a contested re-description of following the Council's rules of decision making as a violation of the political *point* of the Charter. This is an incident of the over-exclusiveness of Article 27(3) of the Charter: it sometimes excludes action in cases where some people think action is needed. There may well be, as intimated in the UN Secretary-General's General Assembly speech in September 1999, good reason to set aside the correct procedure in order to act.[47] But although to explain this as an implementation of the "deep" logic of the Charter is a part of the diplomatic practice never to say one is actually breaking the law, it still remains the case that a beneficial illegality today makes it easier for my adversary to invoke it tomorrow as precedent for some somber scheme of his. Hence, of course, the anxiety of Western lawyers about Kosovo when Russian diplomats have used it to defend Russia's action in Georgia or Ukraine.

Step 8: (The Turn to Ethics). For such difficulties, many people believe that even as law is not just formal texts and precedents, its informality cannot be reduced to utilitarian calculations, absolute rights, or procedural techniques, either. The relevant considerations are situational. One version of such attitude follows Max Weber's analysis of the failure of legal formality in the conditions of complex modernity, and highlights the way bureaucratization focuses on the decision maker's preferences or alliances. To grasp decision making in an environment deprived of determining rules, Weber made his famous distinction between an ethics of ultimate ends and an ethics of responsibility. According to him—and to many others—the latter provided the more appropriate framework for decision makers in a case such as now exemplified by Kosovo.[48] The argument might be—and I have myself sometimes made it in this way—that in the context of 1999, with the experience of passivity in Kigali and in Srebrenica, Western European officials had to take action. If formal law is in any way unclear and cannot be separated from how it is interpreted, then much speaks for the individualization of Kosovo. A decision has to be made, and that decision—as one of Weber's close readers, Carl Schmitt, the Kronjurist of the Third Reich, the theorist of the exception, would say—is borne out of legal nothingness.[49] What counts is the experience of the decision maker and his or her sensitivity to the demands of the situation. The problem is not about criteria or process, but about something that might be called "wisdom."[50]

That we seem left with decisionism is nicely illustrated in the tortured efforts of academic writers, proponents and adversaries, to make normative sense of the status or content of the responsibility to protect, efforts that have tamed it from a normative criterion into a set of bureaucratic programs. In a recent overview, one of the leading R2P specialists, Alex Bellamy, for instance, pointed out that the contrasting interpretations—intervention as an instrument of imperial domination and intervention as the expression of a novel humanitarian order—have gone nowhere but "disagreement abounds."[51] Analysts keep counting the incidents where UN bodies, especially the Security Council, have mentioned the notion in their documents and report on institutional developments—the appointment of special representatives, the production of thematic reports, and so on. Having observed that while the principle "has had little success in mobilizing timely and decisive international action," Bellamy thinks it is best seen as "a policy agenda in need of implementation rather than as a 'red flag' to galvanize the world into action."[52] The crises in Libya (2011) and Syria (2013) have again drawn attention to the dilemmas of military action. If in the former situation, the applicability—so far, the only clear application—of responsibility to protect seemed initially quite warranted, indeed almost a textbook example, the conduct of the operation raised the question whether in fact Resolution 1973 (2011) "opened the slippery slope to 'do anything.' "[53] And yet, there is no doubt that sometimes *only* regime change will attain the goal of protecting a population. In Syria again, but perhaps elsewhere as well, the very characterization of the conflict as humanitarian, so as to raise the issue of responsibility to protect, will erase the sense (that it has for many of the participants) that at issue was a social and political revolution.[54] But today again, skepticism if not cynicism prevails, not least with the new cold war driving the great powers apart and freezing the possibilities of action by the Security Council. But maybe such action was in any case impossible to agree upon—many Third World actors insisting that enhanced military activity under the Council could take place only once its membership has changed the world more equally.[55]

That last point resurfaces the specter of decisionism. Whatever the standard, it suggests, there are exceptional cases, situations that call for action never mind the bureaucratic context, moments when the person that decides must simply do the right thing—as Hammarskjöld was assumed to think about his role in the Congo.[56] The great problem in such a turn lies in the implied suggestion that the proper realm of the important lies in the personal, subjective, even emotional—in the conscience of those whom the dictates of power and history have put in decision-making positions. Let me paraphrase Schmitt again. For him, legal normality was dependent on the power of the one who could decide on the exception: legal normality—rules and processes—was only a surface appearance of the concrete order that revealed its character in the dramatic moment when normality was to be defended or set aside. Behind the tranquility of the *pouvoir constitué* lay the founding violence of the *pouvoir constituant*—a *coup d'état*, a revolution.[57] From this perspective, the bombing of Serbia and the regime change in Libya were moments of "exception" that revealed, for a moment, the nature of the international order, which lay neither in the Charter nor in principles of humanitarianism but in the will and ability of a handful of Western civilian and military leaders to have their way. The sacrifice of 500 civilians in Belgrade, or the chaos in Libya, would then appear as a violent reaffirmation of the vitality of a concrete international order created sometime after World War II and in which what counts as law, or humanitarianism, or morality, is decided with conclusive authority by the sensibilities of the Western Prince.

NEW NORMALITY

However, to reduce the nature of social order to the mental activities or moral states of Princes—the "purity of heart" that St. Thomas held as an indispensable ingredient of the just war—is to blind oneself to the injustice that is produced by social normality. To credit the decision makers as having been involved in an emotional process about their moral obligations is to make precisely that mistake of fact (of being in a position of power) for right, for which Rousseau once accused Grotius, "it is possible to imagine a more logical method, but not one more favourable to tyrants."[58] "Man was born free and he is everywhere in chains," Rousseau also wrote, bearing in mind the religious binds of an *ancien régime* that were finally loosening in his time. The Enlightenment that we associate with him sought freedom through rational rules and public decision-making processes, and relegated morality into one's conscience. To extrapolate the nature of the international order from the moral dilemmas—however real—of the statesmen involved in great events makes us blind to the political and moral problems of a normality that has lifted those people in decision-making positions in the first place, and leaves the rest as passive spectators or sometimes sacrificial victims on the altar of their superior moralities.[59]

This leads me to observe an ironic reversal of the relations between the normal and the exception. For the classical realists, the founding violence of law—the violence that could not be encompassed by law because it was its precondition—was an act of physical force, sending in the military to occupy a territory or to overthrow (or uphold) a government, war aggression, sovereignty; great moments of historical significance. These were the *a priori* on which the law was based and that could not, therefore, be captured within law. How different it all seems today. It is hard to think of a more central concern for the profession than military intervention, a more normal conference topic or item of polite conversation than war, crisis management and peace enforcement, punishment and sanctions. The wide concept of security promoted by UN officials and European crisis managers has blurred the line between military and civilian matters—thus expanding the jurisdiction of military experts, making talk about forcible intervention a matter of bureaucratic normality. If every concern is a security concern, then there are no limits to the jurisdiction of the security police.[60]

What this new normality has done, like every normality, is to relegate its own founding violence into the shadow. But what about the violence of a global system in which, according to a recent study by Oxfam, 1 percent of the world's population owned 48 percent of its wealth, and the least prosperous 80 percent a mere 5.5 percent. In 2016, the ratio of the 1 percent would exceed half of the world's wealth.[61] We deal with military intervention, peace enforcement, or the fight against terrorism in the neutral language of legal rules and humanitarian moralities, and so come to think of it in terms of a policy of a global public realm—forgetting that it is never Algeria that will intervene in France, or Finland in Chechnya. The peace that will be enforced will not be racial harmony in Los Angeles, and the terrorism that shall be branded as the enemy of humanity will not be a migration regime that allows thousands of Africans to sink into early death while attempting to cross the Mediterranean. Our obsessive talk about humanitarian force makes invisible the extreme injustice of the system of global distribution of wealth, reducing it to the sphere of the private, the unpolitical, the natural, the historically determined—just like war used to be—a "social," "cultural," or "economic" *condition* of law, which therefore cannot be touched by law.[62]

So, it is precisely at the moment when we focus on the moral conscience of world leaders that all serious ambition has been renounced to attain a critical grasp of the concrete order of global distribution of power and wealth. It is tempting to think that the very conditions that underlie the debate on justifiable military action are the ones that make it impossible to deal with that founding violence. If international law is centrally about the informal management of security crises by diplomatic and military experts, then of course it is not about global redistribution: it is about upholding the status quo and about directing moral sensibility and political engagement to waging *that* battle. Civilian deaths in domestic crises, civil wars, and terrorist attacks spell anxiety, a recognition of the insufficiency of existing rules and principles, a call for moral sensibility. Hunger and poverty do not. The more international lawyers are obsessed by the effectiveness of the law to be applied in "crises," the less we are aware of the subtle politics whereby some aspects of the world become defined as "crisis" whereas others do not.[63] Despite the rhetoric of universal international law, the rise of humanitarianism at the center of new global law, only the tiniest part of the world is encompassed by our attention. Even as law now arrogates to itself the right to speak the language of universal humanitarianism, it is spoken only by a handful of experts fascinated about matters military and technological, the targeting of missiles and press conferences with uniformed men who speak clearly. Should their moral sensibilities now be the lawyers' greatest concern?

ALTERNATIVES

What alternatives are there? The eight steps traced above might seem to describe a logic that, after successive failures to attain normative closure, leads into the spontaneous and the private; "moral duty" will tell us what to do. Such an understanding celebrates the emotional immediacy of the inner life as the sanctuary of the true meaning of dramatic events that cannot be captured within law's technical structures. This would, however, involve an altogether groundless belief in the primacy of the subjective, or the ability of emotion (in contrast to "reason") to grasp some authentic form of life to be contrasted to the artificial structures of the law. However, the conventions of the subject, and the related disciplines of psychology and identity politics, are no closer to or distant from "authentic reality" than the conventions of public life, including formal law, sociology, or market. Moreover, as I have argued elsewhere, the very claim that one is arguing from the position of authenticity—for example, a given notion of human right, or self-determination—involves an objectionable attempt to score a political victory outside politics.[64] The subjective and the spontaneous form a symbolic order just like the realm of the objective and rational. Neither occupies an innocent space that would be free from disciplinary conventions and ambitions and at which international lawyers could finally grasp the authentic.

The merit in the "turn to ethics" lies in the way it focuses on the indetermination of official behavior by rational standards and criteria and thus, inevitably, brings to the fore the *political* moment in such decisions. It reveals the way such decision making is an aspect of social antagonism, instead of something neutral or "rational" in the way liberal internationalism has often assumed. Intervention remains a political act, however much it is dressed in the language of moral compulsion. On the other hand, however, that cannot be the end of the matter, either, although this is how many critics of liberalism—including Carl Schmitt and Hans Morgenthau— have often suggested. Neither the opposition between the friend and the enemy nor the lust for power shares the character of a final, foundational truth about society or politics. Existentialism, too, is just a symbolic order, a language.

So the turn to ethics, too, is a politics. In the case of international law's obsession about military crises, war, and humanitarianism, it is a politics by those who have the means to strengthen control on everyone else. The idiom of "protection," as Anne Orford has shown, is one born in European absolutism, offering a deal in which the civil society's part has to do with unquestioned obedience.[65] The more open-ended the standards thorough which international executive authority operates, the more the leaders are called upon to examine their "moral conscience" in order to sympathize with humanity, the more you and I have reason to be wary about what is to come. The unforeseen dismantling of privacy protections and expansion of unaccountable secret operations by domestic and international bureaucracies around the world could not have been possible had not the calls of moral conscience over formal legal procedures resonated so well in yet another period that likes to think of itself as "crisis." In such a situation, insistence on rules, processes, and the whole culture of formalism may turn into a strategy of resistance, and of democratic hope. Why? Because formalism is precisely about setting limits to the impulses—"moral" or not—of those in decision-making positions. It cools the sense of "crisis" by looking to past experience and the power of what is being done as a precedent for the future. It casts decision makers as responsible to political communities and is especially obsessed about the effects any decision will have on other members of the community. Of course, the door to a formalism that would determine the substance of political outcomes is no longer open. There is no neutral terrain. But against the particularity of the ethical decision, formalism opens a horizon of communication, embedded in a *culture* of restraint, a *commitment* to listening to others' claims and seeking to take them into account.[66] The reference to "moral duty" in the justification of military action is objectionable because it signifies retreat from such commitment into the private life of the conscience, casting political adversaries as immoral monsters with whom nothing is shared and against whom no measures are excessive.[67]

In a related context, David Kennedy once characterized analogous arguments in terms of modernity's "eternal return," the way they reduce professional history into the repetition of familiar moves: from formalism to anti-formalism and back, from interpretation to literality and back, from emotion to reason and back, from sociology to psychology and back, from apology to utopia and back—with "no exit and existential crisis."[68] If this were all, then a move to formalism like the move to ethics would indeed only repeat certain modernist tropes that we have seen over the years being performed with some regularity in art, philosophy, and politics as well as in law. But this need not be so. Modernity is unstable, and every move it makes is always already split by reflexivity against itself. Formalism can no longer be blind to its own politics. Having shed the pretensions of objectivity, it must enter the political terrain with a program of openness and inclusiveness, no longer interpreted as effects of neutral reason, but of political experience and utopian commitment, as *articulation* of what might be called the "sedimented practices constituting the normative framework of a certain society."[69] To be sure, formalism cannot believe that it merely translates this framework to particular decisions. This is why it does not suffice only to provide a hearing to the claims of the political other, but also to include in political contestation the question about *who* are entitled to make claims and *what kinds* of claims pass the test of validity. Without such self-reflexivity, formalism will freeze into the justification of one or another substantive policy—just like democracy may do. Such a formalism lives on a paradox, split against itself inasmuch as it recognizes itself as "culture"—an aspect of the human, dependent on psychology and politics, uncertain and partial, yet also seeking to articulate something universal and shared. This "split" holds up its utopian moment, suggesting an exit from the anxiety of the "eternal return" and redeeming cosmopolitanism and emancipation as aspects of a properly political project.

For many years now, international lawyers have been called upon to assume the role of technical policy advisers, participants in a global culture of effectiveness and control that underwrites the objectives projected onto the unipolar world by those in hegemonic positions. Now their ethical commitment has been directed to military enforcement as part of the gradual naturalization of an economic system that sustains the hegemon. However, the turn to ethics has also revealed a vulnerable spot in the latter. If law is inevitably always also about the subjective and the emotional, about faith and commitment, then nothing prevents re-imagining international law as commitment to resistance and transgression. Having learned its lesson, formalism might then re-enter the world assured that whatever struggles it will have to weigh, the inner anxiety of the Prince is less a problem to resolve than an objective to achieve.

NOTES

Portions of this chapter have been adapted from M. Koskenniemi, " 'The Lady Doth Protest Too Much': Kosovo, and the Turn to Ethics in International Law." *The Modern Law Journal*, Vol. 65, No. 2 (2002), pp. 159–175.

1. M. Wight, "Why Is There No International Theory?" in H. Butterfield and M. Wight, eds., *Diplomatic Investigations: Essays in the Theory of International Politics* (London: Allen and Unwin, 1966), p. 33.

2. ICJ, *Legality of the Threat or Use of Nuclear Weapons*, Advisory Opinion, Reports 1996, [90]–[97] and [105 E] (dispositif).

3. G. Abi-Saab, "Whither the International Community," *European Journal of International Law*, Vol. 9 (1998), p. 264.

4. Out of the wealth of writings on the matter, see J. M. Sears, "Confronting the 'Culture of Impunity': Immunity of Heads of State from Nuremberg to *ex parte Pinochet*," *German Yearbook of International Law*, Vol. 42 (1999), pp. 125–46.

5. See E-U Petersmann, "The WTO Constitution and the Millennium Road," in M. Bronkers and R. Quick, eds., *New Directions in International Economic Law: Essays in Honour of John H. Jackson* (The Hague: Kluwer, 2000), pp. 111–33; and Petersmann, "Constitutionalism and International Adjudication: How to Constitutionalize the UN Dispute Settlement System?" *New York University Journal of International Law and Politics*, Vol. 31 (1999), pp. 753–90. Astonishingly, many international lawyers continue to interpret the UN Charter as a "constitution of mankind"; e.g., B. Simma and A. Paulus, "The 'International Community' Facing the Challenge of Globalization," *European Journal of International Law*, Vol. 9 (1998), p. 274.

6. See for example, Jan Klabbers, Anne Peters, and Geir Ulfstein, *The Constitutionalization of International Law* (Oxford: Oxford University Press, 2009).

7. See especially O. Corten, "Les ambiguités de la reference au droit international comme facteur de légitimation portée et signification d'une déformalisation du discours légaliste," in O. Corten and B. Delcourt, eds., *Droit, légitimation et politique exterieure: l'Europe et la guerre du Kosovo* (Brussels: Bruylant, 2000), pp. 223–59; and A. Orford, "Muscular Humanitarianism: Reading the Narratives of the New Interventionism," *European Journal of International Law*, Vol. 10 (1999), pp. 679–711.

8. There is no reliable exact number to the civilian deaths of "Operation Allied Force." The Human Rights Watch estimates that about 500 civilians were killed in

approximately 90 incidents. See Amnesty International, *NATO/Federal Republic of Yugoslavia: "Collateral Damage" or Unlawful Killings? Violations of the Laws of War by NATO during Operation Allied Force* (Amnesty International, June 2000), p. 1.

9. NATO Press release (1999) 041 (March 14, 1999).

10. Ruti G. Teitel, *Humanity's Law* (Oxford: Oxford University Press, 2011), p. 111.

11. The completeness of international law was the focus of much of the interwar reconstructive jurisprudence. For Hans Kelsen, completeness was an outcome of the formal principle of the exclusion of the third. More influential has been the theory of material completeness that forms the heart of one of the most important books of twentieth-century international jurisprudence, H. Lauterpacht, *The Function of Law in the International Community* (Oxford: Clarendon, 1933).

12. This naturalist position is expressly taken in H. Lauterpacht, "The Grotian Tradition in International Law," *British Year Book of International Law*, Vol. 23 (1946), pp. 1–53.

13. This argument is expressly made, e.g., in A. Cassese, *"Ex iniuria ius oritur:* Are We Moving towards International Legitimation of Forcible Humanitarian Countermeasures in the International Community?" *European Journal of International Law*, Vol. 10 (1999), pp. 23–30. For nuances, compare B. Simma, "NATO, the UN and the Use of Force: Legal Aspects," *European Journal of International Law*, Vol. 10 (1999), pp. 1–22. For particularly useful discussions of the international lawyers' reaction, see S. Schieder, "Pragmatism as a Path towards a Discursive and Open Theory of International Law," *European Journal of International Law*, Vol. 11 (2000), pp. 663, 691–98; and Corten, "Les ambiguités de la reference," pp. 223–59.

14. See A. Pellet, "Brief Remarks on the Unilateral Use of Force," *European Journal of International Law*, Vol. 11 (2000), p. 389.

15. UN General Assembly, Resolution 2625 (XXV) (October 24, 1970).

16. Unsurprisingly, the customary law argument enjoys wide support among U.S. lawyers such as Lillich, McDougal, or Reisman. The problem with that argument is that it has to be made against the authority of ICJ, *Nicaragua Case (Nicaragua v. US)* (Merits) (1986), ICJ Rep 109. Apart from Kosovo, practice is still scarce of cases in which the acting state itself would have understood (or justified) its action as humanitarian intervention. See D. Kritsiotis, "Appraising the Policy Objections to Humanitarian Intervention," *Michigan Journal of International Law*, Vol. 19 (1993), pp. 1010–14. For a balanced overview and assessment, see S. Chesterman, *Just War or Just Peace? Humanitarian Intervention and International Law* (Oxford: Oxford University Press, 2001), pp. 53–86.

17. See G. Ress, "The Interpretation of the Charter," in B. Simma, ed., *The Charter of the United Nations: A Commentary* (Oxford: Oxford University Press, 1995), pp. 42–43.

18. This is the argument in M. Walzer, *Just and Unjust Wars: A Moral Argument with Historical Illustrations*, 2nd ed. (New York: Basic Books, 1992), pp. 101–8.

19. M. Reisman, "Sovereignty and Human Rights in Contemporary International Law," in G. Fox and B. Roth, eds., *Democratic Governance and International Law* (Cambridge: Cambridge University Press, 2000), p. 245.

20. T. M. Franck, *The Empowered Self: Law and Society in the Age of Individualism* (New York: Oxford University Press, 1999), p. 272. For the policy objections, see Kritsiotis, "Appraising the Policy Objections," pp. 1020–34.

21. P.-M. Dupuy, "L'enfer et la paradigme: libres propos sur les relations du droit international avec la persistance des guerres et l'objectif idéal du maintien de la paix," in *Mélanges offerts à Hubert Thierry* (Paris: Pedone, 1998), pp. 199–200.

22. See P.-M. Dupuy, "L'obligation en droit international," *Archives de philosophie du droit*, Vol. 44 (2000), p. 218.

23. The view that human interests or wants are essentially compatible, and that social problems are thus ("ultimately") problems of scientific or technical co-ordination, lies at the heart of the traditional (liberal) interdependence-based explan-ations of the possibility of international law. It is precisely that assumption—the harmony of interests—that was the basis of the "realist" critique of international law and the tragic view of the human predicament propagated by leading "realists." See E. H. Carr, *The Twenty Years' Crisis 1919–1939*, 2nd ed. (London: Macmillan, 1946), especially pp. 40 et seq., 80–88; and H. Morgenthau, *Scientific Man vs. Power Politics* (Chicago: University of Chicago Press, 1946).

24. See further Martti Koskenniemi, "Faith, Identity and the Killing of the Innocent: International Lawyers and Nuclear Weapons," in *The Politics of International Law* (Oxford: Hart, 2011), pp. 198–218.

25. This is what makes the recent obsession about "compliance control" with international agreements so frustrating. In the interesting cases, noncompliance is not a technical or a bad faith problem, but a political one; substantive disagreement about what the party accused of noncompliance undertook to comply with.

26. A good example of this is the 1997 UN Convention on the Law of the Non-Navigational Uses of International Watercourses (July 8, 1997) UN Dec A/RES/51/229. The treaty merely lays down a general standard of "equitable and reasonable uti-lization" that reserves the determination of permitted and prohibited uses to an open-ended multifactor calculation, "taking into account the interests of the watercourse States concerned, consistent with the adequate protection of the watercourse" (Article 5(1) *in fine*).

27. T. Nagel, *Mortal Questions* (Cambridge: Cambridge University Press, 1979), p. 59. For a good account of the problems of utilitarian arguments about killing in war, see R. Norman, *Ethics, Killing and War* (Cambridge: Cambridge University Press, 1995), pp. 44–50.

28. The idea of rights as "political trumps held by individuals" is famously defended in R. Dworkin, *Taking Rights Seriously* (Cambridge MA: Harvard University Press, 1977).

29. ICJ, *Threat or Use of Nuclear Weapons* (Advisory Opinion) Reports 1996 24]–[25].

30. See Chapter 7 of this volume.

31. See C. Brown, "Universal Human Rights: A Critique," in T. Dunne and N. J. Wheeler, eds., *Human Rights and Global Policies* (Cambridge: Cambridge University Press, 1999), pp. 111–14.

32. Which is how they are defended, e.g., in M. J. Perry, *The Idea of Human Rights: Four Inquiries* (Oxford: Oxford University Press, 1998), pp. 11–41. For the classical critique, see E. Burke, *Reflections on the Revolution in France*, ed. J. C. D. Clark (Stanford, CA: Stanford University Press, 2001), pp. 217–21.

33. For a long list of references to academic studies that propose the development of "criteria," see P. Malanczuk, *Humanitarian Intervention and the Legitimacy of the Use of Force* (Amsterdam: Spinhuis, 1993) p. 30 and p. 69 fn. 298. See also Kritsiotis, "Appraising the Policy Objections," pp. 1022–24.

34. Report of the International Commission on Intervention and State Sovereignty (December 2001), p. 16.

35. *In Larger Freedom*, Report of the UN Secretary-General, Doc A/59/2005 (March 21, 2005); *2005 World Summit Outcome*, UN Doc A/RES/60/1 (October 24, 2005).

36. For a good overview, see Pekka Niemelä, *The Politics of Responsibility to Protect: Problems and Prospects* (Helsinki: Erik Castrén Research Reports, 2008).

37. Anne Peters, "Humanity as the Alpha and Omega of Sovereignty," *European Journal of International Law*, Vol. 20 (2009), p. 523 (referring to a talk by the initiator of the ICISS at the American Society of International Law, Gareth Evans).

38. J. Stone, *Conflict through Consensus. UN Approaches to Aggression* (Sydney: Maitland, 1977).

39. UN General Assembly, Resolution 3314 (XXIX) (December 14, 1974).

40. See ICC Review Conference, Kampala Resolution RC Res. 6, Adoption to the Elements of Crimes (June 11, 2010). For some of these basic points, see Andreas Paulus, "Some Second Thoughts on the Crime of Aggression," *European Journal of International Law*, Vol. 20 (2010), p. 1121.

41. For the way the understanding was intended to cover the U.S. concern that the use of force for "humanitarian" purposes might be made illegal as aggression, see Claus Kress & Leonie von Holtzendorff, "The Kampala Compromise on the Crime of Aggression," *Journal of International Criminal Justice*, Vol. 8 (2010), pp. 1204–7.

42. "Humanitarian Intervention," Report by the Dutch Advisory Council on International Affairs (AIV) and the Advisory Committee on Public International Law (CAVV), No. 13 (April 2000), p. 29. For a much more skeptical discussion, see Danish Institute of International Affairs, *Humanitarian Intervention. Legal and Political Aspects* (Copenhagen, 1999), pp. 103–11.

43. See also T. M. Franck, *The Power of Legitimacy among Nations* (Oxford: Oxford University Press, 1990), pp. 67–80.

44. The way in which the legislative choice between (automatic) rules and (evaluative) standards is influenced by the frequency of the conduct being regulated has been much debated in law and economics, including international trade law. The point is that the less frequent the behavior, the less appropriate automatic rules for regulating it are. J. Trachtman, "Trade and ... Problems: Cost-Benefit Analysis and Subsidiarity," *European Journal of International Law*, Vol. 9 (1998), p. 37.

45. This move is usefully described in F. Kratochwil, "How Do Norms Matter?" in M. Byers, ed., *The Role of Law in International Politics: Essays on International Relations and International Law* (Oxford: Oxford University Press, 2000), pp. 37–42.

46. Morgenthau, *Scientific Man vs. Power Politics*, p. 119.

47. "If . . . a coalition of states had been prepared to act in defence of the Tutsi population, but did not receive prompt Council authorisation, should such a coalition have stood aside and allowed the horror to unfold?" UN Press Release SG/SM/7136, GA 9596.

48. For the strong recommendation for statesmen to shun from absolute principles and to act on an honest appreciation of the concrete effects of one's decision, see M. Weber, "Politics as Vocation" in *From Max Weber: Essays in Sociology*, trans. and ed. H. H. Gerth and C. Wright Mills (London: Routledge, 1967), pp. 77–128. For the application in international relations, see D. Warner, *An Ethic of Responsibility in International Relations* (Boulder, CO, and London: Rienner, 1991).

49. C. Schmitt, *Political Theology* (Cambridge, MA: MIT Press, 1985), pp. 31–32.

50. H. Morgenthau, *Politics among Nations* (New York: Knopf, 1948), p. 444. An excellent analysis of the way Western argument in Kosovo went beyond positivism but fell short of natural law "theory" is in Corten, "Les ambiguïtés de la reference," pp. 233–59 (n. 7).

51. Alex J. Bellamy, "The Responsibility to Protect—Five Years On," *Ethics and International Affairs*, Vol. 24 (2010), p. 144.

52. Ibid., pp. 165, 166.

53. F. K. Abiew & N. Gal-Or, "Libya, Intervention and Responsibility. The Dawn of a 'New Era'?" in Carsten Stahn and Henning Melber, eds., *Peace Diplomacy, Global Justice and International Agency: Rethinking Human Security and Ethics in the Spirit of Dag Hammarskjöld* (Cambridge: Cambridge University Press, 2014), p. 556.

54. As suggested by Hani Sayed, "On the Humanization of the Syrian Question. A Critique of International Legal Responses," talk at the Erik Castrén Institute, University of Helsinki, November 14, 2013.

55. Bellamy, "Five Years On," p. 148.

56. As suggested in Ove Bring, "Hammarskjöld's Dynamic Approach to the UN Charter and International law," in Carsten Stahn and Henning Melber, eds., *Peace Diplomacy, Global Justice and International Agency: Rethinking Human Security and Ethics in the Spirit of Dag Hammarskjöld* (Cambridge: Cambridge University Press, 2014), pp. 153–54.

57. Schmitt, *Political Theology* (1985), pp. 5–15.

58. Jean-Jacques Rousseau, *The Social Contract* (Harmondsworth: Penguin, 1968), p. 51.

59. For the ideological nature or standard narratives about humanitarian intervention that "depend upon the acceptance of gendered and racialized metaphors," see Orford, "Muscular Humanitarianism," Vol. 701 (1999), pp. 689–703.

60. See M. Koskenniemi, "The Police in the Temple. Order, Justice and the UN: A Dialectical View," *European Journal of International Law*, Vol. 6 (1995), pp. 325–48.

61. *Even It Up: Time to End Extreme Inequality* (Oxfam: London 2014).

62. For this argument in a more general form, see D. Kennedy, "Putting the Politics Back in International Politics," *Finnish Yearbook of International Law*, Vol. 9 (1998), pp. 19–27.

63. See Hilary Charlesworth, "International Law: A Discipline of Crisis," *The Modern Law Review* Vol. 65 (2002), pp. 377–92.

64. M. Koskenniemi, "What Use for Sovereignty Today?" *Asian Journal of International Law*, Vol. 1 (2011), pp. 61–70.

65. Anne Orford, *International Authority and the Responsibility to Protect* (Cambridge: Cambridge University Press 2011). Orford's discussion of the extension of international executive authority as a moral quest is interestingly discussed in Carsten Stahn and Henning Melber, eds., *Peace Diplomacy, Global Justice and International Agency: Rethinking Human Security and Ethics in the Spirit of Dag Hammarskjöld* (Cambridge: Cambridge University Press, 2014), especially by Spiraty and Barker.

66. The arguments here draw inspiration from recent debates about the possibility of a left universalism that would not only recognize but enhance claims of identity and the reality of politics as ("agonistic") struggle. Out of a flourishing recent literature, see C. Mouffe and E. Laclau, *Hegemony and Socialist Strategy* (London: Verso, 1985), and J. Butler, E. Laclau, and S. Žižek, *Contingency, Hegemony, Universality: Contemporary Dialogues on the Left* (London: Verso, 2000). I have discussed the culture of formalism at more length in *The Gentle Civilizer of Nations: The Rise and all of International Law 1870–1960* (Cambridge: Cambridge University Press, 2002), pp. 449–509.

67. This "Schmittian" point is also made in Žižek, *The Fragile Absolute* (2000), pp. 56–60.

68. See D. Kennedy, "The Nuclear Weapons case" in L. Boisson de Chazournes and P. Sands, eds., *International Law, the International Court of Justice and Nuclear Weapons* (Cambridge: Cambridge University Press, 1999), pp. 468–72.

69. E. Laclau, "Identity and Hegemony: The Role of Universality in the Constitution of Political Logics," in *Contingency*, pp. 82–83.

12

Human Security[*]

Shahrbanou Tadjbakhsh

Thomas Hobbes, in *Leviathan* (1651), argues that in order to escape the "nasty, brutish and short" life, people must forge a social contract by agreeing to live under common laws where they collectively and reciprocally renounce the rights they have against one another. They must, at the same time, entrust someone or persons with the authority and power to enforce this social contract. In exchange for submitting to the authority of the "sovereign," the latter will act in the name of the common good and maintain people's physical safety. People therefore rationally surrender the whole or part of their freedom and rights to an authority in order to gain the common security of self-preservation. In turn the authority guarantees to protect lives, property, and certain liberties.

The Leviathan, or the commonwealth, as the metaphor for the state, is represented as an artificial man whose body is made up of all the bodies of its citizens, with a sovereign as the head whose power was conceived through a social contract by people. The Leviathan, having been created and made up of people in the first place, is supposed to protect them from abuses by and to one another; in order words, to provide "security" from themselves. It is the sum of responsible, rationale, secure individuals.

By the time Hobbes thought of his social contract between people and between them and their representation as a state, another contract had been forged between nations, which had led to the Peace of Westphalia (1641)

*Parts of this article have appeared in Shahrbanou Tadjbakhsh, "In Defense of the Broad Approach of Human Security," in Mary Martins and Taylor Owens, eds., *Routledge Handbook on Human Security* (Milton Park, UK: Routledge, 2013); Shahrbanou Tadjbakhsh, "Human Security and the Legitimization of Peacebuilding," in Oliver Richmond, ed., *Palgrave Advances in Peacebuilding: Critical Developments and Approaches* (Houndmills, UK: Palgrave Macmillan, 2009); and Shahrbanou Tadjbakhsh, "Human Security Twenty Years On," Norwegian Peacebuilding Resource Center Paper, Oslo, Norway, June 26, 2014.

and the ensuing Westphalian international legal order. Since then, security has been a prerogative of the state, which had been given the assurance of peace within in exchange for protection from war abroad. The social contract, associated with the nation-state in the Westphalian model, legitimizes the sovereign use of armed forces by the state to protect its citizens internally and against other states externally. The threat of violence from citizens against each other is regulated by the social contract and the very prerogative of the state as the only one with the monopoly of use of force, while the Westphalian system pacifies international relations by recognizing the state as the sole sovereign and legitimate military power in world politics.

But what happens when threats are nonexistential—when they may not threaten the survival of the state but its functioning and legitimacy, disabling the capacity of the state to perform its role in protecting its population? What if the state, the Leviathan, and its sovereign fail to protect their citizens? Hobbes's men, in order to avoid misery and fear and to secure order, self-protection, and self-preservation, enter into a contract to voluntarily surrender some of their rights to an authority. But what if their insecurities are not only from the fear of violence instigated by other men and by other states, but also by their inability to keep and sustain the gains made in satisfying their basic needs and rights? In other words, what if peoples' sense of security is broader than limited sense of order and lack of violence? What if escape from the nasty, brutish, and short life they seek entails the right to live a dignified life—free from violence, yes, but also from needs, wants, and indignities? What happens when a state fails to provide the minimum, safety from violence, but also the other parameters of a dignified life? The social contract can be revoked, in Hobbes's view, and people recover their ability to protect themselves. In other words, when states cannot or will not abide by their responsibility as states vis-à-vis their citizens, then another type of social contract is necessary for the provision of security. That other type of social contract is an opportunity to revise the very meaning of security, because living free of fear of violence is not enough for a life secured with dignity.

DEFINITIONS AND PARAMETERS

Security, "an essentially contested concept"[1] by itself, is in the eye of the beholder. For Buzan, security is a political process, "when an issue is presented as posing an existential threat to a designated referent object."[2] The *Oxford English Dictionary* (OED) instead highlights the subjectivity inherent in security as a "feeling" for individuals: "The condition of being protected from or not exposed to danger; safety. . . . Freedom from care, anxiety or apprehension; a feeling of safety or freedom from an absence of danger."[3] That feeling of safety from care, anxiety, and apprehension has relative connotations in different contexts: For some, it entails from a sudden loss of access to jobs, health care, social welfare, etc. For others, it can stem from violence, conflicts, displacement, etc. From people's perspective, security needs to be defined as a subjective experience at the micro level to gain meaning. This experience may be decidedly different from that of states' concerns for their national security.

For states, security comes with sheer force, power, and defense (the protection of borders, buildup of armies, etc.). For individuals within states, security can be the assurance that what has been gained today would not be lost tomorrow: Insecurity, therefore, can refer to the loss of guarantee of access to jobs, health care, social welfare, education, etc., as much as it can to the fear, objective and subjective, arising from domestic violence, political instability, crime, displacement, etc. The meaning of security for a refugee fleeing war, a farmer losing his crops to drought, an elderly couple losing their assets following a bank crisis, and a woman scared of her violent husband is decisively different from the way it can be palpated for a state at the brink of collapse, failure, or invasion. To be meaningful, therefore, human security needs to be recognized at the micro level in terms of people's everyday experiences.

Dominant state-centered security theories rest on the protection of territorial integrity and national sovereignty against existential threats posed by other belligerent states. The human security approach instead proposes that state-focused security fails to address all the gamut of possible insecurities of individuals within a state in a comprehensive manner, and that by extension, security for the state does not automatically trickle down to that of people. Human security is a concept that engages with the security of people and communities instead of solely that of states and institutions. Once the referent object and subject of security is moved down to individuals, the notion of "safety" then broadens to a condition beyond mere existence (survival) to life worth living, hence, well-being and dignity of human beings.

Human security threats include both objective, tangible elements, such as insufficient income, chronic unemployment, and dismal access to adequate health care and quality education, as well as subjective perceptions, such as the inability to control one's destiny, indignity, fear of crime and violent conflict, etc. They can be both direct (those that are deliberately orchestrated, such as systematic persecutions) and indirect (those that arise inadvertently or structurally, i.e., underinvestment in key social and economic sectors such as education and health care).

By putting individuals at the center of analysis, security threats (or, in other words, insecurities) are recognized in terms of their ability to hamper people's *survival* (physical abuse, violence, persecution, or death), their *livelihoods* (unemployment, food insecurity, pandemics, etc.), and their *dignity* (lack of human rights, inequality, exclusion, discrimination, etc.). By extension, it also recognizes nontraditional threats that can menace states' essence in ways similar to that of individuals: by hampering states' *existence* (territorial integrity), their *functioning* (whether they have the resources and capacity to function and develop as a state), and their *sovereignty* (legitimacy and recognition).

Rather than an empirical or positivist theory like realism or neorealism, human security does not proclaim to be amoral. With its "human" accolade, it more comfortably belongs to the field of ethics in international relations (IR) and normative theory, dealing with what ought to be and how the world should be ordered and the value choices decision makers should make.[4] As such it can be considered as an evaluative framework. If realism is supposed to explain why states compete in a competitive anarchical system, human security could be seen as making value judgments on whether this behavior is morally acceptable, judged against the outcomes for individuals and communities as the "content" of states.

In its most common understanding and usage, human security is a people-centered approach to identifying—and responding to—threats to the security of people and communities as opposed to that of states, institutions, and the regional/international system. Thus, human security, in its broadest form, consists of three components that simultaneously delineate its scope: *freedom from fear* (conditions that allow individuals and groups protection from direct threats to their safety and physical integrity, including various forms of direct and indirect violence, intended or not); *freedom from want* (conditions that allow for protection of basic needs, quality of life, livelihoods, and enhanced human welfare); and *freedom from indignity* (conditions in which individuals and groups are assured of the protection of their fundamental rights, allowed to make choices and take advantage of opportunities in their everyday lives).

TOO BROAD TO MEAN ANYTHING, OR NOT BROAD ENOUGH TO CAPTURE LIFE?

Human security is often described as a vague concept with no analytical or practical utility; so broad that it includes everything, and therefore, nothing; and a new nemesis from northern countries, wrapped in an excuse to launch "just wars" and interventions in weak states.

Three schools of thought have evolved in academia and echoed in the policy world: A first group argues that human security lacks analytical rigor and, consequently, is at best a "rallying cry" and at worst as unadulterated "hot air" as a mere political agenda.[5] Among the most adamant critics are realist scholars who, in the tradition of Kenneth Waltz, warn against the securitization of what is not, essentially, an existential threat. A second school, while accepting the term, insists on limiting the definitions to "freedom from fear" and direct threats to individuals' safety from tangible violence and to their physical integrity: armed conflict, gross violations of human rights that lead to fears such as imprisonment and death, public insecurity, and organized crime.[6] Such a minimalist approach has been adopted by Canada as its principle for foreign policy and by the report of the International Commission on Intervention and State Sovereignty, *The Responsibility to Protect* (2001), in its discussions around conditions conducive to the legitimization of international interventions. A third school, to which this author belongs, argues for a broad definition as essential for understanding and dealing with the entire gamut of threats and crises in the everyday lives of people, regardless of whether the concept is "workable" or not. The broad definition comprises of freedom from want, freedom from fear, and freedom from indignity. The maximalist approach has been adopted by the UNDP in its 2004 *Human Development Report*, by the government of Japan, and by the Commission on Human Security (2003). It concentrates on threats, both direct and indirect, both objective and subjective, which come from traditional understandings of insecurity but also from underdevelopment and human rights abuses. Even though adopting the narrow definition facilitates the researchers' work, threats such as poverty or disease can have an equally severe impact on people's lives and dignity as does tangible violence. Broad proponents argue that when agency is returned to people, it is the localized, subjective sense of the security of individuals that in the last analysis is of paramount importance, not the limited domain of possibility for action by politicians, interventionists, or assistant givers.

One way to gauge the academic debate is to consider it as representative of the two different approaches that Robert Cox has labeled as problem-solving and critical theory.[7] From a problem-solving perspective, Robert Paris argues that a broad definition, which includes components ranging from physical to psychological, without a hierarchy of security needs, presents difficulties for policy makers to prioritize among competing goals.[8] From such a problem-solving point of view, competing demands present challenges for policy makers who need to allocate attention and resources on specific solutions to specific issues. Andrew Mack warns that a broad definition does not allow for an examination of variables and the analysis of violence and poverty, for example, as separate issues.[9] Most of these positivist scholars above, who tend to accept the narrow approach, dwell in fact on its practical implications in the guise of taking a shot at the analytical nature of the broad concept. Basing themselves on Buzan and Wæver's conception of security threats as informed by urgency, priority, and gravity,[10] they assume that securitizing some issues changes their status in the policy hierarchy, making them worthy of special attention, resources, and immediate resolution, including by military means.

From a critical perspective, on the other hand, the so-called problem of lack of prioritization and hierarchy of threats, assumes that responsibility for "action" rests only with political actors limited by competing demands for their attention and resources. Yet, policy making is not only a vertical process, but can be a networked, flexible, and horizontal coalition of approaches corresponding to complex situations. Furthermore, to hierarchize and prioritize among human insecurities may be a futile exercise, as threats are interdependent and the eradication of any one of them in isolation is of little effect.

ADDED VALUE TO SECURITY, DEVELOPMENT, AND HUMAN RIGHTS

The broad human security approach hence combines the security, human development, and human rights frameworks by adding elements to them. At the same time, it locates itself as a convergence of the three approaches.

The human security approach can be considered an ethical rupture with traditional security paradigms (by making the security of people and communities as the ultimate goal), and a methodological one (with the idea that by securing individuals, the security of the state, the region, and the international system can also be better ensured). As such, the framework postulates different answers to the three questions that have preoccupied security scholars: Security of whom? Security from what? And security by what means?

Security of Whom?

Individuals in addition to the state are the "referent objects" of security, and by implication, their security is the ultimate goal to which all instruments and peripheral actors are subordinated. Human security thus poses a moral challenge to realism, for whom the moral argument is the *raison d'état* itself.

Security from What?

The broad approach recognizes menaces beyond violence and concentrates on threats to the survival, well-being, and dignity of individuals. It postulates three assumptions about threats: (1) that equal weight has to be given to underdevelopment and human rights violations as threats alongside traditional insecurities, (2) that threats are interlinked and interconnected, (3) that these linkages mean that instead of looking for priorities, the connections have to be sought out in order to make sure that interventions in one domain do no harm in others at worst, and multiply positive externalities at best. Consequently, the answer to "security from what" can only come from an analysis of the given context and find meaning in subjectivity. Contextual analysis would recognize the relative security of a person living under $4 a day but who is well integrated in family and community, lives in a peaceful environment, and disposes of a minimum of social security. On the other hand, it would also recognize the insecurity of a person with income and wealth who lives in a conflict situation, or one whose health insurance relies on his or her job in a volatile labor market.

Security by What Means?

As the main author of the 1994 *Human Development Report*, Mahbub Ul Haq saw a simple solution: human security can be achieved through development, not through arms. When the survival, well-being, and dignity of individuals become the ultimate goal, constructs such as the state, institutions of political democracy, and the market are relegated to secondary status as means to achieve that goal. Hence, insecurity should not be dealt with through short-term military or policing solutions, but a long-term comprehensive strategy that combines protection, provision of welfare, and emancipation.

Within the field of development studies and political economy, the human security concept made an international debut in 1994 by the same team that coined the human development approach through the UNDP HDRs in 1990. For its authors, Ul Haq, Amartya Sen, and others, the distinction was simple: Human development refers to the process of widening people's choices to be who they want to be and do what they want to do; in other words, the enhancement of capabilities and functioning. It can be ensured through economic growth strategies that include distribution, equity, and enhanced freedoms. Human security, by contrast, refers to the condition that enables people to exercise these choices safely and freely, and to be relatively confident that the opportunities they have today will not be lost tomorrow. In essence, human security introduces an element of insurance to the development process and assurance that the process and outcome of development is risk-free. Human development can be summarized as "growth with equity," human security as "downturn with security." The human security approach concerns itself with the "stability" of goods provided within the human development framework against risks of sudden changes for the worse, as opposed to their levels or trends.[11] In the words of Ul Haq, "Human security is not a concern with weapons. It is a concern with human dignity. In the last analysis, it is a child who did not die, a disease that did not spread, an ethnic tension that did not explode, a dissident who was not silenced, a human spirit that was not crushed."[12] Human security also puts additional focus on identification, prevention, and mitigation of risks that are often overlooked in development strategies. In a nutshell, the concept refers to the sustainability and stability of development gains.[13]

In the policy world, human rights and human security are the two frameworks that most reinforce each other. The two frameworks share many similarities: Both are pursuant of human dignity, evoke morality, and stress the universality of rights and their indivisibility. They also share content: Human security threats in the broad definition—fear, want, and indignities—find echo in the first- (civil and political rights), second- (economic and social rights), and third-generation human rights (solidarity rights). If the 1948 Universal Declaration on Human Rights included the broad gamut of rights, Cold War politics saw a division between first- and second-generation rights supported by the two sides of the bipolar divide. Their reconciliation was not official until the Vienna Conference in 1993, which disclaimed any priority of rights by declaring that "All human rights are universal, indivisible and interdependent and interrelated."[14] It is therefore not a coincidence that the following year, the flip sides of these rights were coined as threats in the 1994 HDR, which took as indivisible, universal, and interrelated freedom from fear (first-generation rights) and freedom from want (second-generation rights). In subsequent years, the added definition of freedom from indignities was reminiscent of the third-generation "solidarity" rights related to self-determination, cultural rights, and the right to peace. Yet, there are also differences between the two concepts: human rights are rooted in legal norms and international covenants and agreements; human security raises alarms about threats and potentialities but does not have a normative/obligatory framework. At the context-specific level, human security helps identify the rights at stake in that particular context.[15] In a simplified nutshell, the human rights framework is the prerequisite and platform for human security, while human security is a condition for human rights to be fulfilled.

HS AND INTERNATIONAL POLITICS

If human security, in the original writing of Ul Haq, was supposed to be a convergence of the North-South differences, the subsequent definitional debates and its adoption as a foreign policy tool by some states only served to reinforce the divergence.

Immediately after its international outing in the 1994 UNDP HDR, the concept was adopted, and hence relegated, as foreign and aid policy tools. Japan, Canada, and the EU, for example, by adopting the concept in their external affairs, treated the concept as a functional tool with the premise that the security of people in "other" states or regions would trickle out to security at home. The 2004 Barcelona Report *Human Security Doctrine for Europe* presented by the LSE study group to Javier Solana as part of his quest for implementing the Common Foreign and Security Policy (CFSP), for example, called on the EU to take on an "enlightened self-interest" in its "collective responsibility to intervene" in the "black holes" outside of the Union, which were generating insecurities for the citizens of the EU. Far from Ul Haq's universal and cooperative understanding of global justice, human security as a foreign policy tool became a "good" that some better-off countries could provide for "others." It implied, falsely, that human insecurity was not a problem within industrialized societies, and the concept was not adequate enough to be promoted as a domestic strategy. No country in the industrialized world, including Canada and Japan, adopted the concept of human security as a principle for national policy making. The EU doctrine, for example, failed to talk about the pockets of poverty within its own countries, urban riots, the crisis of multiculturalism, and damning immigration policies.[16]

Another miscue of the concept in international politics has been the association of its narrow approach with the Responsibility to Protect (R2P) doctrine, which reinforced the North-South divide in international relations. Human security, when associated with R2P, has been seen in the South as yet another attempt by the West to impose its liberal values and political institutions on non-Western societies, an excuse for intervention in states' domestic affairs and for conditionality on Overseas Development Assistance (ODA). The main conceptual criticism to the R2P doctrine is that it stems from a narrow definition of human security, which solely emphasizes extreme violations while ignoring other important fears and threats to everyday life. Among the seven categories of the 1994 HDR, only personal, political, and community insecurities were considered as threats grave enough to the core of all human lives to justify interventions, while other threats such as poverty, famine, diseases, and man-made environmental disasters did not warrant action by the international community. The broad approach to human security, instead of advocating the use of military force for humanitarian interventions, would argue for an *a priori* engagement by the international community to share responsibility for prevention rather than dealing with crises that are already underway.

HOW CAN THE CONCEPT HELP LEGITIMIZE PEACEBUILDING AND STATEBUILDING?

Can applying a particular type of human security framework help in the legitimization of the peacebuilding that supposedly comes after interventions and, ultimately, in the development of this "ethic of non-hegemonic engagement"?

In evaluating the impact of the role of international organizations in post-conflict environments, at least two different angles of query can be used. One relates to questions of efficiency and effectiveness of peacebuilding efforts.[17] Another has to do with the rationale for assistance provided to post-conflict countries, the model of the ultimate state presumed in statebuilding efforts, whether there is consensus among different actors on the supremacy of this model, and sufficient legitimacy for imposing it as conditionality for assistance. Ultimately such a query would have to scrutinize the model and assumptions permeating in the ideology of aid, which, increasingly, has been based on a consensus around the model of "Liberal Peace" used by peacebuilders.[18]

For inquiries into the problematic of legitimacy of peacebuilding, as opposed to questions of efficiency, three lines of enquiry can be used: (1) how the models used in peacebuilding and their underlying norms are valued among local populations, (2) how much they have been successful in improving people's everyday lives, and (3) how much have they involved beneficiaries of interventions—i.e., people—directly in the design and implementation of peace. The definition of legitimacy, using the human security perspective, rests therefore squarely on the point of view and perceptions of local populations.

Legitimacy, as opposed to efficiency-oriented queries into peacebuilding, has at its root an engagement with ethics. Understanding what peacebuilding means to the persons affected is crucial to ethical reasoning. The subjects of peacebuilding matter as aims in themselves and not as objects or means to the preservation of an international order where the peacebuilders themselves are the primary subjects. Legitimacy, from the human security point of view, then depends on the consensus around the validity of the models and their content used in peacebuilding by local populations as well as how populations perceive of the success of changes in improving people's their everyday life.

By putting its focus on individuals' perceptions of needs, aspirations, and opportunities, as opposed to models, states, and institutions as referent objects and subjects of peace, human security can answer the legitimacy problem of peacebuilding. The more populations and their perceptions of the common good are included, the more difficult it would be to simply impose particular ideals, values, or models deemed universally applicable but proven to be problematic. But this does not mean a mere adherence to the principles of participation, as utilitarianism would see it, to improve the success of reforms or to prevent inertia at best and hostile response at worst. Perceptions count not because sentiments of mistrust against "imposition or broken promises can result and spark a local backlash that undermines the legitimacy of reforms and may even result in violence."[19] They count because perceptions respond directly to moral judgments by populations of affected countries, whether they are liberal, illiberal, or aliberal. The local gains moral ownership by virtue of being the primary subject and object of insecurity, in its broad form.

From an ethical perspective, something is considered legitimate if it is considered as so by unanimous opinion, or consensus around a common good, presumably that of peace. The ethical question is embodied in the possibilities as answers to these processes: Why peace? How peace? Whose peace? And which peace?

- *Which type of peace?* One that responds to local people's understandings of culture, or to the culture of hegemony, or for the security of institutions, power, etc.? An institutional peace or an emancipatory one?
- *Whose peace?* That of external actors engaged in peacebuilding, or that of local beneficiaries?
- *Why peace?* For instrumental, utilitarian reasons (like international security or the security of systems and regimes), or for emancipation of individuals and communities?
- *How peace?* Through force and coercion, through imposition/installment of liberal institutions of the state and the market, or through welfare, participation, inclusion, and plurality? Through changing local culture along universal norms, or preserving diversity? Through adhering to international law, to domestic norms in the home country of the peacebuilding practitioners, or to the norms of the people affected by these actions?

The emancipatory human security approach would then answer these ethical questions with a focus on the individuals and communities living the everyday perceptions.

- *Which type of peace?* Peace not merely as end of violence, but as a condition that allows for emancipation from insecurities in the broad sense.
- *Whose security/peace?* That of people whose insecurity is at stake and who need to feel secure, as opposed to that of external actors in a peacebuilding situation, or of hegemony, power, and institutions (including the state, the international system, and also models and ideas such as liberal democracy and market economy).
- *How security/peace?* Through empowering people, transforming them into agents of change, protecting them, and providing welfare. A departure from viewing the liberal state as the precondition to peace and international security, by focusing not on the existence or not of such a state, but on its responsibilities.
- *What type of security/peace?* A peace that responds to emancipation from insecurities in everyday life, be they basic threats to survival and bare life, functional threats that hamper livelihoods, and those concerned with dignity. The emancipatory, everyday peace that has local meaning, as opposed to the cosmopolitan liberal, individualistic peace focused on the validity of institutions or the neorealist preoccupation with international stability.

The very legitimacy of the ultimate end state assumed in statebuilding exercises bears similar tensions: The nation-state is caught between legitimacy from the outside and legitimacy from inside. Legitimacy to adhere to international norms and to be recognized as a "stable democracy" worthy of its name by the international community of nations requires the state to play by certain criteria—open and liberal institutions, overruling of corruption, the monopoly over the use of force and neutralization of deviant nonstate actors, defending sovereignty, etc. But legitimacy is also and especially viewed from inside: whether the state can provide, protect, and empower its own citizens, and how it responds to them and upholds the social contract. Far from the Weberian concept of the state, such foundation of legitimacy comes from the fulfillment of expectations and needs of the population. The state finds its meaning and moral legitimacy, its *raison d'etat*, only in its response to the people. Legitimacy is eroded when a state is highly dependent on foreign aid and answers to the needs of external institutions instead. It is also eroded when the state relinquishes its power to other actors, such as international organizations, NGOs, and private companies, out of weakness or force. In an ideal world, the two should coincide; but the challenge of statebuilding in post-conflict situations is precisely the tension that exists around the universal demands on a centralized, rule-creating state with modern institutions, and perceptions from local, traditional and fragmented societies manned by populations with large expectations on the state to provide and protect. Coinciding what can be called universal legitimacy with local legitimacy is the challenge.

From an emancipatory human security point of view, the emphasis is on the perceptions of people within a state rather than the existence, power, or nature of the state itself. The legitimacy comes therefore not from the institutions of leadership, of good governance, of the openness of markets and availability of capital, but perceptions about justice, empowerment, and space provided for participation, in addition to the important indicator of satisfaction with the delivery of public goods. By human security definition, a weak state is one that cannot exercise its primary function of social protection and therefore fails in its duty to protect, provide, and empower its citizens.[20] A "failed state," therefore, is one that is weak in the eyes of its own citizens primarily. Fragility is "dangerous" not because it menaces international security or challenges the institutions of liberal governance and markets, but because it threatens the survival, livelihood, and dignity of the population.

CONCLUSION

Despite the frequent characterization of the human security approach as too broad or ambitious, its essence is ethical: to prevent threats and mitigate their impacts when they materialize. Human security should not be reduced to lists or to a narrow definition, but should remain flexible enough to allow for a deeper understanding of the root of insecurities and capacities to address them. Would it be fair to judge the concept obsolete and impractical, when the failure to put it into practice is dictated not by necessity, ethics, and values, but by *Realpolitik*, resources, and interests? Despite its opponents, this concept still deserves defense, because it is a noble, humanist idea that trumpets the overarching superiority of human beings over other ends such as institutions, market, states, and society.

In the political world, critics of the concept include both countries of the North, which would seek an agreement on enforcement mechanisms, and countries from the South or the emerging world, who mistrust the concept out of fear of new conditionality, unwarranted interventions, and violations of state sovereignty. Yet, domestic human security policies or strategies need to be developed in order to show that the concept is as relevant to address the problem of French banlieux as it is for South Sudan or Afghanistan. Within academia, the variety of human security approaches is a necessity for critical debates. Deliberations help clarify a number of other open questions, such as: the value of normative IR theory, interdisciplinary convergences, what constitutes power and its legitimacy, the prerogative of states, what dignity means, and how it can be measured.

NOTES

1. Steve Smith, "The Contested Concept of Security," Working Paper no. 23, Institute of Defence and Strategic Studies, Singapore, May 2002, pp. 1–26.

2. Barry Buzan, Ole Wæver, and Jaap de Wilde, *Security: A New Framework for Analysis* (Boulder, CO: Lynne Rienner Publishers, Inc., 1998), pp. 23–24.

3. Gary King and Christopher Murray, "Rethinking HS," *Political Science Quarterly*, Vol. 116, No. 4 (2001).

4. Paul R. Viotti and Mark V. Kauppi, eds., *International Relations Theory: Realism, Pluralism, Globalism, and Beyond*, 3rd ed. (New York: Macmillan Publishing Company, 1999).

5. Roland Paris, "Human Security: Paradigm Shift or Hot Air?" *International Security*, Vol. 26, No. 2 (Fall 2001), pp. 87–102, at p. 91.

6. Taylor Owen, "Human Security—Conflict, Critique and Consensus: Colloquium Remarks and a Proposal for a Threshold-Based Definition," *Security Dialogue*, Vol. 35, No. 3 (2004), pp. 373–87; King and Murray, "Rethinking HS," note 7.

7. Robert W. Cox, "Social Forces, States and World Orders: Beyond International Relations Theory," *Millennium—Journal of International Studies*, Vol. 10, No. 2 (1981), pp. 126–55.

8. Paris, "Human Security."

9. Andrew Mack, *Report on the Feasibility of Creating an Annual Human Security Report* (Cambridge, MA: Program on Humanitarian Policy and Conflict Research, Harvard University, February 2002).

10. Buzan, Wæver and Wilde, *Security*, pp. 21–26.

11. Des Gasper, "Securing Humanity: Situating 'Human Security' as Concept and Discourse," *Journal of Human Development*, Vol. 6, No. 2 (2005); Sakiko Fukuda-Parr, "The New Threats to Human Security in the Era of Globalization," in Lincoln Chen, Sakiko Fukuda-Parr, and Ellen Seidensticker, eds., *Human Insecurity in a Global World*, Global Equity Initiative, Studies in Global Equity (Cambridge, MA: Harvard University Press, 2003), p. 8.

12. Mahbub ul Haq, *Reflections on Human Development* (New Delhi: Oxford University Press, 1999).

13. For a more complete comparative table, see Shahrbanou Tadjbakhsh, "Human Security," in *Human Development Insights*, Issue 17 (New York: UNDP HDR Networks).

14. UN General Assembly, Vienna Declaration and Programme of Action, A/CONF.157/23, July 12, 1993.

15. Gerd Oberleitner, "Porcupines in Love: The Intricate Convergence of Human Rights and Human Security," *European Human Rights Law Review*, No. 6 (2005), pp. 588–606.

16. For an alternative view, see J. Peter Burgess and Shahrbanou Tadjbakhsh, "The Human Security Tale of Two Europes," *Global Society*, Vol. 24, No. 4 (2010), pp. 135–51.

17. See Espen Barth Eide et al., *Report on Integrated Missions: Practical Perspectives and Recommendations*, Independent study for the expanded UN ECHA core group; and Alex J. Bellamy and Paul Williams, eds., *Peace Operations and Global Order* (Milton Park, UK: Routledge, 2005). See also Roland Paris, *At War's End: Building Peace after Civil Conflict* (Cambridge: Cambridge University Press, 2004), where he focuses on building a liberal democratic state and the role of institutions, rather than on the question of the legitimacy of the model.

18. Shahrbanou Tadjbakhsh, ed., *Rethinking the Liberal Peace: External Models and Local Alternatives* (Milton Park, UK: Routledge, 2011).

19. A. K. Talentino, "Perceptions of Peacebuilding: The Dynamic of Imposer and Imposed Upon," *International Studies Perspective*, Vol. 8, No. 2 (2007), pp. 152–71.

20. Shahrbanou Tadjbakhsh, "State Failure through the Human Security Lens," in Jean-Marc Chataigner and Hervé Magro, eds., *Etats et Sociétés Fragiles* (Paris: Karthala, 2007).

13

Drone Ethics

Martin L. Cook

Unmanned combat aerial vehicles (UCAVs), popularly often referred to as "drones," have dramatically altered air war in recent years. Originally designed and intended by the United States and other early innovators as platforms for long-duration battlefield intelligence, surveillance, and reconnaissance (ISR), the Predator was first fitted with a Hellfire missile by the CIA and used to destroy a car and its inhabitants in Yemen in 2002. Although extremely culturally resistant to embracing UCAVs due to a powerful bias in favor of humanly piloted fighter aircraft, the U.S. Air Force was forced by the utility and cost effectiveness of UCAVs (and strong pressure from the Secretary of Defense)[1] to incorporate them into its force structure and operating concepts. Cultural resistance is by no means gone and has significant implications for the future of the promotion system in the service. The U.S. Navy successfully landed its own UCAV on an aircraft carrier, and the U.S. Army and the U.S. Marines developed their own shorter-range battlefield Unmanned Aerial Vehicles (UAVs) for battlefield ISR. All of the services have or are developing rotary-wing UAVs as well as the better-known fixed-wing models. The types of unmanned vehicles available to the U.S. military continue to expand well beyond the original Predators to include the more powerful Reaper and the long-distance Global Hawk. Other nations have entered the "UCAV race." We can anticipate that drones will be a significant component of battlefield technology in the near and midterm future.

While the ISR mission of UAVs is a major aspect of their utility, this chapter will focus on the ethical and legal aspects of weaponized UCAVs. I begin with a note on the cultural challenges of recruiting, retaining, and rewarding operators. As noted above, it was the CIA rather than the military services that first pressed unmanned vehicles into the weaponized role, and in some theaters still operates them. Since the CIA is by definition a clandestine service and often operates outside the bounds of local law, international law, and current law of armed conflict, it falls fall into its own somewhat unique legal and ethical space. It appears to be the case that many in government and in the intelligence services believe that the CIA has somewhat lost focus on its primary mission of intelligence gathering and that operation of UCAVs might better be left to the armed services.

Within the U.S. Air Force, however, the need for operators has raised numerous cultural challenges. First, since the 1970s, the culture and leadership of the USAF has been built around its most prestigious personnel: the fighter-bomber pilots. By and large, Air Force senior leadership is dominated by them. Initially, the ranks of UCAV operators were drawn from the bank of already-trained fighter pilots. It eventually became apparent that the extreme expense involved in training a fighter pilot was not in fact necessary to prepare a perfectly competent UCAV operator, and now Air Force officers are brought directly into UCAV training. But a further strong cultural bias in the Air Force is that all "pilots" (including UCAV pilots) must be officers—even though the other services allow enlisted personnel to operate them. Indeed, the Air Force often attempts to insist on this culturally important point by designating these platforms as "remotely *piloted* aircraft" to emphasize the "pilot" in the system.

This raises a still deeper issue because UCAV operators do not enjoy the respect and prestige of other kinds of pilots.[2] This is a challenge for morale, but also leads many to feel (rightly up until now) that being in the UCAV community is a barrier to promotion to the upper ranks in the officer corps. And on top of that, there is growing evidence from the Afghan and Iraq and other wars that UCAV pilots can suffer burnout, low morale, and even high levels of posttraumatic stress over long-duration missions.[3] The latter point is especially important and interesting because it belies the commonly held belief that UCAV warfare is emotionally detached and clinical. However, when one thinks in some detail about the experience of a UCAV operator, it becomes quickly clear why this may not be so. Unlike a fast-moving fighter pilot, who comes in a high speed, drops ordnance, and is quickly out of the area, a UCAV operator observes the target for extended periods of time—sometimes literally days—and acquires a kind of familiarity with the individual who is the target. Furthermore, once the weapon is fired, they loiter over the site and observe in graphic detail the effects of their weapons on the target area. So what might for many seem counterintuitive turns out to be true: they often experience the horror of the death and destruction of the enemy more viscerally than their fast-mover colleagues, or bombardiers in early wars, such as those Allied crews ordered to carpet bomb cities in Germany and Japan during World War II.

All of this suggests that the challenges of incorporating UCAVs into the routines of the Air Force will require further study and significant cultural changes. It will have to design rewarding career paths and long-term expertise in the use of these platforms, as well as psychological conditioning and mission-specific ethical training. Technological advancements will make future UCAVs more highly autonomous in the routine aspects of flying, and probably will enable swarms of UCAVs to communicate among themselves such that humans can orchestrate the activities of a group of UCAVs, replacing the labor-intensive mode of operating a single vehicle at present.

But even more importantly, the world's experience of the use of UCAVs in recent years is about to be made much more complicated by the fact that since 2002's appearance of the first U.S. weaponized UAV, the technology has spread widely around the world. Regardless of how one assesses the ethical and legal basis of the way the United States used UCAVs when it had a near monopoly on their use, the future is one where lots of actors, both government and nongovernmental, will have access to at least some of the technology. So the ethical and legal issues of their use in future conflict loom large.

This chapter will first survey the ethical issues involving the ways the United States has used UCAVs, and then conclude with some thoughts about the future of UCAVs as they become ubiquitous around the world. It then views the ethics of UCAVs through the standard lens of the three levels of military analysis: tactical, operational, and strategic. This approach will usefully illustrate some of the difficulties of thinking clearly about UCAVs because, as shall be seen, the issues shift considerably depending on the level of analysis one uses.

THE TACTICAL VIEW

The first level of analysis is to see the legal and ethical legitimacy of UCAVs as no different from any other weapons system on the battlefield. A weapon delivered from a UCAV is, one might argue, no different than a bomb dropped from a humanly piloted aircraft, a missile from a helicopter, a round of artillery, or rifle fire from ground forces. It can be humane or inhumane. That is a separate issue from whether the pilot is humanly present, detached at a great distance, or absent.

Viewing the use of UCAVs from the battlefield level of tactics, the analysis goes as follows. We know for certain that the individuals in the target area are, indeed, terrorists actively engaged in planning attacks either in the theater or in the United States. Although they are not conventional soldiers, and we are not in a conventional war, we are engaged in an ongoing armed conflict with this group, so they are legitimate targets. The UCAV will fire a precision-guided missile with a small circular error probable (CEP, i.e., measure of accuracy).

In this straightforward tactical case, the UCAV/hellfire system is a perfectly morally and militarily acceptable weapons system. Its use conforms to the *jus in bello* requirements of discrimination and proportionality as well as or better than any other weapons system. Indeed, as measured by those standards, it is preferable to most of the alternative means of attacking the target. It is certainly more accurate than artillery fire or machine gun fire from an AC-130 gunship. It is more accurate and the blast effect smaller than a precision-guided munition (PGM) dropped from manned aircraft such as an F-15. There is therefore good reason to think collateral damage will be less. Only close ground attack with eyes on the target might be even more discriminate and proportionate. But using ground forces vastly increases risk to our forces. In addition, attack by ground forces may often be *more* likely to cause undesired casualties because the situational awareness of ground forces will generally not be as good as that of a long-loiter UCAV. The UCAV operator is able to see the entire scene from above and for an extended period of time. Lastly, one also has a moral obligation to protect one's own forces from unnecessary harm when doing so does not impose disproportionate risk on noncombatants. Therefore, there is a strong *prima facie* case for using the weapons system that best protects one's own forces: a UCAV.

In this first case, we assumed we had specifically identified the individuals to be attacked personally and are sure they are legitimate military targets. How does the case vary when the attack is instead a "signature strike" (i.e., a strike justified by observing a pattern of action that indicates the individuals being observed are preparing an attack, although not individually identified)? This case is a bit more ethically murky. There is clearly more room for error in signature strikes than in targeting of clearly identified specific individuals. On the other hand, the long-loiter capability of the RPV makes it the best possible platform for careful observation of the target for a long enough period to make a good-faith determination regarding threatening behavior and preparation.[4] A standard that simply declares all fighting-age males in an area where some individuals are known to be actively planning attacks is far too permissive, yet one that appears to have been used in some real-world cases. But if one observes a group preparing, for example, IEDs (improvised explosive devices), loading them on vehicles, and beginning to drive them toward American forces, that seems to me a perfectly reasonable "signature" and pattern of behavior warranting and justifying a strike, even though the individuals are not identified. It is in principle no different that, in a conventional conflict between regular armies, one observes a unit of unknown individuals advancing on a position in armored vehicles. One does not to wait to receive fire from those vehicles before they may be legitimately targeted. In this case as well, tactically the UCAV may well be, ethically and legally, the best weapons option.

THE OPERATIONAL VIEW

The operational view approaches the question of the justification and utility of UCAV strikes with a somewhat larger aperture than the tactical view just examined. Viewed through the operational level of war lens, we are examining the utility of UCAV strikes as advancing our military objective in a given operational area or theater of war. For example, given the issue of IEDs, used in attacks against coalition forces and Afghan government forces in Afghanistan, how do we assess the legitimacy and effectiveness of using UCAVs to attack groups supporting ongoing attacks from a country across the border from the area of immediate combat, or even in areas of the country not readily accessible to other forces? For the purpose of this level of analysis we are setting aside considerations of third-country sovereignty. Here I am asking only about the military utility of a program of UCAV strikes in advancing the operational goals in an active combat theater.

For example, after 9/11, clearly there were groups inside the territorial boundary of Pakistan but not under the effective governance of the Pakistani government, supplying weapons, personnel, and ideological support to the ongoing struggle in Afghanistan. One ground rule of counterinsurgency campaigns is that, if the insurgents have effective sanctuary into which to retreat, counterinsurgency is not likely to be effective. Therefore, the operational logic for attempting to eliminate a third-country sanctuary in a counterinsurgency campaign is clear.

The logic is similar for disrupting ongoing plans for attacks directly against the United States being hatched in remote areas of Yemen, Mali, and the Horn of Africa. More troubled areas will likely get new UCAV bases, either for weaponized UCAVs, or for regional ISR, or both. The purpose of attacks is not to defeat the group in question decisively. Instead, the goal is to disrupt its operational plans and to place its leadership at risk at all times. Insofar as an ongoing pattern of attack and threat of attack forces the adversary to devote ever-larger resources and time to defense and evasion, those strikes serve a very valuable purpose to any state with long-range drone capabilities.

In all these cases, the ethical issue turns on proportionality. In the case of Afghanistan, my opinion is that, while they might have been justified when there was some reasonable hope that the Afghan government would emerge strong enough to handle insurgency on its own, if or when that political goal becomes unattainable, then the rationale for ongoing UCAV strikes begins to diminish. Much depends on what the Afghanistan-U.S. pattern of cooperation will be after the United States has officially ceased all combat operations in the theater. If the United States remains committed to the defense of what passes for an Afghan central government, the legitimate targets are considerably broader than if the sole purpose is disrupting and preventing attacks directly on the United States or on U.S. forces in the region.

On the other hand, the "whack-a-mole" aspect of the global threat posed by al Qaeda and similar groups is probably a feature of the ongoing conflict as far down the road as we can see. One would have to be privy to highly classified information to know how to do the proportionality calculation involved to justify the killing of emerging leaders of al Qaeda affiliates, versus the probability of civilian deaths involved and the impetus such strikes provide to recruitment of new participants. But it does not seem likely that that threat will be eliminated by the use of air power alone. As long as al Qaeda and its affiliates or ISIL or some other such organization retain the intent to attack U.S. and Western targets, interests, and citizens, some of their capability will always escape intelligence gathering. President Obama essentially acknowledged all these points in his National Defense University address on UCAV use policy on May 23, 2013.[5]

THE STRATEGIC VIEW

We shift now to the larger strategic view. When one asks strategic questions, one is inquiring into the long-term effects on the global system of patterns of UCAV use. One is asking whether that pattern of use of UCAVs is achieving national goals and contributing to a sustainable pattern of international practice.

The global threats to the international system posed by al Qaeda and similar groups are endemic and enduring. They do not depend on any single location or leader—or even, at this point, on the existence of "al Qaeda central," as bin Laden's original organization was called. They pose an ongoing threat not only to the United States, but also to most developed nations as well as the many weak or failed states where they seek to find a foothold. Although there is a military dimension to responding to this threat, getting the balance right between the proper military aspect and all other aspects of national and international power is a significant challenge. There are economic, diplomatic, law enforcement, and even soft-power cultural influence factors that all play a part in isolating, disrupting, and disempowering terror threats to that globalized international system.

While it is hard to know the extent, if any, to which UCAV strikes recruit and motivate new members to join in with al Qaeda and its affiliates, intuitively it seems plausible that such effects are likely. A Stanford University study, "Living under Drones," suggests that the continual presence of UCAVs over an area stresses populations in ways that are likely to induce fear and hatred in local groups, regardless of whether they are actually at risk of direct attack.[6] Presumably that fear itself will motivate some number of individuals to take up the cause and join the fight against what is seen locally as the primary cause of distress.

From a strategic perspective, the main goals of U.S. actions remain to disrupt pending attacks directly on the United States and its assets, and in the long run to reduce or eliminate the threat posed by al Qaeda and similar groups globally. Clearly, as long as the ideology and narrative that drive people to Islamic extremist groups continue to have appeal, these groups and these threats will continue to provoke military and other responses from the United States and its allies. We might also expect a widening set of players as other countries that face Islamic terror threats also turn to active measures to stop or prevent them: China, India, Israel, and Russia, among many others. What is the role of UCAV warfare in advancing those goals?

If we are in possession of reliable intelligence that a specific group or individual is actively planning or preparing a specific attack, direct action to disrupt or eliminate the threat of that is legitimate (again, setting aside questions of the sovereignty of the state into which the attack must be made). Whether attack by a weaponized UCAV is the preferred mode of attack is a question of the means chosen for that disruption. Alternatives include direct action by Special Forces or the armed forces of the country within whose borders the attackers reside—approaches that, if within acceptable risk parameters, have the advantage of providing great intelligence, but also require facing issues of detention and prosecution of captured individuals. Which is preferable, ethically speaking—a matter of balancing concerns with collateral damage, proportionality, and risk to one's own forces. It is likely that often the result of that calculation will trip in favor of use of the UCAV.

However, the longer-range strategic goal of reducing or eliminating the threat posed by such groups is not achievable by use of the military force. That goal is achieved only when the will and intent to mount such attacks is dissipated at its root—i.e., it is a political and cultural goal. To the extent that UCAV attacks perpetuate the political environment that sustains the will of the adversary to continue to plan attacks or, still worse, recruits new attackers to the cause, UCAV attacks at some point are strategically unwise, regardless of their more short-term tactical and operational effectiveness. To the extent that the adversary perceives UCAV warfare as dishonorable or cowardly, it may indeed perpetuate negative images of the United States and its allies that prolong the conflict at the strategic level.

In summary, we can see that the ethical permissibility and military utility of a pattern of UCAV strikes looks rather different depending on the level of analysis one applies. On the one hand, the UCAV, properly used, offers a relatively high degree of precision and discrimination. It permits application of military power with a degree of force protection bordering on impunity (apart from the possible financial cost of the loss of a relatively inexpensive aircraft). On the other hand, no number of UCAV strikes will ever eliminate a threat grounded in fundamental narratives of resistance and resentment against the West that drive Islamic extremism.

But of course the fact that the use of UCAVs in recent experience has almost entirely taken place in the context of the conflict with al Qaeda and similar groups (including ISIL in Syria and Iraq) should not blind us from the realization that it is a general-purpose weapons system. UCAVs will rapidly become more technologically advanced and the technology will spread to more and more state users, and perhaps nonstate users as well. The aircraft themselves will become more sophisticated and more autonomous, and their control systems will rapidly improve. These facts in and of themselves mean that ethical responses will also have to move, adjusting to new methods and possibilities as well as new wars, actors, and motivations,

We turn now to a more general discussion of the role of UCAVs in future conflict, and to the implications for the global system of their widespread availability to nations and even to nonstate actors. It is obvious there is nothing especially ethically troubling about the use of UCAVs in the context of a conventional interstate armed conflict between the military forces of sovereign states. In that context, they are simply one among many weapons systems. All are governed by the existing Law of Armed Conflict, and UCAVs look pretty good ethically and legally compared to other weapons systems that might be employed in such conflicts, assuming they are aimed at legitimate military targets in such a conflict (a uniformed military unit, a piece of military equipment, a military headquarters, to name a few). They are clearly far more discriminate and proportional that ballistic artillery or mortars, for example. They are vastly superior in accuracy to unguided gravity bombs dropped from aircraft operating at high altitudes.

Things get more uncertain, however, when we think about their use in other contexts. UCAVs have been used extensively in the past for targeted killing of specific individuals, including U.S. citizens. Often these are individuals judged on the basis of intelligence sources to be engaged in planning and encouraging attacks against the United States and its allies.[7] This practice raises a series of ethical and legal questions and may be setting a dubious precedent if U.S. practice is to become a general international norm. First, few of these individuals are "combatants" in the normal sense. At the very least they are not uniformed combatants on a battlefield of an ongoing international armed conflict. The basis for making them targets is entirely grounded in intelligence sources of varying degrees of reliability. Further, as was noted above, in some cases they are targeted not on the basis of specific intelligence regarding them as by-name individuals, but rather on the basis of observed suspicious activity (so-called "signature strikes") that in some cases has been misunderstood innocent activity. Lastly, specifically regarding U.S. citizens, it is a stretch at best to see how such killings are consistent with the "due process of law" requirements of the Constitution.[8]

If one attempts to state a general rule for international law that could be extrapolated from this pattern of U.S. practice, it would have to be something along these lines: "Any state may target individuals for killing inside sovereign states with whom it is not at war whenever, in its sole determination, it deems them a sufficient threat to its interests." Clearly, such a rule, were it to become customary international law, would be seriously destabilizing to the international system. One can only hope, therefore, that as more and more states come into possession of versions of UCAV technologies, some more sustainable international standards of legitimate uses of these technologies can be established in the international system by treaty, UN conference, or some other means.[9]

But it is also important not to restrict consideration of these technologies to the confines of their use by states—either in interstate conflict, or even in the individual targeted killing missions we have witnessed in recent years. The costs and technological requirements of a relatively low-tech UCAV are well within the reach of a well-funded nonstate actor such as ISIL or al Qaeda. Since they are small, and are capable of flying low and slow, they can be operated in ways that are difficult to detect on radar and difficult to intercept and destroy.[10] And of course some drones already commercially available would be capable to carrying weapons.

All of these possibilities point to a significant challenge posed to national security and law enforcement by the mere existence and proliferation of UCAV technologies. At a minimum these possibilities suggest a pressing need to devise technologies to better monitor airspace over large public events such as football games, political rallies, and government events. These thoughts are not speculative: already a drone was flown into a German political rally and landed at the feet of Prime Minister Angela Merkel. In this case, it was merely a political stunt, but it does not take a great deal of imagination to imagine a much darker and potential disastrous outcome to the event.[11]

CONCLUSION

The development, diversification, and proliferation of UAVs and UCAVs is unstoppable. The technological and security logic of developing relatively low-cost platforms that give militaries and nonstate actors capabilities to strike targets with relative impunity is unstoppable. When such weapons are merely added to the arsenal of the militaries of nation-states operating in conventional warfare environments, UCAVs can indeed be seen as "just another weapons system," governed by standard *jus in bello* ethical standards of discrimination/distinction and proportionality.

But as we have seen, UCAVs also offer nearly unique capabilities to do a wide range of other things for which either the legal and ethical rules are unclear or, in some cases, which would not be considered or even possible absent the existence of this technology. They allow targeted killing of individuals inside the territory of sovereign states with which the attacking state is not at war—an "act of war" under existing international law. They provide a means for assassination and terror attack that are almost uniquely difficult to protect against and might be extremely difficult to attribute to a specific source if the attack was well conceived. They offer low-cost capability to small states and to nonstate actors that potentially enable them to offer threats against much larger and more capable opponents they simply could not have if they were required to match conventional military capability symmetrically.

The short window in which the United States had something resembling a monopoly on UCAV technology has already closed. Some aspects of the pattern of use the United States established in that small span of time would, if generalized and deemed to establish customary international law regarding UCAV use, be extremely destabilizing and dangerous for the international community. This points to a need, sooner than later, to begin an international conversation about the legitimate and illegitimate uses of UCAV technologies with a view to establishing international norms.

NOTES

1. "Unloved Aerial Vehicles," *Armed Forces Journal*, November 2012, http://www.armedforcesjournal.com/unloved-aerial-vehicles/.

2. See, for example, the controversies over the proposal to award combat medals to UCAV pilots (and cyber warriors). So disruptive was this to the culture of the service that the medal had to be withdrawn! See Sam LaGrone, "Pentagon Cancels Controversial Unmanned and Cyber Medal," *USNI News*, April 15, 2013, http://news.usni.org/2013/04/15/pentagon-cancels-controversial-unmanned-and-cyber-medal.

3. "Dilbert at War: The Stressful Lives of the 'Chair Force,'" *The Economist*, June 21, 2014, http://www.economist.com/news/united-states/21604608-stressful-lives-chair-force-dilbert-war.

4. Of course it is the inherent uncertainty of most signature strikes that provided one of the reasons President Obama elected a risky SEAL team assault on bin Laden's compound over the far safer PGM bombing approach. In addition, of course, he wanted positive confirmation that it really was bin Laden (which could not be known for a certainty from observation at a distance) and also that he was in fact killed, rather than merely injured as might have resulted from a bombing approach.

5. "Obama Drone Speech Delivered at National Defense University (FULL TRANSCRIPT)," *Huffington Post*, May 23, 2013, http://www.huffingtonpost.com/2013/05/23/obama-drone-speech-transcript_n_3327332.html.

6. See "Living under Drones," Stanford International Human Rights Conflict Resolution Clinic, http://www.livingunderdrones.org/.

7. Jonathan Masters, "Targeted Killings," *Council of Foreign Relations*, May 23, 2013, http://www.cfr.org/counterterrorism/targeted-killings/p9627.

8. A review of the legal arguments put forward can be found in Masters, "Targeted Killings."

9. As an example of the proliferation of the technologies involved, already the Chinese are reported to have considered a targeted killing strike by UCAV against a drug lord inside Myanmar. Jane Perlez, "Chinese Plan to Kill Drug Lord with Drone Highlights Military Advances," *New York Times*, February 20, 2013, http://www .nytimes.com/2013/02/21/world/asia/chinese-plan-to-use-drone-highlights-military -advances.html?_r=0.

10. See, for example, news reports that Iran is developing low-tech "suicide drones" intended only to crash into their targets and explode, such as Matt Novak, "Iran Tests Suicide Drone," *Gizmodo*, December 27, 2014, http://gizmodo.com/iran-tests-suicide- drone-during-week-long-military-exer-1675586041. For concern about the use of drones by terrorist groups, see "NYPD Scanning the Sky for New Terrorism Threat," *CBS News*, October 29, 2014, http://www.cbsnews.com/news/drone-terrorism-threat -is-serious-concern-for-nypd/. See also Tom Brooks Pollock, "Drones 'Could be Used as Flying Bombs for Terror Attack on Passenger Jet,'" *Telegraph*, December 12, 2014, http://www.telegraph.co.uk/news/uknews/terrorism-in-the-uk/11290086/Drones-could -be-used-as-flying-bombs-for-terror-attack-on-passenger-jet.html.

11. Jason Bittel, "German Pirate Party Uses Drone to Crash Angela Merkel Event," *Slate*, September 18, 2013, http://www.slate.com/blogs/future_tense/2013/09/18/ german_pirate_party_uses_drone_to_crash_event_with_chancellor_angela_merkel .html.

14

Ethics and Targeted Sanctions

Joy Gordon

Targeted sanctions—"smart sanctions"—began in large measure as a response to the UN Security Council sanctions imposed on Iraq from 1990 to 2003, after Iraq's invasion of Kuwait. Although sanctions had regularly been used as a tool of foreign policy, during the Cold War their impact had been limited: if the Soviet Union sanctioned a country, it could simply trade with the Western countries, and vice versa. While the sanctioned country might not be able to get particular goods, or have unlimited access to the markets, the humanitarian damage was never so extreme or visible as to trigger ethical concerns.

The sanctions on Iraq were a different matter. They were virtually comprehensive, in every regard: for the first five years, Iraq could export no oil; could import no goods except food and medicine; and because the sanctions were imposed by the UN Security Council under Chapter VII, every nation in the world was required to participate in their enforcement. In combination with the destruction from the bombing campaign of the Gulf War, the UN sanctions were devastating. There was not sufficient equipment or materials to treat water for human consumption, to grow and distribute food, or to operate hospitals or schools. The result was that there were ongoing epidemics of cholera and typhoid, widespread malnutrition, and the near collapse of health care and education.

In the wake of this humanitarian crisis, there were efforts in many venues to think about designing sanctions that would not have the humanitarian impact of broad trade sanctions; that would impact the leadership rather than the population as a whole, and as a result would also be more politically effective. These targeted sanctions included arms embargoes, financial sanctions on the assets of individuals and companies, travel restrictions on the leaders of a sanctioned nation, and trade sanctions on particular goods. Many viewed targeted sanctions as an especially promising tool for foreign policy and international governance; they do not entail the risks and costs of military intervention, nor, it seems, do they did raise the same ethical problems as broad trade sanctions. Many still see targeted sanctions as the best solution to a broad array of difficult situations.

Since the mid-1990s, the sanctions imposed by the UN Security Council have not seemed overly broad or indiscriminate. But it would be a mistake to think that targeted sanctions are used so extensively, and implemented so well, that sanctions overall no longer raise ethical concerns. While UN sanctions, at least on their face, are more narrowly focused on military and security concerns, the sanctions imposed by nations against other nations can be explicitly indiscriminate, with broad prohibitions affecting shipping, banking transactions, the target state's energy sector, imports in general, and exports of critical commodities. This is true, for example, of Australia's sanctions on Syria's energy sector, Canada's sanctions on Syria and North Korea, the EU's sanctions on Iran, and the U.S. sanctions on Cuba, North Korea, Burma, Sudan, and Iran.

But in addition, even where sanctions are designed to target only the leadership or military goods, they may fail, and this may occur systematically. Targeted sanctions may be unsuccessful both in impacting the leadership or preventing access to arms, and they may be unsuccessful in that the civilian population as a whole is still affected on a structural level.

THE HISTORY OF "SMART SANCTIONS"

As the UN Security Council sanctions began to take a toll in the early 1990s, there was growing attention to the need for mechanisms that would reduce the humanitarian damage done by sanctions. In 1995, UN Secretary-General Boutros Boutros-Ghali proposed that there be assessments prior to imposing sanctions that would gauge their likely impact, as well as monitoring throughout the sanctions regime, to minimize the collateral damage.[1] The following year, the Organization for Security and Cooperation in Europe (OSCE) held a round table to review the humanitarian impact of the Security Council sanctions imposed on the former Yugoslavia.[2] In 1997, consultants from Brown University and the University of Notre Dame issued a set of recommendations that included monitoring public health indicators as well as economic indicators, population displacement, increased crime, and political repression.[3] Over the next several years, there were workshops and symposia to develop mechanisms for targeted financial sanctions, bringing together key academics, government officials, UN practitioners, and banking officials.[4] In 1998 and 1999, the Swiss government facilitated a series of discussions on targeted financial sanctions, known as the "Interlaken Process." It looked at the scope of targeted financial sanctions, as well as the legal and administrative structures for their implementation, and produced a manual for practitioners. In 1999 and 2000, there was a series of expert seminars and working groups, known as the Bonn-Berlin Process, sponsored by the German government and the UN Secretariat, focusing on arms embargoes and sanctions related to travel.[5] In 2001, the International Peace Academy held a policy forum on targeted sanctions in conjunction with a special session of the Security Council regarding sanctions.[6] In 2002, the Swedish government and Uppsala University sponsored the "Stockholm Process," a series of meetings involving over 100 experts to refine targeted sanctions.[7] In 2005, the Security Council set up a working group on sanctions issues, which made recommendations on the effectiveness of sanctions, including the design of sanctions regimes, the use of expert panels, and monitoring mechanisms.[8] In the sanctions regimes it imposed, the UN Security Council began establishing panels of experts to monitor its sanctions regimes.

Thus, a great deal of effort and expertise has gone into formulating targeted sanctions that would be more effective in impacting the decision making of political leaders, or would more successfully prevent the flow of the goods that would escalate a conflict, while avoiding harm to a civilian population or to third parties.

THE DISAPPOINTMENTS OF TARGETED SANCTIONS

Where those imposing sanctions have in fact tried to craft them narrowly to target specific goods or individuals, the track record of sanctions in regard to effectiveness has been mixed. In 2002, Tostensen and Bull surveyed the difficulties with effectiveness and implementation of the various types of targeted sanctions.[9] More than a decade later, many of these problems remain unresolved.

Arms Embargoes

It would seem that arms embargoes are exactly what we envision when we speak of targeted sanctions: the arms and military materials that will likely escalate a conflict are themselves targeted, thus the civilian population is not impacted, and we expect that cutting off arms will certainly reduce the conflict or deny an abusive regime of the means to commit a human rights violation. However, arms embargoes in fact do little to actually reduce the flow of weapons. On the contrary, the prohibition creates a black market for weapons, with opportunities for higher profits than in the legal arms trade. Embargoes are more likely to be effective when they restrict the sale of major weapons systems, such as ballistic missiles, in part because these are easier to detect, but also because they are more likely to be manufactured by state enterprises,[10] with greater accountability and documentation. However, most armed conflicts at present involve small and light weapons, such as semiautomatic weapons and rocket-propelled grenades. These are manufactured privately, in vast quantities, and their transport can easily elude detection. Neighboring countries may collude with arms traffickers, providing safe haven or transport routes. Cargo planes may file false air routes, and ships may use "flags of convenience" to disguise their origin.[11] Monitoring the sale and shipment of arms also requires considerable resources and commitment on the part of neighboring countries and those where shipping routes are found, or where banking transactions take place. Monitoring and enforcement would require the commitment of police and judicial systems as well as sufficient technological resources and sophistication to monitor communications, fund transfers, and transport routes of illicit arms traffickers. UN experts reported, for example, that more than half the member states in the UN did not file timely reports, or did not file reports at all, regarding their implementation of the UN restrictions on arms sales to North Korea, due to a lack of resources, or the lack of awareness or interest.[12]

Consequently, it is unsurprising that arms embargoes do not often result in any actual changes in the behavior of the target state. SIPRI, the Swedish research institute on armed conflicts, found that in one study involving 27 cases of mandatory arms embargoes, the behavior of the target state changed only one quarter of the time.[13] A more extensive study, of 74 arms embargoes in effect between 1990 and 2005, found that the target changed its policy only 8 percent of the time.[14] Thus, while arms embargoes seem to be an attractive and promising response to reduce conflicts or deprive aggressors or human rights violators of the means to pursue wrongful policies, in fact they are generally ineffective and disappointing.

Travel Restrictions

Travel restrictions primarily take two forms: visa bans on individuals, and aviation bans. Visa bans accord with the goal of targeted sanctions of imposing measures on individual wrongdoers, rather than broader measures that would affect others indiscriminately. However, visa bans are relatively mild measures, causing inconvenience or embarrassment to individuals seeking to travel abroad, but studies suggest that visa bans rarely cause a political or military leader to change his policies or practices.[15] In addition, just as there are fraudulent means for ships and aircraft to avoid detection, the same is true of individuals, who may use aliases and hold multiple passports or fraudulent passports.[16]

Aviation bans present a different set of issues. There are problems with both implementation and overbreadth. On one hand, aviation bans are quite porous, particularly for cargo flights, which are subject to far less regulation and oversight than commercial passenger flights. As with arms embargoes, the profits to be made on importing goods to an embargoed country are so great that there is considerable incentive to use false flight plans or other means of evading detection while violating the ban.[17] On the other hand, to the extent that there is compliance with an aviation ban, there may also be humanitarian effects that are problematic. Any measures that impact transportation infrastructure will certainly be indiscriminate in their impact. In the case of Iraq, for example, the enforcement of no-fly zones meant that humanitarian aid workers, and their supplies, had to drive 14 hours from Amman to Baghdad in grueling conditions, rather than taking a one-hour plane flight. The passenger flight ban imposed on Haiti was justified as a means of preventing the wealthy from traveling abroad to shop for luxuries; but it also meant that Haitians trying to flee the country to find safe haven had no safe means to do so.

Targeted Trade Sanctions

Where there are particular natural resources tied to a corrupt regime, such as oil, timber, or diamonds, targeted trade sanctions are seen as a way of cutting off the flow of wealth to the regime. In such cases, it may well be true that the regime and its corruption are dependent on this and that cutting off income from exports will be costly to the political leadership. However, where that is true, it is also likely that there is little diversification within the economy, and that the nation as a whole is also highly dependent on the same commodity export. For example, in the case of Liberia, UN Security Council sanctions targeted diamonds and timber, eliminating 50 percent of the country's commodity exports, undermining development efforts, and triggering an increase in unemployment due to the withdrawal of logging companies.[18]

At the same time, there are difficulties in implementing sanctions on commodities, in ways that are similar to the problems facing arms embargoes. Because many commodities are fungible, it is difficult to track whether particular shipments of timber or minerals are derived from a sanctioned country; and illicit trafficking is feasible and profitable in the same ways as illicit arms trafficking.

Humanitarian Monitoring

In the aftermath of the sanctions on Iraq, UN agencies and NGOs called for humanitarian monitoring. The Stockholm process in 2003 recommended periodic humanitarian assessments, to determine the impact of the sanctions and distinguish the harm caused by the sanctions from that caused by other factors.[19] A United Nations handbook published in 2004 provided an outline and methodology for conducting humanitarian assessments with rigor and methodological integrity. It provided guidelines for selecting reliable indicators in the areas of food, water, health care, and education.[20] It also suggested language for Security Council resolutions that would ensure that these assessments take place regularly, and would mandate reports and recommendations.[21] The 2006 report of a Security Council working group on sanctions addressed some of the issues that were most problematic in the case of the Iraq sanctions, such as the arbitrariness and lack of transparency regarding humanitarian exemptions.[22] It suggested that humanitarian impact be addressed in the initial design of the sanctions regime.[23]

For the most part, these recommendations have not been implemented in Security Council sanctions, much less those imposed by the United States or other nations. Lopez argues that while there may not be pre-sanctions assessments of the possible humanitarian impact, there are nevertheless extensive monitoring mechanisms: "UN missions, the special representatives of the Secretary-General, and the panels of experts for each UN sanctions case all focus on monitoring in ways that did not exist a decade ago."[24] With such extensive systems of monitoring, the expectation is that if the sanctions were triggering humanitarian problems, this would be quickly apparent. However, for various reasons, the resolutions establishing the sanctions committees and monitoring groups typically focus on sanctions violations and do not include humanitarian monitoring in the mandates. If they do mandate humanitarian monitoring, it concerns other issues, such as whether militia groups are interfering with humanitarian assistance. In many cases, there is no one on the panels of experts with expertise in humanitarian issues. Where there is a clear humanitarian crisis taking place, neither the Security Council resolutions nor the practices of the committees mandate an analysis of whether the sanctions themselves are a contributing factor. Where other factors contribute to the target state's economic problems, such as the target state's economic policies, or additional sanctions imposed unilaterally by various nations, the monitoring groups and sanctions committees have no mandate, and show no interest, in seeking to disentangle the damage done by the various actors.

Overall, the efforts, and track record, of the Security Council in monitoring the humanitarian impact of its use of sanctions have varied considerably. The Council and other UN bodies sometimes address humanitarian effects of sanctions explicitly. In other cases, the resolutions themselves are viewed as drafted narrowly to target only weapons, and there are no institutional mechanisms to monitor the humanitarian situation. In some cases, Security Council resolutions are invoked to *justify* national measures that cause extensive, direct humanitarian damage. This is the case, for example, with Iran; the United States, Canada, the European Union, and a few other nations invoked the Security Council's vague references to the need for "vigilance" in dealing with Iran to justify large-scale sanctions against Iran's entire financial system, energy sector, and all imports and exports.

Asset Freezes

Asset freezes, or financial blacklisting, are often viewed as a particularly powerful tool within the spectrum of targeted sanctions. The image of seizing the bank accounts of dictators seems to offer an ideal solution: the individuals responsible for the most egregious acts of wrongdoing are the ones who suffer the punishment, and it is the kind of punishment that will cause them significant harm, and therefore cause them to want to change their ways. At the same time, it seems that asset freezes cannot possibly do the kind of indiscriminate harm to the innocent that is seen in broad trade sanctions. Yet financial blacklisting has resulted in the most significant challenges to sanctions under international law.

The most controversial asset freezes have been those imposed by the UN Security Council under Resolution 1267, which targeted persons, companies, and organizations on the bases of their ostensible ties to terrorism, and in particular Osama bin Laden, al Qaeda, and the Taliban. Unlike criminal penalties, asset freezes do not punish those who have actually committed crimes, but rather seek to effectively bankrupt those who *may* commit acts of terrorism or other prohibited acts. In this case, individuals were subject to financial blacklisting if they were deemed to be "associated with" bin Laden or al Qaeda. It was five years before the Security Council articulated what was meant by "associated with," and even then did not provide a great deal more guidance.[25] After September 11, 2001, hundreds of names of ostensible terrorists were added to this list, primarily by the United States. For these individuals and companies, being blacklisted meant that every member state of the United Nations was required to adopt regulations prohibiting their banks from releasing the funds in these bank accounts. There was no end date, and there was no procedure that allowed the blacklisted individuals to challenge these measures against them before an impartial body. Indeed, because the blacklisting was preemptive—it targeted those who *might* commit acts of terrorism—there were no factual claims of criminal acts that could be disproven. The determinations to freeze an individual's assets were based upon claims made by members of the Security Council that sometimes consisted of nothing more than associations or inferences. Perhaps the most significant case involved Yasin Kadi, a Saudi businessman, who was blacklisted in part on the grounds that he owned stock in a bank where "planning sessions for an attack against a US facility . . . may have taken place."[26]

In accordance with the Security Council resolutions, the European Union adopted regulations requiring its banks to freeze the assets of individuals blacklisted by the UN Security Council, including Kadi. They did so, and Kadi challenged the legality of these regulations in the European courts. In their rulings in *Kadi* and similar cases, the courts initially refused to intervene. Their reasoning was that under Article 25 of the UN Charter, states are unconditionally obligated to implement any measures required by Security

Council resolutions under Chapter VII, which concerns aggression and threats to peace. Thus, even if the Security Council requires a member state to adopt regulations that violate its own constitution, or that violate international law, the state is obliged to do so, and has no recourse to decline or question the demands made of it by the Council.[27]

There were widespread criticisms of the lack of due process. In 2005, the General Assembly asked the Security Council "to ensure that fair and clear procedures exist for placing individuals and entities on sanctions lists and for removing them, as well as for granting humanitarian exemptions."[28] The following year, the UN's Office of Legal Affairs released a study by international legal scholar Bardo Fassbender, which concluded that the Council should adopt "fair and clear procedures" for the blacklists, which would include the right of the individual to be informed of the measures taken against him; the right to be heard by a body of the Council within a reasonable time; and the right to an effective remedy, before an impartial body.[29] The Security Council committee responded to these criticisms by incorporating changes that allowed somewhat greater opportunity for individuals to appeal their inclusion on the blacklists to the Security Council itself. However, the Security Council has refused to adopt any measures that would entail the establishment of an impartial body that could hear evidence and determine whether or not it was sufficient to justify blacklisting a particular individual.

But as Kadi and others continued to raise challenges, the European courts shifted their position. In 2013, the European Court of Justice invalidated the EU regulations that implemented the Security Council's blacklist on the grounds that they violated fundamental rights, including due process.[30] The implications are startling: the European courts in effect found that the UN Security Council was requiring member states of the United Nations to violate human rights and international law, and then invalidated the implementation of the Security Council resolutions (within the European Union).

Thus, the story of "smart sanctions" has taken a surprising turn. Asset freezes are the measures that seem to most embody what targeted sanction are intended to be—narrowly circumscribed, causing considerable disruption to wrongdoers, with no possibility of harming the innocent. Yet it is clear that there are occasions on which they fail on all three counts. Further, they have opened the door to challenging the legitimacy and legality of the Council's powers in a way that is unprecedented.

CONCLUSION

There is a way in which targeted sanctions have terminated the conversation on the ethical problems of sanctions, without in fact resolving them. The post-Iraq efforts to require humanitarian monitoring have very much fallen by the wayside. At the same time, targeted sanctions are politically ineffective in many regards. Further, as the asset freezes demonstrate, however narrow and well-crafted these measures may seem, the lack of impartial oversight means that enormous damage can be done to individuals and organizations, without any real recourse. It seems that targeted sanctions are not nearly as "smart" as many would think.

NOTES

1. Boutros Boutros-Ghali, "Report of the Secretary-General on the Work of the Organization, Supplement to an Agenda for Peace: Position Paper of the Secretary-General on the Occasion of the Fiftieth Anniversary of the United Nations," A/50/60-S/1995/1 (1995), para. 75.

2. United Nations Security Council, "Letter Dated 24 September 1996 from the Chairman of the Security Council Committee Established Pursuant to Resolution 724 (1991) Concerning Yugoslavia Addressed to the President of the Security Council," S/1996/776 (1996), 16, para. 95.

3. Larry Minear et al., "Toward More Humane and Effective Sanctions Management: Enhancing the Capacity of the United Nations System," Occasional Paper #31 (Providence, RI: The Thomas J. Watson Jr. Institute for International Studies, 1998).

4. Watson Institute for International Studies, "The Targeted Financial Sanctions Project at the Watson Institute," http://www.watsoninstitute.org/tfs/targetedfinsan.cfm.

5. Michael Brzoska, ed., *Smart Sanctions: The Next Steps* (Baden-Baden, Germany: Nomos Verlagsgesellschaft, 2001).

6. Watson Institute for International Studies, "Targeted Financial Sanctions Project."

7. Department of Peace and Conflict Research Uppsala Universitet, "Special Program on the International Targeted Sanctions," http://pcr.uu.se/research/smartsanctions/.

8. Informal Working Group of the Security Council on General Issues of Sanctions, "Report of the Informal Working Group of the Security Council on General Issues of Sanctions," S/2006/997 (December 18, 2006).

9. Arne Tostensen and Beate Bull, "Are Smart Sanctions Feasible?" *World Politics*, Vol. 54, No. 3 (April 2002).

10. Michael Brzoska, "A Framework for the Analysis of the Effectiveness of Arms Enbargoes," in Brzoska and Lopez, eds., *Putting Teeth in the Tiger: Improving the Effectiveness of Arms Embargoes* (Bingley, England: Emerald Publishing 2009), p. 12.

11. Maraike Wenzel and Sami Faltas, "Tightening the Screws in West African Arms Embargoes," in Michael Brzoska and George A. Lopez, eds., *Putting Teeth in the Tiger: Improving the Effectiveness of Arms Embargoes* (Bingley, UK: Emerald Publishing, 2009), p. 115.

12. "Letter Dated 12 May 2010 from the Panel of Experts Established Pursuant to Resolution 1874 (2009) Addressed to the President of the Security Council," S/2010/571, para. 36.

13. "Foreword," in Damien Fruchart, Paul Holtom, Siemon T. Wezeman, Daniel Strandow, and Peter Wallensteen, *United Nations Arms Embargoes: Their Impact on Arms Flows and Target Behaviour* (Stockholm: Stockholm International Peace Research Institute and Uppsala University, 2007).

14. Michael Brzoska, "A Quantitative Analysis of Arms Embargoes," in Brzoska and Lopez, eds., *Putting Teeth in the Tiger: Improving the Effectiveness of Arms Embargoes* (Bingley, England: Emerald Publishing 2009), p. 207.

15. See, e.g., Anthonius W. DeVries, "European Union Sanctions against the Federal Republic of Yugoslavia from 1998 to 2000: A Special Exercise in Targeting," in David Cortright and George A. Lopez, eds., *Smart Sanctions: Targeting Economic Statecraft* (Boulder, CO: Rowman & Littlefield, 2002), p. 99.

16. Peter Wallensteen, Carina Staibano, and Mikael Eriksson, eds., *Making Targeted Sanctions Effective: Guidelines for the Implementation of UN Policy Options* (Uppsala, Sweden: Department of Peace and Conflict Research, Uppsala University, 2003), p. 115.

17. Ibid., p. 119.

18. "Letter Dated 7 August 2003 from the Acting Chairman of the Security Council Committee Established Pursuant to Resolution 1343 (2001) Concerning Liberia Addressed to the President of the Security Council," S/2003/779 (2003), para. 9.

19. Manuel Bessler, Richard Garfield, and Gerard McHugh, *Sanctions Assessment Handbook: Assessing the Humanitarian Implications of Sanctions* (United Nations, Inter-Agency Standing Committee, 2004), back cover.

20. Ibid., p. 28.

21. Ibid., p. 68.

22. Informal Working Group of the Security Council on General Issues of Sanctions, "Report," pp. 4 and 9.

23. Ibid., II.A.3.(a), p. 4.

24. George A. Lopez, "In Defense of Smart Sanctions: A Response to Joy Gordon," *Ethics and International Affairs*, Vol. 26, No. 1 (Fall 2011), p. 142. Lopez cites David Cortright et al., *Integrating UN Sanctions for Peace and Security*, Fourth Freedom Forum and Kroc Institute for International Peace Studies (October 2010), pp. 12–26.

25. Resolution 1617, in 2005, held that "associated with" al Qaeda, bin Laden, or the Taliban included participating in the financing or facilitating of acts in conjunction with or in support of them, or "otherwise supporting acts or activities" of al Qaeda, bin Laden, or the Taliban ("Resolution 1617," S/RES/1617 (2005), para. 2), which arguably could include "inadvertent and indirect funding." Andrew Hudson, "Not a Great Asset: The UN Security Council's Counter-Terrorism Regime: Violating Human Rights," *Berkeley Journal of International Law*, Vol. 25, No. 2 (2007), p. 20.

26. *Kadi vs. European Commission*, General Court of the European Union, Case T-85/09, para. 157 (2010).

27. See, e.g., *Kadi v. Council of the EU and Commission of the EC*, T-315/01 (2005).

28. "World Summit Outcome," A/RES/60/1 (September 16, 2005), para. 109.

29. Bardo Fassbender, "Targeted Sanctions and Due Process: The Responsibility of the UN Security Council to Ensure That Fair and Clear Procedures Are Made Available to Individuals and Entities Targeted with Sanctions under Chapter VII of the UN Charter," Office of Legal Counsel United Nations Office of Legal Affairs, (March 20, 2006), 8, para. 12.

30. *Kadi & Al Barakaat vs. Council & Commission*, Judgment of the Court (Grand Chamber), July 18, 2013.

Selected Bibliography

NOTABLE ARTICLES/BOOK CHAPTERS

Annan, Kofi. "Two Concepts of Sovereignty," *The Economist*, Vol. 352, No. 137 (September 18, 1999).

Beitz, Charles. "Bounded Morality: Justice and the State in World Politics," *International Organization*, Vol. 33 (1979).

Bellamy, Alex J. "The Responsibility to Protect—Five Years On," *Ethics and International Affairs*, Vol. 24 (2010).

Bennett, Edward M. "Ethics and Foreign Policy," *Phi Kappa Phi Journal*, Vol. 45 (1965).

Berlin, Isaiah. "Realism in Politics," *Spectator*, December 17, 1954.

Best, Geoffrey. "World War II and the Law of War," *Review of International Studies*, Vol. 7 (1981).

Blatter, Ariela, and Paul D. Williams. "The Responsibility Not to Veto," *Global Responsibility to Protect*, Vol. 3, No. 3 (2011).

Bull, Hedley. "Recovering the Just War for Political Theory," *World Politics*, Vol. 31 (1979).

Burgess, J. Peter, and Shahrbanou Tadjbakhsh. "The Human Security Tale of Two Europes," *Global Society*, Vol. 24, No. 4 (2010).

Butterfield, Herbert. "The Scientific vs. the Moralistic Approach in International Affairs," *International Affairs*, Vol. 27 (1951).

Carr, E. H. "The Moral Foundations for World Order," in Ernest Llewellyn, ed., *Foundations for World Order*. Macmillan, 1950.

Catholic Bishops, United States National Conference of. *The Challenge of Peace. Pastoral Letter on War and Peace.* Washington, 1983.

Charlesworth, Hilary. "International Law: A Discipline of Crisis," *The Modern Law Review*, Vol. 65 (2002).

Clinton, W. David. "The National Interest: Normative Foundations," *Review of Politics*, Vol. 48 (1986).

Cox, Robert W. "Social Forces, States and World Orders: Beyond International Relations Theory," *Millennium—Journal of International Studies*, Vol. 10, No. 2 (1981).

Cutler, A. Claire. "The 'Grotian Tradition' in International Relations," *Review of International Studies*, 1991.

Cutler, Lloyd. "The Right to Intervene," *Foreign Affairs*, Vol. 64 (1985).

DeVries, Anthonius W. "European Union Sanctions against the Federal Republic of Yugoslavia from 1998–2000: A Special Exercise in Targeting," in David Cortright and George A. Lopez, eds., *Smart Sanctions: Targeting Economic Statecraft*. Rowman & Littlefield, 2002.

Donelan, Michael. "Reason in War," *Review of International Studies*, Vol. 8 (1982).

Doyle, Michael. "Liberal Institutions and International Ethics," *American Political Science Review*, Vol. 80.

Doyle, Michael. "Liberal Internationalism," in Cathal J. Nolan and Carl C. Hodge, eds., *Shepherd of Democracy? America and Germany in the Twentieth Century*. Greenwood Press, 1992.

Dunne, John C. "Realpolitik in the Decline of the West," *Review of Politics*, Vol. 25 (1959).

Forsyth, Murray. "Thomas Hobbes and the External Relations of States," *British Journal of International Studies*, Vol. 5 (1979).

Fukuda-Parr, Sakiko. "The New Threats to Human Security in the Era of Globalization," in Lincoln Chen, Sakiko Fukuda-Parr, and Ellen Seidensticker, *Human Insecurity in a Global World*. Harvard University Press, 2003.

Gasper, Des. "Securing Humanity: Situating 'Human Security' as Concept and Discourse," *Journal of Human Development*, Vol. 6, No. 2 (2005).

Gooch, G. P. "Bismarck's Legacy," *Foreign Affairs*, Vol. 30 (1952).

Gross, Michael L. "The Second Lebanon War: The Question of Proportionality and the Prospect of Nonlethal Warfare," *Journal of Military Ethics*, Vol. 7, No. 1 (2008).

Hartigan, R. S. "Non-combatant Immunity: Reflections on its Origins and Present Status," *Review of Politics*, Vol. 29 (1967).

Hudson, Andrew. "Not a Great Asset: The UN Security Council's Counter-Terrorism Regime: Violating Human Rights," *Berkeley Journal of International Law*, Vol. 25, No. 2 (2007).

Jackson, Robert H. "Dialectical Justice in the Gulf War," *Review of International Studies*, Vol. 18 (1992).

Kennan, George F. "Morality and Foreign Policy," *Foreign Affairs*, Vol. 64 (Winter 1985–1986).

Kennedy, D. "Putting the Politics Back in International Politics," *Finnish Yearbook of International Law*, Vol. 9 (1998).

King, Gary, and Christopher Murray. "Rethinking Human Security," *Political Science Quarterly*, Vol. 116, No. 4 (Winter 2001–2002).

Lopez, George A. "In Defense of Smart Sanctions: A Response to Joy Gordon," *Ethics & International Affairs*, Vol. 26, No. 1 (Fall 2011).

Lynch, Colum. "The Ten Worst UN Security Council Resolutions Ever," *Foreign Policy* (March 21, 2010).

McKenna, Joseph C. "Ethics and War: A Catholic View," *American Political Science Review*, Vol. 54, No. 3 (1960).

Minear, Larry, et al. "Toward More Humane and Effective Sanctions Management: Enhancing the Capacity of the United Nations System." Occasional Paper #31.

Providence, RI: The Thomas J. Watson Jr. Institute for International Studies, 1998.

Morgenthau, Hans J. "The Evil of Politics and the Ethics of Evil," *Ethics*, Vol. 56 (1945).

Morgenthau, Hans J. "National Interest and Moral Principles in Foreign Policy," *American Scholar*, Vol. 18 (1949).

Morgenthau, Hans J. "The Moral Dilemma in Foreign Policy," *Yearbook of World Affairs* (1951).

Morgenthau, Hans J. "The Dilemmas of Freedom," *American Political Science Review*, Vol. 51 (1957).

Morgenthau, Hans J. "To Intervene or Not to Intervene," *Foreign Affairs*, Vol. 45 (1967).

Oberleitner, Gerd. "Porcupines in Love: The Intricate Convergence of Human Rights and Human Security," *European Human Rights Law Review*, No. 6 (2005).

Owen, Taylor. "Human Security—Conflict, Critique and Consensus: Colloquium Remarks and a Proposal for a Threshold-Based Definition," *Security Dialogue*, Vol. 35, No. 3 (2004).

Pangle, Thomas. "The Moral Basis of National Security: Four Historical Perspectives," in Klaus Knorr, ed., *National Security Problems*. University Press of Kansas, 1976.

Pape, Robert. "When Duty Calls: A Pragmatic Standard of Humanitarian Intervention," *International Security*, Vol. 37, No. 1 (Summer 2010).

Rosenthal, Joel H. "Rethinking Morality and Foreign Policy," in Charles W. Kegley Jr., ed., *Realism and the Neoliberal Challenge*. St. Martin's Press, 1995.

Sandholtz, Wayne. "The Iraq War and International Law," in David Armstrong, ed., *Routledge Handbook of International Law*. Routledge, 2011.

Schmitt, Michael N. "Human Shields in International Humanitarian Law," *Israel Yearbook on Human Rights*, Vol. 38 (2008).

Slater, Jerome, and Terry Nardin. "Nonintervention and Human Rights," *Journal of Politics*, Vol. 48 (1986).

Tadjbakhsh, Shahrbanou. "Human Security," *Human Development Insights*, No. 17 (2008).

Tadjbakhsh, Shahrbanou. "Human Security and the Legitimization of Peace-buillding," in Oliver Richmond, ed., *Palgrave Advances in Peacebuilding: Critical Developments and Approaches*. Palgrave Macmillan, 2009.

Tadjbakhsh, Shahrbanou. "In Defense of the Broad Approach of Human Security," in Mary Martins and Taylor Owens, eds., *Routledge Handbook on Human Security*. Routledge, 2013.

Tadjbakhsh, Shahrbanou. "State Failure through the Human Security Lens," in Jean-Marc Chataigner and Hervé Magro, eds., *Etats et Sociétés Fragiles*. Paris, 2007.

Talentino, A. K. "Perceptions of Peacebuilding: The Dynamic of Imposer and Imposed Upon," *International Studies Perspective*, Vol. 8, No. 2 (2007).

Tilchin, William N. "Morality and Presidency of Theodore Roosevelt," *The Long Term View*, Vol. 3 (Fall 1996).

Tostensen, Arne, and Beate Bull. "Are Smart Sanctions Feasible?" *World Politics*, Vol. 54, No. 3 (April 2002).

Vincent, R. J. "Human Rights and Global Politics," Paper #24 in *Global Politics*. Open University, 1989.

Walker, J. Samuel. "The Decision to Use the Bomb," *Diplomatic History*, Vol. 14 (1990).

Wenzel, Maraike, and Sami Faltas. "Tightening the Screws in West African Arms Embargoes," in Michael Brzoska and George A. Lopez, eds., *Putting Teeth in the Tiger: Improving the Effectiveness of Arms Embargoes*. Emerald Publishing, 2009.

Wolfers, Arnold. "Statesmanship and Moral Choice," *World Politics*, Vol. 1 (1945).

MONOGRAPHS, COLLECTED ESSAYS, EDITED VOLUMES

Acton, John (Lord). *Essays in the Liberal Interpretation of History*. University of Chicago Press, 1967.

Acton, John (Lord). *The History of Freedom and Other Essays*. Books for Libraries Press, 1907; 1967.

Allhoff, Fritz, Adam Henschke, and Bradley Jay Strawser, eds. *Binary Bullets: The Ethics of Cyberwarfare*. Oxford University Press, 2016.

Angell, Norman. *The Great Illusion*. Penguin Books, 1908; 1939.

Aron, Raymond. *Peace and War*. Doubleday, 1966.

Aron, Raymond. *Politics and History*. Free Press, 1978.

Aron, Raymond. *History, Truth, Liberty: Selected Writings*. University of Chicago Press, 1985.

Bailey, Sydney. *Prohibitions and Restraints in War*. Oxford University Press, 1972.

Beitz, Charles R. *Political Theory and International Relations*. Princeton University Press, 1979.

Beitz, Charles R., et al., eds. *International Ethics*. Princeton University Press, 1985.

Bell, Coral. *President Carter and Foreign Policy: The Costs of Virtue?* Australian National University, 1980.

Bellamy, Alex J., and Paul Williams, eds. *Peace Operations and Global Order*. Routledge, 2005.

Berki, R. N. *On Political Realism*. Dent, 1981.

Berlin, Isaiah. *Four Essays on Liberty*. Oxford University Press, 1969.

Best, Geoffrey. *Humanity in Warfare: The Modern History of the International Law of Armed Conflicts*. George Weidenfeld & Nicolson, 1980.

Blair, Tony. *A Journey*. Hutchinson, 2010.

Boisson de Chazournes, L., and P. Sands, eds. *International Law, the International Court of Justice and Nuclear Weapons*. Cambridge University Press, 1999.

Brown, Chris, ed. *Political Restructuring in Europe: Ethical Perspectives*. Routledge, 1994.

Brown, Seyom. *International Relations in a Changing Global System*. Westview Press, 1992.

Brzoska, Michael, ed. *Smart Sanctions: The Next Steps*. Nomos Verlagsgesellschaft, 2001.

Bull, Hedley. *The Anarchical Society*. Macmillan, 1977.

Bull, Hedley. *Justice in International Relations*. Hagey Lectures, University of Waterloo, 1983.

Bull, Hedley, ed. *Intervention in World Politics*. Oxford University Press, 1984.

Bush, George W. *Decision Points*. Random House, 2010.

Butterfield, Herbert. *Christianity and History*. Charles Scribner's Sons, 1950.

Butterfield, Herbert. *Christianity, Diplomacy and War*. Epworth Press, 1953.

Butterfield, Herbert. *International Conflict in the 20th Century: A Christian View.* Harper & Brothers, 1960.

Butterfield, Herbert, and Martin Wight, eds. *Diplomatic Investigations.* Allen & Unwin, 1966.

Buzan, Barry. *People, States, and Fear.* University of North Carolina Press, 1983.

Buzan, Barry, Ole Waever, and Jaap de Wilde. *Security: A New Framework for Analysis.* Lynne Rienner Publishers, Inc., 1998.

Byers, M., ed. *The Role of Law in International Politics: Essays on International Relations and International Law.* Oxford University Press, 2000.

Canham, Erwin D. *The Ethics of United States Foreign Relations.* Fourth series, Paul Anthony Brick Lectures. University of Missouri Press, 1964.

Carr, E. H. *The Twenty Years' Crisis: 1919–1939.* Harper & Row, 1939; 1946.

Chesterman, S. *Just War or Just Peace? Humanitarian Intervention and International Law.* Oxford University Press, 2001.

Church, William. *Richelieu and Reason of State.* Princeton University Press, 1972.

Cingranelli, David L. *Ethics, American Foreign Policy, and the Third World.* St. Martin's Press, 1993.

Clark, Ian. *Reform and Resistance in International Order.* Cambridge University Press, 1980.

Claude, Inis. *Power and International Relations.* Random House, 1962.

Claude, Inis. *Swords into Ploughshares.* Fourth edition. Random House, 1984.

Cohen, Marshall, et al., eds. *International Ethics.* Princeton University Press, 1985.

Cohen, Marshall, et al., eds. *War and Moral Responsibility.* Princeton University Press, 1974.

Crabb, Cecil V. *American Diplomacy and the Pragmatic Tradition.* Louisiana State University Press, 1990.

Cranston, Maurice. *What Are Human Rights?* Basic Books, 1962; 1973.

Cohen, Roberta, and Francis M. Deng. *Masses in Flight: The Global Crisis of Internal Displacement.* Brookings Institution Press, 1998.

Corten, O., and B. Delcourt, *Droit, légitimation et politique exterieure: l'Europe et la guerre du Kosovo.* Bruylant, 2000.

Danish Institute of International Affairs. *Humanitarian Intervention. Legal and Political Aspects.* Copenhagen, 1999.

Decosse, David, ed. *But Was It Just? Reflections on the Morality of the Persian Gulf War.* Doubleday, 1992.

Deng, Francis M., et al. *Sovereignty as Responsibility: Conflict Management in Africa.* Brookings Institution Press, 1996.

Dinstein, Yoram. *The Conduct of Hostilities under the Law of International Armed Conflict.* Second edition. Cambridge University Press, 2010.

Donelan, Michael, ed. *The Reason of States.* Allen & Unwin, 1978.

Donnelly, Jack. *The Concept of Human Rights.* St. Martin's Press, 1985.

Donnelly, Jack. *Universal Human Rights in Theory and Practice.* Cornell University Press, 1989.

Dougherty, James E., et al. *Ethics, Deterrence and National Security.* Pergammon Brassey's, 1985.

Dunne, T., and N. J. Wheeler, eds. *Human Rights and Global Policies.* Cambridge University Press, 1999.

Ekirch, Arthur. *Ideas, Ideals and American Diplomacy.* Appleton, Century & Crofts, 1966.

Elfstrom, G., and N. Fotion. *Military Ethics.* Routledge and Kegan Paul, 1986.

Ellis, Anthony, ed. *Ethics and International Affairs.* Manchester University Press, 1986.

Elshtain, Jean, ed. *Just War Theory.* New York University Press, 1992.

Falk, Richard. *The Vietnam War and International Law.* Princeton University Press, 1971.

Falk, Richard, ed. *Human Rights and State Sovereignty.* Holmes and Meier, 1981.

Falk, Richard, et al., eds. *Toward a Just World Order.* Westview Press, 1982.

Farer, Tom. *Toward a Humanitarian Diplomacy: A Primer for Policy.* New York University Press, 1980.

Fawcett, James. *Law and Power in International Relations.* Faber and Faber, 1982.

Ferguson, J. *War and Peace in the World's Religions.* Sheldon Press, 1973.

Figgis, John N. *Studies of Political Thought from Gerson to Grotius.* Cambridge University Press, 1956.

Finnis, John, et al. *Nuclear Deterrence, Morality, and Realism.* Clarendon Press, 1987.

Fishkin, James. *The Limits of Obligation.* Yale University Press, 1982.

Forsythe, David. *Human Rights and World Politics.* University of Nebraska Press, 1983.

Forsythe, David. *Human Rights and U.S. Foreign Policy.* University of Florida Press, 1988.

Forsythe, David. *The Internationalization of Human Rights.* Lexington Books, 1991.

Fossedal, Gregory. *The Democratic Imperative.* Basic Books, 1989.

Fox, G., and B. Roth. *Democratic Governance and International Law.* Cambridge University Press, 2000.

Frost, Mervyn. *Towards a Normative Theory of International Relations.* Cambridge University Press, 1985.

Frost, Mervyn. *Ethics in International Relations: A Constitutive Theory.* Cambridge University Press, 1996.

Gallie, W. B. *Philosophers of War and Peace.* Cambridge University Press, 1978.

Garrett, Stephen A. *Ethics and Airpower in World War II.* St. Martin's Press, 1993.

Gong, Gerrit. *The Standard of "Civilization" in International Society.* Clarendon Press, 1984.

Goodwin, Geoffrey, ed. *Ethics and Nuclear Deterrence.* Croom Held, 1982.

Gould, Lewis L. *The Presidency of Theodore Roosevelt.* University Press of Kansas, 1991.

Gross, Michael L. *Moral Dilemmas of Modern War.* Cambridge University Press, 2010.

Gross, Michael L. *The Ethics of Insurgency: A Critical Guide to Just Guerrilla Warfare.* Cambridge University Press, 2015.

Grotius, Hugo. *De Jure Belli ac Pacis Libri Tres.* Translated by F. W. Kelsey. Oceana, 1964.

Gulick, Edward. *Europe's Classical Balance of Power.* W. W. Norton, 1955.

Halle, Louis J. *Civilization and Foreign Policy.* 1955.

Halle, Louis J. *Foreign Policy and the Democratic Process.* University Press of America, 1978.

Halle, Louis J. *History, Philosophy and Foreign Relations.* University Press of America, 1987.

Halle, Louis J., and Theodore Hesburgh, eds. *Foreign Policy and Morality.* 1979.

Halperin, Morton, et al. *Self-Determination in the New World Order*. Carnegie Endowment for International Peace, 1992.

Haq, Mahbub ul. *Reflections on Human Development*. Oxford University Press, 1999.

Hardin, Russell, et al., eds. *Nuclear Deterrence: Ethics and Strategy*. University of Chicago Press, 1985.

Hare, J., and Carey B. Joynt. *Ethics and International Affairs*. St. Martin's Press, 1982.

Hart, H. A. L. *The Concept of Law*. Oxford University Press, 1972.

Henkin, Louis. *How Nations Behave: Law and Foreign Policy*. Council on Foreign Relations, 1968; 1979.

Henkin, Louis. *The Age of Rights*. Columbia University Press, 1990.

Henkin, Louis, et al. *Right vs. Might: International Law and the Use of Force*. Council on Foreign Relations, 1989; 1991.

Herz, John. *Political Realism and Political Idealism*. University of Chicago Press, 1951.

Hinsley, F. H. *Power and the Pursuit of Peace*. Cambridge University Press, 1963.

Hoffmann, Stanley. *The State of War*. Praeger Publishers, 1965.

Hoffmann, Stanley. *Duties beyond Borders: On the Limits and Possibilities of Ethical International Politics*. Syracuse University Press, 1981.

Hoffmann, Stanley. *Janus and Minerva: Essays on the Theory and Practice of International Relations*. Westview Press, 1987.

Hoffmann, Stanley. *The Political Ethics of International Relations*. Carnegie Council on Ethics and International Affairs, 1988.

Holt, Victoria K., and Tobias C. Berkman. *The Impossible Mandate? Military Preparedness, the Responsibility to Protect and Modern Peace Operations*. The Henry L. Stimson Centre, 2006.

Howard, Michael. *War and the Liberal Conscience*. Rutgers University Press, 1978.

Howard, Michael, ed. *Restraints on War*. Oxford University Press, 1979.

Howard, Rhoda. *Human Rights and the Search for Community*. Westview Press, 1995.

Hunt, Michael H. *Ideology and U.S. Foreign Policy*. Yale University Press, 1987.

Huntington, Samuel P. *The Dilemma of American Ideals and Institutions in Foreign Policy*. American Enterprise Institute, 1981.

Jackson, Robert H. *Quasi States: Sovereignty, International Relations and the Third World*. Cambridge University Press, 1990.

Jackson, Robert H. *The Global Covenant: Human Conduct in a World of States*. Oxford University Press, 2000.

Jackson, Robert H., and Alan James, eds. *States in a Changing World*. Oxford University Press, 1993.

Jensen, Kenneth, and Elizabeth Faulkner, eds. *Morality and Foreign Policy: Realpolitik Revisited*. United States Institute for Peace, 1991.

Johansen, Robert C. *The National Interest and the Human Interest*. Princeton University Press, 1980.

Johnson, James Turner. *Ideology, Reason, and the Limitation of War: Religious and Secular Concepts, 1200–1740*. Princeton University Press, 1975.

Johnson, James Turner. *Just War Tradition and the Restraint of War*. Princeton University Press, 1981.

Johnson, James Turner. *Can Modern War Be Just?* Yale University Press, 1984.

Johnson, James Turner. *The Quest for Peace*. Princeton University Press, 1987.

Johnson, James Turner. *Morality and Contemporary Warfare*. Yale University Press, 1999.

Johnson, James Turner, and John Kelsey, eds. *Cross, Crescent and Sword*. Greenwood Press, 1990.

Johnson, James Turner, and George Weigel. *Just War and the Gulf War*. Ethics and Public Policy Center, 1991.

Jones, Dorothy. *Code of Peace: Ethics and Security in the World of the Warlord States*. University of Chicago Press, 1991.

Kaplan, M., and Paul Ramsey, eds. *Strategic Thinking and Its Moral Implications*. University of Chicago Center for Policy Study, 1973.

Kavka, Gregory. *Moral Paradoxes of Nuclear Deterrence*. Cambridge University Press, 1987.

Kegley, Charles W., and Kenneth L. Schwab, eds. *After the Cold War: Questioning the Morality of Nuclear Deterrence*. Westview Press, 1991.

Kennan, George F. *American Diplomacy: 1900–1950*. University of Chicago Press, 1951.

Kenny, Anthony. *The Logic of Deterrence*. University of Chicago Press, 1985.

Kipuis, Kenneth, and Diana T. Meyers, eds. *Political Realism and International Morality*. Westview Press, 1987.

Kirkpatrick, Jeanne. *Dictatorships and Double Standards: Rationalism and Reason in Politics*. Simon & Schuster, 1982.

Kissinger, Henry. *A World Restored*. Houghton Mifflin, 1957.

Kissinger, Henry. *Diplomacy*. Simon and Schuster, 1994.

Klabbers, Jan, Anne Peters, and Geir Ulfstein. *The Constitutionalization of International Law*. Oxford University Press, 2009.

Korey, William. *The Promises We Keep: Human Rights, the Helsinki Process, and American Foreign Policy*. St. Martin's Press, 1993.

Kratochwil, Friedrich. *Rules, Norms, and Decisions*. Cambridge University Press, 1989.

Ku, Charlotte, and Paul F. Diehl, eds. *International Law*. Lynne Rienner, 1998.

Kubalkova, V., and A. A. Cruickshank. *Marxism-Leninism and the Theory of International Relations*. Routledge & Kegan Paul, 1980.

Kubalkova, V., and A.A. Cruickshank. *Marxism and International Relations*. Clarendon Press, 1985.

Lackey, Douglas. *Moral Principles and Nuclear Weapons*. Rowman & Allanheld, 1984.

Lacroix, W. L. *War and International Ethics*. University Press of America, 1987.

Lang, Anthony F., Albert C. Pierce, and Joel H. Rosenthal, eds. *Ethics and the Future of Conflict: Lessons from the 1990s*. Pearson/Prentice Hall, 2004.

Lauterpacht, H. *The Function of Law in the International Community*. Clarendon, 1933.

Lee, Steven P. *Morality, Prudence, and Nuclear Weapons*. Cambridge University Press, 1993.

Lefever, Ernest. *Ethics and United States Foreign Policy*. Meridian, 1957.

Lefever, Ernest, ed. *Ethics and World Politics*. Johns Hopkins University Press, 1972.

Lefever, Ernest. *Morality and Foreign Policy*. Georgetown University Ethics and Public Policy Center, 1977.

Lefever, Ernest. *The Apocalyptic Premise*. Georgetown University Ethics and Public Policy Center, 1982.

Levi, Werner. *Contemporary International Law*. Westview Press, 1991.

Lifton, Robert J., and Richard Falk. *Indefensible Weapons*. Basic Books, 1982.

Lillich, Richard B. *Humanitarian Intervention and the United Nations*. University Press of Virginia, 1973.

Lopez, George A., and Drew Christiansen. *Morals and Might: Ethics and the Use of Force in Modern International Relations*. Westview Press, 1995.

Luard, Evan. *War in International Society*. Yale University Press, 1986.

Luper-Foy, Steven, ed. *Problems of International Justice*. Westview Press, 1988.

MacFarlane, S. Neil, and Yuen Foong. *Human Security and the UN: A Critical History*. Indiana University Press, 2006.

MacIntyre, Alasdair. *A Short History of Ethics*. Routledge & Kegan Paul, 1967.

Malanczuk, P. *Humanitarian Intervention and the Legitimacy of the Use of Force*. Spinhuis, 1993.

Marks, Frederick W., III. *Velvet on Iron: The Diplomacy of Theodore Roosevelt*. University of Nebraska Press, 1979.

Mastny, Vojtech, ed. *Helsinki, Human Rights, and European Security*. Duke University Press, 1986.

Mastny, Vojtech. *The Helsinki Process and the Reintegration of Europe, 1986–1991*. New York University Press, 1992.

Maxwell, Mary. *Morality among Nations: An Evolutionary View*. SUNY Press, 1990.

Mayall, J., ed. *The Community of States*. Allen & Unwin, 1978.

Mayers, David. *George Kennan and the Dilemmas of U.S. Foreign Policy*. Oxford University Press, 1988.

McCleary, Rachel. *Seeking Justice: Ethics and International Affairs*. Westview Press, 1992.

McDougal, Myres S., and Florentino P. Feliciano. *Law and Minimum World Public Order*. Yale University Press, 1961.

McElroy, Robert W. *Morality and American Foreign Policy*. Princeton University Press, 1992.

McMahan, Jeff. *Killing in War*. Oxford University Press, 2009.

Mearsheimer, John J. *The Tragedy of Great Power Politics*. W. W. Norton, 2001.

Meinecke, Friedrich. *Machiavellianism: The Doctrine of Raison d'Etat and its Place in Modern History*. Yale University Press, 1952; Westview Press, 1984.

Melzer, N. *Interpretive Guidance on the Notion of Direct Participation in Hostilities under International Humanitarian Law*. International Committee of the Red Cross, 2009.

Midgley, E. B. F. *The Natural Law Tradition and the Theory of International Relations*. Harper & Row, 1976.

Miller, Linda B., and Michael J. Smith, eds. *Ideas & Ideals*. Westview Press, 1993.

Miller, Richard B. *Interpretations of Conflict: Ethics, Pacifism, and the Just War Tradition*. University of Chicago Press, 1991.

Minear, Larry, and Thomas G. Weiss. *Mercy under Fire: War and the Global Humanitarian Community*. Westview Press, 1995.

Minear, Richard. *Victor's Justice: The Tokyo War Crimes Trials*. Princeton University Press, 1971.

Morgenthau, Hans J. *Scientific Man vs. Power Politics*. University of Chicago Press, 1946.

Morgenthau, Hans J. *Truth and Power*. Praeger Publishers, 1970.

Morgenthau, Hans J. *Human Rights and Foreign Policy*. Council on Religion and International Affairs, 1979.

Morgenthau, Hans J. *Politics Among Nations*. Sixth edition. Edited and revised by Kenneth W. Thompson. Alfred A. Knopf, 1985.

Mueller, John. *Retreat from Doomsday: The Obsolescence of Major War*. Basic Books, 1988.

Muravchik, Joshua. *Uncertain Crusade: Jimmy Carter and the Dilemmas of Human Rights Policy*. Hamilton Press, 1986.

Nagle, W. *Morality and Modern Warfare*. Helicon, 1960.

Nardin, Terry. *Law, Morality, and the Relations of States*. Princeton University Press, 1983.

Nardin, Terry, and David R. Mapel, eds. *Traditions of International Ethics*. Cambridge University Press, 1992.

Neibuhr, Reinhold. *Moral Man and Immoral Society: A Study in Ethics and Politics*. Charles Scribner's Sons, 1932.

Neibuhr, Reinhold. *Christianity and Power Politics*. Charles Scribner's Sons, 1940.

Neibuhr, Reinhold. *The Children of Light and the Children of Darkness*. Charles Scribner's Sons, 1944.

Neibuhr, Reinhold. *Reinhold Neibuhr on Politics: His Political Philosophy and Its Application to Our Age as Expressed in His Writings*. Edited by H. R. Davis and Robert C. Good. Charles Scribner's Sons, 1960.

Newsom, David, ed. *The Diplomacy of Human Rights*. University Press of America, 1986.

Nichols, Bruce, and G. Loescher, eds. *Moral Nation*. Notre Dame University Press, 1989.

Niemelä, Pekka. *The Politics of Responsibility to Protect: Problems and Prospects*. Erik Castrén Research Reports, 2008.

Nolan, Cathal J. *Principled Diplomacy: Security and Rights in U.S. Foreign Policy*. Greenwood Press, 1993.

Norman, R. *Ethics, Killing and War*. Cambridge University Press, 1995.

Novak, Michael. *Moral Clarity in the Nuclear Age*. Thomas Nelson, 1983.

Nye, Joseph S. *Nuclear Ethics*. Free Press, 1986.

O'Brien, William Vincent. *Nuclear War, Deterrence and Morality*. Newman Press, 1967.

O'Brien, William Vincent. *War and/or Survival*. Doubleday, 1969.

O'Brien, William Vincent. *The Conduct of a Just and Limited War*. Praeger Publishers, 1981.

O'Callaghan, Sorcha, and Sara Pantuliano. *Protective Action*. Humanitarian Policy Group, Overseas Development Institute, 2007.

Osgood, Robert E. *Ideals and Self-Interest in America's Foreign Relations*. University of Chicago Press, 1953.

Osgood, Robert E., and Robert W. Tucker. *Force, Order and Justice*. Johns Hopkins University Press, 1967.

Oxfam International. *Beyond the Headlines: An Agenda for Action to Protect Civilians in Neglected Conflicts*. Oxfam GB for Oxfam International, 2003.

Paris, Roland. *At War's End: Building Peace after Civil Conflict*. Cambridge University Press, 2004.

Pettmann, Ralph, ed. *Moral Claims in World Affairs*. St. Martin's Press, 1979.

Phillips, Robert L. *War and Justice*. University of Oklahoma Press, 1984.

Pipes, Daniel, and A. Garfinkle. *Friendly Tyrants*. St. Martin's Press, 1990.

Potter, Ralph B. *War and Moral Discourse*. John Knox Press, 1969.

Power, Samantha. *A Problem from Hell: America and the Age of Genocide*. Basic Books, 2002.

Ramsey, Paul. *War and the Christian Conscience*. Duke University Press, 1961.

Ramsey, Paul. *The Just War: Force and Political Responsibility*. Charles Scribner's Sons, 1968.

Rappoport, David, and Y. Alexander. *The Morality of Terrorism: Religious and Secular Justifications*. Pergamon Press, 1982.

Robin, Ron. *The Making of the Cold War Enemy: Culture and Politics in the Military-Intellectual Complex*. Princeton University Press, 2001.

Rosenthal, Joel H. *Righteous Realists: Political Realism, Responsible Power, and American Culture in the Nuclear Age*. Louisiana State University Press, 1991.

Rosenthal, Joel H., ed. *Ethics and International Affairs: A Reader*. Georgetown University Press, 1995.

Rothstein, Robert L., ed. *The Evolution of Theory in International Relations*. University of South Carolina Press, 1992.

Rubin, Alfred P. *Ethics and Authority in International Law*. Cambridge University Press, 1997.

Russell, Greg. *Hans J. Morgenthau and the Ethics of American Statecraft*. Louisiana State University Press, 1990.

Seckinelgin, Hakan, and Hideaki Shinoda, eds. *Ethics and International Relations*. Palgrave, 2001.

Shue, Henry, and Peter Brown, eds. *Boundaries: National Autonomy and Its Limits*. Rowman & Littlefield, 1981.

Sims, Nicholas A. *Explorations in Ethics and International Relations*. Croom Helm, 1981.

Singer, Peter. *Practical Ethics*. Cambridge University Press, 1980.

Smith, Gaddis. *Morality, Reason, and Power*. Hill & Wang, 1986.

Smith, Michael J. *Realist Thought from Weber to Kissinger*. Louisiana State University Press, 1986.

Stahn, Carsten, and Henning Melber, eds. *Peace Diplomacy, Global Justice and International Agency: Rethinking Human Security and Ethics in the Spirit of Dag Hammarskjöld*. Cambridge University Press, 2014.

Sterling, Richard. *Ethics in a World of Power*. Princeton University Press, 1958.

Stoessinger, John G. *Crusaders and Pragmatists*. W. W. Norton, 1985.

Tadjbakhsh, Shahrbanou, ed. *Rethinking the Liberal Peace: External Models and Local Alternatives*. Routledge, 2011.

Teichman, J. *Pacifism and the Just War*. Basil Blackwell, 1986.

Teitel, Ruti G. *Humanity's Law*. Oxford University Press, 2011.

Terry, Fiona. *Condemned to Repeat? The Paradoxes of Humanitarian Aid*. Cornell University Press, 2002.

Thompson, Kenneth W. *The Moral Issue in Statecraft: Twentieth Century Approaches and Problems*. Louisiana State University Press, 1966.

Thompson, Kenneth W. *Ethics, Functionalism and Power in International Relations*. Louisiana State University Press, 1979.

Thompson, Kenneth W. *Morality and Foreign Policy*. Louisiana State University Press, 1980.

Thompson, Kenneth W. *The Moral Imperatives of Human Rights*. University Press of America, 1980.

Thompson, Kenneth W., ed. *Moral Dimensions of American Foreign Policy*. Transaction Books, 1984.

Thompson, Kenneth W., ed. *Ethics and International Relations*. Transaction Books, 1985.

Thompson, Kenneth W. *Moralism and Morality in Politics and Diplomacy*. *University Press of America*, 1985.

Thompson, Kenneth W. *Moral and Political Discourse: Theory and Practice in International Relations*. University Press of America, 1987.

Thompson, Kenneth W. *Traditions and Values in Politics and Diplomacy*. Louisiana State University Press, 1992.

Thompson, W. Scott, and Kenneth M. Jensen. *Approaches to Peace: An Intellectual Map*. United States Institute of Peace, 1991.

Tilchin, William N. *Theodore Roosevelt and the British Empire: A Study in Presidential Statecraft*. St. Martin's Press, 1997.

Tucker, Robert W. *The Just War*. Johns Hopkins University Press, 1960.

Tucker, Robert W. *Just War and Vatican Council II: A Critique*. Council on Religion and International Affairs, 1966.

Tucker, Robert W. *The Inequality of Nations*. Basic Books, 1977.

Tucker, Robert W., and David C. Hendrickson. *The Imperial Temptation: The New World Order and America's Purpose*. Council on Foreign Relations, 1992.

Valls, Andrew, ed. *Ethics in International Affairs: Theories and Cases*. Rowman & Littlefield Publishers, 2000.

Van Dyke, Vernon. *Human Rights, the U.S. and World Community*. Oxford University Press, 1970.

Vann, Gerald. *Morality and War*. London, 1939.

Vasquez, John. *The Power of Power Politics: A Critique*. Rutgers University Press, 1983.

Vaux, Kenneth L. *Ethics and the Gulf War: Religion, Rhetoric, and Righteousness*. Westview Press, 1992.

Vincent, R.J. *Nonintervention and International Order*. Princeton University Press, 1974.

Vincent, R. J. *Human Rights and International Relations*. Cambridge University Press, 1986.

Viotti, Paul R., and Mark V. Kauppi, eds. *International Relations Theory: Realism, Pluralism, Globalism, and Beyond*. 3rd ed. Macmillan Publishing Company, 1999.

Waltz, Kenneth. *Man, the State, and War*. Columbia University Press, 1959.

Waltzer, Michael. *Just and Unjust Wars: A Moral Argument with Historical Illustrations*. Basic Books, 1977; 1992.

Waltzer, Michael. *Spheres of Justice*. Basic Books, 1983.

Wasserstrom, Richard A., ed. *War and Morality*. Wadsworth, 1970.

Weisband, Edward. *The Ideology of American Foreign Policy: A Paradigm of Lockean Liberalism*. Sage, 1973.

Welsh, David. *Justice and the Genesis of War*. Cambridge University Press, 1993.

Wheeler, Nicholas J. *Saving Strangers: Humanitarian Intervention in International Society*. Oxford University Press, 2000.

Wight, Martin. *Power Politics*. Edited by Hedley Bull and Carsten Holbraad. Penguin, 1977.

Wight, Martin. *Systems of States*. Edited by Hedley Bull. Leicester University Press, 1977.

Woods, Martin T. *The Morality of Peace and War*. 1974.

About the Editor and Contributors

THE EDITOR

CATHAL J. NOLAN is Associate Professor of History and Executive Director of the International History Institute at Boston University. He specializes in military history and the history of international relations. He has authored 12 volumes of international and military history, including an award winning two-volume *Age of the Wars of Religion* (2006) and a two-volume *Concise History of World War II* (2010). He has edited a half-dozen books on diplomacy and human rights, and two book series on international history and contemporary international relations. He was founding editor and editor-in-chief of the Oxford online database in International Relations and International History. He is currently completing a study of attritional wars: *The Allure of Battle: Decisive Battle, Arcs of Attrition, and Short-War Delusion.*

THE CONTRIBUTORS

DAVID ARMSTRONG held chairs at the Universities of Durham and Exeter. He was founder-editor of the journal *Diplomacy and Statecraft* and editor of the leading British journal, *Review of International Studies* from 2003 to 2007. His books include a landmark study of ideology in China's foreign policy, *Revolutionary Diplomacy* (1977), as well as *Revolution and World Order: The Revolutionary State in International Society* (1993), *Civil Society and International Governance* (2008), *A Handbook of International Law* (2008), and *Force and Legitimacy in World Politics* (2006). He also wrote three earlier books on the history of international organization—*The Rise of the International Orgnisation* (1982), *From Versailles to Maastricht* (1995), and *International Organisation in World Politics* (2004)—and coauthored *International Law and International Relations* (2007).

ALEX J. BELLAMY is Professor of Peace and Conflict Studies and Executive Director of the Asia Pacific Centre for the Responsibility to Protect at The University of Queensland, Australia. He is also Non-Resident Senior Adviser at the International Peace Institute, New York, Fellow of the Academy of Social Sciences in Australia and Secretary of the High Level Advisory Panel on the Responsibility to Protect in Southeast Asia. His books include *Responsibility to Protect: A Defense* (2015) and *Massacres and Morality: Mass Killing in an Age of Civilian Immunity* (2012).

MARTIN L. COOK is the Admiral James Bond Stockdale Professor of Professional Military Ethics at the United States Naval War College. He has previously served as Professor of Philosophy and Deputy Department Head, Department of Philosophy at the United States Air Force Academy, Professor of Ethics and Elihu Root Chair of Military Studies at the United States Army War College, and as a tenured member of the faculty at Santa Clara University, California. He is coeditor of *The Journal of Military Ethics*, and member of the editorial board of *The Army War College Quarterly*. His four published books include *The Moral Warrior: Ethics and Service in the US Military* (2003) and *Issues in Military Ethics: To Support and Defend the Constitution* (2013). He is also author of more than 45 scholarly articles.

STEPHEN A. GARRETT (deceased) was Professor of International Studies in the International Policy Studies Division, Monterey Institute of International Studies. His books include *Bangkok Journal: A Fulbright Year in Thailand* (1986), *From Potsdam to Poland: American Policy toward Eastern Europe* (1986), and *Ethics and Airpower in WWII* (1993).

JOY GORDON teaches philosophy at Loyola University–Chicago, where she holds the Ignacio Ellacuria, S.J. Chair in Social Ethics. She has published extensively in the fields of economic sanctions and international law. Her areas of specialization include social and political philosophy, human rights, international law and global governance, and ethical issues in international relations. She is on the editorial board of *Ethics and International Affairs*. She has published extensively on legal and ethical aspects of economic sanctions, including *Invisible War: The United States and the Iraq Sanctions* (2010).

MICHAEL L. GROSS is Professor and Head of the School of Political Science at the University of Haifa, Israel. He has published widely in medical ethics, military ethics, and related questions of medicine and national security. His articles have appeared in the *New England Journal of Medicine*, *American Journal of*

Bioethics, the *Journal of Military Ethics*, the *Cambridge Quarterly of Healthcare Ethics*, the *Hastings Center Report*, the *Journal of Medical Ethics*, the *Journal of Applied Philosophy, Social Forces*, and elsewhere. His books include *Ethics and Activism* (1997); *Bioethics and Armed Conflict* (2006); *Moral Dilemmas of Modern War* (2010); an edited volume, *Military Medical Ethics for the 21st Century* (2013); and *The Ethics of Insurgency: A Critical Guide to Just Guerrilla Warfare* (2015). He serves on regional and national bioethics committees in Israel and has lectured on battlefield ethics, medicine and national security for the Dutch Ministry of Defense, the U.S. Army Medical Department (Walter Reed), the U.S. Naval Academy, the International Committee of Military Medicine, and the Medical Corps and National Security College of the Israel Defense Forces.

CARL C. HODGE is Professor of Political Science at the University of British Columbia–Okanagan, Canada. He is widely published in journals of history, comparative politics, and international relations in Europe and the United States. His books include *Shepherd of Democracy? America and Germany in the Twentieth Century* (1992), *The Trammels of Tradition: Social Democracy in Britain, France, and Germany* (1994), *All of the People, All of the Time: American Government at the End of the Century* (1998), *Redefining European Security* (1999), *NATO for a New Century* (2002), *North American Politics* (2003), *Atlanticism for a New Century* (2004), *U.S. Presidents and Foreign Policy from 1789 to the Present* (2007), *The Encyclopedia of The Age of Imperialism, 1800–1914* (2008). He is currently at work on *War, Strategy and the Modern State, 1792–1914*.

MARTTI KOSKENNIEMI is Academy Professor at the University of Helsinki, and Director, Erik Castren Institute of International Law and Human Rights. His areas of special interest are international law, international legal history, state succession, and human rights, all fields in which he has published extensively. He served previously with the Ministry of Foreign Affairs, Finland, as a diplomat and councilor specializing in international law and in human rights. He has advised and consulted on major issues of international law as a member of the United Nations International Law Commission, the Asian Development Bank, and at the International Court of Justice. He is the recipient of multiple Visiting Professorships and legal awards. Among his more recent books are *The Cambridge Companion to International Law* and *The Politics of International Law*.

ARTHUR S. LINK (deceased) was the George Henry Davis 1986 Professor of American History, Emeritus, Princeton University, and Director and Editor-in-Chief of the authoritative, 69-volume document collection, *The Papers of*

Woodrow Wilson (1966–1993). He was the author and/or editor of numerous other books about Wilson and his times, including *Wilson* (5 vols., 1947–1965), *Woodrow Wilson: Revolution, War, and Peace* (1979), and *The Deliberations of the Council of Four* (1992).

PAUL MARANTZ is Professor Emeritus of Political Science at the University of British Columbia, where he also served as the chair of its International Relations Program. He is the author of *From Lenin to Gorbachev: Changing Soviet Perspectives on East/West Relations* (1988) and is coeditor of *The Decline of the Soviet Union and the Transformation of the Middle East* (1994).

OTTO PFLANZE (deceased) was an editor of *The American Historical Review* and Emeritus Professor of History, Indiana University and Bard College. He was widely regarded as the foremost writer of his generation on Bismarck. He wrote several landmark works, culminating in his magnum opus, *Bismarck and the Development of Germany* (3 vols., 1990). Other topics in his works included characteristics of nationalism, practices and tactics of *Realpolitik*, German-American relations, and the philosophy of history.

JOEL H. ROSENTHAL is president of Carnegie Council for Ethics in International Affairs, adjunct professor at New York University, and chairman of the Bard College Globalization and International Affairs (BGIA) program. He is editor-in-chief of *Ethics & International Affairs*. His books include *Righteous Realists: Political Realism, Responsible Power, and American Culture in the Nuclear Age* (1991). He is coeditor of *Ethics and International Affairs: A Reader*, 3rd ed. (2009), and *Ethics and International Relations* (2009). He is author of numerous scholarly papers, chapters, and forewords on ethics in international affairs.

SHAHRBANOU TADJBAKHSH leads the Specialization on Human Security at the Institute of Political Studies (Sciences Po) in Paris. She has taught at Columbia University and as a visiting professor or researcher at universities in Kabul, New Delhi, Pretoria, Moscow, and Dushanbe. She is a consultant for the UN Regional Center for Preventive Diplomacy in Central Asia on Counter Terrorism Strategy, and Research Associate with the Peace Research Institute Oslo (PRIO). She is coauthor of *Human Security: Concepts and Implications* (2007) and editor of *Rethinking the Liberal Peace: External Models and Local Alternatives* (2011) as well as the author of numerous other books and articles on human security, Afghanistan, Central Asia human development, and peacebuilding. She worked at the United Nations Development Program, Regional Bureau for Europe and the CIS, based in

Tashkent and Bratislava; and at the Human Development Report Office at UNDP in New York. She contributed to National Human Development Reports (NHDRs) on Afghanistan, Pakistan, Iraq, Iran and Nepal.

WILLIAM N. TILCHIN is Associate Professor of Social Sciences in the College of General Studies at Boston University. He is author of *Theodore Roosevelt and the British Empire: A Study in Presidential Statecraft* (1997) and many essays on Roosevelt's presidency and diplomacy. He is coeditor of *Artists of Power: Theodore Roosevelt, Woodrow Wilson, and Their Enduring Impact on U.S. Foreign Policy* (2006) and editor of *Theodore Roosevelt Association Journal.*

Index